JACK WHITE

HOW HE BUILT AN EMPIRE
FROM THE BLUES

JACK WHITE

· · · · · · · · · · · · · · · · · · · ·

HOW HE BUILT AN EMPIRE FROM THE BLUES

· · · · · · · · · · · · · · · · · · · ·

NICK HASTED

OVERLOOK OMNIBUS

This edition published by Omnibus Press and distributed in the United States and Canada by The Overlook Press, Peter Mayer Publishers Inc, 141 Wooster Street, New York, NY 10012. For bulk and special sales requests, please contact sales@overlookny.com or write to us at the above address.

Copyright © 2016 Omnibus Press
(A Division of Music Sales Limited)
14/15 Berners Street,
London, W1T 3LJ, UK.

Cover designed by Fresh Lemon
Picture research by Sarah Datblygu

ISBN 978-1-4683-1377-2

Every effort has been made to trace the copyright holders of the photographs in this book but one or two were unreachable. We would be grateful if the photographers concerned would contact us.

Printed in the USA.

A catalogue record for this book is available from the British Library.

Cataloguing-in-Publication data is available from the Library of Congress.

Visit Omnibus Press on the web at www.omnibuspress.com

*For my mum, Ann Hasted, who got me to Detroit,
and my wife, Deborah Nash*

Contents

Introduction

JACK and Meg White had something precious in 21st century rock: mystery. Seeing the White Stripes for the first time in 2001 at London's Astoria, the childlike colours of their costumes – red, white, black – and the volume and force of the music they thrust from the stage seemed inexplicable. The duo's leanness, tension and crayon-bright vividness were almost blindingly exciting.

When the siblings we thought we were watching turned out to be an ex-married couple, the public and media were wilfully slow to believe incontrovertible court documents, preferring the almost forgotten tang of ambiguity and myth. This wasn't the great rock'n'roll swindle of an earlier era, but a yarn boldly spun by Jack White, a man who valued discretion and discipline over rock's usual currency of excess, and had no intention of giving his own game away.

The man his marriage certificate called John Gillis was born in Detroit in 1975. That city's musical wealth, material devastation and archaic and anarchic character are inseparable from all he's achieved. Travelling to this battered, dangerous, resilient American place, I met veterans of the bohemia where Jack nurtured ideas too eccentric to survive London or LA's glare. Only a few dozen in number, these denizens of Zoot's, the Gold Dollar and other now-lost sanctuaries built a community around obscure records, urgent conversation, gigs and booze-laced, haphazard nights, as stimulating and consuming for those in it as Soho and the Bowery were for punks in 1976. "We were just a bunch of outcasts making weird music, and felt completely apart from society," Matt Smith, who produced Jack in the band the Go, told me. Detroit's streets are changing by the minute from the ones John Gillis walked, ripped up and reformed by new corporate cash of uncertain intent. But almost every musician he knew then still plays, and buzzed with the old days' energy when we spoke.

Jack learned his trade and honed the White Stripes in this scene. But the voices of some of those I approached went dead and unresponsive at his name, feeling burned by the international gold rush which followed his band's startling success, the bitter rows when Jack subsequently quit Detroit or the way he still overshadows the city.

Even in Detroit's community of outsiders, Jack had, anyway, felt secretly separate. It was the same in his large family, and the school and workplaces where he was bullied. Shy, unreadable Meg supported him for seven years of musical life after married life became intolerable; a unique, quietly loving partnership. But even after a second marriage and divorce, to model and musician Karen Elson, and two children, he's pondered being permanently alone.

The more Jack has gradually revealed of himself, between matador feints of further subterfuge, the more bracingly strange he appears. He grew up crushed by insecurity, yet has approached idols from garage-rockers the Gories to Neil Young with nerveless confidence. He's scrupulously polite in person, especially to the great swathes of the public who still don't know who he is in rock stardom's dying days. But he struggles to rein in a galloping ego. His ideas of chivalry can explode into violence and stumble into misogyny, but he regularly, fruitfully works with female musicians. His efforts to be one of the gang with the Raconteurs and the Dead Weather only emphasised his prolific power. He once found hip-hop oppressive, but now makes records for Jay Z. If he occasionally seems too interested these days in being a mogul consorting with some-times-dubious businesses, perhaps it's just the demeaned adolescent inside insisting on his adult worth.

Unable to find a place he fitted, he has built his own kingdom in his adopted Nashville home. Third Man Records is, like the Xanadu of the lonely magnate in his favourite film, *Citizen Kane*, a monument to his pleasures and taste. But instead of hollow hedonism, it's a centre for records, films and carnival curiosities, with iron-studded secret doors and crazy-angled corridors. Run with transplanted Detroit friends and family, it offers a colourful, physical world around his sounds as, with initially sparse resources, he always has. The happy reverence for music he shared in the Gold Dollar's penniless obscurity has been faithfully maintained in this functional millionaire's folly.

Outside Nashville he lives and records in a more private home play-ground. Probably, he cares most about his young children. But he believes he signed an unbreakable Faustian pact long ago, which gave him other, artistic responsibilities. He rises early each morning to keep up his old skills as an upholsterer, and tirelessly crafts and invent songs and artefacts, fame and fortune simply means to unchanged ends.

The White Stripes began by releasing two 7-inch singles in 1998, and the new century's journalists derided Jack for his analogue absolutism and conviction that the digital present was a regression. But in 2016, his innovative vinyl albums are champion-sellers of a resurrected format. It's significantly due to Third Man Records that the nearby vinyl factory, which once subsisted on minor orders such as White Stripes 45s, now runs around the clock. Jack White is music's King Canute, determined and inventive enough to actually turn back the tide.

He has kept other things alive. In a pop culture that favours obsequiously pleasant entertainers when it's not cutting stars down to size, he won't apologise for his abrasive character and art. As the fine new rock'n'-roll still being made to express misfit natures is shunted back into the margins, Jack stands for how far a musician can still force a singular, unreasonable vision.

This is more impressive when you realise where he began.

1

Mexicantown

THE highway sign points you down to Mexicantown. The name of the Detroit neighbourhood where Jack White grew up sounds like a defiant remnant of his city's brazenly racist history. Actually, it was renamed as part of an Eighties PR drive, intended to entice more of the Mexicans annually swelling the area's population. Surrounded by black American districts in cliff-fall decline, Mexicantown was meant as a statement of success. But its growth made it an alien and lonely place for Jack, a stray white boy fighting for his place in a schismed, destitute city.

The civically sanctioned name for his southwest Detroit home isn't as blunt as Black Bottom, the lower east side's old alias, also ironically called Paradise Alley, back between the World Wars when black Americans migrating in vast numbers from the depressed, vicious South were segregated anew, packed increasingly high into a deteriorating ghetto. When the factories of the mighty car industry that had attracted them retreated into the suburbs in the Fifties, starting an accelerating decline and exodus, white Civic Associations patrolled the ghetto's invisible walls, hemming in their black would-be neighbours with racist real estate covenants and violent threats.

Detroit's powder keg blew on an oppressively hot July night in 1967, when the police raided a black after-hours drinking joint. The inferno that followed was more indiscriminate than, say, 1965's Watts race riots, as the ignored rage of the oppressed ran high enough to incinerate black- as well as white-owned businesses. It took a general from Vietnam and 5,000 paratroopers to quell the rioters. Forty-three citizens were killed, 30 by law officers. There were 7,231 arrests and 2,509 buildings were looted or razed. "It looks like Berlin in 1945," Mayor Jerome Cavanagh said in the ruins.

Like the layer of ash under London, a scar in the soil to mark Boudicca's vengeful erasure of its Roman streets, 1967 still visibly wounds Detroit. A quarter-century later, over 10,000 houses and 60,000 lots stood empty.

5

Detroit's 1950 population had dropped by a million. Two-thirds white in 1967, it was 80 per cent black in the Nineties. Appalled white citizens, whose racist fears and actions had set the fuse on the inferno, fled behind the new border of 8 Mile Road. Relatively prosperous suburbs above this avenue were deemed separate, tax-retaining cities, continuing the old racial covenants. The real city was left to rot. Walking in 2002 towards the abandoned art deco skyscrapers of the one-time 'Paris of the West', I felt like I was touring Pompeii after the volcano, or perhaps Atlantis. Roofless buildings looked stained and soggy, as if recently dredged up. In the eerie early evening the only sound was the fluttering of rubbish, and it took 15 minutes to glimpse another, distant soul.

The years between 1967 and Detroit's ambiguous 2013 salvation through a declaration of bankruptcy (helping new investment to switch those sky-scrapers' lights back on) are summed up by an ex-resident, White's Raconteurs bandmate Brendan Benson. "Historically," he tells me, "the mayors have been famously corrupt – almost celebrities for it, with a big mansion, a bunch of cars, and affairs with assorted, weird women – they were like rock stars. While the rest of Detroit was left kerbside."

The reeling home of Motown, Madonna, the Stooges, the MC5 and techno (and before them, an African-American treasure-house ranging from John Lee Hooker to John Coltrane's drumming dynamo Elvin Jones) had its profile revived by three men at the millennium's turn. Kid Rock, who helped create the rap-rock/nu-metal phenomenon with *Devil Without A Cause* (1998), wilfully fled to the ghetto from Detroit's furthest, quaintest, very white village, Romeo. Eminem, who dragged hip-hop's gravitational centre from the East and West Coasts to his forgotten Midwest home when *The Marshall Mathers LP* (2000) made him the music's greatest star, spent much poverty-stricken time below 8 Mile. But he was equally formed by suburban, white Warren, where he went to high school. Only the last of these stars to gain eminence, Jack White, is a true son of the city.

In his friend Jim Jarmusch's beautifully decadent 2014 vampire film *Only Lovers Left Alive*, Tom Hiddleston's undead, reclusive rock star Adam, cruising Detroit's ghost-streets at night with his 3,000-year-old lover Eve (Tilda Swinton), decides not to show her the Motown Museum, instead choosing an address which feels more resonant. "That's Jack White's house. That's where he grew up," he informs her of a sky-blue, wooden home surrounded by darkness, a light in the porch beneath its balcony and one barely glowing inside giving it a haunted look.

"Ooh, I love Jack White," Swinton, whose character has been a familiar of great artists throughout history, gasps, star-struck. "Aaah . . . little Jack White," she coos as they leave. "Do you know he's actually his mother's seventh son?" Hiddleston asks, referring to the supernatural powers a seventh son's seventh son is said to possess. "That figures," says Swinton.

Visited one winter afternoon in 2014, the haunted glimmer Jarmusch gave to 1203 Ferdinand Street, where White lived until he was 28, is, of course, gone. The three-bedroomed house has an attic and back garden, a touch of rust on its porch and a lawn at its front. It's in a street of basically decent homes behind grass-bordered, tree-lined pavements. Wear and tear to structures has been patched up, the extreme poverty and rot very nearby kept at bay. Most of the landmarks in White's early life can be walked to. Except that he wasn't Jack White then. Like Bobby Ritchie, who became Kid Rock, and Marshall Mathers, who slipped on Eminem and Slim Shady's masks, he started as someone else.

John Anthony Gillis was born here on July 9, 1975, the tenth child and seventh son of Teresa and Gorman Gillis, who named him after John the Baptist. The family soon called him Jackie. He was "tacked on", he remembered, surely not planned by his 45-year-old mother; his youngest sibling had been born seven years before, the eldest in 1957. "My brothers are barrel-chested, ass-kicking lumberjack types," he told *Mojo*'s Andrew Male. "I'm on the lighter side of that. They're men's men." He remembered his parents as "senior citizens" who were "pretty tired by that stage", leaving his siblings to take up the slack of raising him. "It could be brutal at times," he told *The New York Times*. "I don't recall hearing the words 'good job' very often." Though he was loved and looked after, he also felt outnumbered, unheard, even derided. "We had a big family, I didn't have that many friends, and I was paranoid," he remembered to *Mojo*. "I thought everybody was talking about me all the time." Having nine siblings ahead of him in every queue left him pressed down with guilt. "When nice things happen to you," he told *The Guardian*'s Alexis Petridis, "you're rarely allowed to enjoy them."

He struggled to be alone or in control in a boisterous, chaotic home. "It's just a given, you're going to be sharing all day long," he said in the documentary *It Might Get Loud*. "Hand-me-down clothes, hand-me-down toys, different interests, and everyone's in and out all the time. Some people are walking to work, some are taking the bus." He learned to battle for what he wanted. "Competition, fighting for food. You push each other over. You muscle your way into situations."

He expanded on being the runt of the litter, living under the thumb of two-fisted "lumberjacks", to the *Daily Telegraph*'s Ben Thompson. "You've got a lot of people telling you what to do, and there's nobody below you to blow the steam off on – you're the end of the road as far as that goes . . ." Thinking for a moment, he added: "And if you delve into it in a deeper way, I could possibly be the last one alive. That's a lot of people I love who maybe one day I'm going to bury."

Jackie's platoon of surrogate parents alongside his elderly real ones weren't merely men's men. They pursued determinedly individual jobs including child psychiatrist, pastry chef, postal inspector and keyboardist in an oldies band. Brother Leo Gillis had the appreciation of eccentric, inventive craft that would characterise the adult White, adoring the spiritually questing American designer and architect Buckminster Fuller, and living for a while in Detroit's only one of Fuller's geodesic domes (a self-supporting, sometimes transparent and spherical structure). He built it in 1998, painted blue to resemble the Earth from space, across a scrubby field from looming, gutted Michigan Central train station. Even in a city largely abandoned to its own devices, that would have stood out. "We love this neighbourhood, and we wanted to make a statement that innovators live here," Leo, who physically resembles Jack, told a visiting journalist. A musician married to an artist, with two children they didn't want raised in "boxes", Leo's dome included a studio where his punk band the Teenage Alcoholics and Gillis family bar band Catalyst recorded. Eldest brother Ray, 18 when Jackie was born, made a particularly strong impression. "He was a Redemptorist brother, a priest [the sort that ran the local Most Holy Redeemer church], for a while," White told *The New York Times*. "After that he became a private investigator and opened a spy shop in Detroit. We spent a lot of time together growing up. He'd take me to the movies – he was the only person who took me to the movies, as a matter of fact."

The Gillises' next-door neighbour, upholsterer Brian Muldoon, was among the few others immune to white flight's panicked pressure. They were a stubborn, small minority in Mexicantown. "I don't think my family are the kind of people who would run with the crowd," White tried to explain to Barney Hoskyns. "We don't have that kind of mentality. But at some point I think maybe it wasn't very healthy." He ascribed a sort of quixotic nobility to the decision in *It Might Get Loud*, as if they saw the words 'white flight' as an insult, or challenge. "My family had a stiff upper lip, like, 'We're not leaving. We're not running away like everyone else.'" As a child, he looked out of his bedroom window to watch a neighbour's blazing car lighting up the street. In a city where municipal powers had collapsed, abandoned buildings were regularly torched, adding to the blocks left as ash-bordered, barren grass squares since 1967. Burning the car meant it would finally be towed away.

His brother Eddie, born in 1966, remembered growing up there with less worry than Jackie. "There were a lot of big families like ours," he told *Turn It Down*'s Rich Tupica, "a fairly close-knit community that was mainly Catholic but at the same time pretty diverse by today's standards, definitely a melting pot. There were a lot of factories, heavy industry and churches that would eventually decline." Even the sanguine Eddie knew being soft there wasn't advisable. "It was a fun atmosphere but you still needed to acquire, and keep a certain sense of toughness about yourself as you wandered around."

Their father's roots were Scottish, his ancestors stopping in Nova Scotia for several generations before crossing into the US for work in Detroit's car factories. The family of Teresa, also the youngest of 10 children, were Polish Catholic; her mother had come to the USA from Poland in 1905, and 'Happy Birthday' was sung to Jackie in Polish. Both his parents worked for the Most Holy Redeemer Church at 1721 Junction Street, two blocks west of the family home, and once the largest Catholic parish in North America. Gorman was the Archdiocese's head of maintenance, while Teresa was secretary to Cardinal Edmund Szoka, also of Polish origin, and a power at the Vatican, where he later became President of the Pontifical Commission. His parents' eminent employer loomed large in Jackie's childhood. "It was definitely a ring-kissing situation," he laughed, speaking to Barney Hoskyns of his brushes with the Cardinal.

The family's religious life wasn't simple. Gorman was a born-again Christian and Teresa a "hard-nosed Catholic", White told Pamela Des Barres, making their home a puzzling "Christian group battleground". It was a conservative environment founded in his parents' Depression-era childhoods, he believed, "like this remnant of a dying age of life, a golden age like Eisenhower, right-wing, John Birch Society, Christianity thing going on, but it was 1990, and didn't really apply."

His parents' formal turns of phrase stuck with him. "When I was a little boy and did something good," he once told a fan, "my dad would say, 'Jackie, you're a gentleman and a scholar.'" In adulthood he would expand such decorum into studied politeness, and archaic, chivalrous codes. Though he felt distant from the details of his parents' differing faiths, he kept their belief in a Christian God. Talking to the similarly spiritual Des Barres, he spoke eagerly about core values he shielded from cynical, atheistic rock journalists. "I'm just glad I got God out of all of that," he reflected of his upbringing. Claiming openness and respect to all faiths but "defaulting" to the Jesus of his childhood, it was God as a creative being that he bowed and prayed to: God the greatest craftsman and artist. "We can only take the wood that he put here and make something out of it," he explained. "We can't create from nothing." Even building the Pyramids was pathetic compared to conjuring planets. "So that's what compels me to him all the time. That's my daily thought about God." He would dig into arcana beyond the Bible when he was older, reading the putative Gospels of Mary Magdalene, James and Doubting Thomas. He admired martyrs and saints, he told *The New York Times*, for their devotion and pure sacrifice. His favourites were St Sebastian and St Rita, respectively patron saints of imagination and the impossible. Christianity was a vital layer often missed by listeners to his later music.

"I have three dads," White told *Rolling Stone*'s David Fricke. "My biological dad, God, and Bob Dylan." His brothers introduced him to the third in that trinity. They played old Dylan records "for him", he remembered, suggesting he desired to hear them. His first musical memory was singing along to 'Tombstone Blues', when he was three or four. The second song on *Highway 61 Revisited* is rich and exciting music, with its rapid downhill clatter of drums, carnivalesque organ and imagery, the wild, ringing thrill of Mike Bloomfield's electric guitar and Dylan's exultant, implacable sneer. The album's first song was 'Like A Rolling Stone', which Dylan recalled composing in "vomitistic" fashion, and the similar, surreal torrents of language in 'Tombstone Blues' would be too much for even the most precocious three-year-old to master. Its repeated chorus, though, with shoeless momma working in the factory and daddy in the alley looking for food, could be easily grasped and happily yelled along to. Probably that was Jackie Gillis' first performance. Dylan LP sleeves would have been seen by him too, with Daniel Kramer's photos of young Bob staring out silk-shirted from *Highway 61*, and surrounded by his own piles of records and magazines on *Bringing It All Back Home*, with the red-dressed, sphinx-like beauty Sally Grossman sat behind him, cigarette poised in hand. These were rich and colourful sounds and images for a child to ponder. They were rare, too, in Mexicantown, part of a cosmology with few adherents outside the large Gillis tribe.

Dylan was Jackie Gillis' first gig, aged just 10, doubtless taken along for the

10

ride by his brothers on either June 30 or July 1, 1986, at the 15,000-seater Pine Knob Stadium in the prosperous rural suburb of Clarkston. Tom Petty & the Heartbreakers were both support and backing band, in what must have been a powerful, riotous event for a child. 'Like A Rolling Stone' was played, 'Tombstone Blues' wasn't. Jackie sat in seat 666.

More portents quickly followed. From the age of five till 13, Jackie attended Holy Redeemer Grade School, which had a faculty including nuns from the Servants of the Immaculate Heart of Mary, and adjoined Holy Redeemer High School and his parents' church workplace, where he was an altar boy. The same year that Dylan played Clarkston, Donald Sutherland arrived in Mexicantown to film a religious thriller, *The Rosary Murders*. Most Holy Redeemer's church and schools were its main locations, and Jackie Gillis was glimpsed as an extra.

William X. Kienzle, an ex-parish priest from southwest Detroit, had set his novel *The Rosary Murders* in the neighbourhood's heart. The film's screenplay, by Kienzle, director Fred Walton and Detroit pulp laureate Elmore Leonard, has pungently effective moments, as a serial killer with a grudge against the Catholic church murders nuns and priests, torturing Sutherland's Father Koesler by admitting his spree in the sanctity of the confessional. Walton, best known for the early slasher film *When A Stranger Calls* (1979), has an atmospheric feel for the Eighties streets where Jackie grew up. Detroit's dull, dirty-white winter light falls on a priest's misty, fatal early morning jog past a junkyard piled with rusting cars, smoking factory chimneys, cranes and a disused railroad. The glass-and-concrete skyscrapers of General Motors' Renaissance Center loom greyly in the distance.

The film is dedicated to "all of those wonderful people on the corner of Junction and Vernor", which Holy Redeemer dominates. Low, brick video and liquor stores and pizza places can be seen as Donald Sutherland dodges traffic at that crossing. He meets a detective among regulars at the Pegasus Greek Bar and Diner, giving another flavour of the working-class environment in which the adult Gillises moved. There's little sense, though, of the neighbourhood's Mexican dominance. This is a white Catholic world of Poles and Irish for the priests, nuns and killer.

It's a snapshot of a Detroit that, like the Gillises stubborn stand in Mexicantown, was doomed. The city's Catholic high schools, counted in the hundreds when 80 per cent of the population were adherents in the Fifties, would number four in the 21st century. A major part of the maintenance job Jackie sometimes tagged along to watch his father perform in the Eighties was the emptying of abandoned churches and schools. Holy Redeemer High itself closed its gates in 2005 with just 200 pupils. The explicitly Latino Cristo Rey High replaced it in 2008. *The Rosary Murders*, presumably filmed at both High and Grade buildings, as White remembered his school being used, gives fascinating glimpses of their long, narrow, institutional corridors, theatrical stage and balcony, which seem lonely, gloomy spaces to Koesler.

Most Holy Redeemer Church is the scene of the film's major set piece, and Jackie Gillis' film debut. The police expect the killer to strike again on Good Friday, leaving the priests, played by Sutherland and Charles Durning, vulnerable as they give mass to a packed congregation. The church's cream-and-gilt arches, gold, blue and red stained-glass windows and vaulted ceiling were a grand, weekly backdrop to Jackie Gillis' childhood. He is one of five dark-haired altar boys in the red cassocks and white surplices they wore at special services, watching as the two film stars pass close by; Jackie is tall and still, holding his candle steadily.

The boy he desperately wished to be is the one everyone notices: pudgy Keith Brooks, who nods off, dropping the giant cross he's carrying onto Charles Durning's back, sending him sprawling and causing hidden, heavily armed cops – sure the killer has struck – to abseil from the rafters. "I wanted to be that kid real bad," White told Pamela Des Barres. Mixing a 10–year–old's incompetent cunning and striking confidence, he stepped forward between takes, and picked the cross up himself. The startled director explained that they already had someone for the task. "I said, 'Oh, I thought maybe we could take turns or something, and whoever did the best take would be in the film,'" he remembered. "Showbiz, already showbiz. The other boy was a part of it. He was a part of what was happening. He was creating, and I was an innocent bystander holding a candle nearby."

After Dylan and Donald Sutherland, Jackie had an even closer encounter with the Pope. John Paul II had scheduled his 1987 visit to the USA around its western and southern states. But Cardinal Szoka used his Vatican influence to campaign for a Midwest detour for his Polish compatriot. So the Pope met the Detroit masses on September 18, at the Pontiac Silverdome in the city's still substantially Polish Hamtramck neighbourhood (where a new generation of garage-rock groups were just beginning). He also met invited congregants at a mass at the Cathedral of the Most Blessed Sacrament. The 12-year-old son of the Cardinal's secretary found himself on the guest-list. And as the Pope processed into the cathedral, he stopped in front of him. "My mother said, 'His name is John' – which was also the Pope's name obviously – and the Pope hugged me," he told the *Daily Telegraph*'s Ben Thompson. "I was shocked. I didn't hug him back because I didn't know you were allowed to. It was a confusing moment, and quite intense. Even though he actually spoke to my mum in English, it sounded like Polish to me."

1203 Ferdinand was a musical home. Eddie Gillis remembered hearing a "wide range of music" in his Seventies childhood, when Gorman Gillis was a more active presence than the tired pensioner Jackie knew. Their dad was an "amateur audiophile", Eddie told *Turn It Down*, building speaker cabinets, repairing radios and playing an impressive collection of records and "reel-to-reel tapes of every variety of big band and Broadway artists you could think of." Eddie didn't need to buy many records or a stereo, as "there always seemed to be one around." Deep Purple, Dylan, KISS and the Stones' *Aftermath* and *Beggars Banquet* were among the classic rock played around the house by the older Gillis brothers. Hank Williams, Johnny Cash and Roger Miller's country albums, too.

The sometimes disorientating, giddy swirl of his large family's life also swept Jackie up in relentless music making. Eddie got an acoustic guitar aged 13 in 1979, and began jamming with a shifting cast of family and neighbours. "My cousin came by one day, he was into Jethro Tull quite a bit and could play flute and guitar very well," he remembered to *Turn It Down*. "And I had an older brother who had been playing keyboards and another brother who had been writing poetry – he eventually took over vocals and playing bass." Eddie wrote a song for a blues trio with whom he gigged around Detroit in 1989, the year before he married and left home, and much later played with next-door neighbour Brian Muldoon in their own lo-fi garage band, Tin Knocker. Before that, Eddie was part of the older brothers' prog-rock/jam band, Catalyst, who started practising in the Ferdinand Street basement in 1984, and gigged for the next two years in bars such as Paycheck's and Old Miami. Also in the basement was a piano, bought by Gorman for $100 from one of the vacant Catholic schools he'd cleared out. Aged 14, Jack began to write songs on it.

He'd already learned to play with his brothers on a drum kit found in the attic when he was about five in most tellings, 11 in some. His early drumming idols included the jazz extrovert Gene Krupa, a hero of his father's in Benny Goodman's big band, the Police's Stuart Copeland and Deep Purple's Ian Paice. He also met his life-long friend Dominic Suchyta when both were 11. "Dominic was probably the only one I knew who liked rock'n'roll at all," White claimed to Barney Hoskyns. Both would race their bikes west to Dearborn to buy musical equipment to jam with in Jack's basement, and Suchyta would play him records made before they were born. "In the fifth grade [aged 11], he was already wearing Doors T-shirts," Suchyta recalled to the *Detroit Free Press*, "and by the sixth grade, Pink Floyd and Zeppelin shirts. So we were listening to stuff really early."

Asked later if playing music had been fun, White struggled with the concept, equating it instead to the intense imaginative world he'd had playing soldiers, since becoming a Second World War-obsessed "Army freak" aged five or six. Both hobbies absorbed this sometimes-lonely child. But developments in his musicianship excited him. "Every time I sat down to play, something new was happening," he told Barney Hoskyns. By the time he was 14, this feeling had become more important than sleeping on a bed, which he replaced in a bedroom only 7 × 7 feet with a length of foam, laid diagonally against the door between two drum kits, a 4-track reel-to-reel tape recorder, three amps, a stereo and a PA. "I got really into drumming, playing along to the records," he said in *It Might Get Loud*. "Those rhythms got into me early. 100 per cent only caring about music and rhythm." In a crowded, chaotic house he had carved out his first tiny musical kingdom.

In 1989, the 14-year-old almost left to study for the priesthood in Wisconsin (probably at St Lawrence Seminary High School). But he couldn't bear to leave behind a new amp he'd just bought. He needed to hear his guitar more than he needed to save souls. Later, aged 18, his military fascination nearly lured him into the US Marines. "Then I got scared," he told *Entertainment Weekly*, "'cause the sergeant came to my house. I just changed my mind instantly." This seventh son made choices with a keen sense of fate and tradition. "Some teacher once told me," he explained to *Mojo*, "that in older times the first son would always take on the father's trade, the second one would join the military and the third one would be expected to become a priest."

The temptation to live in distant isolation also resulted from intensive viewing of boarding school films. He pined for these boys' spartan, regimented lives, so different from his anarchic home. "You came down [from the dormitory] and you had breakfast – where everybody sat down at the table – and then you went to class," he said longingly to *The Guardian*'s Alexis Petridis. "I loved the idea of that structure, it seemed secure to me."

Not wanting to go to Wisconsin meant attending Cass Technical High School. Cass Tech today is a gleaming, modern structure, built in 2005; but Jack attended the old Cass Tech it replaced, a six-storey Gothic landmark from 1917, with traditional classrooms that were starting to crumble, heated in Detroit's deadly winters by sputtering, unreliable radiators. "Going to school there at 14 was like all of a sudden you were going to Harvard or something," White supportively told NPR in 2011, when the fate of the grand old building hung in the balance, before its final demolition late that year. By Detroit public school standards, Cass was Harvard, a "magnet school" with enhanced specialist classes and a good academic record, notably in music. Suchyta, renamed Davis and the bassist in Jack's solo band when he reminisced 20 years later, called Cass a "great school" he passed an exam to enrol in, where, he told *Epiphone.com*, "you picked a major and got to take the classes you wanted to take. I became immersed in art and music and was given plenty of time to work on it." Jack played drums and trombone in the school band, and learned marimba (an arcane skill used on the White Stripes' *Get Behind Me Satan*).

But he felt alienated there. He suffered minor social embarrassment ("When I was in high school my parents were the same age as my friends' *grand*parents," he told Hoskyns; when he left Cass, his mother was 63). More significantly, in his teenage years his minority status, unimportant as a child, made him feel cut adrift from his peers. "We were like a white family from the Twenties or something," he told *The Guardian*'s Petridis, hinting at an eccentricity in his clan that went deeper than colour. "My parents had this bizarre, different way of looking at things from the people that surrounded us. I went to an all-Mexican grade school and an all-black high school . . . Their families didn't watch the same TV shows my family watched."

Cass' wide catchment for strong pupils meant it reflected Detroit's large black majority, more than Mexicantown's ghetto within a ghetto. "Going to a school where I was in the minority did expose me to some music I wouldn't have heard otherwise," Suchyta/Davis told *Epiphone.com* of his positive experience as a white boy there, "and that helped a great deal. I learned as much from listening to [Miles Davis'] *Kind Of Blue* as I did from [A Tribe Called Quest's hip-hop classic] *Midnight Marauders*."

"The school was Mexican and black and they were all into rap and house music, which I couldn't stand," Jack told *Mojo*'s Andrew Male, with contrasting gloom. He found rap sexist, foul-mouthed, alien, and part of a black world that wasn't his, leaving him a pariah. "Some people will just

15

fall into that culture – you know, white people pretending to be black people or whatever," he explained to *Spin*'s Chuck Klosterman, "because they're involved in an environment where they want to fit in and they want to have friends, so they decide to like what everyone else likes and to dress how everyone else dresses." Instead, he was "picked on", he recalled in *It Might Get Loud*.

On a summer night in 2015 I'm drinking in the backyard of the Lager House, the bar in Mexicantown's adjacent neighbourhood, Corktown, where the adult White spent many nights. There I meet a leary, lanky, baseball-capped man who casually tells me just how Jack was "picked on". "A graffiti artist friend of mine used to beat Jack up every day on the way home from school," he says happily. "'Cause he was white. I'm white!" When Jack shuddered with apparent prudishness in later interviews at the thought of hip-hop and Eminem in particular, saying "he reminds me of kids I went to school with", that bully must have been on his mind. The Gillis family's eccentricity was targeted in other ways. "I broke into that dome of his [actually brother Leo's geodesic dome]," my new acquaintance continues, "just to see what was in it, and there was nothing there – it was mouldy . . ."

Blending in, as most teenagers do, would have betrayed something fundamental in White: values, and what sounds like pride, or an antique notion of honour. "I had such a stiff upper lip about it for 18 years," he sighed to *Mojo*. "I don't know why I didn't just break down and have some friends, but I just couldn't do it."

Feeling alone at school, his siblings defined him even more. "I had so many older brothers and sisters and I cared what *they* thought so much," he told *Esquire*'s Miranda Collinge. "I was indoctrinated to assume that if I was ever going to attempt anything new in my life, it would have to be approved through that committee." Unable to adapt to his neighbourhood, his family became his community.

In the late Eighties, in places such as the Hip-hop Shop on 7 Mile, Marshall Mathers joined a vital, underground Detroit version of the rap culture repelling White at Cass. White just looked back on his days of white, working-class ethnic struggle (and mutual musical closed minds) as unhealthy. "I can't really decide whether it was good or bad," he pondered to Barney Hoskyns, of adolescence in Mexicantown and Cass. "It's like saying I was in the Bataan death march in the Second World War and it made me a better person – I mean, it's still a horrible experience, you know?"

The action, anyway, was outside school. Aged 15, he started as a busboy then a pizza chef at the Fox Theatre, a recently renovated, vast cinema and venue built in 1928 on Detroit's main thoroughfare, Woodward Avenue. In another brief portentous brush, he cooked a pizza for Mike Ilitch, the city's remaining billionaire merchant prince, owner of a pizza franchise, the Fox, and Detroit's baseball and hockey teams. Standing in front of the Fox today, with its marquee topped by a proud neon griffin and eight brass double-doors, you can see the new Cass Tech a short after-school walk away. White experienced a surviving example of the old downtown splendour of a city he would form complex feelings for. "That whole block felt like Detroit from the 1940s, as golden age as it could be, even if across the freeway [where he lived] it became a different story," he fondly reminisced to Brian McCollum in *The Tennessean*. When the restaurant emptied for shows, he saw major bands in the theatre, Keith Richards' X-Pensive Winos among them. "I saw a lot of acts there," he said. "I remember watching the Black Crowes soundcheck there when I was 16." He was also transformed by watching *Citizen Kane*.

Orson Welles' 1941 debut is a wonder of wide-open, achieved ambition. Herman Mankiewicz and Welles' screenplay conducts a media investigation into the life of a media magnate, Charles Foster Kane, whose flaws drag him short of greatness in the American Century, and whose secret – buried beneath the Spanish-American War his newspaper helps start, his barnstorming empire-building, daring and ego – is the livid wound of a lost childhood. The words have wit and dazzle enough, but Welles also sends Gregg Toland's camera vaulting through ceilings, falling among raindrops onto skylights, peering up at trampling, bloated Kane in old age. Sound echoes in a library like a mausoleum, butlers murmur from the sides of mouths, and light, shadows and smoke are suggestively angled. Kane's Californian estate, dubbed Xanadu in a newsreel, becomes a Pharaoh's tomb, haphazardly stuffed with treasures turned to junk. The film sparks with the pleasure of invention. It is an organic, mechanical, electric marvel, 1941's analogue cinema carelessly hurled to its limit.

Young Jack watched this in the dark of a picture palace old enough to have shown the film a half-century before. "Mind-blowing," he remembered to Pamela Des Barres. "Midway through it I thought, 'I shouldn't be liking this, at 15 . . . why is a movie from 1940 doing this to me?'"

Welles the actor, in his first role in front of a camera, is *Citizen Kane*'s charismatic core: a big man, a doer, a one-man band sweeping lesser mortals up in his wake. The credits at its start tell you whose film it is: A

17

Mercury Production by Orson Welles. The cast was filled by Welles' Mercury Theatre company who, all in their early twenties, had already conquered the American stage and now cheekily played grand old men, as if this revolutionary film was a wonderful jape. And for all the fine talents who had actually helped him, one man declared himself the author, as few in Hollywood had before.

Welles was 24, a prodigy who had been performing since 10 and hood-winked his way to stardom aged 16 at Dublin's Gate Theatre. RKO Pictures had begged him to leave Broadway for Hollywood, finally handing this novice the prize of final cut. "When you honestly didn't want to go," he explained to an interviewer, "the deals got better and better. In any case, I didn't want money. I wanted authority." Everything afterwards would be hard and heartbreaking for Welles. But he managed to insist on owning his flourish of film genius. He made it exactly the way he wanted, ensured no one could stop him and lived to be proved right, as it outlasted and outranked its rivals.

White read and absorbed all this. Sneaking into film classes aged 18 whenever *Citizen Kane* was shown, he astonished professors with his knowledge. By 2001 he'd watched it three-dozen times. When his direc-tor friend Jim Jarmusch interviewed him in 2003, this obsessive absorption of cinema was ongoing; White had just watched *Rosemary's Baby* for the third time in two days. "It's hard for me," he told Jarmusch of the need for control he'd grasped from Welles, "because I'm constantly battling what's good and bad about ego. But because Orson Welles is such a big idol of mine, I love that whole auteur aspect. He was given complete control to do *Citizen Kane*. With [the White Stripes], being a two-piece band and because the songs are generated from me, it seems wrong to get a producer involved."

White seriously considered a cinema career after his *Kane* epiphany. "I wanted to be a filmmaker when I was a teenager," he told *Comingsoon!*, "and I started to work as an assistant on commercials just to get some quick money in Detroit. I started to realize, especially having been in a couple films [since], it's the most difficult art form of all . . . So many people to weed your vision through, to keep it pure is so hard. I lost my dream of that a long time ago." It didn't help that, when he tried to join in this collective endeavour, the commercials' crew bullied him, he told *The Guardian*, "to the point of tears." In the classroom and here, groups vio-lently rejected him. He just didn't fit.

He attended a film class when he was 18 at Wayne State University, near his home. He told an interviewer he'd quit after one semester due to disgust at his classmates' lazy lack of interest, a contrast to his own drive he'd also hated at high school. More prosaically, he told Des Barres that he couldn't afford it (though he snuck into later lessons to watch *Kane*). The class provided him with one further, life-changing revelation. They were shown the title sequence of *The Graduate* (1967), in which Dustin Hoffman is numbly transported along an airport moving walkway. Director Mike Nichols then cuts to Hoffman's luggage moving down its similar conveyor belt. The professor freeze-framed the luggage belt's briefly glimpsed sign to passengers, asking of their luggage tickets: DO THEY MATCH?

"My mind was blown," he told the *Daily Telegraph*'s Ben Thompson, still electrified by the memory. "I actually emoted out loud – a kind of semi-yell – to the point where people around me stopped and stared. That was it, man! It took that long for me to realise that people put those things in there on purpose!" The idea of symbols opened to him. Suddenly, the religious carvings and mosaics of Most Holy Redeemer were filled with meaning. He could consciously structure, secrete and connect elements. His future art could resonate.

Two other sides of his life developed together, as he explored then-abandoned cinema. His next-door neighbour Brian Muldoon introduced him to upholstery, and a vastly expanded music world. "There were seven Muldoons and 10 Gillises living over on Ferdinand Street," Muldoon reminisced to the *Metro-Times*. He learned upholstery as both a career and vocation from an older local, W.E. Klomp. "He did work for my parents – I really loved it." Muldoon first asked Jack to help rip up furniture at his workshop, which became a three-year apprenticeship starting when he was 15 in 1990. The pair wore matching blue Muldoon Studio overalls; a photo shows Jack behind a full-face visor, in a workshop of steam and sparks. "He'd pick me up from school," he remembered in *It Might Get Loud*. "I'd start tearing down the furniture, ripping off fabric and cotton off of old chairs. Gluing fabric to foam . . . [he'd say] 'Here's how you sew a fly-strip on the back of a decking . . .'"

Muldoon was 16 years older, an age range Jack's siblings made him comfortable with. He was starting to seek out older company in bohemian Hamtramck, too. Distant at school, he was socially precocious elsewhere. "I was looking for something more mature," he believed.

White told Des Barres of being "resigned" to being an upholsterer as a teenager. Rock music careers just weren't being made in Detroit any

19

more. But he also shared Muldoon's love for the work. He learned "perfectionism to the hilt" from his employer, he told Hoskyns. And when he turned full-time at 18, in Muldoon's shop then his own, he saw the long hours as complementary to his music. "I could create, make something tangible, it's physical labour," he explained to Des Barres of the job's attractions, "and all that fantasising about what you could be doing besides this. It's all happening at the same time, so it's kind of perfect." As his nephew Ben Blackwell, who worked in White's shop, told *Kerrang!*'s Stevie Chick: "He wanted to be as creative with his upholstery as he was with his music."

As he became sympathetically familiar with furniture from throughout the 20th century while patching it up, White learned about style, and schools of minimalist design and art such as Bauhaus and De Stijl. He also discovered an apparently universal principle. A quarter-century later he could still envision the pink, silver-threaded Vladimir Kagan couch he was fixing when revelation struck. "I had a piece of fabric wrapped around [it]," he remembered to *NME*'s John Mulvey. "There were three staples on it. One for the middle and one for both sides and that held it down." This was the minimum requirement for furniture to hold together. He sat still for 10 minutes, mesmerised by the implications. He swiftly extrapolated a philosophy in which three was the magic number. From a stool that stood up to colours and music, everything could work with three elements. The White Stripes were built from this principle (duo status apart). "It's really important," White told Mulvey. "It means perfection to me."

This was an early example of a monomaniacal, absolutist bent he had to consciously control. As he confessed to Des Barres, he abandoned reading Bob Dylan's autobiography because he knew he'd become lost in each sentence's implications. Despite his adult status as a prolific producer, let him understand how a mixing desk worked and he'd be pulling it apart like a mad mechanic. He even had to limit his record-buying. "I get scared because I know I could go into it and have 100,000 of them," he told Des Barres. "Then I'll be this guy with goggles in my basement." Everything he loved was a Pandora's Box he had to resist.

The deliberate constraints and hurdles that would characterise his art sound like a strong-minded check on such obsessive traits. These checks were themselves pursued with useful obsession. His favourite writer at school was unsurprising. "I grew up on Poe," he told Hanspeter Kuenzler. "That's my thing." Poe's focused yet baroque stories of singularly fixated characters must have seemed familiar to Jack, like fever dreams of his own tendencies. Suffocating in malarial, Southern Gothic, blackly comic atmosphere, with emotions hysterically heightened yet reduced to their essence, White's only stated literary influence mingles easily with the blues in his work.

All White's future enterprises – Third Man Upholstery, Third Man Studio, Third Man Records – kept faith with the theory found among the staples of Muldoon's workshop. Welles' most famous role as Harry Lime in *The Third Man* was also plainly an influence. Muldoon, though, recalling the local lineage started by W.E. Klomp, remembered a simpler reason. "That's where the Third Man thing came from," he told the *Metro-Times*. "He was the third man in our neighbourhood to become an upholsterer."

Muldoon had a more lasting influence. During work, music played. And after work was over, the dismembered couches would be cleared away, and Jack and Muldoon would play themselves. As his boss was a drummer, Jack fell back on an instrument he'd had little interest in (because, in what would become characteristic strategising, it was too commonly played to let him stand out): the guitar. When his brother Joe, the manager of a St Vincent de Paul charity thrift shop, asked Jack to pick up a fridge in his upholsterer's work van, Jack's reward was the Kay Hollowbody guitar he'd play with Muldoon, and would keep for the White Stripes' whole career. Joe had also given him the 4-track reel-to-reel tape recorder in his tiny bedroom. He'd started playing guitar there, to have something to add to the drums he regularly recorded. From the first year of his apprenticeship in 1990, he was the after-work guitarist, too, with his best friend Dominic Suchyta on bass alongside Muldoon. In 1993, when Jack turned 18, concluding his apprenticeship and time at Cass, Suchyta left for Michigan State University in East Lansing. That left guitar and drums. Jack and Muldoon continued for another three years, playing out only once. They called themselves Two Part Resin.

The guitar made Jack even more of a freak in Mexicantown. Strumming it on the family porch, as if already understudying for the role of out-of-time bluesman, underscored his family's place as square-peg hillbillies. Passing schoolmates derided him. "It was uncool to play a guitar," he said in *It Might Get Loud*. Only DJs and rappers counted. "There was no record store. No guitar shop. Nobody liked rock'n'roll or blues music."

But in the privacy of Muldoon Upholstery, only rock'n'roll counted. Jack and Suchyta had gravitated to the classic rock Jack heard from his older brothers, admiring Hendrix and the Who as well as the Doors and

21

Pink Floyd. Both had also bonded over a Howlin' Wolf tape dug up when brother Eddie wanted the three of them to play Wolf's take on 'Sittin' On Top Of The World': Jack's first, appetising taste of the blues. They also loved Fugazi's idealistic post-hardcore punk – the band was Jack's first major gig as a teenager. "Jack didn't have a record collection then," Muldoon told Brian McCollum, *Detroit Free Press*. "He was into Helmet, AC/DC and, like most 17-year-olds, Led Zeppelin."

The scale of Jack's Zeppelin debt would be underplayed later. Muldoon, anyway, let him draw from a deeper well. "He exposed me to punk music," White remembered. "The Velvet Underground, the Cramps. He really took me under his wing, to be an employee and play music together." The singing of Rob Tyner, the main vocalist of Detroit proto-punks the MC5, was also a "real influence" on Jack, Muldoon told McCollum. Tyner was hoarse, hectoring, imploring, an amateur soul man and revolutionary with jazz chops, who sang in the moment with the vocal needle all the way in the red. "Some nights it would be like he was singing in Arabic," MC5 guitarist Wayne Kramer fondly recalled. "And he didn't speak Arabic!" White would be just that sort of front man: unpredictable, improvisatory, taking each performance and his vocals to their limit.

"He became fascinated by Dick Dale, the Flat Duo Jets, the Stooges and the Gories, which influenced us a lot," Muldoon also remembered. The Flat Duo Jets were the most obscure of these vital keys to what Jack White would become. "They were showing people what was possible in a live performance and on record," he remembered in Tony Gayton's documentary on the band, *Two-Headed Cow* (2006). "It was obvious, when you just watched Dexter [Romweber] perform, that he didn't care what people thought of him." Romweber was singer-guitarist, and Chris "Crow" Smith the drummer (a bassist broke this symmetry for a couple of years). Similarly to White, Romweber grew up in the often-parentless company of six older siblings, who in his case traumatised him with what he darkly termed "crossed boundaries". He based the Flat Duo Jets on Fifties rock'n'roll, the most "pure" sound he'd heard. "I still think there's a way to do the old music that's new," he said. Footage from the mid-Eighties shows his method, playing rockabilly as an overdriven, speeding, howling clatter, its vintage respectability and breaks torn off, Elvis' joyous Fifties danger mangled, dirtied and resurrected by punk. He grimaces carelessly, hair flying as he stomps the stage; crowds would wait for the moment when his eyes rolled back in his head. Smith watches intently from the drums, tuned to him with a "hell of a radar", Romweber remembered, and the singer regularly prowls up and plays at him with intimate drama. They weren't the only drum-guitar duo on the circuit. Still, it's just like watching the White Stripes' interaction, with the melodrama and sensual undercurrents from Meg's side removed. Romweber played a 1965 Silvertone guitar with an amp in its case, a cheap thing made for the Sears department stores' household products line, with a lipstick tube for a pickup and bathroom tiles for sides. The Kay guitar brother Joe gave Jack was a near equivalent, sold in the Fifties by Montgomery Ward department stores, the red 1964 Silvertone which became his primary White Stripes guitar still closer to Romweber's instrument.

When the Flat Duo Jets toured the US with the Cramps in 1990, Romweber remembered being consumed by isolation and madness, and reading Knut Hamsun's angst-ridden, early 20th century interior monologues, Rimbaud and Baudelaire, and biographies of Jerry Lee Lewis, Elvis and Errol Flynn – "real heavy partiers and wreckage-makers", he said in *Two-Headed Cow*. This was around the time teenage Jack saw the band in Detroit.

"I went and saw him play, and was blown away," White remembered in *It Might Get Loud*. "There was nothing onstage, there was nothing there. Just a little amp and a Silvertone guitar, heading in what I would have thought of at the time as a backwards direction. I had to reassess what backwards meant." Whether just before or more likely after he got his Kay, that night "opened up a whole new world of inspiration about the guitar. I started leaving the drums alone a bit."

Muldoon also had his brother post a box full of cassettes from New York, 90-minute blasts of *The Teenage Wasteland*, hosted since 1979 on New Jersey radio station WFMU by DJ Bill Kelly, the "Guru of Garage". This was a cheap crash-course in garage-rock, the abrasive, fuzzed-up, high-energy reaction of thousands of North American teenagers to the British Invasion – mostly forgotten R&B and rock'n'roll singles played with often amateurish zeal. The Kingsmen's 1963 version of 'Louie Louie' was the smash hit, pre-Invasion prototype. Listing the White Stripes' key influences to *Mojo* years later, White recommended the Sonics as "the epitome of 60s punk" ("Life becomes better after buying a Sonics record. Or at least more *tolerable*"); costumed, thuggish GIs the Monks; and the Rats' lone single's B-side, 'Rat's Revenge Part 2', his favourite garage record. He loved the Rats for crystallising the sound of "a group of teenage boys working on something together . . . having a blast." He would search, finally in vain, for that simple camaraderie among his peers.

"It wasn't long before Jack was writing his own songs," Muldoon remembered to McCollum of the 17-year-old he partnered and tutored in Two Part Resin. They worked privately on their sound at night with the care they used on upholstery by day. "We were very determined about the way feedback should be, the way things should sound," Muldoon explained. "We were never just goofing around." Jack's schooling in laborious craft and punk abandon at the shop stayed with him. "If you have a mix of [punk] with the perfectionist side," he told Barney Hoskyns, "then something interesting can happen."

White remembered how impressed his older friend became with him, as his unhappy school days wore down. "Brian Muldoon said 'You're gonna take this music somewhere,'" he told *Mojo*'s Andrew Male. "I thought, 'Well, that's a polite thing to say but that's fucking ridiculous.'"

It seemed even more absurd that the smashed, abandoned city in which he lived could help. But the Detroit Jack Gillis explored as an adult was becoming garage-rock's secret capital.

2

Detroit Rock City

DECEMBER 2014. The stairway leading up to the Magic Stick is decorated with a faded cutting from *GQ*'s January 2002 edition. "Detroit Rock City", the headline reads. "America's Most Beleaguered City Tunes Up."

The club is dark upstairs tonight. Its floor is blue and white, with booth-style seating around the walls, two stages and a curved, bowling ball-decorated bar. It holds 500, but rarely gets that many now. A doorman wanders over to see what I'm doing, and points to a spot by the pool table next to the bar. "You writing a book about Jack White?" he asks. "He beat the shit out of that other guy, right there."

He means the moment on December 13, 2003 when White knocked Von Bondies singer Jason Stollsteimer to the ground, and the unity of the local scene the White Stripes heralded to the world seemed to fall with him. But the roughly curtained-off, homely Musicians' Lounge that serves as backstage, with its own small bar and two companionably facing sofas, suggests more typically happy nights at a venue vital to the supportive, resurgent rock culture in which White musically grew up.

The Magic Stick is part of the Majestic Theatre Center, gradually bought up by the Zainea family since the grandfather of current owners Dave and Joe left a poker game to buy its Garden Bowl bowling lanes in 1946. It has ridden out those high days for Detroit and lower ones, when its part of the city's central Woodward Avenue was all but derelict. In 2014 it includes the grand, art deco Majestic Theatre venue, a downstairs cafe, pizza place and bar. The Magic Stick opened as a nightclub and pool hall in 1992. But it was the Garden Bowl where Jack hung out in his early twenties, plotting his next move but rarely drinking at the bar where I'm sitting, or playing solo. "He used to play right in that corner over there," Dave Zainea tells me, pointing between two mostly glass doors onto the street. "Right by the alcove in front of that mirror. And he played numerous times upstairs. At the first one there were maybe 50, 60 people, and

25

we paid him $75." Mostly he'd just go bowling, among those at the tables watching the action and drinking beer pitchers, the ball-and-skittle decorated carpets and the framed pictures of bowling balls smashing into Detroit's grand old buildings. "He was a pretty good bowler," Zainea recalls.

Woodward is the eastern edge of the Cass Corridor, bordered in the north, the White Stripes' early producer Jim Diamond tells me, by Warren, just before Wayne State University and the city's library and museums, and to the south by Michigan Avenue. Others place its southern start at the I-75 highway, which tore up Black Bottom's ghetto and the Hastings Street John Lee Hooker strolled down on the way to blues business in 'Boogie Chillun', and these days plunges you into Mexicantown. New Wayne State students in the Eighties and Nineties were vainly ordered not to walk off campus into its badlands. These are the streets where the rock'n'roll Jack White joined, boiled and bubbled over.

Walking up from a downtown currently being swiftly, unrecognisably remade with new money on a warm Sunday morning in September 2015, it feels like the Detroit Jack knew will, like crumbling old Havana after the blockade, be lost soon. The city is still like nowhere else. Lone white joggers power through empty, concrete canyon wind-tunnels and carless car parks. White guests on the steps of revived hotels and poor black pedestrians trail very different bags. A squirrel skips onto the steps of the grand Comerica Bank at the bottom of Cass, while below the female statuary and classical tracery of the dead Twenties skyscraper, the Book Tower, its rusted gilt doorway lamp is an informal pigeon coop.

Jim Diamond's Ghetto Recorders studio, where dozens of Detroit classics including *The White Stripes* were produced, was until its 2015 closure to the rear of the Fillmore (formerly the State Theatre). The sprawling Comerica Park baseball stadium, whose 2002 opening helped jolt downtown back to life, faces the Fillmore's Woodward side. Cross from Woodward into Cass and you enter a wilderness. Daisies grow and butterflies alight in an earthen heap studded with rubble. There is a low, twittering hum in the air, blending electricity and bird song. A couple of once fine old homes have their street numbers scrawled in pen, signifying inhabitants. Many others, huge and turreted, have been smothered and reclaimed by leaves. There are empty parking lots, gaps in streets, building sites for unspecified purposes. The Masonic Temple, a true castle where the White Stripes played and Jack's mother once worked as an usher, backs onto the derelict American Hotel. Its wall-painted advert boasts of '300 Rooms With A Bath', but its masonry looks wrenched off. Nearby graffiti declares: 'Cass Corridor Okay – Never Broke Again – Fuck The City'. Underneath a payphone painted wholly over in grey as if fossilised, a sticker asks 'Remember the Cass Corridor'. The Temple and Stream in the Wilderness bars are the last businesses I see as I walk up Cass. There is almost no traffic. The few black pedestrians include an unnatural number rolling in wheelchairs or limping on crutches. A lone cyclist passes me on rusting wheels.

I'm seeking the Gold Dollar, where the White Stripes played their first gigs, and a rock scene cohered to conquer the world. My first search for it at 3129 Cass Avenue defeats me, as street numbers leap confusingly in a city where whole blocks have disappeared. This rock ruin also seems to have sunk into the Earth. "The building's still standing," the Gories' Dan Kroha wryly assured me in London, "believe it or not . . ."

This time, I see it. Past two more ivy-covered homes, the broken rafters beneath their rotting, Gothic roof gables open to the blue sky, are two modern, low buildings, with every inch recently daubed mud-brown. They look camouflaged, like they've been painted into the street. The Gold Dollar is on the right, with a garage-style rolling entrance, flaking wooden top and metal frame on its roof. Its single storey is wide but shallow. There's a tiny yard, and parking spaces to the side where another squirrel skips. It looks like a last paper gig bill has been painted into the front. Nondescript and almost invisible, this is Detroit rock'n'roll's Pharaoh's tomb, where revolution was once in the air.

Perhaps appropriately, Jack Gillis found his first hit of Detroit rock in a skip. He was 16, and *The Stooges* had been thrown there by one of Brian Muldoon's punk-loving clan. Iggy Pop's band's 1969 debut was one of punk's founding tablets. Made in two days, vampire cape-wearing producer John Cale smoothed some abrasion from its metallic sound, but didn't mask the emotionally blank, delinquent sneers of songs such as 'No Fun'. Jack quickly covered 'I Wanna Be Your Dog' on his bedroom reel-to-reel, and bored his boss at the Fox with his new obsession while cooking pizzas. But it was the Stooges' second album, *Fun House*, that became his touchstone. The lurid red and gold sleeve, with a topless, sweat-haired Iggy horizontal, holding his mic in fetish-gloved hands and seemingly smeared into another photo of his own giant, open-lipped face, looks pornographically illicit; a red-light album for a teenager.

The music didn't disappoint. The Stooges had recorded it almost live in LA. Free Jazz influences absorbed from the MC5 came through in Steve Mackay's sax, and the music was mantric yet chaotic, doomy and ritualistic. They had Jack at the first track, 'Down On The Street'. Iggy moans like a monkey and whoops like a hillbilly hunter, leering at 'a pretty thing'. America's great primitive punk guitarist Ron Asheton slashes into the staccato beat with insolent, quick and dirty wails. Later tracks are increasingly assaultive and oppressive, stretching out like the Doors mired in Michigan mud. Scott Asheton's drums crash out of time on 'Dirt' and no one cares, and the guitar becomes a buzzsaw vibration in the gloom. It was a further template for Jack of how direct and unadorned music should be. "Nothing is more raw rock'n'roll than ['Down On The Street'], and no other rock album can hold a candle to *Fun House*," he later told *Harp*'s Jaan Uhelszki. "Iggy Pop is the quintessential Detroit rock performer." In Paul Trynka's liner notes for its reissue, White called it "by proxy the definitive rock album of America."

But such chance finds, even when added to Brian Muldoon's punk and garage-rock tutelage, still left White feeling slow and out of step with the peers he met in his late teens. "Most of the garage-rockers in Detroit were record collectors, and I was envious of them," he told Barney Hoskyns. He had grown up with his brothers' classic rock and country hand-me-downs, but this new community were mostly from the suburbs, where they'd shared record listening sessions after school with "lots of friends", then worked at record stores. "I was jealous because I felt like I was 10 years behind these guys," White remembered. "They just knew – from going to work every day – what albums to get and what albums *not* to get."

Walking through the solid suburb of Ferndale, just off 9 Mile Road, I pass another former White Stripes haunt, the Magic Bag. Starting as a cinema in the Twenties, it specialised in porn by the Eighties and closed as the Deja Vu strip club in 1989. Turned into a venue by Jeremy Haberman in 1996, just in time for Detroit's rock rebirth, its neon sign with a cat and sparkling bag shows it soldiers on. A few doors down is another hangout of the old days, Como's pizzeria, its cocktail bar a shadowy contrast to the afternoon sun.

I'm in the neighbourhood to meet Troy Gregory, who has played with bands from Swans to Spiritualized, and Detroit groups only he can keep count of, including the Dirtbombs. His main band the Witches' second LP, *Universal Mall* (2001), is one of the city's finest, a heady brew of

stomping, echoing glam-garage, spooked harmonies, Roxy saxes, supernatural strangeness and resistant attitude. They were the Gold Dollar's
heartbeat, playing there 20 times. Sitting in his darkening front room, he
sips beer and snaps his lighter on a fresh cigarette at each new reminis-
cence. He saw the scene Jack joined from beginning to end. He confirms
that others in it grew up differently from Mexicantown's plain rock'n'roll
diet. He starts to rattle through the connections some were making even
in childhood.

"I played with this guy Michael Alonso," he begins. "He was in [White
Stripes-predating guitar-drums duo] Bantam Rooster for a little while
later, Five Points Johnson and this other band Speedball that toured with
Motörhead, and he drums in the Electric Six now. Anyway, I was 10, he
was 12, and Matt Smith, who produced the first Go album that Jack's on,
and was in Outrageous Cherry and the Volebeats, he was about 12, too.
This was over in Warren, on 10 Mile by Hazel Park, on the corner right
by the racetrack. We were listening on the 8-track to Black Sabbath's *We
Sold Our Soul For Rock'n'Roll*. I already had a bass. And kids round there
had discovered other kids who knew who the Monkees were, and Paul
Revere & the Raiders, some of those old records, but were also hip to
Alice Cooper. Now we're talking '76, and all I cared about was music.
And guys were also into horror movies. They could talk to you about
Peter Cushing and they knew who Ingrid Pitt was. But Matt turned up at
12 and he had [Captain Beefheart's] *Trout Mask Replica*. This was at a time
when kids were smoking dope and listening to Foghat. Matt had the latest
Leslie West record, and Beefheart, and 'Oh, man, did you hear this new
band, Devo?' and just blew us away. So those guys I always stayed in touch
with, and Matt always kept the pulse on what was happening. Even if it
was only two people going to see this one band somewhere, and they
were really great. What this is leading to, really, is, just like in every
'scene', it was just a bunch of record geeks. What came of age in the
Nineties was the rock'n'roll record-buying kids. [Gories singer] Mick
Collins' whole house is filled with albums, Matt Smith's has records everywhere. A lot of people do."

"Compared with a lot of people I knew like Mick Collins," Jim
Diamond agrees, "I probably had one of the smaller record collections. I
only had 1,000."

Nineties figures such as Gregory and Smith were literally 10 years ahead
of White, listening to Beefheart while he was still in nappies. The city's
music ebbed and flowed as he grew up. Future influences and bandmates,

through age or precocity, were already in its midst in the Eighties. The scene then centred on the historically Polish, relatively bohemian urban enclave of Hamtramck. David Feeny, who quit a steel plant in 1982 to start the enduring studio Tempermill, supported the White Stripes in Blanche and worked on Loretta Lynn's White-helmed album *Van Lear Rose*, lived and partied in Hamtramck in the Eighties.

"I thought the coolest thing in the world was when I first went to Bookie's in 1979," he tells me of Detroit's first punk club, which burned down in 1988. "There wasn't shit to do in the suburbs, and it opened my eyes to all the freaks in the city. The energy was overwhelming. Then, Hamtramck was a fantastically alive place to be in the Eighties, it wasn't just one style of music, it was where all the freaks came after Bookie's, Nunzio's and the Freezer Theater closed down in the city. There were hardcore punk bands, New Wave, neo-garage, psychedelic and early electronic. There were other places to play all over town as well – Alvin's, St Andrew's Hall, Blondies, Traxx. But the three clubs in Hamtramck were the most consistent – Paycheck's, Lili's and the Hamtramck Pub. They were all kicking on the weekends. Rent was cheap and a lot of musicians lived there."

Sitting at the bar at Jack White's old near-local, the Lager House, around closing time one night, I bump into Steve Nawara, who casually mentions he was once the White Stripes' bassist. This Detroit mainstay also tasted international success with the Electric Six. Raised in the Detroit suburb of Berkley and born, like Jack, in 1975, he was in the melee by 1987. "My first gig ever was at a place called Blondies," he remembers. "Our mom dropped us off in the middle of the ghetto. I was 13 years old and going upstairs to talk to Roosevelt, the guy who owned the place. 'We're a bunch of kids, can we play your show?' 'Yes, of course.' 'All right!' I had friends sneaking me into punk gigs all the time. I saw [shit-eating, crowd-assaulting provocateur] GG Allin when I was 14 years old. It was definitely a wilder, different time back then."

"I started playing bars in Detroit in 1981, when I was 15," says Gregory. "There were only a couple of bars for original music in really shitty parts of town. Blondies, and there was this old punk place, the Kishma Grotto out in Flint, and the Hungry Brain and the Greystone, where Swans and Einstürzende Neubauten played, but mostly punk bands like Black Flag and the Misfits. The larger clubs only played national acts. Around that time, all those bands that became like Guns N' Roses were starting – I was in LA when they came through, and I said, 'Man, there's so many bands in Detroit like this.' Guys who grew up listening to Aerosmith and Led Zeppelin, a little bit of light metal, and then Hanoi Rocks came out and they started dressing that way and drinking whisky. I graduated in '84, and moved away."

Punk's Stooges and MC5 roots were sometimes still close enough to touch. "Some were hip to them, some weren't," Feeny remembers. "I wasn't especially at first, but [MC5 singer] Rob Tyner became a fixture in the scene in the mid-Eighties. I did a lot of work with Rob, he was bringing bands in that wanted him to produce them. He ended up working a lot with my band the Orange Roughies. He was just a super-powerful singer and presence."

The band Jack Gillis loved the most then were the Gories. "The best garage band in America since the Sixties," he told *Mojo*, listing the White Stripes' prime influences. "Very primitive, very good, and not very good . . . They definitely laid down the law in Detroit." When their singer Mick Collins stood behind Jack in a record store queue in 1997, long after they'd split, he was giddily thrilled. "The Gories are so obviously, directly influential," Nawara adds. "And their sound became the prototype of all Detroit garage-punk later. They were stripped down, and no one really understood it at the time. The White Stripes pretty much copied the Gories. Real simple, tribal beat and really raunchy guitars." Tim Purrier, who White played with in the Hentchmen, agrees. "I felt that the Gories were more of an influence on the White Stripes than what was going on currently when they started. I mean, Jack *loved* the Gories. The Gories and the Flat Duo Jets, at least early on, were a huge, huge influence on him."

"People always had a strong feeling about the Gories," Feeny remembers of their Detroit reputation in their prime. "They either loved them or hated them. I loved them and the song 'Thunderbird ESQ'." In that one, Mick Collins declares, 'I'm gonna get in my car, and find some place to be alone,' so he can sink the titular, cheap fortified wine.

With Collins – one of the scene's few black figures – and Dan Kroha as singer-guitarists, and drummer Peggy O'Neill, the Gories lasted from 1986 to 1992. *The Gories At Garageland*, filmed for a local public access TV show on November 5, 1987, shows O'Neill is an obvious anteced-ent of Meg White's White Stripes role. She, too, had to be talked into drumming. Deadpan, gum-chewing, herself channelling the Velvet Underground's Moe Tucker in beatnik black jersey and beret, she keeps the beat steady for the film's 49 minutes. Kroha is foppish in green jacket and yellow trousers, Collins sharp in black jacket, white shirt and shades.

31

With their coloured costumes and the studio's crazy-tiled backdrop, they could be a Sunset Strip band in 1966. They play a tense boogie, with room for exploratory solos from Collins against the relentless rhythm. He can sing low and smooth. Kroha tends more towards a bratty shriek, yet another source for White's hysterical vocals. Collins' blues drawl on John Lee Hooker's Detroit anthem 'Boogie Chillun', with low asides and a nagging, stinging guitar solo, shows another angle White loved. The band grin between takes, not taking it seriously, missing the crowd at Paycheck's.

The Shaw Tapes: Live in Detroit 5/27/88, "recorded by Jim Shaw in a building (long-since torn down) on the southwest corner of Faber and Joseph Campau Street, Hamtramck" and released by White on Third Man in 2013, is probably a truer picture. The crowd slur into the mic, a fuse blows and the bootleg tape enhances a sound of amateurish mess, stapled together like one of Jack's chairs by a minimal, sufficient beat. It's needling, boozy, falling-down rock'n'roll you can't fake.

When the reformed Gories play London's Dirty Water Club on July 28, 2015 (as the White Stripes famously did at its old Tufnell Park pub home in 2001), Camden's Jazz Cafe is jammed with garage-rock fans cheering and dancing to a band they now deem Detroit legends. The sound is a wall-flattening R&B rumble, Collins starting with giant Bo Diddley chops, with Kroha on crackling guitar backup and howls. "We wanna do some gay-rage for ya, baby," Kroha says, but is soon covering electronic proto-punks Suicide, equally familiar in Collins' vast record collection. "That shit sounds like the Gories," Collins nods approvingly as they move into an abstract, fuzzed drone and slow, whipping feedback. The night is a loving, far more coherent representation of the band they once were.

Backstage, Kroha has an understated loucheness, like a dandy who no longer bothers with the clothes, and a clear core of decency. It's said the Gories grew out of Detroit's Eighties Mod scene. Just how many Motor City Mods were there? "Aah, three!" he laughs. "I had a couple of other buddies from a nearby suburb who were into that stuff, and it was mainly 'cause we liked the Who and the Jam. We used to go see *The Kids Are Alright* at the midnight movies, and *Quadrophenia* got me through my senior year of high school. Listening to that album, man, it really meant a lot to me, and I started raiding my dad's closet and finding clothes from the Sixties, and when I was a senior I started wearing vintage clothing, and one guy who had lived in England said, 'You look like a Mod!' And I thought, 'Ooh, wow, that sounds cool, I've gotta find out what this

32

means!' And I found that listening to classic rock radio, the stuff that I was really attracted to was mid-Sixties music, like 'You Really Got Me' by the Kinks, and 'It's All Over Now' by the Rolling Stones, and 'For Your Love' by the Yardbirds. In the age of Journey and REO Speedwagon, that's what I started getting into."

Collins remembered the *Back From The Grave* compilations (1983's first accurately boasting 'Rockin' 1966 Punkers!' and including White favourites the Rats) hit Detroit "like a bombshell." But a local inspiration was already playing. "We knew this really good garage band that was really influenced by *Pebbles*-type stuff [like *Nuggets*, Seventies LPs rounding up more varied Sixties garage and psychedelia than . . . *Grave*], and the really great local Sixties garage group 45s that their older brothers and sisters had, like the Unrelated Segments and the Woolies, all these great local hits from the Sixties that were just lying around – they were called the Hysteric Narcotics. We used to go see those guys all the time, they were really, really good, much more musically accomplished than we were. They had a 12-string guitar and a keyboard, and they did harmonies, and they could play those two Unrelated Segments songs, 'Story Of My Life' and 'Where You Gonna Go', like, perfectly."

"Danny Kroha and Peg were at every Hysteric Narcotics gig," confirms Feeny, their keyboardist/guitarist, of a band who debuted at Paycheck's in 1983, then added a light show from the city's Grande Ballroom's psychedelic heyday. Footage of them shows the careless, speeding energy, spontaneous guitar, caveman beat and shrieks that would finish infecting the city's underground a decade later. "They were always in the front row singing along," Feeny continues, "Danny often jumped up for encores, he was a fireball. His band Start [in homage to the Jam] and later the Onset used to open for both the Hysterics and the Orange Roughies. I also did some early recording sessions with Mick [Collins] in the first incarnation of my studio The Tempermill in my parents' basement. It was some weird sampled electronica; his musical knowledge is astounding! So I knew them all from before the Gories and I saw them a bunch, at the after-hours club the Red Door and other underground parties."

"The Hysteric Narcotics were five years older than us," Kroha remembers. "And I didn't have any older brothers or sisters, but Mick was the youngest of five kids, by 10 years, so there was an incredible record collection from the Fifties and Sixties, and he had all the Detroit soul hits from the Sixties in his basement, just lying around. So he knew that stuff, and he turned me onto a lot of it. But he was also collecting by mail order the compilations that were just starting to come out in the Eighties of obscure British R&B. There was this one called *Dimension Of Sound*. It had stuff like [the Joe Meek–produced] 'Crawdaddy Simone' by the Syndicats on it. You know, all these obscure British Sixties white R&B bands. We were getting into that stuff, too."

The Gories' White-appreciated blues side, though not the acoustic sort he revered, flowed naturally from this. "We were discovering the whole Chess catalogue at that time," Kroha says. " 'Cause I loved *Having A Rave Up With The Yardbirds*, and I thought, 'God, these songs are so great, I wanna know where they came from.' Looking at the label, it said C. Burnett wrote this one. M. Morganfield, E. McDaniel. So I thought, 'All right, man, I gotta find out who these guys are.' So I find Bo Diddley, Muddy Waters, Howlin' Wolf, Chuck Berry, and I started discovering Mods weren't actually into the Who and the Jam, but the roots of Mod were all these soul records that were just lying around us everywhere."

The Gories had many of the right ingredients, but were John the Baptists for what was coming in Detroit. No real audience was ready for them. "No, no, no. I felt like we were out in the wilderness," Kroha says with feeling. "We were a band in Detroit for almost seven years, and in the first five, six years of our existence 20 people would come see us. We played just regular bars. And it wasn't until around 1990, '91 that 40 or 50 or maybe even 75 people might come and see us, and that was a lot. But we were already close to breaking up by then, because we'd been beating our heads against the wall that much."

The Gories disintegrated, literally at each other's throats, on a 1992 European tour. But in 1991, Kroha had already co-founded a second White-adored band, Rocket 455. "That was our response to the grunge years," he says. "Because all these bands like Mudhoney and Nirvana were coming up, and starting to talk about the Stooges and the MC5. That's when the Stooges and the MC5 became an influence. I thought, 'There's got to be a Detroit band that's influenced by this kind of sound.' "

Footage from the year before they split, at a Magic Bag show on February 6, 1998 with the Hentchmen and the Wildbunch (likely the Friday when they helped drink half the venue's weekend beer supply), shows singer Mark Walz roaming the stage and maniacally, sometimes incoherently testifying like a slightly winded Rob Tyner, pausing to down a glass of "rocket fuel" as Jeff Meier's guitar buzzes and bucks. "I was a fan of the band before I was in it," remembers Steve Nawara, by then bassist in the Wildbunch (later renamed the Electric Six) and Rocket 455. "They were

34

a nasty, Stooges, MC5, deeper Detroit sound [than the Gories], there was more punk. And the guitarists were just on fire, a real finding trouble sound. They were a force to be reckoned with, and everyone who saw it knew it. Mark looked like a businessman who was too wound up at work and was going nuts onstage. And finally one day they asked me to play, and I was terrified. I couldn't believe how nice everyone was at rehearsal. Mark was a very down-to-earth, well-centred guy. Then I get onstage, and I got hit in the face by the singer in my first gig! And he would sit there choking himself with the microphone cord, and go up and hit the guitarist in the face, and hit me. This is what happens." Meier blacked out after the best show they played. "I guess I hit Dave Buick [who released the White Stripes' first singles] in the face," he told the *Metro-Times'* Brett Callwood. "There were naked girls involved and torn shirts."

As Hamtramck's rock'n'roll scene faded in the Nineties, Rocket 455 helped kick things off in the Cass Corridor. Kroha agrees, but argues Cass was already alive. "The Gories started out there, too. Because the first gig we ever did was Rob Tyner hosting an open mic night at St Thomas Church on the Wayne State campus. The Gories played down there a lot. We played the Old Miami [a bar just south of the Majestic over on Cass Avenue], and there was an old funeral home across from there that had an open mic thing we played a lot. There was a pub down there called Murphy's where we used to play, before they opened the Magic Stick across the street, and an art gallery in Cass called the Willis we played quite a bit."

"That was our headquarters, that area," Meier stated to Callwood of Rocket 455's early Nineties. "Nobody our age was playing rock'n'roll. They were all playing whatever was popular. One year it'd be U2. The next year REM . . . We always liked the Hysteric Narcotics, but they were over with. The Gories were over with . . . There was more stuff happening in Ann Arbor and Ypsilanti at the time. Garage stuff like the Hentchmen was all around Ann Arbor. There wasn't shit going on in Detroit that I recall."

Ann Arbor, a more salubrious, left-wing, college city west of Detroit, was the Stooges' actual birthplace, and a bolthole from police heat for the revolution-minded MC5. The Hentchmen, who Jack would gig and record an album with, favoured garage-rock's buoyantly melodic Mod side, centred on John Szymanski's fairground-giddy Farfisa organ and skinny, speccy, knee-dropping kid guitarist Tim Purrier. "We were super-young when we started in 1992, so we were playing parties, not bars," Purrier remembers, "and we had friends going to college in Ann Arbor. There were a couple of garage bands there into the same kind of stuff we were, like the Monarchs. John's dad lived in Detroit, and John ended up taking over that house, and that [soon known as the Hentch House, post-Cass-gig party central in Hamtramck] was our base for a while. And what we wanted to do with our ability was primitive garage stuff. Within our first year we started meeting people like Rocket 455, and playing Detroit as well. There was a lot of common ground, record collecting and all that stuff. And we were fans of the Gories before we even started. Seeing a local band that primitive gave all of us inspiration to play – none of us could before we started the band, we were in it for fun. Things were pretty small back then. We'd play in Detroit and there'd be 15 people there. Early on, there were a few clubs we played in Cass. But it didn't really grow. There was a veterans' bar a lot of bands would play. This is '93, '94. There'd be someone sitting at the bar grumbling about kids with blue hair and loud music. And sometimes old-timers would kind of like us, because there was a direct correlation to old rock'n'roll." This was Vietnam veterans bar the Old Miami: Missing In Action In Michigan.

Looking back, Gregory can see clearly how the foundations for the rock'n'roll revival that nurtured Jack White were laid, brick by brick. "Around '91, '92," he says, "I moved back from New York. I'd be home visiting Matt [Smith], and this friend of mine Monica said, 'You've got to meet Mick Collins, 'cause you guys are into a lot of the same shit.' And we'd write songs, or go play Alex Harvey songs or something like that at the Hamtramck coffee shops. I found that a lot of bands I'd be introduced to were all unique among each other. That was why I moved back here, I noticed that right away. It was a wave of people just doing their own thing, and very few of them were dicks. It wasn't like where I'd been in New York or LA, when the first time you get together they're all talking about how big their limo's going to be."

The Gold Dollar wasn't open yet, but Gregory still found himself down in the Cass Corridor. "There was a place that was really important called Zoot's," he explains. Zoot's Coffee House was in a Gothic-looking home on 4504 2nd Avenue, with a small stage space in a bay window. On Mondays, dance promoter Adriel Thornton, gay and black and full of imagination, ran EXAT (a night of "EXperimental Audio Transmissions"), a chance for weekend clubbers to detox and actually talk, and reconnect with the progressive spirit of the city's techno pioneers. A photo from one of those nights shows people of student age sinking into armchairs or cross-legged on the floor, holding candles for light, with objects piled haphazardly on a table, like it's a house party. They look subdued, zonked or, in some cases, bright with happiness that they're young and in just the right, comfortable place. The crack-zone outside is another world. And this wasn't the only crowd that mingled at Zoot's, which became a true bohemia.

"Zoot's was in a house," Gregory remembers. "A guy from a band owned it, lived upstairs and turned downstairs into this venue-type place. And what I really liked about Zoot's was that the bills were always really interesting. It was an unsaid criteria that as long as someone was doing their own thing, they can play there. And so I started hanging out there first. And it was great because it was all-ages, but it was right in Cass in a badass area. Right next to the Bronx Bar, on the corner. There was a noise band, Wolf Eyes [an album of who's Jack White released in 2015], who did really well. And we would play there, with Matt Smith's Outrageous Cherry, and the Laughing Hyenas, and the Demolition Doll Rods, who Danny Kroha had just got together."

"The Demolition Doll Rods started in about '93," Kroha says. "Margaret [Gomoll], my friend and girlfriend at the time, said she wanted it to be an all-girl band, but she wanted me to be a girl in it, which I thought was brilliant. And the early Nineties seemed like it was a gender-bending, glam sort of time, and I really wanted to do something crazy. Margaret loved the Gories, so we based it on their sound, but added more Seventies punk and Velvet Underground influences. The Doll Rods got fairly popular fairly quickly, so I left Rocket 455. And because the Detroit Cobras started coming up, and the Paybacks started coming up, there started to be a little bit of a Detroit rock explosion around 1992 or so." Gomoll led the Doll Rods on a path of initially boozy, often near-nude, burlesque attempts at sexual confrontation and liberation, Kroha often enthusiastically androgynous in just a black leather jockstrap. His electric guitar and the most basic drum kit were the bare musical bones of their gaudy, heartfelt, *Playboy* Americana. As Jack Gillis began his barely noticed rise, the Doll Rods were the Detroit band people thought would really make it.

"When any band would play," Gregory adds of a typical night at Zoot's, "the audience was either people who were in bands or wanted to be in bands, or who were sick of being in bands. So then you got people dating each other, because there were a lot of males and females in a lot of the groups. So of course at parties afterwards at somebody's house in the neighbourhood, where you can go till the sun comes up and be really loud and nobody gives a fuck because the houses are empty, of course when that happens you introduce a lot of drinking and bad decisions and pot, and maybe cocaine's happening in the bathrooms, too. So then people say Detroit's an incestuous city – well, yeah, a lot of people were screwing."

Other sorts of useful regulars mingled at Zoot's. "There were all these different vinyl stores with owners who sold and played records that reflected their taste," says Gregory. "There was Car City Records in St Clair Shores where Tommy Potter from Bantam Rooster and Matt Smith worked, and Mick Collins and Jeff Meier every now and again. Bob Setlik owned it, and Bob put on the more avant-garde shows that came to town. He let us do a John Cale tribute one time, and he actually paid for [LA rock entrepreneur-magus and Svengali of female rockers the Runaways] Kim Fowley to come here and record. And there was Stormy Records in Dearborn, and Off the Record in Royal Oak, where Brendan Benson and [Italy Records'] Dave Buick worked. And these guys unwillingly became tastemakers, and they'd sit at the bar at Zoot's and talk with each other. You'd get people who were really having arguments for two or three hours over the Stooges' *Raw Power* and *Fun House*. Some people embraced the rock'n'roll, Little Richard vibes in the Stooges and MC5, and some people liked that but also gravitated towards the fact that it was its own vocabulary that would fall under art, for lack of a better word. And younger kids going into record stores for Nirvana were being told, 'Nah, check out this Monks record, or the Fugs.' And there were younger kids doing it. Even when I was running Borders' blues section, working on my record at home and getting this Charles Dickens bitterness, wishing someone would put spiders down some cat's chimney, if a friend put out a record, I'd make sure it was in the listening stations."

Word got out in other ways. "I also worked at this store called Repeat the Beat run by this guy Willie Wilson," Gregory continues, "who had just got a DJ gig with [Wayne State-based public radio station] WDET. Willie ordered in a lot of that stuff, then played it on WDET as well. And [fellow presenter] Liz Copeland was also hanging out down at Cass and shopping at Willie's store, and playing the Doll Rods or Outrageous Cherry on her show. So things are being set up. Not only was there at least a venue or two that would let you play. Even though you maybe couldn't get arrested, or you'd get a tiny little review of your 45 in [fanzines] *Tape Opera* or *Big Takeover*, you had people playing your records, and places where you could get it. Stuff started getting played, and Zoot's started getting packed."

Some in the outside world noticed, even this early. "The funny thing was," Gregory says, "when Detroit started getting written about, the buzz-word wasn't garage, it was space-rock. Kier MacDonald's Medusa Cyclone did this split-recording with Pavement, and John Peel started playing Kier's stuff, he really liked it. So then when Ian Carl's band Fuchsia, this space-thing, and the Witches were just starting up, people started saying 'Detroit space-rock' – but the Doll Rods would play on the same bill."

Further necessary elements started to be drawn to Detroit, as a still wholly underground scene imperceptibly approached critical mass. "The Witches played this 'garage' festival in Lansing [a college town northwest of Detroit]," Gregory says, "and we did a couple of Banana Splits covers, and Jim Diamond was doing sound, we didn't even know each other. And Tommy Potter from Bantam Rooster and the Dirtbombs and this guy John Linardos, who does the Motorcity Brewing Company and eventually put out the *Ghettoblaster* compilations with Detroit groups on, were all there and living in Lansing. And they were like, 'Oh my God, you played Banana Splits!' so we made friends with them, and this girl from the Fondas and this girl Alicia who was in this band Slumber Party, which [future Von Bondies guitarist and Jack White girlfriend] Marcie Bolen was in for a little while. Basically, a bunch of girls came round. And these Lansing folk we got along with then moved to Detroit. We were playing in Zoot's, and Jim handed me liquor in a bag, and said, 'I live here now, and I've got this studio, you've got to come and record.'"

"When I moved in there in '96 there wasn't much going on," Diamond remembers of setting Ghetto Recorders up at 60 West Elizabeth Street, a chicken processing factory in the Twenties, now deep in a Cass Corridor where literal tumbleweed once blew by him. "There were just a few liquor stores in the area. It was isolated and desolate."

"He would get people to record but make it a party, with people there," Gregory recalls. "John Linardos had the brewery there and was supporting him, and he'd get Ghettoblaster beer-kegs, and you'd meet all these other musicians. The Wildbunch started hanging out, and these young guys who were the Go, and the Sights, who were only 18. And it wasn't like a ski lodge, it had a really nice atmosphere. And around that time a lot of the other studios were becoming very Pro Tools, and having tape to record like Jim did was becoming an anomaly. There was a machine-shop echo in the room, and Jim had a reverb-trap in what used to be an elevator shaft, behind the State Theatre. People would knock on the door after shows, thinking it was backstage. On every single Jim record unless they took it out, you can hear the bell. On our records, we turned it up. So now you've got a studio and it's inexpensive, and people can even hang out. So we're getting there."

3

Golden Years

AUTUMN, 1994. 19-year-old Jack Gillis parked his car on Cass Avenue. Walking towards his film class at Wayne State, he could almost see his life stretching ahead. "There was a moment I just took a really deep breath, and everything was in front of me," he said, looking back 20 years later to Brian McCollum in *The Tennessean*. "I could do whatever I wanted to do. I wasn't in high school any more. I didn't have to mess around with people who were just goofing around in life." He could go to his class, or not. Discuss something, or build something, maybe wander across to the College of Creative Studies and pursue his fascination with architecture. "I ended up dropping out of that and doing my own thing ever since then. But there was a moment there where I realized, 'Wow, now I am on my own, and I can do it myself. But I am by myself, and I will always be by myself in these thoughts.'"

His adult liberty was isolating. If he spoke a thought out loud, he feared it would be contaminated, or condemned. He had been beaten up at school, reduced to tears by co-workers on a film crew. He was a pale, tall boy – 6 feet 2 inches by now – with a high, Woody Woodpecker laugh, and a self-honed way of thinking that others let him know was abnormal. "Something I've battled with my whole life is how to present myself to other people," he confessed to *Mojo*'s Andrew Perry. "When I'm 'having a blast', enjoying myself socially, saying whatever comes in my head, I will very quickly be told to stop. Someone in the room will have a bad expression on their face."

He was 19 when all this came to a head. It was a fissure in his life, an internal earthquake he fought to survive. It was the last year he let himself relax. "I was 18 or 19," he told *The Observer*'s Tim Lewis, "the last time I woke up and was like, 'Ahhh! I guess I'll play chess today.'" Afterwards, his drive to work and create consumed him. Sitting exhausted in a Tokyo restaurant on a White Stripes promotional trip, he gave *Q*'s John Harris a rare glimpse of the boy he had been, and the cost of his self-creation. "I can remember," he said, "when I think back to being a teenager, forcing myself to change." As well as his overwhelming older brothers and elderly parents, he had always sought out older acquaintances and role models, from experienced musicians to, he once said, "senior citizens or European artists in their forties and fifties." All the signs of an 'old soul', impatient with his peers. But, he told Q, much of what he saw of adult life also dismayed him. "There were so many characteristics of [these older people] that I did not want in my life. And I forced myself so much and became so self-conscious – I constantly changed, on purpose, over and over."

He was "really political" as a teenager, he surprisingly revealed, "and I just stopped: stopped myself having an opinion about politics and opening my mouth about it." He observed ego, temper, drunkenness and druggery in his elders – expressive traits usually assets in rock'n'roll – and felt repelled. "It got to the point where I was so self-conscious that I had a breakdown when I was 19. I couldn't handle it: I was becoming very paranoid and very anti-myself . . . I wouldn't let myself enjoy anything." This conflicted Puritanism stayed with him.

As he burned through acceptable identities, Jack also explored different art forms, never really just a musician. The lyrics of his 2014 album *Lazaretto* were sparked by a pile of plays and short stories he wrote aged 19. Two songs seem to borrow Jack's teenage voice. 'Entitlement' finds him feeling like the only person on Earth 'cut down to my knees' when he tries to do what he wants. In 'Alone In My Home', he loves friends though they let him down, feels himself turning into an ephemeral ghost, and pulls the shutters down on an uncaring world: 'I build my own home/ To be sure/ That nobody can touch me now.'

The album's lyric sheet starts with an excerpt of a one-act play named *The Admitting of Patience*, dated ''9-'94'. The first character's dreams of institutional discipline in work camps, hospital wards and the military were certainly his, growing up. The second speaker begins, "I don't feel very good about myself", declaring: "Nobody can stand me for very long." He wishes he could chop off his tongue, "or take out the part of my brain that has opinions. Or cares. I wish I could be simple." He believes he's in an unloved limbo between being a wallflower and Elvis Presley. He isn't able to be shy and quiet enough to be the former: he can't shut up. But lonely, adolescent Jack can't believe he's a rock star, either. Though he's halfway to it.

That September play must have been written within weeks of Jack Gillis' sunburst revelation of life's widening potential as he walked onto campus for almost the last time. He was painting and sculpting now, too, admiring Michelangelo almost as much as Iggy and Orson Welles. "The perfection of what he did . . .," he later marvelled to Jim Jarmusch. "He chiselled everything down, but left just enough to show a vein."

Jack was also 19 when he met Meg White. Born December 10, 1974, she was seven months older than him. She worked as a barmaid at the Memphis Smoke, a two-storey barbecue joint in Royal Oak, a pleasant suburb north of 9 Mile. She was also a habitué of the second-hand record shops where Detroit's gathering clan of musicians worked and met. She always owned much more music than Jack, Dylan and country albums especially. They spent time together leafing through the dusty racks at Car City Records in St Clair Shores, just north of her home in Grosse Point, an upper-class enclave far from Mexicantown. But their different backgrounds never seemed to matter. "No, Meg's not like that," Dan Kroha tells me. "And the part of Grosse Point that she's from isn't like the really old-money part of Grosse Point. There's different parts. Meg's very down-to-earth for a Grosse Pointer." Meg was a wallflower when she wasn't happily drunk, both more shy and able to relax than Jack. She was his first girlfriend, Italy Records' Dave Buick remembered.

Jack had already begun playing publicly, bringing his guitar with its amp and case to coffee houses when he was 18. "There was this place, Shadowbox in Hamtramck, where you could just go in and sign up and start playing," Troy Gregory remembers. "It wasn't so much all folk, it was just that it was a small place so they didn't really have a lot of amps, so it was more acoustic guitar. But they would have people doing things like Roky Erikson and Screamin' Jay Hawkins songs, as well as your local Joni Mitchells. Matt Smith says we saw Jack around there in the early Nineties. I *vaguely* remember . . ."

"I met Jack then," Smith says, "but at an Orson Welles movie – I think *Touch Of Evil*. I knew Meg's sister, Heather; I ran into her and she was with Meg and Jack, and introduced me to him. He looked like a young punk-rock kid, with dyed-blond hair. And I heard he and Meg used to bump into each other at the Gotham City Coffeehouse, in Ferndale on Woodward and 9 Mile, which was the haunt of my band the Volebeats and various others. Before the early Nineties, there wasn't any coffee house culture in Detroit, it was all people hanging out in bars or their basement." Smith recognises Jack's talk of meeting "European artists in their forties and fifties" in this new bohemian milieu. "I met a painter from New Zealand, and I remember some crazed, Seventies Polish jazz musician on the lam from some sort of sordid thing. It was an environment with a lot of artists and odd characters hanging around. You'd go in Zoot's and Roy Brooks, a major post-bebop jazz drummer who used to play with Thelonious Monk, would be jamming. It wasn't all teenagers and indie bands. It was experimental music, and people playing acoustic guitars who weren't your normal open-mic crap, and completely underground. That was a really good time to be in an up-and-coming band, there was so much stimulus."

Jack was trying on the guise of folk singer in many of these places, directly imitating the early days of the man whose debut, *Bob Dylan* (1962), he'd just got. "I learned every song on that record and I played it in coffee houses in Detroit . . . from start to finish, all the time," he told Pamela Des Barres. "That was my gateway even more, that folk . . . it's such a great gateway to all that other music." Dylan at 20 was a good model for Jack at 18 and 19. The album's unique in the way Dylan's voice strives for intensity, his early persona not quite set. You can almost see the joins, and his teeth gritting into an outraged gravel growl on Bukka White's 'Fixin' To Die', overcompensating to match the bluesman. He takes running jumps at songs, favouring rattling guitar attack over accuracy. Only on the sexy, funny beauty 'Baby, Let Me Follow You Down', and the masterly narration of 'House Of The Rising Sun', a brothel song moving from weary bitterness to rasping resentment over tense, pacing guitar, does Dylan rival his idols. Otherwise, he barks and yodels, a young voice out of control as it tries to be old. Jack, too, let his immature voice fly. The wry, struggling musician sketch of 'Talkin' New York', and the liner notes portraying the then unknown Dylan as a death-haunted college dropout, playing guitar since the age of 10, seeking out the older Woody Guthrie for advice and swapping ideas with fellow singers in coffee houses, must have resonated with Jack as he mixed with his peers, and sang these songs himself to general indifference. Dylan's idea of American folk was also entwined with blues, as it would be for Jack. "I consider us a folk band," he'd tell *Rock Sound* of the White Stripes.

In 1994, 19-year-old Jack also joined his first professional band. Goober & the Peas had been going since at least 1989. Led by singer-guitarist Dan John "Goober" Miller, they'd already released one well-received album, *The Complete Works Of Goober & The Peas* (1992), supported Dylan at the Fox Theatre in 1990, and were among the few local acts popular enough to tour out of state. They were a darkly comic country band with punk energy, who cartoonishly skidded through hay bales live. "There was a pretty great rockabilly scene in the early Eighties that had been part of the mix in the indie club scene, but it fizzled out," Feeny says, considering the band's Detroit place. "But Goober was a different animal completely, undeniably entertaining, and they quickly became the biggest draw in town. A lot of folks didn't know what to make of them, and a lot of the other bands hated them for being so popular. They definitely knew their old-time country history." According to Gregory, "there were a couple of bands with country elements. The Volebeats [formed by Matt Smith in 1988], who were a big influence on Wilco, put out a thing called *Ain't No Joke*. Goober & the Peas were more like a party band, a show, pub, almost novelty act. Even though they had some catchy tunes. They would dress in the Hank Williams sparkly outfits, and there was a great deal of humour involved – they had a song called 'Hot Women (Cold Beer)'. They had hay onstage, that kind of thing."

Jack's successful audition as their drummer was a coup for him. "We knew we'd be touring a lot, so we wanted someone whose personality we liked, too," Miller told *Detroit Free Press'* Brian McCollum. "Jack was a lot younger than we were. He wasn't the most technical drummer, thank-fully. I do remember the first show when he played drums: for an encore he came up and sang some Elvis song. People were just shocked by his passion for it." Troy Gregory remembers opening for them, and his sur-prise at seeing "John, Jack – whoever!" drumming; he was billed as John "Doc" Gillis, replacing Damian "Doc" Lang in the Peas' arch cast. Dave Feeny met him for the first time at a Tempermill session. "Nice kid, he was kinda quiet," he remembers. "He came to the studio with them just to hang out one day and brought his pet rat. Kinda weird." Jack played on their final album, and his first, *The Jet-Age Genius* Of Goober & The Peas*, released on January 24, 1995. His drumming is unobtrusively skilful, nothing like his guitar. It was the last time he would blend in with a band. Even then, he chafed at its democracy. "He'd want to change songs night to night, even as the drummer," Miller recalled.

The enduring highlight of the experience is the video for the single 'Loose Lips'. The band play out of time cowboys, walking with slow-motion suspicion through Hollywood, squinting uncertainly at TVs, then running for the hills. Intercut live footage shows them booting blizzards of hay. Miller's future career as an actor (he played Johnny Cash's guitarist Luther Perkins in *Walk The Line*) doesn't surprise, but Jack, too – his all-black costume topped by a Stetson, his boy's face ghost-pale – acquits himself well. It looks like great fun. Miller's considered aesthetic, from the costumes to the video's vintage film scratches, fits Jack's later groups. He also learned the basics of stagecraft and road work. "I think it was a good thing for him just to see what it was like to be in a band that toured," Miller told McCollum. The future Nashville resident and Best Country Album Grammy-winning producer absorbed further lessons. "Goober & the Peas definitely opened my eyes to a lot of things about showmanship and the other side of the tracks of country music," he told McCollum in *The Tennessean*. The way Grand Ole Opry musicians "dressed and presented themselves" had seemed Vegas-fake. Goober & the Peas showed him "that world was very cool and very beautiful."

During the band's stay in Hollywood, on a tour that surely took Jack from the Midwest and maybe Michigan for the first time, he entered a Melrose Avenue bookshop and stared longingly at Iggy Pop's autobiography, *I Need More*. With two bucks in his pocket, so did he. Then with his regular fated luck, he found a $100 bill neatly folded nearby. Buying and reading Iggy's book, he somersaulted on the hotel lawn to celebrate its "rock'n'roll spirit". The band stared, amazed at their drummer's child-like ecstasy. So often controlled, the desperate emotions that churned in him could pour out.

Miller met Jack at the far side of the riptides of self-conscious change that had crippled him and made him break down. He had decided how he would go on. "It was weird, knowing him at 19," Miller reflected in *Detroit Free Press*, "[with] these clear-cut goals for how he wanted things to go in his life, musically and otherwise. I remember him saying, 'I really want to be proud of everything I do.'"

"My brain feels 19 all the time," Jack told McCollum, when he was 39. "And that's a good spot." In many ways, Jack White was born in that pivotal year.

Goober & the Peas drifted apart in 1996. Back in the Cass Corridor that year, media-stoked police raids were hitting Zoot's, the victim of a wave of anti-rave hysteria. It had helped lay the kindling for a scene ready to catch light. In 1997, the flame sparked off the newly opened Gold Dollar. "Neil Yee was always a regular at the Hamtramck Pub," David Feeny remembers, "even as the Hamtramck scene was disintegrating in the Nineties. We would stop in there at the end of the night, and it was typically dead, and he was always talking about opening a club. I thought, 'You're nuts, the scene is dead.' And of course, he opened the Gold Dollar."

"So you walk in," Kroha says, shutting his eyes backstage in London and sketching lines in the air as he remembers, "and it was not that long, and fairly narrow, kind of like a shoe box. The stage was on the right, the bar was on the left, the bathrooms were at the back wall, and that was it. And there were some tables in the middle. And the whole thing was maybe 25 feet wide from wall to wall, and maybe 60 feet long. So it was little. And it had been a drag-show bar in the Fifties, Sixties, maybe into the Seventies, and it had these cool, old silver dollars on the mirrors, you know. So it had this cool history of a subversive culture. All these kids who hung out there were too young to know that, but it somehow added to the vibe of the place.

"One thing a lot of people don't know," Kroha adds, "is that the guy who started it did not intend it to be a rock'n'roll club. Neil Yee wanted to make this eclectic little performance space where he could have plays and movies and poetry, and maybe music, too. But it was such a great little dive bar, and the rock'n'rollers in the city needed a great little dive bar right at that time. So it quickly got taken over by all the rock'n'roll bands. I think that Neil was never happy with the direction that it went in."

"I started the Gold Dollar because I really wanted to have a place to put in all kinds of music that no one else would book," Yee told the documentary *Candy Coloured Blues.* "What paid the bills was the Detroit garage-rock scene." The eight people who turned up for Canadian post-rockers Godspeed You! Black Emperor's austerely intense improvisations may have been more to Yee's taste. But the eclecticism of such nights, like those at Zoot's (where pioneering promoter Greg Baise once glanced up from playing Trivial Pursuit to heckle Autechre's chilly Rochdale electronica), was anyway part of the new garage-rock's freewheeling, home-made spirit.

"Zoot's was starting to get some hassle," Gregory remembers. "And Neil was hanging out there, and he's like, 'I'm opening up this place, want to play?' 'Sure . . .' And he would take these young guys like the Wildbunch, and the Witches, and the Sights and the Go. And all of a sudden bands like the Clone Defects [thrashing, sleazy glam-punk extremists led by the obnoxious, regularly barred Timmy Lampimen] were just popping up at that place. It all seemed like the same people, who worked together at record stores and knew each other. But suddenly, you'd got another place to play. And almost right away, people started getting interested that there were a lot of bands in there. But mostly friends. That's how it usually works, especially around Detroit. Who comes to see you?

47

Well, mostly people that know you, so if you don't know many people no one really comes, for a while."

For some, the Gold Dollar immediately became a new kind of home. "The Gold Dollar was the birthplace of many things," Steve Nawara says with undiminished fondness. "In high school you felt like you were this isolated punk rocker and everyone hated you, and all of a sudden you found the Gold Dollar. It was a revelation, to know that there were other people out there like you. I remember talking about the MC5 at high school and people going, 'Oh, whatever, who the hell is that?' We coincidentally ended up in the same place. It seemed such a freak of nature thing to happen. Everything that's happening now is a result of that meeting. All the different studios, all the different little scenes that are happening today is the result of the Gold Dollar and a handful of bands, like the Dirties, the Gore Gore Girls, the White Stripes, the Wildbunch, Rocket 455, Demolition Doll Rods. Oh my God, we were really just in love with each other, and we hung out every day. It was like I'd found a family. Like I was a lost soul Indian, and I'd found my tribe."

"When the Gold Dollar opened, things started to grow," the Hentchmen's Tim Purrier remembers. "There were a few more bands starting up. There was this new kind of energy. Neil [Yee] was trying to do more of an eclectic thing, but our rock'n'roll scene took it over, for better or worse. It was a tiny, tiny place, though. Over the next couple of years, people started doing more shows at the Magic Stick, which was much larger, and only a few blocks away. There would be shows at the Gold Dollar, but it was really, really packed. But it was always fun to play – it had a dive charm. For a band like us, that was the best. I never really expected to do much more than play some small clubs, and put out some records that 100 people were going to buy. It was all very small-time."

"It opened up at the same time as a scene was developing," says Jim Diamond. "It was a good place to have, where like-minded bands could play in a crappy little shit-hole. I had a lot of fun there, believe me."

"So there were all these bands around that always seemed to sound really good," Gregory says of the scene's expansion. "And then there was this guy Jason Schusterbauer who started booking over at the Magic Stick. That place wouldn't touch you before. And he could see the Sights pulling this many people at the Gold Dollar, and the Go, and Outrageous Cherry. So he put them on the same bill at the Magic Stick, and started bringing people in." According to Diamond, "the Gold Dollar was more to see specific shows, the Magic Stick was more if you were going out drinking, to hear a lot of good music. A friend of mine called Ko Melina would bar-tend there." Melina would soon lead Ko & the Knockouts, join the Dirtbombs, become Meg White's housemate and ask Jack to sing solo at the Garden Bowl when she was bored on quiet Sunday nights.

"There suddenly seemed to be more people coming out and actually going to shows," Gregory reflects. "And there was a long festering time when people became friends, or jammed on each other's projects, or got drunk with each other. It was an unsaid thing that you think your band's the shit in this city. Everyone always talked shit about each other, but not in horrendous ways. 'Oh, man, I really like that guy — [back of hand] too bad his band sucks!' And because no one could remember people's names, everyone was known by band names. So it was always Bobby Go, Johnny Hentch."

"We were brutally honest with each other," Nawara says of the style of camaraderie. "It wasn't just like little girls showing their artwork to the family and them going, 'Oh, that's really good.' That was not the thing. It was, 'That sucks.' 'This lacks sincerity.' 'This doesn't have an edge.' It was the brutal honesty that really shaped things, and made them more poignant."

"It's something inherent in being more than just a band on a treadmill," Gregory considers of the prevailing spirit. "Someone picks up [a] guitar and other people join in. You've got musos like me, and others saying, 'I just got a guitar last week, and I want to be in a band', and they would be in that band with you. And they weren't all guys. A lot of the women who hung out in that whole Gold Dollar scene were tougher than all the guys anyway. It wasn't a macho scene of fellas at all!" Gregory laughs. "The record geeks, they'd call ya!"

"It was one of those type of places where there was no security," he says of the Gold Dollar's ambience and appeal. "The bar guy, Aaron, was the sound guy right where you walk in. And Neil was always there, and he was a super-nice guy. He didn't charge a lot at the door and bands would get it, and Neil would pay the sound man. Beer was cheap if you played there, you got a dollar Pabst and Faygo pop for free — so you get the pop with Well Whiskey so it's all set in there, and a Pabst or two," he says, mentally mixing a typical round. "And the bar girls were all really nice, and some were also girls from other bands. When you walked in the 'backstage area', there were these old theatre mirrors. But no one ever used it. I think people went back there to do drugs or screw around. But you'd just put the equipment aside and hang out. There were a lot of drunken shows like that."

Yee also managed to sustain some of his avant-garde, random intentions, in what became a chaotic clubhouse as much as a venue. "Neil put together these silly things like the Rock'n'Roll Prom," Gregory remembers, "where he'd pick names out and mix up groups, so it'd be me and Johnny Hentch and Joe from the Electric Six. 'What are we gonna play for this thing?' 'I dunno, a Monkees song?' 'Okay!' 'Or we'll just make noise . . .' 'All right!' And then these artists around town did this thing called Aces High. They all dressed as [Kiss singer] Ace Frehley, from different eras, playing only Ace Frehley-written songs, and doing all the moves. And Deb Agolli, the drummer in Outrageous Cherry, made all these outfits – they looked really incredible, but they were all stone drunk out of their minds.

"I've spent my whole life in dingy rock clubs," Gregory concludes warmly, "but I liked going to the Gold Dollar. I don't remember any fights. I'm sure there probably were. When I think about it now, I remember it as being friendly. I kept going back, just turn up no matter who was playing. There was always someone to talk to, or drive you home if you got too drunk."

About the time Goober & the Peas ended, John Gillis became Jack White. Marrying Meg on September 21, 1996, he took her surname – part of a typically difficult feminist streak that could dance close to misogyny in his music. "It was like a 1960s gathering," Meg's Uncle Doug told *The Sun* of the "Small . . . real sudden" wedding. "Meg was barefoot in a lacy, frilly white dress. She had flowers in her hair, daisies which she picked out of their garden." Meg's sister, Heather, was friends with Yee, and they were around the Gold Dollar from the start. The White Stripes would soon make their debut there, and make it their home, as Nawara felt it was his. "I had seen them through other connections, with Meg and all that," Yee said in *Candy Coloured Blues*. "And I kind of forgot he was in a band, and then he came in on one of our open-mic nights and played drums, and he was really good."

"Jack's not a quiet, wallflower kind of guy," Kroha says of his first impressions. "He was very outgoing when I first met him. He came right up to me and said, 'Hey, you're in the Gories, right?' And he seemed really happy to meet me, and because of that I was really happy to meet him."

"The first time I met him, he was hanging out at the Gold Dollar. He was very big in stature, a *very* big guy," Nawara say, laughing. "And you could tell. He had that look where he knew what he was doing, he knew where he was going. I'd call him a perfect gentleman. He was attentive, he would listen to what you had to say. Just a good dude, through and through. I really admire Jack for his personality in general. But you also knew that he knew what he wanted and you weren't going to stop him. He was driven, but in a courteous manner – as much as you could when you're that driven. He had a very specific idea of what he wanted."

The parallels between the Gold Dollar and CBGB's, the punk-gestating club in a rotting part of Seventies New York that had similarly nonplussed its country and blues-loving owner, Hilly Kristal, seem obvious now, after the White Stripes' rampaging break-out. But in the late Nineties it was the centre of a tiny scene, now self-sufficient enough to let the outside world vanish. The prospect of that world caring remained remote.

"You're being excited by some guy you kind of know's band more than by what you hear on the radio," Gregory remembers, "and you've already forgotten about record companies, you figure they aren't going to touch you anyways. A couple of indies were starting around town, guys at least saying, 'Oh, I'll put out a 45.' But even people who worked in the industry here, label reps, weren't coming down to shows at the Gold Dollar, not at all. It's not like when Atlantic had scouts in town to find Aretha Franklin. The [free weekly equivalent to the *Village Voice*] *Metro-Times* for a while wouldn't write about any of those bands. But eventually another writer came in there. So there were some people interested in the music who got into the right gigs at the right time.

"I think it was about 50 people," he says of the scene's personnel, "that somehow had their hands on the toys."

The unknowable extra factor in the music everyone made lay outside the Gold Dollar. When I walked there on a Sunday morning in 2015, there was something restful to a visitor about the area's continuing, overgrown dereliction. But even now, as development and gentrification eat at the edges of the Cass Corridor, I wouldn't walk down that part of Cass Avenue at night. And I can remember how still more spookily deserted the Corridor was in the daytime in 2002. In the dark, drugs, prostitution and ruins surrounded the Gold Dollar. First impressions to an outsider were apocalyptic.

"Yeah, absolutely," says Kroha. "And because of that, the signs of life that you see are that much more poignant. And it makes living more poignant, in a way, too. Because you have to make something happen. But another cool thing about Detroit is it's not a super-hip place. So you could do things and be left alone, and be really outside of the hip culture.

We were always five years behind New York. But we had our own time and our own place to come up with our own thing."

"Detroit's unrecognisable from when I grew up," Nawara states. "I remember when I was a kid it being beautiful, and people walking their kids down the street, greeting people, smiling, and people gardening. And I remember it turning to complete shit in the Eighties, and it went like that through the Nineties. But it was definitely ghet-to, ghet-to round the Gold Dollar. Very rough. And even today where it is, on Peterboro and Cass, it's still total ghetto. Back then, because of all the crime and all the filth, it made you feel like an outlaw. It made you feel like a badass, I guess. Like, 'Yeah, we're tough.' Everyone was much more tough back then! And actually, you had to be, because at the time it was still predominantly black, and we were living in an old-school African-American world. In the Gold Dollar, we were the only white kids in the neighbourhood. And it wasn't a very mixed crowd back then. It was a little tiny white oasis, I guess!"

Did the scene get any trouble because of that, for being interlopers?

"There was crime. Lots of break-ins and robberies, and definitely some incidents to people I knew that were not too cool. But for the most part, nothing too major happened."

"It was pretty sketchy," Tim Purrier remembers. "A lot of people's cars got broken into and windows smashed in front of there. And usually you only saw that area at night, because you were only playing there at night, and it was very dark, street lighting wasn't good. It was a little scary. If you parked two blocks away, you were kind of watching yourself. That might have got into the Hentchmen's music."

"When Crime & the City Solution recorded here, Alexander Hacke was saying how much it reminded him of Berlin when he was growing up," says Gregory. "A lot of people romanticise what they call 'ruin porn'. But when you've grown up here, it's just always been that way. It's how you've seen the world. There's burned-out buildings. You almost accept it as part of the landscape, till you go to other cities. But where you first start going to shows and playing, it's just how it is. Like there was a house where the old drummer from the Electric Six, Corey Martin, lived, where the old Tigers Stadium was [near Jack's home]. It was like a fricking mansion, but horrible. Really bad with the crime around that area. But always after shows there'd be parties there, with people hanging out all night."

I ask him if how the Cass Corridor was had any impact on the music being made there. "Well, it was a big crack area between the Gold Dollar and the Masonic," he considers. "And on any of the side-streets there, people got their windows busted out. Neil did have someone watching the lot, and he had a camera on the side of the Gold Dollar. Dion Fischer from the Go got mugged outside, but it was very rare. But you just didn't go walking there. There was a Chinese place you'd walk down the block to eat at" – itself a shuttered ruin now – "and walk back. You weren't really hanging outside. But because it was so far and out of the way, the only people who came really did come for the music. And that's probably why it attracted a lot of musicians. Because a lot of people wouldn't go to a place that was that dodgy, you had to have a reason."

"My friend Dion got pistol-whipped behind some building very close to the Gold Dollar," Fischer's Go bandmate John Krautner confirms. "But the week after, he went back to the club." According to Matt Smith, "Dion had to stand there while a girl he was with got pistol-whipped. I walked outside afterwards and saw the bump on her head."

Jack's perspective on all this was different. He had always lived deep in the city, never travelling far from dodginess when he went home. It's very unfair to portray his new Gold Dollar friends as effete suburbanites, even when most of them went north of 8 Mile to sleep, eventually. Most were white working-class. But they didn't wake up in Mexicantown. Though he loved Detroit in many ways, it often seemed an abusive affair. He saw decreasing romance in its ruins as he grew older. The city's past seemed to berate and diminish him, as he often felt family and others did. "I grew up with the feeling that my environment wasn't good enough or I wasn't good enough," he told *Q*'s Michael Odell. "Everyone would talk about how Detroit was 'before', and I had this feeling you'd missed out because you were in the aftermath."

He found the most friends he'd ever have in the sweaty closeness of the Gold Dollar. But just as he did at school, he also privately guarded against fitting in too well with this new community. The drive towards set goals Dan Miller sensed in him at 19 couldn't be deflected. Since finishing his apprenticeship with Brian Muldoon and quitting Wayne State, White had worked for a number of suburban upholstery firms. When he was 21, the year he married Meg, he had started his own shop, Third Man Upholstery. He also replaced his parents, who'd finally quit Mexicantown, as 1203 Ferdinand's sole, mortgage-paying owner. He had weighed himself down with responsibilities, as he would find ways to for the rest of his life. But as he focused all day on hard physical craft, he came to envy the music-filled lives of his friends, who seemed to drift from one record store job to the next. "I was jealous of them because you just don't have the time in the day to be able to do that," he remembered in Steve Miller's book *Detroit Rock City*. There was, of course, no need to envy a life he could have joined. "I started thinking maybe I should work at one of those places," he admitted. "That's when I made the decision to be careful of myself, to be careful of things like collecting records and emulating other people."

White was also in a new band formed by Dan Miller from the remnants of Goober & the Peas in 1997. Two-Star Tabernacle found him no longer behind the drum kit, but sharing guitars and vocals out front with Miller, whose wife, Tracee Mae Miller, was bassist, with the "Doc" White replaced in the Peas, Damian Lang, on drums. White also had a shock of curly blond hair, in a style wisely never seen again. "Who's the guy with the Split Enz haircut?" Jim Diamond chortled. A 1998 photo shows the quartet in suits, White now sporting more sober rockabilly/GI crew-cut sides and dark hair on top. "Two-Star Tabernacle was a drier more 'serious' extension of Jack and Dan's writing," Dave Feeny remembers. "It was slightly different from Goober & the Peas," says Troy Gregory, "a more spaghetti western kind of sound."

Their only release was a 7-inch on Bloodshot Records in 1998, 'Ramblin' Man'/'Lily White Mama And Jet Black Daddy', featuring Andre Williams. Then 61, Williams was a Fifties star of local R&B label Fortune Records, subsequently working with Chess Records, Ike Turner and George Clinton. It was likely the first released recording from White's living room home studio at 1203 Ferdinand, and sounds like an early dream come true. With Dan Kroha helping on production and Rocket 455's Jeff Meier recording, White takes barrelhouse piano and, on the B-side, delighted backing vocals. Williams is the sort of weathered, salty shouter Dylan wished he was on his debut, admitting, 'Some people, some people might say that I'm not good.' Long acquaintance with this sometimes homeless survivor from the beginnings of Detroit soul could indeed be trying, but 'Ramblin' Man' is the sort of high-energy, high-roughage single Third Man would be proud to release now.

Detroit musicians who'd been around the block such as Williams, and Rodriguez, long before his discovery in the documentary *Searching For Sugar Man* (2012), were part of the new scene White was mixed up in – more elders to admire, or run a mile from. "These older R&B guys were still around," Troy Gregory explains. "And Andre did this record with Mick and Dan Kroha at Diamond's called *Silky* [1998], and everyone around Detroit that was listening to music at that time knew that record. And Jeff Meier got [Williams' Fortune labelmate] Nathaniel Mayer on Fat Possum. Same with Rodriguez, everybody knew those records like *Cold Fact*, and he was always around town, and we liked and respected him. I'd be at shows, and they'd go, 'Oh, fuck, Rodriguez was here . . .'"

A bootleg of Two-Star Tabernacle at the Gold Dollar on January 16, 1998 shows White returned to strong electric guitar. But what's most striking is how his always high, wild voice sometimes tumbles off the high wire into absurdity. When White sings his own song, 'Itchy', his try at speeding excitement becomes an unintelligibly rapid squeal, like a mangled cassette tape. "After the show," a Goober & the Peas fan reflects under this performance on YouTube, "Dan asked me how it was and I told him it was great. I didn't have the heart to tell him the other guitar player sang horribly. He sounded like a cat being strangled." At White's worst here, you can't argue.

He does manage a decent country croon, over a now familiar deep, distorted guitar. And the set-list includes 'Hotel Yorba', soon to be made famous by the other band White formed in 1997, the White Stripes, its depressed lyrics ('All they got inside is vacancy . . .') clearer in this scratchy, country version. A year later, Two-Star Tabernacle played more future Stripes songs, as White's career finally neared singularity, with one band and sound strong enough to take him out of Detroit. But that was also the climax of another long, private struggle since high school, to establish a vision of his own. And he had done it through the blues.

4

Wanting the Blues

"I WOULD much rather have lived in the Twenties or Thirties," Jack White told an early British interviewer, "but that will never be. My dream of being a black man in the Thirties is not going to happen."

This quote struck me as soon as I read it in 2001, and it still suggests the strangest reaches of White's life and music. I'd forgotten in the intervening years that White grinned to *NME*'s James Oldham after he said it, attempting to make his last line a joke. But the look Meg flashed revealed its poor taste. The White Stripes were talking in the balcony of the Bristol Louisiana the morning after their second UK gig, the tidal wave of tabloid attention already rushing towards them, but perhaps hazy on how loaded words can become. Still, White didn't really back off, instead digging into his statement's implications.

"As far as hardships go," he insisted, "at least their lives made sense to them. They were playing for money and they were playing to get by. Music was a form of communication." In contrast to the "mass", instant media of emails and mobile phones in the just dawned 21st century, his blues heroes lived, he thought, in a time that was "a lot more cultured." How that compensated for rural poverty so extreme that some literally ate dirt, working conditions and a lack of rights still much like slavery, and racism so unfettered that Mississippi left lynching legal till 1938, was something the 26-year-old White seemed naively indifferent to.

His relationship with the blues was inextricable from his attitudes to modernity and an idealised American South, where most of the bluesmen he revered had lived. But Jack White's blues began with a series of musical stepping stones, all taken in the streets of Detroit, and leading to a moment of stunning, personal revelation.

The tape brother Eddie found so they could learn Howlin' Wolf's 1957 version of the Mississippi Sheiks' 1930 'Sittin' On Top Of The World', with Wolf rasping the words between harmonica breaks and free-ranging boogie piano, was the first, false start. It was more part of the Fifties

56

Chicago style popularised by Wolf's label Chess than the Mississippi sound of the singer's Thirties youth, which White would come to favour. White was 16 then, and his school friend Dominic Suchyta remembered the blues as their "common ground". During the next two years, White traced rock cover versions of Robert Johnson's Twenties and Thirties recordings back to their source; he was a fan of the Gun Club (who recorded Johnson's 'Preaching Blues') and Stevie Ray Vaughan ('Sweet Home Chicago'). This introduction to the most legendary figure of so-called country or Delta blues "felt really, really compelling and beauti-ful," he assured Barney Hoskyns. "When I heard him, I thought it was okay," he told *Rolling Stone* in a more precise record of his taste's progress. "Then I heard Son House's a cappella song 'Grinnin' In Your Face'. That was a transformative moment."

White's trail there had begun at a Radiohead show when he was 18 (either at Detroit's State Theatre on October 13, 1993, or among 800 others at St Andrew's Hall, on June 9 the following year). The alienation Thom Yorke was describing as his band toured *The Bends*, with the defiantly self-loathing 'Creep' still their most famous song, fitted the late days of grunge (White was already a Nirvana fan). But it wasn't Yorke or Radiohead's guitarist Jonny Greenwood who marked White. It was one of their intro music's songs that haunted him. No one with him recog-nised the stark a cappella sound. When he hunted it down (in the internet's early days, the encyclopaedic Brian Muldoon was surely his source), he discovered Son House's 'John The Revelator'.

Son House (born Eddie James House, Jr. in Mississippi in 1902) was an artistic giant in Thirties acoustic blues, a confidante of the music's original king, Charley Patton, and direct inspiration to younger guitarists, from Robert Johnson to the post-war electric revolutionary Muddy Waters. The song White heard was from his 1965 *Father Of Folk Blues* comeback LP, recorded after House, presumed part of a pre-war blues history only surviving in the scratched grooves of prized 78s, was found very much alive, if a serious alcoholic, in a Rochester, New York housing project. House's abilities were blurred by drink and encrusted by the rust of the decade since he'd played guitar, needing young white blues fan and future Canned Heat guitarist Al Wilson to teach him how to play his own songs. The album nevertheless bleeds genuine, raw power, on 'John The Revelator' most of all. House moved between preaching and playing all his life, and his words ring with a riverside evangelist's declamatory force. 'Tell me, who's that ridin'?' he asks, urgent and echoing in the dark. His voice and handclap beats shake, and he mutters half-formed answers to his question, but his gathered, remaining strength feels gigantic. The words, too, with Adam driven from Eden 'nekkid and ashamed', are ancient and strange.

It was the opening track, 'Death Letter Blues', which White vividly remembered being played. House's almost jauntily springy slide guitar accompanies his journey to view the corpse of his newly dead lover, who he finds 'laying on a cooling board'. His expedition's details grow memorably darker, with '10,000 people standing on the burying ground', a grimly casual adios, 'Farewell, honey, I'll see you on Judgement Day', the revelation that she didn't even love him, and our final glimpses of the singer 'just hugging the pillows where you used to lay', and numbly 'feeling around for my shoes', ready at the circular finish to set off again.

Any songwriter could learn a lot from that. But the next song White remembered being played didn't just change his music, but his life. Son House's only accompaniment on 'Grinnin' In Your Face', as with 'John The Revelator', was a slow, uneven hand-clap, the slapping together of his palms made fleshily clear by Dylan producer John Hammond. 'You know your mother will talk about you/ Your sisters and your brothers too', the old voice advises, as if speaking directly to the listener. 'Yes, don't care how you're trying to live/ They'll talk about you still.' Slap, slap, then the description of indignity deepens. 'You know they'll jump you up and down/ They'll turn you round and round/ Just as soon is your back is turned' – the voice rising in outrage – 'They'll be trying to crush you down.' Somewhere in the world, by contrast, there exists 'a true friend'. So, Son House insists throughout the song's bare two minutes, with malicious-sounding pleasure in his bleakness: 'Don't you mind, people grinnin' in your face.'

White put the record on for Jimmy Page and U2's The Edge in *It Might Get Loud*, shutting his eyes as if in prayer. "I didn't know you could do that, just singing and clapping [off-time]," he said. "It meant everything. I heard everything disappearing." This extended his epiphany aged 15 watching the Flat Duo Jets, when there seemed to be "nothing there", just Dexter Romweber marauding with a crappy guitar and amp. The necessary rudiments of music-making vanished one by one, like a conjuror's trick. Now, all you needed was a human being.

Even more importantly, Son House's words seemed to depict the protecting, muffling, critical screen White's siblings formed between him and life outside Ferdinand Street; and, by showing it plain, demolish it. "I heard the song I'd been waiting to hear my whole life," he told *Mojo*'s Andrew Male. "It said, 'Don't care what people think' . . . we had a big family, I didn't have that many friends, and I was paranoid. I thought everybody was talking about me all the time. It released my life." He thought about what he'd heard for days, digesting its implications. The last Gillis sibling to be born, who often felt like the least, let invisible shackles fall. There was nothing to stop him choosing his own path. Musically and personally, he could stand alone. He mentioned this happening when he was "18 or 19" to *Total Guitar*. This was surely part of the breakdown and focused rebirth he suffered at 19, with Son House at its heart.

"It was as if someone, with a single blow of the axe, had opened up the world to me," *Sonic*'s Lennart Persson remembered him declare of the moment he heard the song. "After that, my life received meaning."

Feeling such powerful truth in 'Grinnin' In Your Face' turned the key into blues as a whole. It was now that Robert Johnson "became extremely beautiful", he explained to *Rolling Stone*. Columbia had released Johnson's *The Complete Recordings* in 1990, a chart hit crowning a posthumous cult, which had been growing since he was dubbed *King Of The Delta Blues Singers* on a 1961 LP. Johnson had been an influential enigma since the Sixties; tales of trading his soul for guitar prowess spun around him. He had died aged 26 in 1938, a jealous husband poisoning him during a gig, and his lingering mystery was further cemented in fact in the Eighties by two recovered photos. One showed Johnson snappy in pinstripe suit and fedora, happily beaming with acoustic guitar in hand; the second revealed a hip, handsome, white-shirted kid, looking coolly at the photo-booth camera, cigarette dangling from his mouth. White saw the former photo on *The Complete Recordings*' cover while bunking off school to buy *The Beatles* (White Album), aged 14. He found it "legitimately scary", reason enough to steer clear of Johnson for years.

But it was the precociously modern, worldly, commanding Johnson of the second photo who was eventually appreciated by White. His guitar can seem stuttering, constricted, then leap down jolting yet fluent lines; hold a bass-line beat, or, as on 'Crossroad Blues', violently, repeatedly slash. It's an instrument of improvised, personal freedom, as it would be for White. His voice leaps into sudden falsetto, croons and growls, in the service of lyrics incorporating Biblical lore, blatant sex spliced to sly modern metaphors ('Phonogram Blues', 'Terraplane Blues'), cocky brags, threats and momentary despair. White ignored the Satan stories to respond to the art he actually heard; the way 'Stones In My Passway', for instance, follows the line 'you laid a passway for me' by seeming to turn to the girl mid–song and softly, conversationally enquire, 'Now, what are you trying to do?' "Amazing natural songwriting," White marvelled to Jaan Uhelszki, also noting its subtly "odd" guitar rhythms. "Johnson inspired and influenced us the most," he told *Mojo* of the blues behind the White Stripes. "A full-ranged, truly beautiful singer. Good and evil are equally present in his songs."

Walking into a Detroit record shop one day, White found blues' full wealth laid out before him. A family had just sold a dead relative's stack of blues reissues on the Austrian Document label. When White arrived, the obvious cream had already been skimmed. "So I got to buy a lot of records I'd never seen before," he remembered to *The Guardian*'s Dave Simpson, "by Tommy Johnson, Blind Boy Fuller, Mississippi John Hurt, Blind Willie McTell . . . I bought as many as I could – 30, 40 of them." White told Document's latter-day, Scottish owner Gary Atkinson that these were the first blues records he bought.

McTell's name had been recently revived twice by another White idol. Bob Dylan's 1983 'Blind Willie McTell' (unreleased till 1991) was his own greatest blues song, abandoned as a demo made with Mark Knopfler, with a Son House-style, foot-stomp beat. Sitting in a drifting, visionary state in the St James Hotel in Reagan's America, Dylan stalks across time and space from East Texas to New Orleans, sniffing out scenes of revival shows, Civil War, torched plantations and whip-crack cruelty: 'Smell that sweet magnolia blooming/ See the ghosts of slavery ships.' This blasted, cursed Southern landscape becomes a symbol of a still fallen world, encapsulated in another's man voice. 'No one sings the blues,' Dylan sings with rising majesty, pounding the piano as if at his own revival meeting, 'like Blind Willie McTell'. His 1993 acoustic blues album *World Gone Wrong* then covered McTell's 'Broke Down Engine' and 'Delia'. His extraordinary liner notes make a Beat manifesto for the blues' ceaseless cultural depth. "It's about variations of human longing," he writes of 'Broke Down Engine'. The best-selling Thirties blues band the Mississippi Sheiks, also covered twice, go against Nineties "cultural policy". Blues, for Dylan, exists "before the insane world of entertainment exploded in our faces". That is the lost world White wants.

The White Stripes' familiarity with Dylan's example was shown when they made a folk song he revived on *World Gone Wrong*'s 1992 companion *Good As I Been To You*, 'Black Jack Davey', a 'Seven Nation Army' B-side. Jack discussed 'Blind Willie McTell' with *The Guardian*'s Dave Simpson in

2013. "Dylan . . . he used McTell's name to make a point that all these things have happened in the world and there is still someone that's going to scream about it."

McTell himself, heard by White on those second-hand Document LPs, is lighter in tone and temperament than the agonised weight White and Dylan put on him. Born around 1898 in Georgia, and literate in braille from several blind schools including one in Michigan, McTell was a teenage runaway and street-singer, learning his trade, too, at medicine shows, carnivals and country fairs where hillbilly, folk and pop would be required in his repertoire alongside blues and ragtime (Robert Johnson would have been similarly flexible and non-purist live). McTell's high, dryly humorous voice suits lyrics of surreal sexual excess and wry acceptance, matched by 12-string guitar of eccentric time-signatures, unexpected accents and sudden, dazzling speed.

His suitability, like Johnson, as a model for White's playing is suggested in this Woody Mann description, quoted in a Yazoo reissue LP's liner notes: "his inconsistent picking approach . . . has almost no order and seems to stem as much from whim as from his vocal inflections. He treats each phrase of his music as a separate entity with its own rhythmical and melodic nuances . . . McTell's musical stream-of-consciousness wanders . . ." This is very different from the more regular rhythms of the electric Chicago blues that were spliced into rock'n'roll's hybrid DNA in the Fifties. White's inspirations were less tethered to structure, more primed for experimentation. "I don't, and never have, liked the electric blues very much," he told *Bangsheet*. "Stuff like B.B. King and Buddy Guy." Even John Lee Hooker's thrilling 1948 anthem 'Boogie Chillun', which walks the listener down the bustling, now long-gone streets of Detroit's Black Bottom where Hooker made his name and echoes right through to T. Rex, was only politely acknowledged by the city's new blues king. Typically, White fell in love with a form constructed from constriction – blues has 12 bars and three-line verses, a haiku-like cage – but heard how, travelling light with acoustic guitar and voice, individuality could be expressed without limit.

Skip James, a Mississippi contemporary of Son House rediscovered alongside him in the Sixties, all spectral falsetto and minor-key guitar, and Blind Willie Johnson, capable of gravel-throated outrage, quavering moans and brief, swampy slide-guitar solos White wished went on "for an hour", were important to him, too. "You pull certain things from those guys," he told *Rolling Stone*. "From Kokomo Arnold [capable of feminine-high notes, and conversationally natural then telescope-squeezed singing], I get the vocal phrasing. From Blind Willie Johnson, it's the slide." Jack White's blues were also found in odd corners. 'St. James Infirmary Blues', covered on *The White Stripes* (2001), was learned from a video cassette of Thirties Betty Boop cartoons he and Meg delightedly watched as a couple; outrageous jazz-pop star Cab Calloway sang it in the guise of Koko the Clown.

But it was Charley Patton who White saw as the final breakthrough in both his blues schooling, and his sense of self. Born in Edwards, Mississippi in 1897 and dead of a heart attack by 1934, Patton was a riotous showman forebear of Little Richard, Jerry Lee Lewis and Jimi Hendrix, riding his guitar or riffing it behind his neck, and prophesying rock, too, in a sharp-suited, quick-burning life of cocaine, liquor and sex. He sounds imposingly masculine, with a deep, rough roar like molten coal; his guitar skips nimbly while seeming to exert relentless pressure. But this has to be deciphered through the crackles and static of especially worn source 78s, like weather patterns reducing an old TV signal to snowy shapes and sounds.

It's no wonder Patton was a step too far for White when he first heard him in 1999, two years after the White Stripes began. When he discussed his blues tastes with Barney Hoskyns a decade later, he loved Patton at last. But what he loved even more was that his conversion was honestly emotional. This contrasted with a Detroit scene he by then saw as a "bizarre filter", where he'd struggled not to "like things just to tell people this is what I like . . . 'I've got this obscure record and you don't.' So to finally have Charley Patton connect with you is such a great thing." He trusted what he felt for Patton as much as he now suspected the refined, record-collector tastes of the garage-punks of Detroit. He sounded like a truly existential loner as he spoke. When others said they shared his pleasure in Patton's murky blues, he had no faith he was truly understood. "You can hope, but you don't really *know*." Only the blues in his head could comfort him.

But blues was a fervently spoken language in the Cass Corridor, the Witches' Troy Gregory remembers. Rummaging in a back room of his Ferndale home in 2015, he digs out two box sets for me: *Screamin' And Hollerin' The Blues By The Masked Marvel*, which compiled Charley Patton and his peers in 2001, and Harry Smith's epochal 1952 roots survey *Anthology Of American Folk Music*, issued on CD in 1997. "Yazoo Records came out and started reissuing people like Charley Patton, Blind Boy

Fuller and Rev. Gary Davis [on CD]," Gregory says. "And those records were awesome, because if you ever found them in record stores in good condition they were pretty damn expensive. So now this stuff was way more accessible. Willie Wilson who ran Repeat the Beat, and was friends with Lee who ran Off the Record where Brendan [Benson] and Dave [Buick] who did [the White Stripes' first label] Italy worked, they would order this stuff into the store. So anyone who appreciated some authenticity in their music was of course snatching those up. I bought a CD player, to play them."

When Gregory first saw the White Stripes and they played 'Death Letter Blues', he appreciated their good taste, but wasn't surprised. Blues was already in the local water. "Yeah. God, a band I had right when I moved back [in the early Nineties] covered 'Soul Of A Man' by Blind Willie Johnson," he remembers. "Another thing at that time was that because that stuff started coming out, blues got popular elsewhere, too. That's why [Mississippi raw blues label and future home of the Black Keys] Fat Possum was able to become a profitable label for a little while, because it found [Mississippi bluesman] R.L. Burnside was still around. And Mick [Collins] knew a lot of those people from the Gories working with Alex Chilton in Memphis, and one of those guys did this movie called *Wayne County Rambling*. Mick's in it, and Danny [Kroha], and R.L. Burnside. R.L. came round here a bunch of times, and played one time in Royal Oak. That stuff was popular enough for that to happen."

White's brief White Stripes bandmate Steve Nawara also remembers Detroit blues clubs surviving into the Nineties, though perhaps not ones to Jack's taste. "They weren't exactly . . . you couldn't really go to them unless you knew someone," he laughs. "There was a place called Garfield's, and they would sell cocaine over the bar. They'd cut it up for you, and there'd be all these old blues guys sitting around and listening to their old 45s, it was like you're going back into the Forties or the Thirties. It was right around the Magic Stick. Right beside the campus area. That was around '95 or so. You'd see a lot of old blues then. There's still a place called John's Carpet House. It's called that because there was a bar that every Sunday held blues jams, that was in such a bad state they held it together by stapling pieces of carpet together, and finally the place just collapsed. And they still wanted to play blues. And so they got a generator and set up in a field across the street [at 2133 Frederick Street]. The city keeps trying to close it down, but they play every Sunday, with barbecues, and a lot of real deal Motown musicians. It's a blast."

There's a deep irony, anyway, to White's eventual dislike of Detroit's record-collector reverence for the cultish and obscure. As Marybeth Hamilton's *In Search Of The Blues* uncomfortably reveals, the idea of country or Delta blues, its great players and the authentically primitive American culture it meant to him was cooked up by a previous generation of record collectors, not in the Thirties, but the Sixties.

Hamilton's book traces a history of audacious white sociologists and adventurers roaming the South throughout the first half of the 20th century, armed with a developing array of Speak-o-Phone disc recorders, experimental aluminium discs and other portable, cutting-edge gear, hunting for what the Library of Congress' 1902 *Negro Blues And Hollers* approvingly called music that was "archaic in the best sense . . . gnarled, rough-hewn, and eminently uncommercial." The story of Huddie Ledbetter, better known as Leadbelly, is this search in extremis. His enduring currency saw his 'Where Did You Sleep Last Night?' sung with a marrow-chilling scream by White's early hero Kurt Cobain on *Nirvana's MTV Unplugged In New York* (1994). But his eventually bitter relationship with the Southern white sociologist who "discovered" him in Louisiana's grim Angola penitentiary, John Lomax, meant Ledbetter couldn't wait to escape his tame rustic role for the fast urban pleasures of Harlem and, later, bohemian Greenwich Village. Similarly, a Lomax 'field' visit to a plantation juke-joint in Clarksdale, Mississippi found customers dancing not to local bluesmen's 78s, but the latest urbane Duke Ellington hit. "Charley Patton probably sold better than any of them in the Twenties," Hamilton says of White's heroes' place in black lives. "In 1941, when Lomax goes to the Delta and draws up his list of what's on the jukebox, Robert Johnson's 'Terraplane Blues' was on there, and that's about it in terms of local singers. None of them really sold at all."

The crowning triumph of white fantasy and taste over blues' black reality came when a small coterie of obsessive New York record collectors, led by their strange guru, James McKune, responded to Sam Charters' *The Country Blues* book and record (both 1959) with cult releases such as *Really! The Country Blues* (1961). Country blues itself was a phrase these white fans had cooked up, part of a full-blown mythology built around primeval Mississippi swamps, decrepit shacks, plantation hollers, raw unknown voices on unbought 78s found in skips and, most of all, the Satan-haunted, then-faceless legend of Robert Johnson (quickly taken up by Columbia Records' *King Of The Delta Blues Singers* and blues-rockers from Eric Clapton to Led Zeppelin). It was now that the previously obscure Skip James, Son House, Blind Willie McTell and Johnson joined Charley Patton – actually popular in his day – on blues' white-run Mount Rushmore. Jack White built his musical life around the authenticity of icons only recently carved into stone.

"There's a direct line between these early folklorists and then these record collectors, and this sense of what the Delta blues is," Hamilton tells me. "It is really late in the day that the Delta becomes the place to go to if you're looking for authentic black music. And it really isn't until the 1960s that the phrase 'the Delta blues' was coined. It's certainly not one Robert Johnson knew. There's this moment in Alan Lomax's *The Land Where The Blues Began*, based on field-work in 1931 but written 50 years later, where he has somebody, Son House maybe, playing in a juke-joint, and when he's finished the man behind the bar says, 'That's the blues. That's the Delta blues.' That's nowhere in his field notes, I've looked. That's completely an invention. That phrase comes out of a later turf-war among collectors."

The 26-year-old White's fond imagining to that English journalist about envied black lives free of "mass" culture, like Dylan's belief *World Gone Wrong*'s songs pre-dated "the insane world of mass entertainment", are just two more fantasies, according to Hamilton. "Alan Lomax had gone into that [Delta] landscape in 1941 precisely because it was so permeated by jukeboxes, by commercial culture, by movies, by cars. He and the white sociologists were interested in going because they wanted to know what the region was like where a 'folk', 'primitive', rural people were being affected by this. So they wrote notes on jukeboxes and they interviewed Muddy Waters about his record collection. They were interested in their worldliness."

White could hear the music of his heroes clearly, studying individual style and content. He went academically deep, digging out John and Ruby Lomax's Library of Congress interview with Blind Willie McTell in an Atlanta hotel room in 1940, and sampling a fragment in which McTell complains of a car crash en route on the cover of one of his songs, 'Your Southern Can Is Mine', which ends the White Stripes' second album, *De Stijl*. He was acutely aware of the recording process that gave these records to him. "The romance of it . . . the timing of it – the recording technology of the time, and the fact that they even bothered to record it – is just so perfect," he marvelled to Barney Hoskyns. "It's like the frame around the picture."

But the idea of these records and their makers as impossible phantasms appealed to him more. "They sound like they couldn't have occurred for real," White told Dave Simpson. "They don't sound like you could have listened to those songs being recorded." Charley Patton, who he'd found so hard to grasp, became an exemplar of the blues' appeal to him in part because of the encrustations like petrified tree bark that filled the grooves holding his voice. "Charley Patton almost seems like he didn't even really exist," he suggested to Pamela Des Barres.

The 'Delta' blues and its Thirties milieu were a dreamland for White, rich in outlandish personalities, extravagant action and complex codes of music and character. In his waking reality he was beaten down by bullies, unwittingly diminished by older siblings and stuck in a city that was a backwater, itself encrusted with mould and ash like a Patton 78. He described hearing 'Grinnin' In Your Face' to Andrew Male as if the record was speaking directly to him. From that moment, *Sonic*'s Lennart Persson remembered him saying on Swedish TV "my life received meaning", which sounds like Holy Communion. The "single blow of the axe" with which Son House cleaves the world open for him in the same interview suggests a superhero origin story: the lightning bolt transfiguration, maybe, which when 12-year-old Billy Batson says "Shazam!" turns him into mighty Captain Marvel, or the walking stick with which crippled Dr Don Blake strikes the ground to become hammer-wielding Thor. Time travel, alternate realities and alter egos were part of blues mythology's potential for him, alongside its concrete musical lessons.

"The Blues is holy, a perfect creation; it is everything that music should be," Persson remembers him saying. "It contains so much that I almost don't dare to mess with it. But I must." He shivered at its power. "I can lie in bed in the middle of the night and feel an ice-cold wind flowing through my body, which makes me start to shake uncontrollably. Then I have to get up and hear Charley Patton or Robert Johnson." This dreamland was inextricable from a second one: "The American South should be regarded as holy land by everyone. Everything which is worth anything comes from there."

Detroit is a historic outpost of Southern emigrants, fleeing declining plantation economies for the city's auto industry from the Twenties till the Sixties. Scraps of their culture, accent and an open helpfulness uncommon in big cities remain. Before Meg informed White of this connection, hearing Southern voices already felt like coming home. "It always felt like, *this is an American*," he told Barney Hoskyns. "When someone has a northern accent you don't know – you could," he sniffed dismissively, "be from Canada." He went further to *The Observer*'s Andrew Perry, declaring the region was "the real America, the last bastion of culture in the country, where people really have American culture."

White also associated the South of his blues heroes with an archaic separation of the sexes when, he told *The Guardian*'s Keith Cameron, "there were a lot of things involving feminine and masculine ideals that were closer to one's own nature." The White Stripes covered McTell's cartoonishly violent, woman-beating 'Your Southern Can Is Mine' instead of "a sweet heartbreak number", he told *NME*'s James Oldham, to emphasise this old reality. "They did lead different lives. They were huge drinkers and they beat their women. Some of their lifestyle makes me wish I was born in the Twenties; at the same time, some of it was bad. Women and men both had different roles then . . . All that machismo kinda interests me." The bluntness of the blues' sexual battles, settled with fists, guns and, in the case of 'Your Southern Can Is Mine', a household brick, fascinated him. But his own songs explored his dismay at modern relationships in terms of disappointed chivalry. 'I'm Finding It Harder To Be A Gentleman', he warned on a 2001 White Stripes song; the subtitle of their biggest hit album, *Elephant*, is 'Death of the Sweetheart'.

The American archetype that most fits his fantasies of courtly decorum is, of course, the South of an even earlier era, grotesquely idealised in the opening lines of *Gone With The Wind*: "There was a land of Cavaliers and Cotton fields called the Old South. Here in this pretty world Gallantry took its last bow . . . Here was the last ever to be seen of Knights and their Ladies Fair, of Master and of Slave . . ." Jack's most significant film role would be in a 21st century cousin to that saga, *Cold Mountain*; he would name a daughter after Scarlett O'Hara, and eventually live in a Southern mansion like a miniature version of O'Hara's home, Tara. If his formative dreams seem split between sipping mint juleps on an antebellum porch and slugging gin in the shacks down below, this is certainly rich and strange ground for rock'n'roll.

As if correcting his outlandish statement to *NME* a year before, White simplified his blues mission to *Mojo* in 2002. "I'm not black, I'm not from the South, and it's not 1930," he confessed. "I'm not interested in copying . . . I'm interested in re-telling the story. I just believe in singing 'John The Revelator' one more time." Jack White, folk singer – the role he'd tried on for size singing Dylan's debut LP in coffee houses aged 18 –

was another aspect of his blues persona. The songs he learned from vintage blues LPs certainly had roots older than recorded music. "Think about how many versions there'd been of something like 'Death Letter Blues'," Troy Gregory suggests, "or what that morphed from, and how lyrical details like disasters were changed by location. 'We don't have floods here, but we have tornadoes.' The murder's with a gun, not a candlestick – the sun rises in the east, not the west, depending what you're looking at. The White Stripes were lucky to have that and draw upon it. Like the Stones and Zeppelin had, they were able to dip into these great old songs and reinterpret them. And you had all these young kids who didn't even know the Zeppelin or Stones versions, so to them it was brand-new and exciting." White felt a responsibility to tend this tradition. "If we can trick 15-year-old girls into singing the lyrics to a Son House song," he told Jim Jarmusch, "we've really achieved something."

But it definitely wasn't 1930, and Jack White's blues didn't grow in isolation. They were also nurtured by the radio and Brian Muldoon's record collection, by punk and his garage-rock peers. Two white Californians had already shown him how blues could be remade as an extreme musical statement at the end of the 20th century. The Gun Club's debut, *Fire Of Love* (1981), was a crucial album to the teenage Jack. Like the Flat Duo Jets' Dominic Romweber, the band's pudgy, bleach-haired singer Jeffrey Lee Pierce seemed desperate and possessed, with a high, lonely, wild voice. His fatally self-destructive course was set by habits described in junkie blues such as White favourites 'She's Like Heroin To Me' and 'For The Love Of Ivy'. On the latter, between goblin moans, Pierce buys a graveyard to fill with his enemies, while Ward Dotson tunnels into the echoing mix with surf and slide guitar (linking him to another teen hero of Jack's, Sixties surf king Dick Dale). Pierce fused blues to LA punk, rockabilly and an insistently dissolute Eighties existence.

Then there was Captain Beefheart. White's co-guitarist during his brief spell in the Go, John Krautner, told him to watch a John Peel-presented BBC Beefheart documentary in 1999, the same year he discovered Patton and the White Stripes recorded their first album. Elaine Shepherd's film, *The Artist Formerly Known As Captain Beefheart*, sketches the story of Don Van Vliet, from a Fifties adolescence in the dull, desert-bordered tract housing of Lancaster, California, where he became obsessed with the blues records of his Southern parents, to local celebrity as Captain Beefheart, a bluesman with a rough bark purloined from Howlin' Wolf; then on to *Trout Mask Replica* (1969), in many ways rock's equivalent to *Citizen Kane*.

Beefheart, a non-musician, exerted total, tyrannical control over the Magic Band of skilled musicians who put his outlandish ideas into practice, constructing and rehearsing the double album's music over 10 months in an old, hilltop bungalow hidden in lush undergrowth. Inside, rubber-covered walls caused dungeon darkness, where time crawled unnaturally and Beefheart was a sleeping ogre, waking mid-afternoon to whistle or murmur shards of riffs and lyrics to 19-year-old drummer John French, who interpreted them for the others. "My personality had been encroached upon and nibbled away until there was a little bit of me left cowering in a corner," French once told me of Beefheart's terror-technique. "I couldn't express an opinion. I was afraid to. So I concentrated on music instead. When the others were playing by themselves, all at once, I could hear each wrong note. I was consumed. It's an awful feeling." He muttered to himself, "It makes me shake," and I saw that he was. "It still makes me shake when I start thinking about it, it makes me . . . tense." This paranoid focus fed blues through a Cubist blender, with Beefheart snapping absurd lyrics over time signatures scribbled by a madman, or the genius the Captain and his abused crew believed he was. This was blues adrift from the Delta, after acid and John Coltrane. White learned this legend, as he did that of Welles' absolute power over *Citizen Kane*. Many years later, he would suggest to the Stooges that he produce their 2007 comeback album with them all locked together in a house. When he was interviewed by Pamela Des Barres, infamous author of *I'm With The Band* and once of Beefheart ally Frank Zappa's groupie super-group The GTOs, he asked, with uncharacteristically timid awe: "Did you ever . . . I suppose you . . . of course you hung out with Beefheart, too?"

But as with the original bluesmen, practical ideas and detail impressed White before the myth. It was the two-second, off-kilter drum intro to *Trout Mask Replica*'s 'Moonlight On Vermont', heard on the VHS he and Krautner sat watching in 1999, which snagged his attention. "I have to hear it three times every time I hear it," White told Des Barres. The obsessive-compulsive, ritual power of three again helped draw White in. He instructed *Mojo*'s readers, like a GP doling out delicate medication, to always play the intro thrice before proceeding further. "It's the structure of it, the conducting of it," he considered.

The Artist Formerly Known As Captain Beefheart held other ideas for the 24-year-old White to ponder. "If he sustained a groove too long," brief Magic Bandmate Ry Cooder explained of the Captain, "it's corny, it was bourgeois. The concept [was] you take the raw blues elements, like the sound of the John Lee Hooker idea, the Howlin' Wolf, down to its purest element . . . a grunt, maybe, and something abstract. And then you take your John Coltrane crazy time-signature, free jazz, Ornette Coleman thing and hybridise it." Jack never got jazz. But such thoughts blew blues open further.

White the painter, poet and sculptor also learned of Don Van Vliet's second, post-Beefheart career as a successful abstract artist, living some-where in the Mojave Desert and no longer speaking to the wondering outside world, protected by this second legend as he focused solely on his work (and gradually succumbed to MS). "I want things to change," White heard Van Vliet say, before that long silence fell, "like the patterns and shadows that fall from the sun." There was so much heady fuel here, for a young man hungry to be an artist.

But the White Stripes were already in action when Beefheart entered the equation. White tended to underplay one last, much more blatant influence on them – the blues-rock idols of 17-year-old John Gillis, Led Zeppelin. Jimmy Page's guitar style can't be heard in Jack's as much as the Thirties blues masters. Page the producer, though, the conductor of the vivid dynamic in their heavy-voltage electric sound, who made John Bonham's drums seem to gut-punch through the speakers as 'Stairway To Heaven' takes off – that is in every Jack White record. Robert Plant's shredded shriek, too. One of the many things that stopped White being a black blues musician in the Thirties was that he was also steeped in what white Britons of the Sixties did to that music, from the Stones to Zeppelin. His love of the acoustic technique and mystique of Robert Johnson, Son House and Blind Willie McTell, after passing through his more contem-porary influences, came out as pounding electric rock. White put a personal, punk straitjacket on its excesses at first. But his classic rock tendencies couldn't be denied. "Sometimes I kinda feel bad because it's like I'm doing some form of that," he agonised to *Bangsheet* of electric blues and its offshoots. "Sometimes it feels like the most natural thing to do, while other times it's like, 'Oh man, we don't want to be Led Zeppelin or Cream or anything like that.'" More than any of their peers, though, they were.

White's Welles-like taste for sleight of hand and smoke and mirrors may have mesmerised himself first of all. Instead of admitting he was in an obvious blues-rock tradition, he decided that a white boy born in Detroit in 1975 playing Thirties blues songs would be ridiculed. "There's this whole new world that's just opened up in front of me, and I have to figure

70

out, how do I get there?" he agonised in *It Might Get Loud* of the blues desire Son House awakened in him. "Am I not allowed to get there?" In 1997, aged 22, he was still missing one thing to start his true work. He needed a willing partner in a magic trick that would make the world listen to his blues. One day, he realised he was married to her.

5

Sister Lover

MEG and Jack White had been married barely six months when she asked to play music with him. They were sitting in the attic at 1203 Ferdinand Street, now their wedded home since Jack's family moved out. The drums her husband had first bashed away at age five suddenly intrigued her, and the woman who, during the public life this act would trigger, rarely said a word, wanted to play David Bowie's 'Moonage Daydream'. Jack and Meg both agreed that her long periods of shy silence meant that when she opened her mouth, her words carried unusual weight. Her casual moment of musical curiosity on an otherwise purposeless afternoon in May 1997 changed both their lives. Jack seized on the opening gratefully.

"I thought, 'Well, that's great,'" he remembered to Barney Hoskyns, "'cause I wasn't doing anything . . . I'll do it because there's someone else who wants to make music for a second, which is hard to find."

Bowie was one of the Muldoon family's fascinations, and Meg was musically voracious enough to know 'Moonage Daydream' anyway. It was the fourth track on *The Rise And Fall Of Ziggy Stardust And The Spiders From Mars* (1972), a concept album with touches of *A Clockwork Orange*-style ultra-violence belied by its warm, Beatlesque sound. Bowie himself, in blue jumpsuit and boots, peered at his Detroit listeners from an equally exotic, wet London street on its front cover, and a red telephone box on its back.

'Moonage Daydream' wasn't the most obvious track. But it was a science-fiction love song that would be fun for two young lovers to play. 'Press your space-face close to me, babe,' Jack sang, then the chorus took them into cosmic hippie jive: 'Freak-out . . . far-out . . . in-out!' On the record, the song climaxes in a swirl of bat-shriek strings and guitar. More pertinently, Woody Woodmansey's drums sound deceptively, invitingly simple. As he does for most of *Ziggy*, he holds a steady, swinging beat, with soft, padded toms reminiscent of Ringo, and regular splashes of cymbal.

Meg had never played drums before. But Jack the ever-ready craftsman and problem-solver saw that if Woodmansey's harder, rapid fills were stripped out, as he might to a sofa in his day job, this was music a child could play.

"I thought, if we just left a lot of space in there and hit the notes here and there," he told Hoskyns, "then all the space would provide something interesting and we wouldn't really need to know how to play these instruments." He claimed, perhaps disingenuously, to still have felt more drummer than guitarist, and relatively amateurish himself as he joined in on the latter instrument. But as they played, something clicked. "It actually felt way better than I expected. I'd been in other lo-fi bands and done recordings but it wasn't like that. It didn't make a point."

Seven years later, when the White Stripes were at the peak of both success and its miserable downside, he listened to the tape of this strange band's first moments, and felt content. "It still sounds raw and cool," he enthused to *Rolling Stone*'s David Fricke. Having begun almost by accident, they pressed on with their improvised session. David Bowie wrote the first White Stripes recording, now Jack wrote the second. Glancing at a red screwdriver on a table, he grabbed the word for a chorus and title. 'Screwdriver' hadn't changed at all when they recorded it for *The White Stripes* in 1999, he told *Rolling Stone*. It begins then with a dirty, Yardbirds-style riff, and him setting out from Ferdinand to 30th Street, on the other side of Michigan Avenue, searching for something to do. He calls up Tommy (maybe his friend Tom Potter of Bantam Rooster), and they head to the pawnbrokers. There's some faintly surreal, associative stuff in what follows, in the blues tradition. But if Jack truly didn't change a word from that first afternoon, elements of the White Stripes were in-built. He tells the listener to 'think about their little sister' when out wandering alone, and loves people 'like a brother'. But that love will only stretch so far. Jack's sense of suspicious isolation from those around him, and a building itch to retaliate, give 'Screwdriver' its force. If someone steps up to him in the street and slices him, he won't 'stand there grinning' as he's wronged. Son House's 'Grinnin' In Your Face' guides the first White Stripes lyric. 'Screwdriver', Jack mutters at that verse's end, as if wrapping his hand round it to retaliate. The musical dynamic is the one he heard from Nirvana when he was 16, quiet followed by explosive noise – an indie-rock cliché. But Meg's blunt, guitar-shadowed thumps add to the tension of verses sung at a constantly hysterical pitch, and Jack's final detonation feels viscerally instinctive. 'I got a little feeling going now,' he repeatedly moans as that feeling grows, till on the final 'now!' his fever breaks in a rush of whipping guitar, and climactic, pounding unity with Meg. Jeff Beck is a stronger ingredient than Robert Johnson, Sixties British R&B possessing Jack's guitar. But Meg's brute simplicity and the nursery rhyme lyrics' singular psychological intensity are this band's own. It can't be true that everything on this 1999 recording was present in the couple's attic that afternoon. But their musical marriage began then.

"When Meg started to play drums with me, just on a lark, it felt liberating and refreshing," Jack told *Rolling Stone*'s David Fricke. "There was something in it that opened me up." Meg's part in the lark, and in a romance Jack hasn't admitted to since 1999, is hard to ascertain. The only scenes from their marriage he has let slip are that afternoon's playing together, and a time they watched old Betty Boop cartoons. Simple, innocent pleasures.

When Jack erased their three years living together from all but his earliest interviews, Meg talked instead of happy childhood memories. While Jack was marshalling battles with his toy soldiers in Mexicantown, she was piling Grosse Point's deep winter snow into mountains to burrow through. In her imagination, this became Superman's Fortress of Solitude. "I was obsessed with it," she told *Mojo*. "It was the best." It sounds a tellingly isolated playhouse for someone who as an adult seemed to strangers abstracted from the world, hardly there at all. The first record she bought as a child was the Steve Miller Band's 'Abracadabra', "because I liked to roller skate to it in my basement when I was six," she also told *Mojo*. "It was one step up from 'Pop Goes The Weasel', which was my favourite basement dance before that. I bought it on 45 at the local corner record store." Quizzed on her favourite Christmas records by *NME*, she remembered her parents having "a huge turntable, it was like a massive piece of furniture" on which she'd play *The Reader's Digest Christmas Album*, a comforting five-LP set of festive songs, "things like Bing Crosby." Like Jack's house, there was a lot of music around. Unlike her future husband, who first bought records in his teens, she started her much bigger collection in second grade. Her adult taste was also rooted in Grosse Point. "I grew up listening to a lot of country music, and Dylan," she told PBS' Charlie Rose. "My mum listened to it. I like any kind of music that has a lot of emotion to it." That included Sister Rosetta Tharpe and the Staple Singers' early gospel records, Willie Nelson and Merle Haggard. More than anything, she loved Dylan's *Blood On The Tracks*, his 1975 masterpiece of atmospheric, scene-shifting heartache, recorded as his marriage collapsed.

"Meg is a sweetheart," Steve Nawara says. "She's just a very gentle soul, and I love her. She's the best. Very quiet, very shy." The Detroit Cobras' Mary Restrepo told Brian McCollum of the *Detroit Free Press* that Meg was "a very cool chick. She's like all the Detroit rock girls – they party hard." Nawara happily agrees. "Oh yeah, she's hilarious. Always funny, and she can throw 'em back with the best of 'em, she can definitely hang with the boys, no question about that! All I can think of is just pleasantness when I think of Meg." Dave Feeny also recalls her being "lovely, a little shy, but she was, and still is, really fun when she felt comfortable around you. She worked at a club in Ferndale, where we would run into her." The Magic Stick's co-owner Dave Zainea fondly remembers her hanging out there. "I always appreciated Meg. She was quiet, and down to earth, and I think she's a fantastic drummer, man, in my estimation. She hits them hard. For somebody that wasn't destined to be a drummer, I think she's pretty damn good. I liked drinking Bud Light with her. Our mutual friend Tina and her both liked Bud Light."

"I worked in the main art film theatre in Royal Oak for a while," Troy Gregory remembers, "and Meg White was working at Memphis Smoke, which was just this" – making a squitting, derogatory sound – "Royal Oakish barbecue bar place. Chris Tate from the Electric Six worked there, too. We used to talk at the bar when she was bartending, always 'What's up with your band?'-type things. We used to rehearse in her house, later. She doesn't talk that much. I'm used to that because my wife doesn't talk that much and I talk a lot," he says, a clue to how Meg's relationship with vastly more voluble Jack balanced out. "But she was friendly. She is extremely quiet, but she's always been all right."

It's tempting to read Mona Lisa mystery into Meg's inscrutability when the White Stripes brought her to a wider public, as she kept impenetrably silent during interviews and head-tossing, onstage duels with her ex-husband. But no one who knows her believes there is any Sphinx-like code to crack. "I actually know Meg better than Jack," says Dan Kroha, "because Meg lives right down the block from my sister, and we spend holidays with Meg and her family. People always talked about how she never talked, and it took a really long time to get to know Meg, she's very private. But I can say now that I'm good friends with her. Meg is like family now. She's really smart, really funny."

"What you see is what you get," Nawara says of her. "Some people," Meg advised *Spin*'s Chuck Klosterman, "put more thought into shyness than necessary."

While Meg worked as a barmaid, Jack laboured at his new shop, Third Man Upholstery, helping to bring in the cash to pay the mortgage he'd taken on from his parents. Such straight-backed adult responsibility was undercut by his decision to colour every bit of the operation yellow, black and white. From power tools to walls to workbench to van, nothing escaped his chosen hues. "I ran my business like a cartoon," he admitted to *Rolling Stone*'s David Fricke. "I didn't care if I made any money. I was so happy to pull up in front of someone's house wearing a yellow-and-black uniform, with a yellow clipboard." Such giddy delight recalls the cartwheels 19-year-old Jack turned after reading Iggy Pop's autobiography in Hollywood. For someone who always felt compelled to be responsible, he also had an impish desire to brighten his world to his own design. Constantly oppressed by the thought of others' opinions, he was also able to cut loose and forget them, to stand on his head and say, "Fuck it." The mostly older, suburban clients who even bothered with his essentially outmoded job (most Detroiters just got another cheap or abandoned armchair) gawped suspiciously when this kid in a yellow-and-black van and, in 1997, dyed-yellow hair proudly handed them a bill scrawled in crayon. Jack was actually a diligent, fully trained artisan, with creative ambition that blurred into his art. "My upholstery shop was half sculpting studio and music rehearsal place," he told Brian McCollum. "That was all going on in that room, and that was going on in my house, too." He slipped his poetry inside sofas, imagining an ancient guild of honourable upholsterers passing secreted messages. 'Your Furniture's Not Dead', his business card promised, a motto which paralleled his wish to revive the blues. A Forties chaise longue or a Twenties tune both held his attention. In the cold world of business in depressed Detroit, an upholsterer who merrily skipped up dressed as a citizen of Toytown was always likely to struggle. But his business' childish, garish idealism was a model for what became the White Stripes.

The shop was also where he passed on friendship and musical knowledge while his nephew Ben Blackwell helped break up furniture, as Brian Muldoon had to him. Blackwell grew up relatively far from Jack, near Grosse Point, and was the right age to be a rare companion to an uncle who, used to feeling demeaned by his peers, could for once be the wise old-timer. "I'm 15, he's 22, he's the cool 'brother', uncle," Blackwell remembered to *Audioboom*'s Damian Abraham. "The shop's where I first heard *Back In The Grave* compilations, the Gories, the Monks and the Melvins. Driving around with him and Meg was where I first heard the

Velvet Underground and the Modern Lovers." Blackwell was the White
Stripes' first fan. He'd pass through roles as their tour driver, default
manager and the Third Man Records vinyl boss he is today, but stayed the
archivist and historian of a band he instantly knew mattered.

Jack and Meg's lark suddenly made music easy. Instead of fighting to
impose his ideas on bandmates, Jack could simply plug in with his wife
once they got back from work, and play. Later visitors to Jack at home
found him among the detritus of a single-minded boy with no grown-ups
left to say no: odd collections of vintage alarm clocks, or springs, the shape
of which he found "restful". "Sometimes I think I have too many
interests," he conceded to *The Guardian*'s Alexis Petridis at a later,
Nashville residence, as he pondered his scissors collection. Such basic
fixations ran riot in the White Stripes. Meg's initially incompetent
drumming was the band's foundation. "We just wanted to work on some
simplistic kind of music, whether it was blues, punk, or just real simple
rock'n'roll," Jack told *Bangsheet*. "That was the main motivation behind it."

Jack refined that line during early interviews. "When we started, our
objective was to be as simple as possible," he told the *Metro-Times*' Norene
Cashen, in their first significant press coverage in May 1999. "Meg's sound
is like a little girl trying to play the drums and doing the best she can." The
immaturity of Meg's playing was constantly emphasised. "I'd been writing
all these childish songs, like 'Jimmy The Exploder' – this story I made up
about this monkey who exploded things that weren't the colour red," he
explained to *Mojo*'s Andrew Perry. "So when Meg started playing that
way, I was like, 'Man, don't even practise! This is perfect.'" He heard
fascinating possibilities in such primitive drumming, an uncluttered base
he found "really cool to work off of, to play guitar off of, and to sing off,"
he explained to *Bangsheet*. "I was obsessed with it," he told PBS' Charlie
Rose. "I didn't want her to change, I didn't want her to practise, and just
stay child-like. It's like that thing of Picasso saying you take a lifetime to
learn to paint like a child. I couldn't drum like that if I wanted to, and I
had never played with a drummer like that." The simplicity of Meg's
ability, at first enforced, also triggered the lesson he'd learned listening to
the Flat Duo Jets, Son House and other early bluesmen, when he'd heard
"everything disappearing", leaving a pure core of minimal sound. "Robert
Johnson tapping his foot on a floor is what's going on with me and Meg,"
he snapped to Rose. In fact, Meg, embarrassed when Jack dragged their
home-made lark onstage, would practise, and become a powerful drummer.

But Jack persisted in praising her style as infantile, keeping the concept fixed.

After toying with Bazooka and Soda Powder, he named their collaboration the White Stripes, a reference to red-and-white, swirling-striped sweets. "We saw a bag of peppermint candies," Jack remembered in *It Might Get Loud*. "I said, 'Well, we should paint that on your bass-drum.'" From the start, they dressed in the colours of these children's treats, soon adding black to red and white. "We decided we wanted to dress up in our Sunday best like a kid would," Jack told the BBC's Chris Jones. "If you tell a kid that they are going to church, they'll always come down in a red outfit or something." This was also putting on a costume for the stage, not dressing shabbily, like they were still in the crowd, a democratic pretence he found revoltingly lazy. "You wouldn't wear your pyjamas to church," Jack primly believed. He also thought red and white were the colours of "anger and innocence", and, he claimed to *Rolling Stone*, "the most powerful colour combination of all time, from a Coca-Cola can to a Nazi banner." In the inner sleeve of *The White Stripes*, the young marrieds stood proudly on 1203 Ferdinand's porch, its bricks, fencing, slats, roof and street-number all painted in alternating red and white. If his Mexican neighbours thought teenage Jack the strumming bluesman looked absurd on that porch, they really had an eyeful now. Third Man Upholstery's Toytown aesthetic soon spread through a home turned into the White Stripes' art project and play-pen. An American flag with no stars, only red and white bars, was draped in the attic where he rehearsed, and used as a stage backdrop.

"It was a cool house," says John Krautner, guitarist for the Go, who practised there as Jack's bandmate in 1998, probably a few months before the LP photos' full-blown transformation. "The kitchen was completely red, and black – or maybe white, but mostly red. He had these two dogs running around. We practised upstairs, in a refinished attic, and that was red too. He had a lot of cool custom amps, like a blue-greenish Tuck and Roll one, with sparkles. You went up there and thought, 'This guy has set this up to where it would be fun to practise with a band.' Most people's practice spaces are used for something else, but this was dedicated. Jack and Meg were married at that point, and the rest of it was just like any other young guy's house. A stack of CDs and a stack of records, and a TV, and some cool posters on the wall. And apart from the almost completely red kitchen and practice space, things in other rooms were blue, too. He was playing with different colours at that time. And one thing in his house

I thought was hilarious; he had a Polaroid of Jack as a boy with his head buried in the robes of Pope John Paul II, when he came to Hamtramck. And this picture was not in a frame. It was stuck with a chunk of silver duct tape to the wall. And I thought, 'Jack, don't you think you should frame this thing? Your family would be proud to have that . . .'" Jack admitted later to misplacing the evidence of his 1987 encounter with the Pontiff. "Probably fell off and got vacuumed," laughs Krautner.

Jack also decided that this smallest possible band-unit, despite having two members, perfectly met his mystic obsession with the number three. It "exemplifies the almost iconic, mysterious perfection that cannot be obtained," he informed *The Guardian*'s Alexis Petridis. Invisibly present like the messages he hid in furniture, the figure was spectral, decodable, universal DNA. "There are three elements to everything, and if you can discover what those three are as your structure, then you're on the right path." Red, white and black; voice, guitar and drums; music as rhythm, melody and storytelling: the Holy Trinity mostly unmentioned by Catholic-raised Jack was alive in the White Stripes.

There was one more thing, which would come to dominate the rest. In this band, Meg would be Jack's big sister. Later, journalists would believe this was to distract them from a marriage which, by the time their fame started, had ended in divorce. Jack himself seemed to support this, in his most explicit statement on rock's grandest bluff. "When they're brother and sister, you go, 'Oh, that's interesting,'" he told *Rolling Stone*'s David Fricke. "You care more about the music, not the relationship – whether they're trying to save their relationship by being in a band."

But the White Stripes were brother and sister even when Jack and Meg were Detroit nobodies with no reporters to think about, playing to friends at the Gold Dollar who all knew the truth. "It was earlier than the divorce," John Krautner confirms. "I think I was there from the very start of the White Stripes, and it was funny. [From the] first, he would say during gigs, 'That's my sister, Meg,' because in Detroit, nobody cares. Everybody who knew him knew. They kissed each other like husband and wife when I was there practising! But I didn't come up to Jack after the show and say, 'Dude, why are you calling Meg your sister? It's kind of weird, isn't it?' I just thought it was Jack's character in full force. We were just entertained by it, and amused. It wasn't something we made him be accountable for, as he later had to be in the papers."

"It was from the start," Matt Smith confirms. "I remember all of us being confused by that. 'Why is he presenting this as a brother–sister act? Is he okay? Is he flipping his wig?' When he got into his musical thing he would get into that character. Everybody in town knew that they were married. But when he would do this, he was in his own world with his music. And I don't remember him ever explaining that to any of us. We just observed and thought, 'That's strange.'"

As 'Screwdriver''s lyrics suggest, this invented relationship was as intrinsic to the band as their costumes' colour. In later interviews, Jack said it was all part of an elaborate distraction, not from marriage, but the music he ached to play. "All the aesthetics about the band and the way that we presented them was a great way for me to get away with playing the blues," he told *Total Guitar*. "People wouldn't notice that I was this white kid born in the Seventies playing the blues because they're wondering why we were wearing black, white and red." He claimed that someone from his background playing the blues was "inherently ridiculous" and "unnatural" – not that that stopped 'Surrey Delta' blues-rock guitarists such as Jimmy Page and Eric Clapton, or his Kentish hero Keith Richards, as Jack well knew. Having felt ridiculed so often, maybe the thought of this reaction to his most cherished music made him double the dare with a show so strikingly outlandish, you forgot to laugh. "We might as well go to the extreme of unnaturalness," he told the *Daily Telegraph*'s Ben Thompson, "and say, 'Here's the presentation – we're in this box. We're gonna only dress in red, white and black, and the peppermint swirl is our mascot, and we're essentially just little children trapped in adult bodies.'"

That last idea was more than a conjuror's trick to let them play the blues. Look at Meg's girlish glee as she whacks Jack with a Barbie doll (in a red–and–white striped outfit, of course) in *NME* photos taken in 2001. That simple innocence would be sustained for most of their joint public lives, and some of it surely was real. "Meg's a very child-like person," Jack informed *Mojo*'s Will Hodgkinson, a personality he felt her drumming expressed. And though Jack plotted a sophisticated aesthetic around this belief, he too could act like an essentially kindly, sometimes naive, brattily stubborn kid. It was he who'd been writing children's songs before Meg looked at a drumstick. In interviews, both sounded out of step with a cynical adult world. People believed they had the closeness of children, not lovers, because it felt true.

"I only got a short window to see how their relationship was," John Krautner says of the private reality, "and what I saw was a typical married couple. We'd all be talking in the living room before or after practice, and she'd come and sit on his lap and look at a book or something. They acted

80

very much like a married couple. She didn't hang out during Go practices, she did her own thing, but I saw them together at our favourite hangouts, the Magic Stick, the Garden Bowl and the Gold Dollar, where Meg's older sister, Heather, was a bartender."

"You'd generally see them out together," Steve Nawara remembers of their wedded days. "Jack was not as big a partier as most people were in Detroit. A lot of the times after the gig he would just go home with Meg. Sometimes Jack would stay out and sometimes Meg would, but they'd typically go home together. Really the after-hours, offstage relationship all seemed to me to be fine. I was surprised that they got divorced."

Removing that reality from the White Stripes still leaves Krautner nonplussed. "To this day I'm a little confused by it," he says. "Because what's wrong with being a husband-and-wife band? That seems kind of cute, and just as innocent." He sees surprising parallels with another female drummer. "I'm a fan of bubblegum, and family bands like the Partridge Family, and the Carpenters. There is something really cool with that. I love seeing Carpenters videos where Karen is acting like the kid sister, and Richard Carpenter's going, 'Ahh, come on, Karen, just get your act together and let's play this song!' Like kids fighting with each other. I don't know if Jack really loves the Carpenters. But he may have thought something like that was really neat."

Nawara believes Jack and Meg's joint innocence in the White Stripes was truthful, matching how they seemed as a couple.

"They were very sweet to each other, and it was very carefree," he remembers. "Like with their band it seemed really at first like they were just having fun. And then obviously it snowballed into something way greater than that. Definitely there was a very childlike wonder to the White Stripes. That was definitely the impression I got, and I think most people did as well." And that fitted how they were together anyway? "I would say so, yeah."

Sitting in the White Stripes' dressing-up box, with its privacy, suited Meg. "I've always kind of lived in my own little world," she said to Jim Jarmusch. "Everything else outside me seems far, far away. We never really cared about the things that other people cared about. I've always been kind of suspicious of the world, anyway."

You don't think about siblings saving a relationship, Jack told *Rolling Stone* of the band bond he'd forged. A brother and sister had stronger ties. "They're mated for life. That's what family is like."

★   ★   ★

On Sunday July 14, 1997, two months after playing 'Moonage Daydream', the White Stripes walked onto the Gold Dollar's stage, wearing red and white. It was Neil Yee's weekly open-mic night "for Poets, Musicians & Performers. Drums, bass amp, guitar amp provided." As usual, Yee taped the performance from the bar.

"All right, er, we're just gonna bore you for two or three songs," Jack nervously begins. There's a lone whoop from the half dozen or so watching. They start with a blues, learned from a cartoon. "This is 'St. James Infirmary' by, um, Cab Calloway." You can hear the hum of Jack's plugged-in instrument in the almost empty bar, then the distorted guitar and drums start a beat that often wobbles uncertainly. Jack uses a light, story-telling voice for this old song of brothels, burial and booze, his words lost whenever the guitar thickens, and one line a gabbled rush. There's a choked, melodic solo. His playing during this brief gig is slower, more halting than you'd expect, maybe fitting into this strange new band. "Thanks a lot," he says. "Gonna bore you with a couple more here. This one's 'Jimmy . . .'" The first publicly heard White Stripes song, 'Jimmy The Exploder', influenced their aesthetic with its anarchic monkey destroying everything that isn't red, even green apples feeling his wrath. Jack nearly laughs and his voice cracks, at the song's absurdity or something lost in time. Though a slightly more complicated rhythm makes Meg stumble badly, the rumbling guitar and manic lyric's momentum build low-wattage excitement, especially when the duo blend with direct force. Jack's gaining confidence with the tiny crowd now. "Do you know 'Love Potion No. 9'?" he asks. "Well, we're gonna do it for you, and it's gonna be the way you never heard it before. The original!" He toys with his higher, hysterical register, and the crowd take the Lieber and Stoller song's familiar chorus. "All right, thank you, we're done," he says. "Thanks a lot." The few present shout, "More, more!" There would be.

Sitting backstage in a Nova Scotian dressing-room on what proved to be the final White Stripes tour in 2007, Jack thought back to that Sunday. "I remember there being seven or eight people there," he said. The band after them on another mixed-up Gold Dollar bill had covered 'Born To Be Wild'. "They were drunk and I was sitting there at the bar with Neil [Yee], and they started the song, which started off note-perfect. Then the singer said, 'Get your motor run-nin'/ Head on down my asshole!'" He and Meg chortled happily at the memory. Yee considered their performance "kind of questionable" in *Candy Coloured Blues*. "If you think she's playing simple beats now, well, they were simpler then, and there were a lot of mistakes and tempo problems." He quickly realised their two-piece, home-made sound needed help. "He had one amp, and it was really thin-sounding. So I would always EQ it quite a bit and do other things to it, 'cause you do need a fuller sound."

Jack soon pressed for a real gig. "John [Syzmanski] and I were coming out of a show and Jack came up to us, we didn't know him," the Hentchmen's Tim Purrier recalls. "He said, 'I've got this little two-piece band, if you guys are ever looking for an opener . . .' And John called him up. 'We're looking for an opener.'" Neil Yee's monthly Gold Dollar flyer lists the Hentchmen and the Insects ("mid tempo 60s kinda sound") on Friday, August 15, 1997. "The show is opened with the debut of the White Stripes, 2 pc original Detroit music. Or was that 2 pc extra spicy?"

They also slipped onto the bill the night before, supporting Rocket 455 and Memphis garage band '68 Comeback. Jack liked to claim he and Meg never rehearsed, favouring simple spontaneity. That's hard to believe, hearing the leap forward from a month before. "Hello, hello, we're the White Stripes," he tells the few Rocket 455 fans not outside the Gold Dollar on this summer night. They start again with 'St. James Infirmary Blues' and 'Jimmy The Exploder', but Jack's voice is more fiercely confident, switching registers as he spins the blues' tale, then cooing eerie nonsense on 'Jimmy', a bolt of feedback separating them. The debt to the crude Gories over their peers' Sixties models is ensured by Meg's out-of-tempo start. An 11-song set with eight originals also shows the White Stripes' own world already well populated. 'Red Bowling Ball Ruth' adds a Garden Bowl-friendly kindergarten anarchist to Jimmy the ape. Feedback bends and quivers before its manic opening lines – 'Pay attention! Pay attention! I love ya! I don't know what you heard!' – then Jack and Meg start a dialogue of electric flicks and thumps. 'I Can Learn', unrecorded till 2001's *White Blood Cells*, is more sweetly strange, Jack crooning over the bassy twang of an early Sixties ballroom ballad, the kind the Beatles played. Meg delicately hits the cymbals, and Jack sounds like Jim Morrison in Sinatra mode at the end. 'Love Potion No. 9' gains a hectic, dismayed vocal, Lieber and Stoller's fine pop confection buried in White Stripes punk-blues. Meg's locked in as much as she needs to be now, showing a glimmer of swing on the lonely boy's lament 'Why Can't You Be Nicer?' 'Marantette Blues' is an early version of the 'Lafayette Blues' riff on Detroit's French street-names, Meg steady just off Jack's galloping pace, only faltering as they slow to a trot. "Don't worry about that, Meg, that's all right," Jack tells her after the Little Richard-quoting

'Jumble, Jumble', flushed with confidence compared with the open-mic's meek apology. The Stooges' 'TV Eye' barely starts finding what his guitar can do with Ron Asheton's primitive genius before it collapses. 'Big Girl' (later called 'Little People') is sung in the voice of a small, bruised boy, the childishness just escaping perversion.

"All right, everybody," Jack informs whoever's bothered to listen. "We'd like to thank Jeff Meier and Rocket 455 for letting us play, and then we're all done. We're the White Stripes, thank you very much." They finish with 'Screwdriver'. Tonight it includes hard rock sludge, studded by rumbling feedback, Meg just anchoring the murky material. There's no mention of being brother and sister, and the set peters out. But after the open-mic's hesitant incompetence, the White Stripes are recognisable.

"The first time I saw them was their second show, opening for us," Tim Purrier says of the following night. "You could tell that they were both uncomfortable, but it was definitely interesting. I know at that early stage a lot of people just laughed them off. I think all three of us in the Hentchmen supported them and said, 'You should take notice of these guys. They're doing something pretty cool.' And whatever they couldn't make up for in just being a two-piece, the simplicity of it at least early on, they didn't try to overcompensate for. A lot of it had to do with their limitations. We felt like we were champions of them. I thought they were these honest kids trying to make a go of this little band."

Opinions varied among the few who bothered to watch the White Stripes open bills in the months that followed. But they were noticed. "At first, I of course thought, 'I've seen this'," says Dave Feeny, "with other two-piece and super-raw bands, like the Gories, Bantam Rooster and Flat Duo Jets. But [Two-Star Tabernacle's] Dan Miller was always raving about how talented he thought Jack was, so the more I saw them the more I liked them."

"When Jack first came up to me and introduced himself, I had heard of the White Stripes," the Gories' Dan Kroha remembers. "Because really, right when they first started, people thought they were good, and people were talking about 'em. But I thought the name sounded really dumb! I did go see 'em fairly early on when there was just a handful of people there still, and I obviously thought that Jack was talented. I found their music to be very plodding, and difficult to dance to. 'Cause I like to dance, that's my thing, to me the R&B stuff the Gories play is dance music. But they had the whole aesthetic, with the red and white, and the zebra head on the stage, and the Mod table and the furniture. You could tell they had some-thing going on right from the get-go."

"I walked into a bar in their early days and went, 'Oh, there's Heather's sister, playing drums,'" Matt Smith says. "I was very impressed with Meg's drumming, and her musicianship, because I'd never heard her play before. I couldn't tell Jack's guitar ability at that point, and in Detroit there's a guitar player on every street corner. The first time I saw 'em it was kinda loose, and Jack looked like he was signalling Meg the whole time. I thought it was okay. Later on, after their album had come out, he had his guitar sound more developed and powerful."

"I just remember telling him, 'You are in the best band in Detroit, right now,'" the Witches' Troy Gregory says emphatically. "We're talking about people who moved on from the MC5-type thing – it was sloppy, and I mean that in a musical sense, in a very charming way. And Bantam Rooster was playing already around town, too, which was just a two-piece, but they had that sloppiness more like Motörhead. The White Stripes were more [notoriously amateurish Sixties female band] Shaggs. But it wasn't just all falling apart. Because Meg was so new to it he had to be constantly cueing her, as well as getting into what he was doing and putting on a show, he had to constantly move the music. This sense of cueing would be there even if this was someone who played drums for 800 years, with those songs. Plus he would just go into songs, and she would know, 'Oh, yeah, that one', or what the feel was. The spontaneity was really nice, and they leaned towards a real noise side, and had original stuff that sounded good, and covers that he picked out from stuff that a lot of other people got into, like when I saw them doing 'Death Letter Blues'. It was great songs."

"There were other two-piece bands who were doing R&B," the Paybacks' Wendy Case said in *Candy Coloured Blues*. "But the White Stripes had this delicate quality."

"They really embraced the band, first off, didn't they, in Detroit?" Jack remembered to Meg 10 years later, in *Under Great White Northern Lights*. "There were a lot of people coming to see us, really right off the bat. I don't know if they particularly *liked* the band," he laughed, with self-deprecating truth. "They were just intrigued enough to go." Meg laughed too. "What the hell," she imagined their first crowds thinking, "are those two doing?"

"Some of the bands had been around a few years, but things were just starting to build at that point," Tim Purrier remembers, of the Detroit scene the White Stripes entered. "I wouldn't say it was really established. Bantam Rooster had been playing around for not even a year in Detroit, the Wildbunch had just started, a lot of things were just starting at that point. And the Detroit Cobras [a soul and rock covers band led by riotous singer Rachel Nagy] had been around for a while, but they were playing out more. So they weren't jumping into this established thing. It's not like any of these bands were playing these huge places, or had this huge following. It was all pretty small-time."

Other nights seemed more crucial then than the White Stripes' beginnings, Gregory remembers. "Ben Blackwell always says what changed his life was Clutch Cargo's in Pontiac, when the Cramps came [on November 21, 1997]. They had the Doll Rods open up for them, but also they had Guitar Wolf on the bill. And Guitar Wolf were off the fricking hook that night. He comes up, getting all this feedback, the bass player's combing his hair. Guitar Wolf's grabbing the microphone, screaming something in Japanese but all you can hear is 'MC5' in there somewhere. It was just this amazing-ass show. And then the Doll Rods started in front of an audience aside from being in the bars of Detroit, people who knew about the Cramps. All of a sudden, there's people going, 'There's bands from around town?' It's funny. That was always the band everyone thought was going to be mega-huge." Inspired by the Cramps' "voodoo sex charge", that night 19-year-old friends Jason Stollsteimer and Marcie Bolen got drunk and formed the band that became the Von Bondies.

As the Doll Rods broke surface in Detroit, the White Stripes slipped across the border to play their first show outside the city on October 14, 1997, in the neon tawdriness of Club Shanghai, in Toronto's Chinatown. The gig was set up by Detroiter Dan Burke, part of a mutually supportive Midwest tour network including Rocket 455's Jeff Meier, the Hentchmen's John Syzmanski and Johnny Walker, who, with drummer Ben Swank, had left Maumee, Ohio to open for the Hentchmen at the Gold Dollar as another guitar-drums punk-blues duo, the Soledad Brothers, on October 11, 1997. Walker and especially Swank quickly became part of Jack's inner circle, as the White Stripes' visibility at last gave him a social life, based, of course, on music, at the Gold Dollar and the Magic Stick.

The Go's bassist, Dave Buick, already saw enough in Jack's new band by the end of 1997 to ask to release a 7-inch on his tiny label, Italy Records. Once Jack had grasped that a label would pay him for a 45, not the other way round, the White Stripes made their recording debut in February 1998. Jeff Meier recorded it at Third Man Studio (aka the Whites' living room, with an 8-track reel-to-reel borrowed from one of Jack's brothers), as he would Two-Star Tabernacle's lone single with Andre Williams, 'Ramblin' Man', the same year.

'Let's Shake Hands' lasts two minutes. You can hear electricity hum when the distorted guitar crackle briefly drops. This sounds like vinyl that will give a static tingle to the touch. Jack's high voice is startled into action then desperately urgent, as he pleads 'put your fingers in my hands,' and, 'just say my name!' Innocent friendship mingles with recrimination to the girl being addressed, ambiguity that would mark the White Stripes. Romantically ignored before he met Meg, Jack retained the bitter frustration of a sensitive wallflower, spurned for cruel jocks by stupid girls. There's a Fifties delicacy to some pleas here, and a speedway grind to his heavy rhythm guitar. Meg's bass drum helps push the hammering finish. The single has the concise structure and leaping attack of early rock'n'roll, and an obscure perversity all Jack's own. If that wasn't enough, the B-side is a Marlene Dietrich number, 'Look Me Over Closely'. Jack takes the female role, sounding like Cruella de Vil with a pinch of Weimar hauteur, to which he adds prancing cabaret piano. As the wife he'll make his sister plays behind him, he can't decide if he's 'the marrying kind'. The Gold Dollar's old drag bar patrons would have put him in their pocket.

Jim Diamond mixed the track at Ghetto Recorders. A total of 500 red vinyl copies were released in March, plenty for Detroit then. Heather White's sleeve photo shows her sister masked by thick black hair as she touches a disc painted in red-and-white swirls by Jack who, in a white T-shirt, and with blonde tufts of hair coloured red like his trousers and lips, shuts his brown eyes. Jack's brother Stephen photographed the attic's American flag on the back. It's a complete, simple statement. Jack remembered it as his first record, something he hadn't realised was possible. "I put it in the bathroom," he told NPR's Bob Boilen, "so that every time I was in there, I could pick it up and look at it. I was just so shocked."

On Saturday, February 7, half a year after their debut, the White Stripes headlined the Gold Dollar, supported by the Soledad Brothers. "A 2 piece festival!" Neil Yee's monthly programme declared. "Stripped down to the basics . . . guitar, voice, and drums . . . A good opportunity to give a little more exposure to Jack's smooth, emotive, & explosive voice and guitar, ably backed by the minimalist percussion of wife Meg." If the sibling routine was set then, no one had told Yee.

6

Master of All Trades

THE White Stripes didn't have Jack's full focus yet. He continued during 1998 as an upholsterer and Two-Star Tabernacle's lead guitarist. And the night before topping the Gold Dollar bill, he appeared with the Hentchmen at Ferndale's Magic Bag, along with the Wildbunch and Rocket 455. "All right, where's Jack White?" Johnny "Hentch" Syzmanski asks, half an hour in. Jack ambles unmissably on, seeming almost freakishly tall, still sporting a curly blond lid of hair on an otherwise shaven head, and wearing a black suit with Teddy Boy lapels. He's lead guitar and singer on the MC5's 'Looking At You', grabbing the chance to be one of his vocal idols, Rob Tyner. Eyes engagingly wide as he enacts the words, he skips Tyner's testifying side. Then it's Richie Barrett's 1962 R&B hit 'Some Other Guy', cribbed from Jack's latest obsession, the Beatles' *Live At The BBC*, but channelling McCartney's high, Little Richard holler, not the record's Lennon. His guitar parts fit the garage-rock and soul at the new Detroit scene's heart, and he politely sits back for Tim Purrier's turn on lead. Arms flopping at his side when not playing, his later volatile stagecraft hasn't yet caught up with his charisma. But all parties look satisfied at his addition to an already exciting gig.

On a subsequent night at the Garden Bowl, Jack and Johnny decided to keep going. Later in February, Jack made his second 7-inch of the month at 1203 Ferdinand, this time with the Hentchmen. 'Some Other Guy' became the B-side to a cover of the Yardbirds' 1966 Jimmy Page-Jeff Beck duel, 'Psycho Daisies'. Here, Jack and Purrier trade solos for the final minute. Like Louis Armstrong's trumpet, White starts at the dramatically high frequencies where others finish, as if playing falsetto guitar. Purrier hovers in the thin air of his orbit, then takes a lower road. The single's sleeve declared this was the Hentchmen Featuring Jack White, as a joke: he was hardly a guest star, yet.

Detroit's anything-goes eccentricity, in which the White Stripes hardly figured as unusual, had been written all over the Gold Dollar's early programmes, as Neil Yee booked avant-garde theatre, local films, comedy, poetry and blues revues, and even featured a toilet historian. "Detroit is divided into sections," the Go's John Krautner explains, "and a healthy section of Detroit music fans love Sun Ra more than the MC5, the Silver Apples more than normal-sounding bands. Detroit advocates for the weird. That's one thing that everyone noticed in the late Nineties and what made that moment special, is that everyone was advocating for the underdogs." But even in the Gold Dollar's first year, 1996, Yee was irritated enough to nag, while plugging a Miles Davis-inspired jazz jam: "Why does the 'alternative' crowd only go see pop music? DO SOMETHING DIFFERENT!!" It was one of his wide-open Sunday nights that let the White Stripes slip onstage. But during 1998, and more firmly the next year, Detroit's burgeoning new rock'n'roll colonised the Gold Dollar.

On July 11, barely a year after the White Stripes started playing, the long-running block party the 4th Street Fair signalled to some how far things had come. "One of the greatest days for Detroit music ever," scene maker and promoter Greg Baise told *Detroit Free Press*. "Almost all the great bands played that day." Jim Diamond agrees. "Oh yeah, that was a lot of fun. The Dirties were doing their insane take on the punk-rock thing, and there was a surf band called the Volcanoes, and a spaghetti-western band called the Hellbenders were playing underneath the trees outside, selling mixed drinks from the porch of their house. A great free-for-all, it was so good." The Hentchmen played, too. "That was the first time I saw the Go, they'd just started," Tim Purrier remembers. "And the Cobras were starting to play a lot more, the Wildbunch were playing, the White Stripes, Bantam Rooster, the Dirtbombs had just started, and the Demolition Doll Rods were playing quite a bit. There were three times the bands that there had been a couple of years before. A peak, it seemed. I remember hanging out with Jack that day, but we saw them all the time back then. That wasn't a stand-out for me." You can see footage of the White Stripes playing 'Red Bowling Ball Ruth' on an improvised stage beneath trees, people strolling past on a sunny mid-afternoon, one intent listener smoking a gigantic joint. But no one I speak to remembers the White Stripes especially that day.

On July 25, Jack played with the Hentchmen again, this time as bassist at Detroit's St Andrew's Hall. Then in August, he was bassist on their *Hentch-Forth* album, recorded by Jeff Meier, again, over a weekend at an old car factory in Pontiac, a suburb at metropolitan Detroit's northern edge. That same weekend, he shut Third Man Upholstery. "Towards the end he just felt drained," Ben Blackwell told *Kerrang!*'s Stevie Chick, of juggling three bands with a job in which he was also creative and driven. "I was happy back in 1999, when I could just tour and play to 20 people and not have to have a day job," Jack told the journalist Hanspeter Kuenzler of the decision's aftermath. "That was success to me."

Around the time of *Hentch-Forth*, the White Stripes recorded a second 7-inch for Italy Records at 1203 Ferdinand. 'Lafayette Blues' hadn't changed much since being played as 'Marantette Blues' at their Gold Dollar debut. Its list of French street names searches for the exotic in Detroit (a city named for the strait – le détroit – that 18th century French trappers passed through). Built around a simply anthemic solo and a fast martial finish which, as she did live, makes Meg stumble as it slows, there's not much to it. The B-side, 'Sugar Never Tasted So Good', is much stronger. Acoustic blues in style and recorded to a single track and microphone, Meg carries the beat on tambourine and cardboard box (unless that dull whomp is Jack smacking his guitar, Son House-style). This is the White Stripes recording closest in its intimacy to the artless, private play with which they began. The words give water and sugar a special tang, and Jack feels like a baby becoming a man while holding a baby. Though some lyrics tangle and obscure his emotion, he sounds quietly ecstatic, and in love. 'What a feeling that's begun,' he exults, in what might be married bliss. If not, it's the start of a child's life that leaves him afloat in natural wonder; or the start of an affair, feeling much the same.

Mixed again at Ghetto Recorders, Dave Buick pressed 900 white vinyl copies, and 100 with red-and-white swirls. They included photocopied inserts by Jack concerning the Marquis de Lafayette, the hero of the French and American Revolutions who gave his name to the boulevard a block south of Ferdinand. The Marquis and Orson Welles were among those thanked for "support and inspiration" on the back sleeve. Both songs were credited to White/White, a momentary, generous acknowledgement of Meg's essential place in a band that, Jack once explained, "play White Stripes covers of Jack White songs." On Friday, October 23 at the Gold Dollar, they played to launch 'Lafayette Blues' and the Hentchmen did so for *Hentch-Forth*, Jack joining them to play Hank Williams' 'Jambalaya'.

"He wasn't really a bandmate," Purrier says. "I feel like that whole time was just pretty much fun. He was just mucking around. And, in retrospect, he probably wanted to hang out with other bands to learn his trade."

Jack's promiscuity was anyway standard in an almost private scene, where line-ups incestuously morphed at the bar. "It was always, 'Someone can't do a show, can you do it?'" Troy Gregory remembers, "and you end up in two or three different groups again. I've ended up in six bands at once." As Rocket 455's Marco Delicato told the *Metro-Times*' Brett Callwood: "It's a Detroit thing. Everyone had to be in two bands or you weren't working hard enough."

In the latter part of 1998, Jack joined a fourth. The Go were far more important than his Hentchmen dalliance. To most observers then, maybe even himself, they seemed more important than the White Stripes. Apart from Brendan Benson, they were the most pop-minded new Detroit band – though the pop of their record collections, not the Britney Spears-ruled charts. Singer Bobby Harlow and guitarist John Krautner formed the group in 1996, gigging from the end of 1997. Jack shared their love of the Stooges, MC5, Velvet Underground, Beatles, Beefheart and Zappa. So too their ambition. "We wanted to zoom to the top. We wanted to be the biggest thing ever," Krautner says. They seemed to offer the comforting gang Jack had often pined for since being ostracised as a teenager. But the Go tested his ability to be in a band he didn't run to definitive destruction.

"A lot happened in a very short amount of time," Krautner tells me. "I would say Jack was in the band about six months. It seemed longer, but I don't think it was. He was pretty busy at that point, in Two-Star Tabernacle and playing in the Hentchmen, and with his own band. But even though he had the White Stripes going, because he was involved in so many other projects, it was hard to see it as his main focus. So I wasn't sure what he really wanted. And that's what made us think, he's involved in so many bands, maybe he wouldn't mind joining one more!"

Watching a Two-Star Tabernacle gig pushed Harlow and Krautner to make their move. "He was very much in the background in that group," Krautner says. "But he had a sort of Split Enz hairstyle that stuck out. For that reason, he was a character we noticed, he wasn't your average Joe-looking guy. And he played like Jimmy Page. You know some people say they love Led Zeppelin, and then you hear them play guitar and you're like, 'You don't like Led Zeppelin, you like some indie-rock crap!' But when Jack played, you actually heard the thing you heard during *The Song Remains The Same* and all that awesome early Zeppelin footage. You saw, right in front of your face, that wow, it was taken from the real stuff, and he was expressing it in a very real way. I think that caught Bobby's ear especially. And it wasn't any kind of a big deal. We went over to Dave

[Buick] our bass player's house, who was friends with Jack and put out Jack's first couple of records. And we said, 'Do you wanna join the band?', and he didn't even think about it. He just said, 'Sure.' It was very cool. He was really easy to play with, because he was so good."

Jack debuted with them at the Gold Dollar on September 18, 1998, but it's their second gig together, backs to the street at the Garden Bowl bar, which sticks in John Krautner's mind. "The first great show with Jack was downstairs there, in a very small section. So just like the Gold Dollar, you're right up against the people watching you, and that's what it was all about for our band at the time – people feeling the sweat bounce off of you. The Magic Stick upstairs was rather nice, good sound system, and the place you wanted to be in front of a lot of people. But it was cooler to play the shittier show down there with the crappy PA that somebody taped together, and the sound was probably terrible, but the energy was there, you could reach out and touch it."

Jack gained immediate practical advantages. "He had complained to us that, 'the White Stripes don't get as much respect as they should,' and that he wished he could've grabbed a better position in a three-band bill," Krautner explains. "They always put him on first because they were a two-piece, and he thought he was getting slighted for that reason. So in the Go, because he was in our gang now, we had him positioned better for a show we played at the Magic Bag. Sometimes the middle slot is best, about 11.30 in Detroit, when people are not all that drunk yet and still up for seeing music, and that's where we put the White Stripes. We thought it was cool that he had his own band too. But Bobby and I had ideas about our band, just like Jack had about his. And before long we were signed to Sub Pop, and that gave us confirmation that we were on the right track."

Sub Pop's Dan Trager, a native Detroiter back in the city for Thanksgiving weekend on November 26, heard a tape of the Go recorded at Jack's home studio, after seeing the band at the Magic Stick. "I'd recorded demos in Jack's living room on his 8-track," Matt Smith remembers. "It wasn't really a studio, we had the instruments and amps spread out in different rooms. But I set up mics where I thought they should be, and Jack was like, 'Oh, man, that mic has got to be closer to the bass drum'. He kept going on about it, and I finally said, 'It's your house, I'll defer to you.' And on the song where the mic was moved, the bass drum sounded louder than the whole band. I'd been producing for over 10 years by then. But it was like Jack kinda would've liked to have been producing this. Then I went over to Jim Diamond's, who let me mix that tape in a half-hour for free, because Kim Fowley had heard the Go's 4-track demos and hoped to get something by them in a Hollywood movie, *Detroit Rock City*. Then Dan Trager, who I'd met in Ann Arbor in the Eighties, came to this Go show, and I gave him that tape I'd mixed in a half-hour from my car, and that's what got them their deal."

The contract offered on Trager's advice by the label, home of Jack's early heroes, Nirvana, would have also given them "right of first refusal on the White Stripes", Trager told Steve Miller in his book, *Detroit Rock City*. In White's memory, he spotted "a little paragraph thing" meaning Sub Pop would "own everything the White Stripes ever did." That ownership would turn the key to his long-term survival and, like Orson Welles, he already knew its power. A sympathetic Trager allowed him to prevaricate. And though label boss Jonathan Poneman took an impressed Go out to dinner, Sub Pop never tried to sign the White Stripes.

When the Go entered Ghetto Recorders to record their debut LP, *Whatcha Doin'* – probably in December, though Krautner remembers summer warmth – they also hit a wall with Jack. Outrageous Cherry's Matt Smith, a scene elder at 34, was a producer with his own firm vision. For the first and only time, Jack endured a whole album as a musical subordinate. "Bobby and I were at the Go's helm, so we had a meeting with Matt alone," Krautner remembers. "And Matt's been in several bands, and worked with crazy people like Crime & the City Solution, and his whole apartment is filled with records. And he brings out the Sweet's *Give Us A Wink*. He put it on, and he said, 'I think we should make what you're doing sound like this record.' And then he brought out a record by a German garage band called [Beatles Hamburg contemporaries] the Rattles, and on that one there was a lot of reverb, the drums were super-loud, and the vocals were really down in the mix. And it was an awkward mix. Bobby and I were looking at each other, and said, 'This is okay with you?' And Matt said, 'It's more than okay. This is one of my favourite records.' So we knew going in that the production was going to be adventurous. And I guess Jack was blindsided by that."

"The most interesting thing that came out of that whole period was the Go," Matt Smith states. "When I first saw them, I thought, 'This is the best rock'n'roll band I've ever heard out of Detroit.' They had the kind of influence and presence in that scene that the MC5 had in theirs. But they ended up being overshadowed, obviously. The whole band came over to my house, and I put on the Rattles' 'I Know You Don't Know', the B-side of 'Devil's On The Loose', a [1971] US 45. It's this absolute simple rock'n'roll thing, with pre-glam production – a really badass record. I thought, 'All these guys need is recording with this single's atmosphere, then we got it.'"

"Matt would say, 'It can't sound a day over 1971!'" laughs Jim Diamond, who engineered the sessions at his studio. "They had recorded the stuff they got signed on at Jack's house, and we re-recorded a lot of those songs, but they ended up preferring a few of the original tracks, then remixed them all here. So there were two versions, and some dispute over which to use. And I remember this well. We were tracking everything live, and then Jack would do his solo, and Matt would say, 'Yeah, let's move on,' because Matt's into the first take being the one. And Jack would want to redo his solo, and Matt would say, 'No no no, that was great!' So that was a sticking point. Then they did some overdubs on top of the mixes – 'Oh, we need to add a guitar or keyboard part' – which is not a real common thing to do."

"The minute Jack joined the band," says Smith, "he was a very nervous and very edgy guy, and he immediately seemed very suspicious of everything that was going on. Jack wanted to be reassured that he could get all his guitar parts the way he wanted. Once we were in the studio, everything seemed fine. But after the whole thing was recorded, he started to seem real unhappy with certain things, and confronted me about it. He questioned his guitar parts, and wanted to relisten to everything and redub some. His musical stuff always sounded great. He just seemed like he was a very uneasy guy. And he didn't get his way because he would never present it in a way that could convince everybody else. He wouldn't say, 'Hey you guys, I've got this great idea . . .' It was, 'I'm nervous about this idea.' It was always in the form of being suspicious about what was happening. And I think it was in the middle of making the record that he and Meg were having some problems. So if he was not real happy with the record, I think he was not real happy in general. I didn't know or ask the details, but I knew something was up with that."

"We were in the studio for about two weeks, then mixing maybe another week," says Krautner. "It was during mixing and the deciding of which tracks stayed where you could see Jack getting visibly upset. And that rang a bunch of bells with the producer, Bobby and I. Because we thought, 'We like the way this is going. How come this lead guitar player's getting so upset over his solos?' And," he sighs, "for everyone else in the band, this was our first experience in a studio, and we were trusting our producer. Matt making our first record sound like his favourite obscure record was something that we were behind. So to see Jack fighting against that was frustrating for us. And Jack, as we all know now, is very in control of his legacy. That's how he works it, and it's worked out well for him. But in that tiny microcosm of a rock'n'roll band that was the Go, it wasn't working well. We were too green to allow him to do that."

"I knew that if I ever was going to be in a studio situation with Jack, he would definitely be the one in charge," says Steve Nawara, who ultimately replaced Jack in the Go. "He'd be, 'I want this, I want that, I don't want this, I don't want that.' I don't think that he had room for other people's opinions. I think if anyone had anything negative to say about him it would just be because he was so specific, and he was not a hippie-dippy dude. God bless him for it, though. I think that's exactly what he had to do."

Whatcha Doin' sounds like a fantasy of the years just before Jack was born, early Seventies glam, heavy pop and boogie soundtracking Bobby Harlow stepping up to hot chicks in the sun to warn, 'Girl, don't you come too soon.' "We'd just gotten into Roxy Music and Brian Eno's first two albums, and thought, 'We've gotta write a song just like that!'" Krautner explains of 'It Might Be Bad''s phased keyboard slur, from which Jack's spot at the top of its three-part harmonies soars clear. You can hear the MC5 at their post-revolutionary tightest in 'Meet Me At The Movies'. The production is subtly imaginative and the melodies nag, on a high-spirited, fuzzed-up guitar album. It's not garage-rock or blues, but a strain in the scene that was written out of history by the White Stripes' success, that just wanted to rock out (knowledgably, in the style of favourite records) and, as a song here says, 'Get You Off'. The solos that left Jack fuming are pointedly brief, like Dave Davies' instinctively brilliant scribbles on early Kinks singles. 'Suzy Don't Leave' shows how he suits the Go's Zeppelin-era style, as his guitar dances jaggedly like a sun-storm over the melody, then takes off like a Texas twister and burrows into the mix. On one of the two songs he co-wrote with Harlow and Krautner, 'Time For Moon', passing meteorites of guitar zoom through in seconds. The melody is from the Sixties, and the arrangement and hedonistic feeling are from the following decade, where the Go abide.

"*Whatcha Doin'* was the record that really did it for me and a lot of people," Nawara remembers. "We couldn't believe how good that record was. The production was a little rough, and Bobby, the singer, was very *cocky* back then! But they were fricking amazing."

Jack's complicated life was speeding up now, many parts of it coming to a head. In January 1999, shortly after making *Whatcha Doin'*, Jim Diamond thinks, he returned to Ghetto Recorders to record the White Stripes' debut LP. They had a handshake deal with Sympathy for the Record Industry, the Long Beach, California label that had also released the first records by Hole and, more recently, the Detroit Cobras. Its owner, maverick rock'n'roll benefactor Long Gone John, heard them when '68 Comeback's Jeff Evans passed on the recommendation of Jeff Meier, now a Cobra as Rocket 455 wound down. "Steve Shaw, who's with the band Detroit Cobras, he had sent them two records that are on Italy Records," was Jack's own memory on WDET. "And [John] liked them but I guess he was pretty busy, so he waited a couple of months and said he'd like to do a full album with us." Jack sat at his usual spot at the Garden Bowl bar to ponder the offer with his friend, Bantam Rooster's Tom Potter. It wasn't Sub Pop, but Jack would own the recordings. Matt Smith remembers him saying he'd signed midway through *Whatcha Doin'*. The White Stripes made their album as soon as possible, only the Go delaying them enough to let the signatures dry.

Jim Diamond sets the scene, already familiar to Jack, which greeted the White Stripes for the four days they took to record. "When you come up to the front door, I tell people, look for the abandoned building. It looks like no one lives there. There's a black door, no handle. I lived there as well, so there's an apartment up there. In the back, for bands with a lot of equipment, I had a big old freight elevator from the early 1900s. But they came in the front, which is like walking through a maze. You'd have to walk through my living room, walk through my kitchen, go downstairs, upstairs, and then you're back in the studio. It's 10 metres by 10, a pretty sizable room filled with amplifiers, keyboards and drums, almost like a used instrument store."

The cavernous echo and presence that is a signature of Diamond's work, from the Witches' *Universal Mall* to *The White Stripes*, was partly due to this forgotten place in the Cass Corridor. "What I really miss, now I've left, is the unique sound in the room," he says. "A lot of the presence on that White Stripes album is down to the reverberation and overall tone of the room for drums and vocals. I always used a lot of that – varying the distance of the mics from instruments to pick up more of the room's ambience, to shape its sounds." Ghetto's analogue set-up was also essential to Jack's ethos. "I'd record everything on tape – 16-track for *The White Stripes*. I always want people to set up like they're rehearsing, so they're comfortable, then do the basic tracks live."

Meg White, her feet bare as she often preferred, picked her way through the broken glass left on the concrete floor after a Dirtbombs session. For the first time, she was recording away from her home. Behind the windowless wall of his control room, Diamond heard the duo struggle. "I think Meg was just very nervous about it, because she wasn't an experienced drummer. So we'd do a lot of takes, because she was brand-new to playing. It took a little while to get down those basic tracks. We did the drums and guitar together, and Jack had to cue Meg a lot on the stops and the starts." Though they spent "less than two grand" of the $3,000 Sympathy provided, according to Long John, Jack's temper sometimes shortened as time and money mounted. It can't have been easy for his shy wife, who he'd thrust into a position where her inexperience was expensive. Already irritated by his lack of control when the Go dragged him to Ghetto, Jack was also suspicious of this 'real' studio's capacity to tamper with the authentic sound he ascribed to his favourite blues records. A Fifties RCA mic "sounds too much like we're in a studio," Diamond remembered him saying. Still, it was a fairly uneventful session, by a band Diamond had no strong feeling for among all those playing and partying at his place. "After we got the takes," he says, "we did some minimal overdubs, and remixed it. They were good. It wasn't like, 'My God, this is the most amazing stuff I've ever heard.'"

The White Stripes begins with a slow, heavily echoing beat in an empty room, an elephantine rasp of slide, and then the dumb rush of 'Jimmy The Exploder', the song of childish anarchy Jack had waiting for the band's accidental start. Then Robert Johnson's 'Stop Breaking Down' states blues intentions not apparent in their early gigs, the scratchy slide-guitar so massive and distorted it seems ready to bust out of the grooves, as certainly as Jack threatens to bust out the brains of a pistol-packing girlfriend. Though his voice is only one almost swamped layer in a super-charged sound, it's the first time he dares to act the part of a bluesman who was similarly young when he recorded it. His new friend Johnny Walker of the Soledad Brothers adds a second slide which contemplatively intertwines with his in the initially drifting, riverside blues 'Suzy Lee', an interlude about a child's note-passing infatuation. It's notable for the oddly arresting rhetoric Jack has learned from blues lyrics – 'To end this tale/ The one I'm speaking of . . .' – and the practicality of Walker's presence here and on the tense, sultry 'I Fought Piranhas'. The iron conceptual limits of the White Stripes as studio duo can still be bent.

'Cannon' stomps with obvious Zeppelin tread, until Jack slips into Son

House's 'John The Revelator', almost cockily asking, 'who's that riding?', and revelling in declaring, 'I've been evil – EVIL!' – itself a bridge to 'Cannon''s twin song about an idiot dance, 'Astro', which finds room for nods to Jack's hero, the underdog electrical pioneer Nikola Tesla, and jibes at his nemesis Thomas Edison. 'Wasting My Time' is an early Sixties-style, operatic ballad with the twang of the Shadows or a Jack Gillis idol, Dick Dale. 'Sugar Never Tasted So Good', included from the previous year's single on CD and later LP versions, adds more intimate shade. So does a Meg-suggested Dylan cover, 'One More Cup Of Coffee' from 1976's *Desire*, with an organ paying clear tribute to the Animals' 'House Of The Rising Sun', itself learned from Jack's Hamtramck coffee house touchstone, *Bob Dylan*. 'St. James Infirmary Blues' began the White Stripes' live career and ends the album, Jack sighing, "Oh, Koko!" in private tribute to Cab Calloway's Koko the Clown guise in the cartoon where he and Meg heard it. This third blues cover is skeletal and relatively upbeat, as Jack plays juke-joint piano, and emphasises the freedom and transformative identity in the death-haunted song: 'I can say whatever I feel like to you . . . take your bones apart and put 'em back together/ Tell your mother you're somebody new.'

Though *The White Stripes* has careful textural variety, Meg's ceaseless steadiness, doubled by Jack's guitar, hammers the album into shape, making it all one thing. Iggy Pop claimed the Stooges' sound was influenced by the pounding of Detroit's car factories (though the band hailed from Ann Arbor). Those factories were long silent, but this album is equally made by the city. 'Screwdriver' takes a walk out of Jack's house. Two other songs dig through the bones of Detroit's past. 'Broken Bricks', co-written by Stephen Gillis, is a fast, spitting urban blues for the city's wreckage. Jack guides you through an abandoned factory's vacant security gates as a cowbell rings – bring out your dead? – and points out still machinery and the ghosts of his listener's family (a listener presumed to be a Detroiter), where they worked hard, violent, lusty years, or just ate lunch. It's a dangerous playground of puddled oil, snapped cranes and tripwire memories – diminished by those who may one day demolish it to 'Building C'. Though he lets the music's angry rush carry his words away, the typed, carefully numbered verses of Jack the poet are inside the LP: 'Broken tooth window panes/ Drip a rusty coloured rain/ To drive a man insane.'

'The Big Three Killed My Baby' is Jack's ultimate word on Detroit, a rare protest song and the album's greatest, pumped by staccato guitar and drum pistons. The three in question are the city's giant car corporations, General Motors, Chrysler and Ford, blamed here for the vast human and material waste of planned obsolescence. The factories and the billions of cars they produce are seen as insanely whirring cogs, an industrial dystopia like something out of Chaplin's *Modern Times*, or Fritz Lang's *Metropolis* (a director Jack revered). Greased by the blood of Preston Tucker, the doomed Michigan auto idealist valorised in Francis Coppola's film *Tucker: The Man And His Dream*, the industry on which Detroit rose and fell is seen as corrupt, lazy, and yet another side of the social contempt revealed to Jack by 'Grinnin' In Your Face'. As in 'Screwdriver', faces here are 'grinning' with shit-eating disdain. It's a maddened manifesto by a man ready to blow, his voice tight and rising, till he roars: 'I found out my baby's dead – yeah, yeah, yeah!'

Jack conceded to *Rolling Stone*'s David Fricke in 2005 that it was one of his most important songs. "I felt I connected with what I wanted to talk about: my city and the evil it contains, the big three automotive corporations." Interviewed by the *Metro-Times*' Norene Cashen after its release as an album-heralding single in April (with 'Red Bowling Ball Ruth' as the B-side), he emphasised how it conceptually fitted into the White Stripes: "Meg's playing on 'The Big Three Killed My Baby' is the epitome of what I like about her drumming. It's just hits over and over again. It's not even a drumbeat – it's just accents." And it was the trinity. "It's three chords and three verses, and we accent threes together all through it."

In that same *Rolling Stone* interview, Jack said he'd never want to write an "exposé" of himself. But he so often did. *The White Stripes*' B-side takes a long look at his tender psychic spots. In 'When I Hear My Name', he wants to vanish at the sight and sound of himself. 'Little People', while seeming to conform to the band's childish concept, is about saying 'hello' across unbridgeable time to a child's apparently untroubled mind, now his hugely self-conscious, ever-whirring adult brain won't shut up. As 19-year-old Jack wrote in a play *Lazaretto* unearthed, "I wish I was simple." 'Screwdriver' ends in a feverish moan at interlopers crowding and demeaning him. And 'Do' is plaintive but increasingly desperate. He can't trust his child's eyes as they look at a mother he can't hear; he despairs of responding to a passing 'hello', making a joke rather than risk his thoughts being ridiculed, or somehow stolen when they leave his head: 'Don't wanna be social/ Can't stand it when they hate me but I know there's nothin' I can do.' In the final verse, his idols – the Detroit adults he sought out as a teenager – disintegrate up close, collapsing on feet of clay, 'destruction of a mystery' he'd learn from and avoid as a star. 'Do' dissects the particular pathology that separates him: the reason he feels alone. It's a cry for help certain it won't be answered.

A close-typed piece of poetic prose with the lyric sheet stated even more explicitly why the White Stripes' aesthetic was childish. Any attempt at adult pleasure merely pined for backyard games "when you first saw others and dreamt that with them you could be happier than you were alone."

"I think our first album is still our proudest with the White Stripes," Jack told *NME*'s Julian Marshall in 2004. "I think it captured something really Detroit-sounding, like the Stooges' *Fun House* felt like Detroit to me."

Heather White was too busy to take her usual sleeve photos, so Garden Bowl barmaid and Ko & the Knockouts singer Ko Melina snapped Meg in a red mini-dress and Jack in red trousers and white T-shirt, hair now floppily grown out and dyed black to match Meg, outside Mexicantown's fire station. Every Jack White record's details would be precise, and the station's fresh red paint had to be photographed before it dulled. Melina also took the inner photo of Jack and Meg standing happily on their married home's red-and-white porch, their pink-and-white Chihuahua in smiling Meg's arms. But before its June 8 release, Jack's wedding ring was digitally removed.

On February 3, 1999, before the White Stripes performed some of their new songs on WDET, the interviewer was the first of hundreds to enquire: "I wanna ask you first of all, are you guys a husband-wife duo, or a brother-sister duo?" Not missing a beat, Jack said, "It's a brother-sister duo." "Uh-huh . . ." The airtime the station tried to give Detroit bands on the way up was easygoing, Jack claiming that with songwriting "we always try to be 50/50 as much as we can", and Meg withering under early interview fire when asked about her drum style: "Well, basically just . . . hitting the drum . . . just little-girl style, I guess." Jack said they were looking forward to March's Blowout music weekend in Hamtramck, when he'd be playing in Two-Star Tabernacle, the Go and the White Stripes. Then shortly before it, the Stripes' March 12 gig was announced as their last. The band was gone with their marriage.

It's impossible to know what caused the separation of a married couple that wouldn't admit they were married. But reflecting after a second divorce years later, Jack boldly conceded his faults. "I'm a very provocative person and very intimidating," he told *The Guardian*'s Tim Lewis. "I'm incredibly complicated, incredibly full of energy, incredibly busy and I never stop thinking, I never stop creating. Sitting next to me in a room or laying next to me in a bed, it could be a lot of work." In another interview he mentioned his need to take charge, to be the one mapping out friends' seats in a restaurant. Asked if she'd heard the comment, Meg said: "Oh, yeah – believe me . . ." Most comments drawn from her in interviews corrected his curmudgeonly thoughts about women's flaws, borne of years of rejection before her. And her passivity, calm and silence could goad this voluble, volatile man. "Having a conversation with Meg, you don't get any answers," he sighed to *The New York Times*, when the White Stripes had really split. "She's the most stubborn person I've ever met, and you don't even get to know the reasons." To Barney Hoskyns, he said: "She's an enigma to me." With cracks appearing in the Go, and the White Stripes making him push a wife still uncomfortable playing through a strained album session, home life must have suffered. All that's sure is that they married young, and it didn't work.

"He spent a lot of time at my house," Dave Buick said in Chris Handyside's *Fell In Love With A Band*. "It was a bad fight. He was pretty bummed out for a while." When Meg pulled out of even that last gig, Jack, Buick and Ben Blackwell rehearsed to fill in. But then the woman who was still Jack's wife, and who had effectively started the White Stripes, said they should play on. Danny Kroha says he urged her to. During little more than 24 hours in Hamtramck, Jack's emotional chaos and complex musical life then simplified and powerfully peaked.

He began the evening of March 12 in Two-Star Tabernacle at Paycheck's, for their final show before he quit a band he hadn't found fulfilling, and was now just in his way. "He didn't stand out in Two-Star Tabernacle, or Goober & the Peas before that," Troy Gregory remembers. "It was more when he was the focal point onstage, and finding his niche, like a lot of bands around then were – experimenting, and always turning into something else, and defining their own thing more with how they sang, rather than forcing atmospheres. In the Go, I really loved his guitar playing. I remember even for the White Stripes in those early days, it was, 'The guitar player in the Go's got this other group . . .'"

'Hotel Yorba' was still in Two-Star Tabernacle's last set-list, as it had been a year before at the Gold Dollar, and they finished with the American folk song 'Wayfaring Stranger', which Jack would return to three years later in unimaginably different circumstances. He also debuted two songs he would keep for the White Stripes' third album, *White Blood Cells*. They had a particular life tonight. 'The Union Forever' was his *Citizen Kane* tribute, built from its two songs and lines in the script that caught his attention during his 36 viewings, which he found began to rhyme. The scenes used include Kane's refusal of the values of old-moneyed banker Thatcher ("What would I like to have been? Everything you hate"), the tatty vaudeville send-off 'Oh, Mr. Kane' and Charlie Barnet and Haven Johnson's 1939 jazz song 'In A Mizz', the theme for the violent dissolution of Kane's second marriage. The music at Paycheck's is low, churning country *noir*. Jack's vocal is the closest he's come to Kurt Cobain's savage blues performance of Leadbelly's 'Where Did You Sleep Last Night?' There's a lot of Nirvana, and his battered marriage, as he keeps returning to the words of 'In A Mizz' with controlled, throat-ripping shrieks: 'It can't be love, well there is no true love!' Dan Miller tries to harmonise, then backs off. Even lines from the jaunty 'Oh, Mr. Kane' are infected, as Jack sings with bitter irony of a man who 'enjoys a *joke!*' It starts to sound like flagellation, then immolation, love burning in the grate of his voice. 'The cost no man can say, but you've gotta love me,' was how he began, but that's all gone. It's music Two-Star Tabernacle can play, but can't contain.

"Hey, here's a song that I wrote the other day," Jack says a bit later, debuting 'The Same Boy You've Always Known'. It's a beautifully sad and fatalistically funny lyric about more lost love, with odd blues lines about death. What really stands out compared with the band's Gold Dollar set 14 months before is Jack's voice. Sometimes laughably high and wild then, now he's a strong, confident balladeer.

Next, he rushed across Hamtramck to play guitar with the Go at the Motor Lounge, the glitzy club now run by the promoter of Zoot's old Monday nights, Adriel Thornton. A mirrored wall for dancers was behind them as they played. "It was an unconventional venue, a techno place," John Krautner remembers. "We'd just recorded our record, and all our friends were in front. And it was the moment when we realised, 'Wow, people really like this band.' And we played a great show, we were wild, we were sweating. A girl got onstage and was very sexual, the way she was moving! Everything about the whole night seemed very rock'n'roll, and very fun, and the energy was there, and it was just a moment. I'm sure every band has that one magical show, and that was ours. We wanted to be rock stars, and that was our glimpse into the world of being a rock star. The crowd with their hands up, screaming."

Steve Nawara remembers the night well. "It was jam-packed, everyone was inside the show. And I was suddenly intimidated by my own friends. It was that incredible a show. It was fricking amazing. And I remember we were all hanging out afterwards, and they knew how good they'd played. They had this Led Zeppelin demeanour. Really like, 'We're the kings now.' And of course Jack was just incredible on the guitar. That one show was a very pivotal moment in Detroit, I think. Things shifted quickly after that. All the trendy girls were at the Go show. And that was something that was unheard of. It was a very important, powerful night, and everyone knew it."

The night after that sweaty rock success, Jack was back at Paycheck's with the wife he'd just separated from. Doug Coombe's photos show him bending to rip out solos, neck straining as he sings, and looking back at a typically impassive Meg, who mostly keeps her eyes closed. As with the Go at the Motor, most of the scene, from Brendan Benson to Jim Diamond, are there.

"Most of the crowd was bands supporting each other," Coombe agrees. "The Sights, the Dirtbombs, the Wildbunch and Bantam Rooster were all there. That Blowout was kind of pre internet and brought a lot of bands together, and made people realise there was a scene going on. The White Stripes really stood out, but they were also part of that scene. I saw Jack in the Go first. I walked in mid-song, and the thing that blew me away immediately was that his playing reminded me of Ron Asheton. His solos were really raw, they blew into the song as an amazing, energetic thing, and then they were over before you realised what happened – like someone pulled the plug out of his guitar. And it left you wanting more. And then I saw the White Stripes, and I realised this guy has amazing, classic songs, and there was also a sense of fun about it. When Jack was soloing or singing, Meg would have a whimsical look on her face, because they were reading each other – 'Is it here I come in?' You could feel some looseness to it. Jack's guitar broke, and he just carried on with one from [fellow Mexicantown band] They Come In Threes. And it's funny, you can see the wedding ring in the photos. It surprised me to hear later that he and Meg had split up. It's crazy to think the White Stripes almost didn't happen. I didn't get any sense of that onstage. There were so many phenomenal bands, I think we were all just high at having such a great night."

"I don't know what Jack considers his magical show," Krautner considers. "But his show with the White Stripes at Paycheck's seemed a little magical to me. I could see Jack playing, and the crowd was starting to sing his song 'Sugar Never Tasted So Good'. And the guy's only got a couple of 7-inch singles out, and vinyl wasn't as popular then as it is now. And I looked at Jack's face, and the look on it was pretty hilarious, because I don't think he was expecting people to sing along with his song. I felt what he was feeling – oh, man, you're having a moment right now! Isn't that crazy?"

As with the glowing aftermath at the Motor, it sounds like a moment where what you wanted suddenly becomes real, and you form an idea of what's possible. A night that can rocket-fuel you forward.

"Yeah. It's like when you win a race. People are crowded around you, and put the medal around your neck. That's the feeling."

"I saw the White Stripes at Paycheck's, and they were great," Nawara agrees. "It was at that point that the mass hysteria around Jack White was happening, and the White Stripes were happening. But Jack being in the Go was definitely a big add-on. And the Go was the gig that weekend that blew me away. And that was the reaction of the crowd at the Motor Lounge, every girl had hearts jumping out of their eyes!" he laughs. "I thought that the Go were going to go further than the White Stripes, and I think many people shared that opinion. Because that two-piece line-up, I couldn't believe it would go further than a full band. It was shocking to me, and I think very surprising to other people as well when that happened. Especially after that Go show at the Motor. But Bobby's got a strong personality, and so has Jack. So I also wasn't surprised when Jack was like, 'Okay, I'm just doing the White Stripes now.'"

Jack's weekend hadn't finished. On the Sunday morning of March 14, after the White Stripes had reaffirmed their future at Paycheck's, he played solo at the Garden Bowl bar, and with another new friend, Brendan Benson. Then in the weeks after the Motor's momentary triumph, the tensions while making *Whatcha Doin'* came to snapping point.

"Towards the end it didn't work out with Jack as a bandmate," Krautner states. "Because you could tell that he wanted more. And he was acting out a little bit in our band. During shows, you could tell he wanted to be more involved in the creative process with the Go. And he was, to a degree. But Bobby and I could feel the control of our baby slipping out of our hands, and we saw Jack getting a little negative. It was passive, not aggressive. I think Jack probably saw his future coming a lot closer than we did, because he knew what he was capable of doing, and he probably couldn't do it in our band. We didn't play that many shows together –

nine. And the last two or three were hard, because there was a frustration, and it was pretty visible.

"We had three more shows after the Motor," Krautner continues. "Our last was in a tiny club in Ferndale called Club Bart. It had an awkward stage. It was actually behind the bar, and very high up and very dangerous, because in front of the stage were all the bar's bottles of booze, and it was like falling into an opera pit. And that show ended when Jack threw his guitar down and broke it, in a Pete Townshend way. And then a mic stand got whipped down, too. Which was all very dangerous-seeming to me, because there wasn't much space on that stage not to fall into that pit of despair! At that time, the tensions were at their peak. And that was it."

Troy Gregory, whose Witches were supporting that night, saw that Jack's appeal was still patchy. "I remember Jack started playing, and he's all into it, he's basically how he is onstage. But there were these two girls up front, and they were laughing at him. I thought, 'That's funny . . .'"

The Ferndale eruption just confirmed that Jack's time in the Go was up. "I remember this like it was yesterday," Krautner says. "It was the worst feeling ever. Bobby and I had talked and talked, and we knew we had to ask Jack to leave, there was too much tension. And it was extremely hard, because why would you let a guy go just when your band is really happening? But we knew that we could not function creatively with Jack having all these frustrations. And it was just like something out of *The Godfather*. We told him to meet us at a restaurant on Cass Avenue, and we sat at this table, and I had this pit in my stomach. And he didn't make it any easier on us, because he acted like he didn't see it coming. Maybe he didn't. The thing I remember most is the innocent look on Jack's face. 'What did I do wrong, I don't understand' – that kind of vibe. As if he was caught unknowingly. Like a little kid who did something bad but he didn't know it was bad. And he had that baby face. It was pretty difficult. And actually, as a person, Jack was cool to hang out with. We all had similar interests, and we laughed at the same jokes. That was probably the hardest part. 'Oh, man, our new friend Jack, we've gotta kick him out.' It sucked."

Having felt compelled to hand their star player the Black Spot, the confrontation wasn't finished. "We'd told Dave Buick we were going to do this, and he really didn't want to be a part of it. But we went to see him, and Jack was waiting at his house! Even more of a *Godfather* moment. So we went in, and it was just so tense. We're all there, having to think about what happened. And Jack gets up and leaves. And then Dave quit, because we fired his friend. We let Jack go, and then our bass player quit that same night. It was terrible. The local papers made us seem like assholes. And we felt like assholes. It's become a joke to people in my world, because of his success – 'Waitaminute, did you just say you fired Jack White from your band?' It was tough, and it put us back several steps. But it was absolutely necessary."

"The only band I've ever been fired from," Jack mused many years later, still sounding affronted. *Whatcha Doin'* was released on September 7, 1999, to disappointing sales, Sub Pop dropping their three-album deal. *The White Stripes* had been released on June 15, dedicated to Son House, to some local interest, the *Metro-Times* calling it a reminder that Detroit's "identity has more options than a membership card to the latest cliché . . . or a one-way ticket to the coast." "*Whatcha Doin'* was definitely the bigger deal," Diamond says, after working on both. "Because it was on Sub Pop." Jack and his former band soon settled their differences, in a close-knit Detroit scene where everyone still had to rub along. "It didn't take terribly long," Krautner remembers. "Jack still had some struggling to do to get his own band out there, and we were both touring at the same time, hitting the same clubs two or three nights behind each other."

October 2's Gold Dollar bill announced: "The White Stripes just keep getting better . . . also on tour with Pavement?!" With Ben Blackwell in the back of his mum's Ford Taurus van with the bass drum, and Uncle Jack and Meg in front, the White Stripes supported Stephen Malkmus' slippery American indie heroes for three dates in the southeast. "I don't know nervousness," Jack told Pamela Des Barres years later. "I've always been able to walk out onstage and [think], 'Yeah, there's a lot of people standing in front of me, so what?" But Blackwell remembers them playing on September 25 at the Recher Theater in Towson, Maryland to 800 Pavement fans, by far the biggest crowd they'd faced. "They were so nervous they played super-fast, and finished in 20 minutes," he told *Detroit Free Press*. The White Stripes made a loss, but Pavement rustled up about $200 to send these nice kids home.

Not everything about the White Stripes was yet certain. Probably in 1999, perhaps previous year, Steve Nawara remembers an experiment that broke the fixed conceptual framework Jack would claim for them. "I don't think I truly got to know Jack in a close relationship," he says, "but we were friends, and we respected each other, to the point where he asked me to play bass in the White Stripes for a couple of shows. But it didn't work out," he laughs. "The simplicity of the drums is very hard to follow as a bass player. It's almost impossible to be a bassist in the White Stripes. A beat going ba–bum–ka–boom–baboomcha . . . what are you going to go the whole time, basically follow it? You could, but it gets rather boring, and it takes away from their sound. I know he missed having a bass there. That's why he started messing around with octave-pedals. But the two of them were powerful enough that they didn't need it. I think it would have dragged the music down." Though he couldn't really add to their equation, the rare experience of being a White Stripe was memorable. And Nawara may have completed their colour scheme. "They were obviously flaunting the red-and-white motif, and I was like, 'I'm not wearing red and white. I'm wearing black. All black.' Jack said, [rapid] 'That's exactly what I was thinking.' We had a chuckle out of that. I couldn't believe how high he was singing. Holy shit, he could sing high. And again, they were amazing. They were popular then, in our little scene. But for those first few years, it was just a little secret among ourselves. Everyone loved them. No one ever thought they'd make it out of Detroit, though. No one."

Jack claimed to have felt similarly about the very particular band he'd created. "It's a limited audience, you know?" he told Pamela Des Barres. "There's like 50 people in every town who might dig this. We thought, that's fine. If we don't have to have a day job, that's not bad."

But when Troy Gregory next saw Jack that year, after watching girls laugh at him in the Go, there was a change. "It was interesting. My wife and I went out, and the White Stripes were at the Magic Stick. And it was packed. But unlike before, it was a lot of kids – 17, 18, 19-year-olds. And it was like, 'When did this happen?'"

On Friday, November 26, the White Stripes headlined over the Go at the Gold Dollar. In footage from the night Meg, 24, looks very young, thrusting her chin forward, chewing her lip, and lost in her work. An early take on Dolly Parton's 'Jolene' is a steely quiver, while as 'Stop Breaking Down' turns into 'Little Bird', Jack declares, "I'm gonna preach the word to ya!" His face expressively narrates 'The Big Three Killed My Baby' even as he sings it with tightly focused fury. He's bouncing, spread-legged, on the small stage. "We were honoured to play with the Go, and the Baby Killers," he announces – the latter group soon to become the Von Bondies, whose guitarist Marcie Bolen will replace Meg as his girlfriend at 1203 Ferdinand, the start of an eventually violent soap opera. For 'Hello Operator', he steps towards Meg, the two looking at each other as she smashes down on the cymbals. What would become an onstage duel, charged with the drama of their unspoken relationship as they played to huge crowds, starts here as a remnant of the visual cueing he gave when she could barely play. Someone shouts "Freebird!", and they finish with the Stooges' 'I'm Sick Of You.' Jack looks almost casually in command.

He and Meg divorced on March 24, 2000. Nothing more was ever said publicly of his marriage with his bandmate, after she decided to play on at Paycheck's and stay by his side; but Brian Muldoon was sure the choice had been harder for her.

"It seemed like they still loved each other," Nawara says. "I could feel that when they were onstage, at least. They wanted two different things, I think. But that's something I really don't know. It wasn't that strange to me that they continued. Because they had a bond, and they both had to see where it was going to take them. It would have to have been tense, but at some point I'd forget that they were even married. I knew they were going to keep playing. It seemed their bond was bigger than a marriage. They were entering the collective unconscious at that point," he says, clearly flashing forward in time. "'Of course we're going to go into there. You do this, and I do that, and we have something that's going to be remembered for eternity.' So of course that bond's going to be stronger."

7

Half a World Away

"THIRD Man Studio, SW Detroit at the turn of the century." The recording dateline noted inside the White Stripes' *De Stijl* was a time of pre-millennial tension, fear of planes dropping from the sky as digital systems failed, and survivalists bracing for Armageddon in the American woods. The Gold Dollar closed on December 23, 1999. "Open again on Thursday January 6," Neil Yee promised, "even if the world as we know it has ended." But while those around him left the 20th century, Jack White found inspiration for the White Stripes' second album at its tumultuous start. A Dutch design movement begun in reaction to the ongoing First World War and American blues of the same vintage merged fruitfully in his mind.

Jack was a one-band man and ex-upholsterer now, a new focus that would bring rapid rewards. His time was divided between continuing to make music in his living room with the wife he was separated from, and the girlfriend who was visiting 1203 Ferdinand in her place. "She moved out and I moved in," the Von Bondies' Marcie Bolen told Steve Miller in *Detroit Rock City*, of a relationship begun in 1999. Everything was happening in his old family home, including *De Stijl*. "I remember he said he wanted to record the next one at home because he didn't want to spend all the money on studio time," Jim Diamond says, "because they had to do a lot of takes on the first one." Ghetto was hardly the money-guzzling Abbey Road it seemed to cost-conscious Jack, and he later regretted the distractions and relative sloth of *De Stijl*'s home recording. But it was a vivid, varied album.

The upbeat opening 'You're Pretty Good Looking (For A Girl)' announces a brighter, broader palette than *The White Stripes*. It's a seamless Sixties patchwork in which Jack sings 'linger on' in tribute to the Velvet Underground's 'Pale Blue Eyes', and slips a sound like the band's John Cale drone beneath the sweet optimism of verses echoing the Beatles and Buddy Holly. His vocal is indulgently happy, the mood that of sunny

1965, before acid's complexities and comedown. The song's title has a schoolboy's defensiveness, as he plots knowing everything about this girl and dodging becoming her 'toy', as she is to the other boys crowding around her beauty.

De Stijl is in part a secret breakup album. Bob Dylan's lacerating *Blood On The Tracks* is the form's template and Meg's favourite LP, which she surely played in these last days of their marriage, given the effect she described in *Mojo*: "in [its] sadness I always find hope, or at least the strength to go on believing in love despite its almost inevitable end, the power to look at different loves as stages in your life which can make you stronger even in their demise."

Jack's approach to a love so partially lost that its object is playing drums behind him is more sanguine than Dylan's. The enticingly warm 'Little Bird', with its formal vocal like Ray Davies in Noel Coward mode, ends with the declaration, 'I think I'll marry you.' The gorgeous 'Sister, Do You Know My Name?' also toys with this sibling act's ambiguity, as scratchy slide guitar accompanies a hopeful, school-bus crush. 'I'm Bound to Pack It Up''s glistening acoustic intro, with Jack's cousin Paul Henry Ossy's violin adding to the feel of a pastoral Zeppelin track, finds Jack as a runaway from a love both lovers know has run its course. 'The bus is warm and softly lit' he sings affectingly as the Greyhound pulls away from his past, like his film class favourite *The Graduate*'s ending turned unhappy. The song ends with a strum of fresh resolve. 'A Boy's Best Friend', all slow-motion slide, tolling piano and lazy cymbal splashes, sees Jack exiled to a room where words meant for a girl who's not there hollowly ring. 'I am all alone, dear,' he assures her. Then his soon to be ex-wife hits the chorus with him in unified power, even as the lyric prefers Mom, pets and cigarettes, who never let you down.

The most explicit tribute he ever wrote to Meg, 'Truth Doesn't Make A Noise', opens Side Two. This girl looks small to him, with bird-like, fragile bones, but unbreakable, quiet self-possession. She's the wife and sister-drummer whose whispering unworldliness and stubborn silences frustrated him, and made him devotedly proud. 'Her stare is louder than your voice,' he tells anyone who'd slight her, ready to rip up the joint in rage at her detractors. This protective, big brother's love would endure till the White Stripes' end.

There are other sides to *De Stijl*. The single that preceded it in May 2000, 'Hello Operator', starts at a pitch of high indignation and heavy irony, as Jack grapples with the Detroit phone system. Even his guitar tone is raspingly sarcastic. While the world outside dreads the internet's millennial collapse, Jack heedlessly taunts the telephone exchange and mailman, stopping for Meg's woody clock-tick interludes on drumsticks, marking his wasted time. The Hentchmen's John Szymanski jumps in on blasting blues harmonica, Jack's guitar becoming a choking rhythm engine as the record steadily picks up steam, Meg taking a second to jump aboard as it pulls away. Seemingly inspired by the loss of a quarter in a payphone, Jack ends by declaring he'd rather rely on canary post. It's unsurprising, on this evidence, that he's never owned a mobile. The tape continues to roll on the 7-inch version, for a few seconds' slice of life in the living room. Meg giggles "I got butter fingers!" followed by a crash of dropped instruments, in a more forgiving environment for her than a real studio.

Her teamwork with Jack belies such clumsiness. In a click-track, machine-beat world, *De Stijl*'s rhythms are able to slide, speed and spin like the mad merry-go-round in Hitchcock's *Strangers On A Train*. No longer cued by him beat by beat, Meg's human responses support and redouble Jack's impact, their interaction now a partnership of two whole personalities. The derision her drumming always attracted, despite its potency and distinction in this context, was already out of date. "At first she wasn't a very good drummer, she didn't keep time that well," Dave Feeny remembers. "But she really stepped up to the plate. She's got a drum sound that's simple. But she's got more style than any of these fancy drummers with gigantic drum kits. She swung. And most drummers don't, these days." Danny Kroha agrees. "I think she really got the raw end of the deal with the White Stripes, man. People said a lot of bad stuff about her, and she was made fun of a lot in the media. You always hear people saying, 'Well, the White Stripes would have been really great if they'd had a decent drummer,' and all this shit. But I always thought she was really good. And I jammed with her one time, and she was driving that bus, man. She's powerful." Troy Gregory adds his support. "I always liked her drumming, and what was she supposed to do in the White Stripes? You can imagine . . ." he says, voicing 'Seven Nation Army''s simple riff then a virtuoso, Sten gun blur of beats. As Steve Nawara found when he added bass, there's no room. "I think even Phil Collins would just come in on snare, and know that would be enough."

Bruce Brand, the British drummer who helped them through their first UK visit, gives the most thoughtful analysis of Meg's style. "Jack told her what to play, and how to do it," he states. "You could tell by how she played that she wasn't tutored in the art of drumming. But she had such a unique style, and it fitted what he did so well." He drums his fingers absently, remembering. "Ringo might not have been the best drummer in the Beatles, but he was the best drummer for the Beatles. And Meg was the best drummer for the White Stripes. Because whenever she hit a cymbal, it was at the same time as she hit something else. None of that hitting a cymbal in between beats business – it was kssshhh, prrshs. No one else does that. And if the timing between them can be imperfect, it gives it tension, it's live, and it's proper."

After initially fearing humiliation, Meg also became certain of her strength. "Ringo knew what was needed," she told Jim Jarmusch in *Interview*, with rare assertion, "down to every little tiny thing needed for that song. It's about what the band needs. When I hear music, I just hear the whole thing. It's the emotion of it that hits me, more than anything technical." Jack envied her ability to switch analysis off, seeing her as the id to his ego, his complementary opposite. "The male and the female onstage and nothing else," he suggested, as if they were archetypes. "I can feel it."

Jack, like Meg, had developed quickly on *De Stijl*. 'Little Bird''s rough waves of woozy slide guitar end by veering between Led Zeppelin and ragtime; the whooping tear-up and post-relationship archness of 'Let's Build A Home' (they'd just had one) tops climbing slide guitar solos with Warner Bros. cartoon "That's all folks!" sproings; and 'Jumble, Jumble' is, by further contrast, the sort of absurd, hammer-swinging punk with which the pair started. Like 'Why Can't You Be Nicer To Me?', it actually dates back to their public debut. Paul Henry Ossy's electric violin on the latter song takes Jack's high parts from that otherwise similar 1997 performance, fleshing out a fuller Seventies arrangement. Then there's 'Hello Operator''s B-side, 'Jolene', which reveals Jack and Meg's shared love of country. With its fatalistically gloomy guitar, Meg on sand-shaker percussion and Dolly Parton's masochistic melodrama making Jack androgynously beg, this studio take would be eclipsed by live versions.

De Stijl's two blues covers were less interesting, although for Jack then, the White Stripes' real point. Son House's 'Death Letter Blues' is played straight on sometimes over-driven slide, only its swaying, lumbering rhythm and breathing, rushing and slowing tempo marking it as this band's. At 24, Jack deepens his voice for blues learned from vastly more experienced Americans, and focuses on the haunting story of a love realised once its object's in her coffin, reducing him to 'hugging the pillows/ where my baby used to lay.' He'd only find the song's grim majesty in concert, as when the White Stripes played Sydney in 2003, when like a hysterical carnival barker he cried, 'Hurry, hurry, the girl you love is dead!', then told Meg, 'It's so hard to love someone who don't love you back' as she nodded, politely sympathetic, head resting in hands. There, this became huge and heavy, bucking and whipping, Meg hammering beside Jack as he vaulted from country hoedown into speed-metal blues, then cut to an a cappella 'Grinnin' In Your Face', becoming a finger-pointing, knee-dropping preacher, forcing home the blues' naked point to a massive crowd.

In 2000, barely a local success, he was a more timid interpreter, daring only in the songs he chose, especially *De Stijl*'s closing, acoustic 'Your Southern Can Is Mine', its woman-beating braggadocio softened by Meg's harmonies. 'When I hit ya, mama, then you'll feel my hand,' Jack faithfully sings. But as with McTell's 'Lord Send Me An Angel', an October 2000 single personalised so 'all the women were crying, Mr Jack, won't you be my man?', straight retelling of these strange, lost tales, casually capable of extremes Jack isn't yet, is the point. "To me, it's a joke," Jack told *Mojo*'s Andrew Male of the single, "'cos everybody who knows me knows that women don't like me that much! But I was toying with the idea that girls are attracted to cockiness, and bad, bad qualities in men. So I feel comfortable with that song, because it's true." The impish surrealism and sexuality available on McTell's versions – as in the variant 'Talkin' To Myself', where 'I even heard a rumblin', deep down in the ground/ It weren't a thing but the women tryin' to run me down', 'mess-around girl made me break my yo-yo string', and the listener is advised 'don't drink no black girl's milk' – is set aside. The loverman persona is as much as young Jack can handle.

De Stijl was dedicated to McTell and Gerrit Rietveld. Rietveld is the reason Jack and Meg, in white with red shoes, seem to stand between the red, white and black planes of a Mondrian painting on the sleeve, and explains the album's title. *De Stijl* was a magazine founded in the neutral Netherlands in 1917 with print runs in the low hundreds, like an underground 45. Its stencilled cover motif is printed twice inside the *De Stijl* LP, along with designs, sculptures and sketches by its editor Theo Van Doesburg and contributors such as Rietveld. Its name was Dutch for 'the Style' but could also mean part of a cabinet-maker's crossing-joint, reflecting its philosophy's combination of utopian yearning in the face of Europe's self-destruction, and practical construction. Piet Mondrian was this movement's early hero and enduring talent, intending "a means for the evolution of mankind" in paintings reduced to the three primary colours (red, blue, yellow) and non-colours (black, white, grey), and erasing evidence of the artist's hand with grids of straight lines and right angles – female, natural, horizontal lines harmoniously meeting spiritual, male, vertical ones. As artificial national lines caused senseless slaughter by the million, universal, spiritually transformative principles were sought. "International unity in art, life and culture," *De Stijl* demanded in 1918.

The appeal to a male-female, tricoloured Detroit rock band is clear, and Jack's feeling that he and Meg are complementary gender absolutes onstage, yin and yang, is very like Mondrian. But it was Rietveld, with his *Red/Blue Chair*, who led Jack to De Stijl. Like Jack, he was both practical and a dreamer, a cabinet-maker by trade who built his own wooden prototypes from cheap materials, but is most famous for a chair you can't sit on. Designed in 1918 after meeting Mondrian and gaining its final colours in 1923, Rietveld meant it as the skeletal essence of an armchair, its thin, straight red back and blue seat joined by overlapping pieces, each function explicit, but the whole so balanced that the chair "stands freely and clearly in space", seemingly weightless, made from nothing but its colours and function. Rietveld designed the Schröder House on the same principles in 1924, furnished with his uncomfortable chairs. It is in some ways the White Stripes' dream home, the colour scheme minimal and unbroken, helping to unify interior, exterior and furniture in explicit, sometimes unlikely functional harmony: home as a "total work of art". Visitors to red-and-white 1203 Ferdinand, and Third Man Records' bizarrely coherent building in Nashville – total Jack – would find the concept familiar.

Jack discovered Rietveld's chair while a teenage upholsterer's apprentice, fascinated by the furniture he ripped and remade. He soon explored the whole De Stijl movement, as well as Dada's contemporary, anarchic reaction to the First World War's rational carnage. De Stijl was influenced by the American architect-designer Frank Lloyd Wright, and was part of a Modernist movement preaching "form follows function" and "truth to materials", extending into Hemingway's blunt sentences and the Hollywood-influenced art deco skyscrapers around Jack in downtown Detroit, whose functional skeletons as they were built fascinated European Modernists. A visit to the city's Ford Factory inspired Chaplin's *Modern Times*, and Jack's film favourites *Citizen Kane* and *Metropolis* were also part of this post-war whirlwind. Jack added blues' functional, unadorned genius in the same American years to the equation. If he looked up at the world around him as the 21st century began, he'd see post-modernism's irony, pastiche and inauthenticity ushering in the digital age, where originality, in rock'n'roll and elsewhere, was over. Eminem, hip-hop and sampling ruled. Jack despised it all. The White Stripes were a Modernist band, still working through ideas that were a reaction to the Somme, and black Modernist sounds sparked from slavery. Form followed function, and with the tools of guitar, drums and voice, storytelling, melody and rhythm, they'd build their own world.

But Jack named their second album *De Stijl* because of that movement's awareness it had to evolve, and his own uncertainty that the White Stripes' austere structure could last. The album added piano, violins, two other musicians and, on 'I'm Bound To Pack It Up', even Jack on verboten (stand-up) bass. He summarised De Stijl's need to mutate on the art-saturated insert: "It descends back to the beginning where the construction of things visual or aural is too uncomplicated not to be beautiful. But this is done in the knowledge that we can only become simple to a point and then there is nowhere else to go." German Dadaist Hans Richter clarified the ideal that defined art between the wars: "to start from the beginning again by returning to the most elementary and basic concepts and to build something new upon the fundamentals." This was why Jack told *Bangsheet*'s Kurt Hernon that De Stijl was his favourite art movement, and "almost the equivalent to what we try to do with our music". What fascinated him now was that it "got so simplistic that they decided to abandon the movement in order to build it back up again from nothing . . . We had wondered . . . how simple we could get with people still liking what we do. And on this record we added some piano and violin." He'd quickly regret such easy excess. Three future songs aside, the White Stripes stayed alone from now on.

Tape fragments linked some album tracks, adding to its unity. A burst of French-Canadian radio (whose presenter later, inevitably sued) introduces 'Jumble, Jumble', while a stunned-sounding McTell muttering of the previous night's car crash is the suggestive finish to 'Your Southern Can Is Mine'. 'Let's Build A Home' is preceded by six-year-old Jackie Gillis in an early, proud performance, warmly encouraged by his parents to sing his party piece, a misheard homily about the devil adapted to his own, long-lasting desires: 'I wish I had a little red box to put my best friends in. I'd take them out, and put them back again.'

Jack mixed *De Stijl* with Jim Diamond, back at Ghetto Recorders. It sounds like it could have been recorded there. "He did all the basic tracks at home, and finished it up at my place," Diamond says, "adding equalisation, reverb, delay effects. That's why I mix a lot of things. Because I give it my own raw presence, so it becomes tough. Some things need a little help. That was the case in that record. Because it was recorded at home, so I had to pull out a lot of tricks to make it have that power."

De Stijl was released on June 20, 2000. On May 28, the White Stripes had made their TV debut on the local public access show *Backstage Pass*, playing 'Apple Blossom' and 'Death Letter Blues'. Jack and Meg spent June 12 on the rollercoaster at the Mall of America, celebrating Ben Blackwell's birthday. Soon afterwards, Jack's nephew quit his journalism degree. Alongside becoming the Dirtbombs' co-drummer, he focused on helping the White Stripes on tour and documenting their nascent career, digging lyric sheets from bins for posterity. "Jack started handing me stuff, realising certain things are important, but he couldn't be bothered to keep them," he told *Audioboom*. Jack spent the rest of the summer preparing for a future not yet quite in focus.

He already had a booking agent, the first of the corner men he'd find early and keep to take on the world. Impressed by the touring ability of his two-piece friends Bantam Rooster, he called their agent Fred Kaplan, boss of San Francisco's Easy Action Industries. "I knew about the White Stripes," Kaplan recalled to *Pollstar*'s Joe Reinartz. "I had friends who worked at Revolver, a record distributorship, and they told me about them. But at this point, if you weren't a record store clerk or a fanzine guy, you probably hadn't heard of them."

On April 13, the Gold Dollar had screened a documentary, *Detroit Rock Movie – Reinventing Sound*. "Remember Detroit music in 1999?" Neil Yee wistfully asked in the programme. "Everything seemed as though it was about to blow up . . . Witness one man's attempt to capture what it was like to be adrift in the whirlwind that was last year . . . the Wildbunch, FEZ, the White Stripes, the Foxgloves, Volebeats, Universal Indians, Rocket 455, and the Immigrant Suns. Maybe you too?" In the giddy, enclosed world of the Gold Dollar, Detroit's moment was deemed to have passed. The spark had, as usual, failed to catch. But the White Stripes were slipping out of the city. On June 13, a tour started on the usual Midwest circuit of the mildly ambitious Detroiter, at a club they'd already played in March, O'Cayz Corral in Madison, Wisconsin. This time they kept going. In Seattle they played Fallout Records then Sit & Spin, a laundromat-coffeehouse-bar where local bohemians washed clothes, ate pizza and listened to poetry and punk bands. Thirty people turned up at the latter, so like the odd clubs back home. Two days after *De Stijl*'s release they played

Spaceland, an ex-gay disco in LA's Silver Lake district, which had nurtured one of Jack's heroes, Beck. Then on the 23rd they reached Long Beach, California, home to their mysterious label boss, Long Gone John. He likely saw his signings for the first time that night at the Foothill club, a Forties honky-tonk with vintage fixtures and barmen, where Johnny Cash and George Jones had played, and rockabilly and roots music now ruled, promoter Steve Zepeda relishing its "David Lynch vibe". "I thought, Jesus Christ, what have I got here," Long Gone John exclaimed. Kaplan had earned his pay with these bookings, giving Jack a fitting taste of Americana.

Returning via Midwest gigs in hip dive-bars in Lawrence, Kansas, Chicago and Champaign, Illinois, homecoming shows were at the Magic Bag in June and the Magic Stick, on July 11 and August 18. These venues were a better fit now than the much smaller Gold Dollar. But even in Detroit nothing was yet guaranteed, as they'd found on March 3. "They played upstairs at the Magic Stick after Yo La Tengo had played at the sold-out [next-door, 1,000-capacity] Majestic Theatre," Doug Coombe remembers. "You could just walk up to the Magic Stick and see the White Stripes for free, and there was barely anybody there. It's hilarious to think about it now."

"I don't think the White Stripes was a long-term concern for Jack at the time," Kaplan told *Pollstar*. "He definitely had no visions of getting a [major] record deal and being famous. People from Detroit just didn't think that way. But they toured with Sleater-Kinney in fall 2000, and that was the first time they went to the northeast. Those dates were really an eye-opener to Jack and Meg." Jack told *Pollstar* that tour was "the turning point."

Sleater-Kinney were an Olympia, Washington trio of post-riot grrrl punk feminists with enormous credibility in the American rock press. In the US punk tradition of good-value bills helping deserving talent, they picked up the White Stripes on September 13 for a 13-date tour through Wisconsin, Chicago, Ohio, Toronto and Montreal, ending among the East Coast's influential media. "We didn't know if it was the same audience as us but at the last second we thought, that's probably the best part," Jack told *Pollstar*. "When they opened for us," Sleater-Kinney's Corin Tucker recalled to *Spokesman-Review*, "we knew that they were definitely on their way to becoming big. And when you have somebody opening for you that's that good, you notice." Fame was still distant, as both bands discovered after playing a college cafeteria and being invited to an after-show party. "Janet [Weiss, Sleater-Kinney's drummer] and I hopped in Jack and Meg's van," singer-guitarist Carrie Brownstein remembered. "This guy walks down the stairs and says to Jack, 'Who are you?' And Jack says, 'Oh, we just played a show on campus.' The guy goes, 'We don't know you guys, you don't go to our school. You need to get out of our party!' Such a humbling experience . . ." But they played two nights at New York's Bowery on September 25 and 26, the White Stripes' calling card to critics there. Jack also arranged to meet Marcie Bolen in the romantic, last-century opulence of Grand Central Station. The tour ended in Washington, D.C. the next night. "Did you see Sleater-Kinney at the 9:30 Club Wednesday?" a fan asked *Washington Post*'s music writer Eric Brace that week on his blog. "Brother-sister act White Stripes opened with power – keep an eye out for them." Brace promised he would.

The tour had been a revelation. "A lot of people showed up just for them," Kaplan told *Pollstar*. "And Jack and Meg were, like, 'Wait. We can actually do this and make money?' They didn't exactly have a lot at the time."

"It was interesting to see how quickly they were able to take off," Troy Gregory reflects. "Sympathy was a good label to be on, it was getting positive reinforcement from magazines. And, we talk about being secluded here in Detroit. A lot of bands were very content to be here, but others didn't have a lot of money to go and play. To make any money at all you're going to have to be out for a bit, but then you'll lose your job. So it's difficult to play outside of Michigan. Even if you packed out the Gold Dollar, you'd make 100, 200 bucks, split with the band, or put to when you play in Canada. But with a two-piece, it's easy as pie to travel. I'm not saying another band who could afford to travel would have had the same success. But if you've got the goods, people don't have to find you. You can go out to them. And getting that Sleater-Kinney tour was a good deal, and people I know that saw that tour said it was like when Van Halen opened up for Black Sabbath, or Metallica for Ozzy Osbourne. Sleater-Kinney were slouching a little bit, and the White Stripes were new and into it still."

Their careful image reached a wider public, too. "A lot of bands round here go, 'Ah, fuck, take a picture of the cat!'" Gregory says. "Every time you saw a White Stripes picture they weren't just against a wall going, 'Oh, don't take a picture of me.' I'm sure Jack saw, 'We look like cartoon characters.' I'm sure he was smart enough to know it made them more iconic-looking, and they became that. He was smart enough to know the magazine would say, 'Shit, who cares what they sound like, this picture makes the magazine look better.'"

White Stripes photos were certainly an easy sell for Doug Coombe. "Jack's style definitely helped. And the other thing is, Meg is gorgeous," he laughs. "People who weren't part of the scene who ended up looking at your photos would go, 'Oh my goodness, who's that drummer?' It was the same with Marcie in the Von Bondies."

White Stripes sleeves were also attracting people in disparate places. Troy Ferguson, a music programmer for 95bFM radio in Auckland, New Zealand, spotted *The White Stripes* in an American record store rack at the end of 1999. "Their visual aesthetic appealed to me straight away," he told Radio New Zealand. "This was a time when no one cared about record covers very much. It really looked like it may be interesting, I didn't know if it was old or new." He didn't buy it, but back home his local record shop, Crawlspace, found him an imported picture disc of 'Hello Operator'. "If I thought there was an interesting art aesthetic to the LP, how the 7-inch looked blew my mind. I was almost too scared to listen to it, because I didn't want to be disappointed." He risked it. "I thought, 'There's a particular aesthetic that goes beyond the visuals and the way they present themselves. If people get the chance to hear this group, they're going to love them. They're going to be thrilled.'"

On January 8, 2000, while leafing through Groningen, the Netherlands' Platenworm record shop, Britain's most nobly adventurous DJ, John Peel, also found *The White Stripes*. "If the sleeve art is good that draws you to it," he explained to Serbia's Radio B92. "The White Stripes LP would be a case in point – you think 'I can see where that's coming from', you develop an instinct, d'you know what I mean? And it looked like the sort of record I would like, so I took it out and I did like it, and started playing it." On January 12, 'Little People' on Peel's Radio 1 show was Britain's introduction to the band. On March 21 he also started played 'Handsprings'. This was on a 7-inch the White Stripes shared with the Dirtbombs given free with the Spring 2000 *Multiball*, a pinball and rock'n'roll fanzine combining Jack's favourite pastimes. The song, a piledriving, teenage pulp vignette in which Jack loses his temper with a love rival at a bowling alley to the sound of red-alert sirens, loses his girl and ponders how age will steal his pinball prowess, is a hoot unique in his writing, surely scribbled at the Garden Bowl bar.

In London, meanwhile, an *NME* freelancer, Stevie Chick, opened his post. "Simon Keeler, who worked at Cargo, the distributor for Sympathy for the Record Industry then, sent me a package with a bunch of CDs, including *De Stijl*," he recalls. "I was aware of the White Stripes because they'd supported Guided by Voices around 2000, and an internet community I was part of were saying how great they were, and I'd flagged that name up. When I put *De Stijl* on, the songwriting was instantly astonishing. I've always loved slide guitar, and it was played with such visceral joy and violence, a virtuosity that's about getting your emotions out through your instrument. Shortly afterwards, stuck at an electronic music festival in a northern seaside town in the off-season, I played *De Stijl* over and over, and it felt timeless. I got an album review commissioned by *NME*, but it sat on the spike, there was no urgency to publish it. I felt I was screaming into the void."

Down in Melbourne, John Baker, a New Zealander who helped promote "low-rent rock'n'roll bands from around the planet" at home, sat alone in a warehouse party after a gig by Californian rockers the Donnas, listening. "It was your typical boozy Melbourne rock'n'roll party, dark, and there was some music not exactly blaring but you could hear it," he remembered to Radio New Zealand. "It was some old ghetto-blaster, and I thought 'This guy's voice sounds out of this world.'" The party faded away as he flipped the cassette to hear more. Taped unnamed over another band's music, *The White Stripes* was a mystery. "Then a guy came up and said, 'Oh, it's a brother and sister from Detroit, you can buy the album through Sympathy.' And that stayed next to my mind, and I returned to New Zealand."

These isolated pressure-points forced the White Stripes to the surface in America, when *Rolling Stone*'s November 23 issue reviewed *De Stijl*. Critic Jenny Eliscu noted "the Stripes' quirks are more delightfully apparent live," a payoff for the year's touring. "If the Who played 'maximum R&B', then you could call the White Stripes' music 'minimum R&B'," she wrote of a "Detroit couple" whose "feisty and clever" music she compared with *Nuggets*, the Sonics and the Kinks. The review helped legitimise the White Stripes in the States. But when it was published, they were half a world away.

"It was really nice when I used to go drink in Royal Oak," Troy Gregory reminisces, "and Meg would give me a heads-up on stuff. Eventually she was like, 'I get to quit my job.' Then one time she said, 'Oh, we're going to Auckland.'"

John Baker was back home in Auckland, as usual trying to book a weird rock'n'roll tour. Finding that the freaky, enigmatic New Orleans one-man band Quintron was an Easy Action act, he contacted Dave Kaplan, who sent him an alphabetised list of his roster. Its last name had stayed with Baker since that Melbourne party. Calling Kaplan, he was told the White Stripes had no agent for foreign tours. He would have to call Jack direct.

"Meg and I had just finished rehearsing," Jack was quoted in Nick Bollinger's definitive Radio New Zealand documentary *The White Stripes In New Zealand*. "We were both at the house when he called and explained that he would like to bring us over to New Zealand." He gave a small, incredulous laugh at the memory. "I had to go check the map again to remind myself where that was. I got off the phone, said, 'There's some guy just called wants to bring us to New Zealand,' and we laughed and thought it wasn't true, and we started wondering how he had gotten our phone number." They forgot the crank call till a soundcheck at a Denver bar two weeks later, when the bar phone was handed to Jack. "It's one of those things from a movie, like, 'Who knows I'm even here?' It was John Baker, he had tracked us down."

"I later found out he held the phone, pointed at it, and was looking at the other people in the room, like, 'Who is this guy?'" Baker told Bollinger. Subsequent email contact was clearly humouring this lunatic. "I got the feeling they weren't taking me seriously," Baker realised. "So I told them I was going to buy plane tickets." With chutzpah Jack came to value, Baker wasn't about to let not having 5,000 New Zealand dollars to fly over an unknown foreign band deter him. Instead he played his friend, Amber Easby, 'You're Pretty Good Looking (For a Girl)', then explained his "business opportunity". "I said, 'Great, you should totally do it,'" she told Radio New Zealand. "'Well then, can you lend me $5,000?' 'No.' He said, 'Well how much do you have?'" Easby was persuaded to empty the $3,000 on her credit card, with the condition that she worked on the tour. Again the White Stripes' minimal, portable line-up helped them. "To pay for two people to go to New Zealand instead of five people is a difference of four or five [US] grand," Gregory explains. And so Jack and Meg left America for the first time.

Eleven New Zealand and Australian dates were booked. They added to the 8,500 miles from Detroit with a Tokyo stopover. The culture shock began there. "We played some tiny little place that held like 20 people in Japan," Jack told Bollinger, "and stayed with a Japanese family, which was our first cultural experience outside the US. We were bathing on the floor of a bathroom with a shower, doing everything wrong at dinnertime, and nobody spoke English very well." At two gigs at Club Shinjuku Jam, they were disconcerted when no one clapped till the end. Then they flew to New Zealand, arriving on Monday, October 30, 2000. Stepping off the plane into a second alien world, the perfect Pacific spring weather bewitched Jack. "It felt like we were on Easter Island."

He made a striking first impression on his hosts. "Out walks this guy, and he's walking quite fast, in a beat-up leather jacket, black cords, and these crazy brothel-creepers," Baker remembered. The duo's other long-term Kiwi fan, Troy Ferguson, also fixated on Jack's Mod shoes, made by Northampton's George Cox, the English shoemaker who created the brothel-creeper in 1949. "They still make very small quantities now cut from the same pattern and suede. When I saw he was wearing George Cox brothel-creepers, I thought, 'This guy knows far more than he's letting on.'"

The Midwesterners looked exotic to the New Zealanders, as they sat smoking and talking. "Oh my God, they're pale," Baker thought. "I've never seen people that white before." Easby's offer of New Zealand's version of a burger, with egg and beetroot, confirmed to the horrified Stripes they were far from home. The next morning, the business of a foreign tour began with their first two TV interviews. Detroit's *Backstage Pass* public-access show was their only experience of the medium. "The brother and sister duo from Detroit have been together four years now," TV3's presenter explained. "Meg wants us to be like Emmylou Harris and Loretta Lynn, and I want us to be like Son House and the Gun Club," Jack said. And just what was their sound? "Blues, duo, blues, simple trash-punk, sludgeabilly . . ." he answered, amusedly reciting early reviews. They sat around the TV with their new Auckland friends that night, excited to see how they'd done. Or at least Jack did. "Meg was so embarrassed at seeing herself on the television," Ferguson told Bollinger, "that she lay on the floor and stared at the ceiling the whole time the interview was playing."

The next morning, November 1, they woke early to appear on Mikey Havoc's 95bFM breakfast show. Jack spent time advising Meg what to wear as they diligently dressed their best for the radio, like formal Fifties BBC announcers, daubed in red and white. It was professionalism you could call naive, or absolute. "Is this a good time for you?" Havoc wondered on-air. "1920s would have been better," Jack answered, sounding jet-lagged and groggy. Better shoes probably, back then . . ." What, apart from footwear, was important to the band? "Oh, a good sense of timing, and not much else," Jack drawled. "We try and colour-coordinate our fingernail polish every day." It wasn't quite the Beatles' first US press conference (perhaps in the mind of a man heavily versed in rock history), but Jack was memorably witty, and revealed nothing.

The White Stripes started their New Zealand tour that night at Hamilton's Mainstreet Rhythm and Blues Bar, where a pole disconcertingly blocked Jack's spot on the stage. Baker booked the Datsuns, a new New Zealand band who'd make their own international impact in the White Stripes' wake, as support. In a small blues bar with a crowd of at most 80, the headliners impressed the Datsuns' Dolf de Borst. "They were pretty primitive and very guttural-sounding, but at the same time it was like folk music . . . tender and naive and innocent," he remembered to Radio New Zealand. "But what turned the whole thing for me was 'Jolene'." As well as Dolly Parton's original, an EP including her song had been a big 1997 hit for Darcy Clay, an Auckland singer-songwriter who killed himself aged 25 the next year. "You couldn't escape that song in New Zealand," De Borst said. The version Jack delivered, like all the tour recordings, is rawboned, impassioned blues, feeding off the crowd's intimacy, a soft, bassy pulse and cymbals pacing piercing words. "Wow, what just happened?" De Bolt wondered afterwards. "One guy in the crowd was saying, 'These guys could be massive. This could be like Beck.'"

A November 3 show at a small club used to garage-rock acts, Wellington's Bodega, was sold out, the owner fielding disappointed calls. "Word had gotten out about the White Stripes," Baker said. De Bolt saw them on November 5, the last of two nights at Auckland's city centre music pub the King's Arms, before they left for Australia. "It was pretty packed," he said. "Word had spread: 'you have to come and see this.'" Jack also began a consuming hobby. "He became interested in taxidermy I think for the first time," Ferguson told Bollinger. "He bought a rabbit. And then we went to a very strange antiques fair at Auckland Showgrounds, and Jack bought a taxidermied finch, which he named Higgins after the character in *Magnum, P.I.*" (Johnny Walker's gift of a mountain goat's head may actually have started this obsession). After five dates around Baker's familiar Melbourne haunts, he recrossed the Tasman Sea with the band for an extra, last-minute Auckland date, organised by Easby at the 60-capacity Pizza Pizza. "I've seen them play hundreds of times, and it's my favourite show," Easby told Bollinger. "Jack opened with an acoustic set. We fit 180 people into that room, and we had noise complaints. It was really hot, and we had to have the windows closed, everyone was sweltering. They were standing on tables and chairs, anything. Nobody could move."

On the way to the airport, Jack asked his first ever tour manager if he'd like to go with them when the White Stripes played the US West Coast and Midwest again in December. "I'll make it up as I go along," Baker replied. That attitude confirmed his place with Kaplan in Jack's loyal inner council. "After about a month on the road I thought, 'Hang on, all the shows are sold out,'" Baker discovered in America. "We were late for a San Diego show, so I called, and the guy at the venue said [sounding too harassed to talk], 'The White Stripes show is sold out', and hung up."

US tours earlier in 2000 and national media attention were bearing fruit. But their weeks in Australasia, ignored except by those who were there, were at least as important. Baker's quixotic invitation had allowed a dress rehearsal for an expedition into the full glare of the British spotlight the following summer. When they arrived there as American unknowns, they were veterans of a victorious foreign campaign.

The White Stripes finished 2000 with December returns to venues including Seattle's Sit & Spin, Madison, Wisconsin's O'Cayz Corral and Chicago's the Empty Bottle, reinforcing support in these cities, and a New Year's Eve show at the Magic Stick with the Detroit Cobras, Soledad Brothers, Von Bondies and Come Ons, celebrating a scene they now clearly led.

In February 2001 they headed south to Memphis, Tennessee, and recorded *White Blood Cells* in three days. It was Jack's first extended trip to the Southland of his dreams, and first recording away from his friends in Detroit. "I got scared thinking if we recorded it in Detroit it would have to feel like it was coming from my neighbourhood, the one I grew up in," he told *NME*'s Julian Marshall years later, comparing their unrepeatable, deep Detroit debut to everything that came after. Further changes were deliberately rung. *De Stijl* had recalled Thirties melodic, piano-based pop to Jack when it came out. "I've always wanted to write songs that people could whistle on their way to work," he'd told *Bangsheet*, brightly. But on reflection, its blues covers and heavy slide guitar seemed a dead end already cornered by others. "Songwriting-wise," he considered to *Uncut*'s Barney Hoskyns, "I was coming from the same places that Jimmy [Page] and Robert [Plant] were – Robert Johnson, Tommy Johnson, Blind Willie McTell . . . [and] if you want this to be powerful *and* feed from these same influences, there are going to be moments where you sound like Led Zeppelin. So we moved on." Jack was also wary of typecasting, wanting to stay slippery, ahead of media games before they'd even begun. "We keep getting put with this bringing-back-the-blues label," Jack told the *Metro-Times*. "There's no blues on the new record," he added to *Spin*. *White Blood Cells* was instead a stocktaking of "songs that had been sitting around . . . these piano-written, 'songwriting'-type songs. I wanted to make a whole album of that."

Easley-McCain Recording was recommended to Jack by both Detroit-frequenting Memphis garage band the Oblivians and Rocket from the Crypt's punk-preacher showman John Reis. Once an adjunct to Memphis' legendary American Studios, Wilco's debut *A.M.* was among its recent sessions. "It was on a dead-end street by the airport," *White Blood Cells'* engineer Stuart Sikes remembers, "and it's not the best neighbourhood in town. It was in the Deadrick Building, a big, two-storey place. It was a beautiful, big, old, pretty amazing studio, the first ever built in Memphis from the ground up. It was a one-room facility, with a large cinderblock live room, probably 30 by 45 feet, with maybe 30-foot ceilings. It still had live echo-chambers built into it from the American days. They came because we had a tape machine and a lot of old equipment. We recorded it on 24-track, 2-inch tape. And we actually split the tape in half, and recorded half the songs on 12 tracks, then the others on the other 12. It's not often done. They didn't really have any money, so it was my way to save some." The $1,700 bill was at least as cheap as their debut, Jack's thrift unshaken by looming success.

He and Meg rehearsed the songs, some familiar from Two-Star Tabernacle and early White Stripes sets, for a week before the rapid recording. "We tried to keep it as unorganized as possible," Jack told *Spin*'s Jennifer Maerz. "We tried to rush this as much as possible to make [the sound] really tense." That was no problem for Sikes. "We did a lot of Sympathy bands at the time," he says, "so we did a lot of fast records, and they were good, dirty rock records. I don't think that Meg knew the songs very well, and I think that Jack wanted it that way. She knew the songs enough to have her part, but she wished she had rehearsed more. I think that was pretty smart of Jack, because the energy of her pushed him, and pushed the songs. That was their third record, so they knew how to play with each other. The idea was to catch that.

"It was gloomy. And cold," he says of those Memphis winter days. "Not Detroit cold – but cold. They stayed with Jack Yarber of the Oblivians. It was fun in the studio, but mostly work, noon to midnight." Jack's role as producer was basic. "They wanted it to sound more of a rock record than the other ones, I guess, but I don't remember him suggesting a sound he did or didn't want. I just set 'em up like I thought they should sound, and adjusted it to what they thought when they came in and listened to the first couple of takes. That was how it went. They didn't do a ton of takes. There wasn't time." You can hear Jack as he sings catching his breath at the pace of events, his voice sometimes rough. "He was going for it," says Sikes. "And some of the songs were kinda high. And he might have been a bit sick."

Did Sikes know anything about Jack and Meg's relationship?

"I knew who they were, but their past? No. And I wouldn't have cared."

Did he think they were siblings?

"No!" he snorts. "I just thought they were two people in a band who had the same name, like the Ramones."

White Blood Cells starts with the rising hum of an amp, preparatory drumstick clicks, the crash of something dropped, then a fuzz-guitar riff with Hendrix's undeniable weight. Dialogue from Meg is left in, adding to on the hoof, studio *vérité* energy recalling *Another Side Of Bob Dylan*, which was recorded in a long night in 1964 and towards the end floats woozily on red wine and tiredness. The only stimulants in Memphis were red-and-white Embassy cigarettes, adrenaline and Jack's songs, full of resentment, fear and momentary bliss. Assembled from four years' work, this is no random deck-clearing exercise, instead revealing consistent quality and concerns. The conceit of writing children's songs is scrapped ('We're Going To Be Friends'' nursery idyll apart), the love complained of here adolescent at least.

'Dead Leaves And The Dirty Ground' backs up that Hendrixesque riff with a pretty mid-Sixties melody, Jack's voice shaky as he showers a girl with adoration, thundering eagerly down the hall to her with a falling piano's noise, willing to lose his sight if he can hear her voice, 'every breath that is in your lungs' received as a precious gift. He wants to equal all she's given in an ideal love song that lasts a pop-perfect three minutes. 'Fell In Love With A Girl' needs less than two minutes of pell-mell punk to express conflicted feelings for a 'red head with a curl' (a passing tribute to Marcie Bolen), the words anyway almost swallowed by rattling guitar and drums, and finally reduced to an idiot chant. 'Hotel Yorba', a tribute to a "really disgusting hotel" the song made a tourist site, is a Two-Star Tabernacle leftover of rickety charm, all campfire strums and biscuit-box beats. Its couple's dream home is in the Michigan woods, but the hotel's 'vacancy', as when he sang it in 1998, is inside him, too.

'I'm Finding It Harder To Be A Gentleman' is the more prevalent flipside of Jack's romantic feelings, the defining shot of a battle of the sexes entwining chivalry and chauvinism. Near-discordant, percussive piano drives wordless choruses abrasively home, while a keyboard's warm, rolling funk supports verses in which Jack sets out his disappointment with a woman. His gentlemanly manners wither in the face of her neediness, complaints and unresponsiveness. Maybe a doctor can 'tell us which one is sane', he suggests, sure his simple masculinity will win. The hypocrisy of silly girls is seen in childish terms – they're not even grateful when they need help climbing a tree. Thinking better of dropping a coat in the mud for her like Sir Walter Raleigh, he dumps the girl in the muck instead. It's Dennis the Menace's answer to Andrea Dworkin, an attitude returned to in 2003's 'Girl, You Have No Faith In Medicine'. That song was sparked, Jack told *The Guardian*'s Keith Cameron, by his irritation at women debating headache cures, symptomatic of a sex prone to "take 25 minutes waddling around looking for her purse" before leaving the house. "Makes me want to smack him. A lot," Meg said of the lyric. "Maybe you're hanging around with the wrong women," she further advised. But her ex feared an unnatural, "androgynous" society, longing for clearly defined men and women "closer to one's own nature", back in his mythical Thirties.

This suspicion of modern women and interest in clashing gender extremes runs through *White Blood Cells*. 'Expecting' is a robotically staccato, sneering account of a trip to Toledo as a labour of Hercules, for a woman weighing her man down with endless requirements. 'I Can't Wait' is a blunt, minor, Nirvanaesque kiss-off, 'I Can Learn' a pensive exploration of the teenage temptation of a midnight kiss, played similarly at their 1997 public debut. 'Now Mary' is ambivalent at best to a lover, but manages this swooning couplet: 'What a season/ To be beautiful without a reason.' The closing 'The Protector' then makes up for earlier gaucheness, finding supernatural, psychological strangeness in being a man. Jack is at the piano, his first words distantly inaudible, but revealed in the lyric sheet as a meditation on a young man realising his protective responsibilities. These take horror film, nightmare form, as the danger a scared girl asks him to watch for in a doorway erupts through the floor. Meg harmonises with rough, demo intimacy, as if being taught the song or just practising scales with Jack as the record spins. They enact an interior monologue which '300 people in West Virginia', standing in surreally for the outside world, will never hear.

Two songs from Two-Star Tabernacle's last show stand out. 'The Same Boy You've Always Known' borrows faintly from 'Bridge Over Troubled Water''s grand melody for its gentle, wintry tale of lost love. Its concluding thought from a modest, abandoned boy – 'If there's anything good about me/ I'm the only one who knows' – is extended in 'Offend In Every Way'. This lacerating cousin to the first album's 'Do' confesses Jack's life-long conviction that he's repulsive, dull company, prone to overcompensate with hysterical torrents of chat. The low self-esteem undercutting his ego only becomes clear in such lyrics. The guitar melody threaded between the song's driving piano and drums ends in sinking despair. 'I Think I Smell A Rat', opening with a mariachi flourish, develops this discomfort with his peers (which no one I've spoken to from those days noticed, or returned). Baseball bat meaningfully in hand and talking like Bogart, Jack's voice quivers with rising contempt for kids who disrespect their parents and 'think they know where it's at'. Such resentment would only grow.

'The Union Forever' stands apart from other White Stripes music, keeping its atmospheric organ swirl and haunted croon from Two-Star Tabernacle. But the emphasis of its *Citizen Kane*-cribbed lyrics has changed. In 1999, his split with Meg still a livid wound, the falsity of 'true love' made Jack roar. Now, lyrics taken from a tawdry tribute to Kane's celebrity are sung with broken numbness: 'With wealth and fame, he's still the same . . .' This is the prospect growing dauntingly large for Jack. 'Little Room', much commented on after the White Stripes' stardom, distils success' price into a 49-second parable (and much of that is wordless yatter). With only Meg's most naive crashing behind him, Jack adopts a desperate blues whine to consider the 'bigger room' good work in his little room might move him to, though the small room is where his inspiration may stay.

The future was intruding on his present in Memphis. "When they were recording, they had made a list of up-and-coming bands to watch for [*Rolling Stone*'s 10 new bands for 2001]," Sikes remembers. "They were both surprised and excited by that." During the session, they listened to T Bone Burnett's hit soundtrack compilation of roots music for *O Brother, Where Art Thou?*. If only that was being released a year from now, Jack told Meg, when they'd be famous enough to contribute. *White Blood Cells'* sleeve parodied the dilemma he saw coming. On the cover, he and Meg are harried and gloomy, backed against a wall by silhouetted strangers. Inside, they grin, Jack's thumb up and Meg's head tossed back like a

Hollywood star, as the black-garbed crowd point paparazzi cameras. The "bacteria" in the second shot look all the friendlier for Marcie Bolen's revealed, pretty face next to Jack. The others included his old Two-Star Tabernacle bandmates, Brendan Benson, Jason Stollsteimer and Jim Diamond, some of whom Jack would truly think of as parasites in time. *White Blood Cells* was named for "this idea of bacteria coming at us . . . or media, or attention on the band," Jack told the *Metro-Times'* Melissa Giannini, pondering approaching success. "Is the attention," he wondered, "good or bad?" His LP liner note looked forward to nostalgically realising that these had been "the good days".

While waiting for *White Blood Cells'* release, the White Stripes played 28 US gigs between February and May. They returned as headliners to the Bowery Ballroom, where they'd supported Sleater-Kinney, and played fabled venues including San Francisco's Fillmore and Hollywood's Troubadour. Jack's relationship with Marcie Bolen was often long-distance, conducted by phone as he and, less often, the Von Bondies travelled. "If anyone's going on tour with their ex-wife, of course it's going to be a little weird," she told Steve Miller in *Detroit Rock City*. "I liked Meg, and I wanted to know that I could trust him with Meg." Once, Bolen shared their tour van for a few days, sometimes driving, both women settling into their odd situation.

The Von Bondies were on Sympathy for the Record Industry themselves now, and in March, Jack returned to Jim Diamond's studio to produce *Lack Of Communication*, his lover's band's debut album. It took two days. It's another Ghetto special, the space's atmospheric sound compensating for lack of time and cash. Jason Stollsteimer's early influences included Otis Redding and the Cramps, and there's a Fifties twang to the guitars, as he sings with an introspectively throttled, rockabilly-soul holler. His monologue of young lust on 'Cass & Henry', his voice seeming to bounce off the Cass Corridor's empty avenues, is dirty Detroit *noir*.

Stollsteimer, like Jack, was from a Polish Michigan family, and Jack helped him develop his guitar playing. *Lack Of Communication's* bitter, carnal songs were inspired by "a breakup that lasted three years" with the woman he later married, and he spoke to *NME* of suffering a "total breakdown" aged 19, as Jack had, which made him hide inside for months. There was a basis for friendship between two quietly alienated young men. After the way things actually ended up, when I contact Stollsteimer he won't talk for what he calls "a John Gillis book", but cautions me against repeating previous, "bland" reports on the Detroit scene. "As a person who was born in the outskirts of the metro Detroit area, I have a different view on what happened," he says, recalling being an "outsider". "They were a little bit younger," the Hentchmen's Tim Purrier reflects on the band he first knew as the Baby Killers. "And they came from Ypsilanti, near Ann Arbor – a different scene."

White Blood Cells' US release date was set for June 25, 2001. With this third album, the White Stripes' recorded output was half done, and almost no one knew Jack White's name. But that summer the clock ticked over, and the big time began.

8

Conquest

WHEN the reporters from *Time*, *Entertainment Weekly* and the rest entered Mexicantown, they found Jack's home subtly adapted to his new situation. An upstairs room was now an office, with stacks of cardboard boxes, press photos, a file-filled computer and fax machine. There were two phone lines to field calls from circling agents, lawyers and major labels including DreamWorks, Elektra and Eminem's home, Interscope. *Entertainment Weekly*'s May 11, 2001, story, which unveiled Detroit's precious, private scene to the mainstream media, mentioned Jack getting 10 enquiries a day. When the *Metro-Times* visited later that month, Meg complained of both phones ringing constantly, despite the New York PR they now employed – a practical step viewed with surprise and eventual suspicion by some in their small community. As *Entertainment Weekly* noted, in Detroit "major-label interest, if and when it comes, will be tolerated, not welcomed." The magazine reported fear of the implosion that ended the booming scene theirs now resembled: "Seattle 1988, right before grunge exploded." Making the comparison was a self-fulfilling prophecy.

Local and national reporters had different impressions of the Gillis childhood home where Jack and a mostly tongue-tied Meg were interviewed: what the *Metro-Times* thought "comfy" was "ramshackle" to *Entertainment Weekly* and "slapdash" to *Time*. It had become something to see, filled ever more intensely with Jack's art and obsessions. Red-and-white junk sculptures were scattered through it. The green living room sofa on which Jack spoke to the press faced a flickering old TV, and a kitchen much as the Go knew it in 1998, with red cupboards, white work surfaces and a red-and-white sugar tin, and sleeveless LPs flanking its clock. A parakeet hung in a cage for a while. A photo of Charley Patton's grave and framed gig posters decorated walls and doors. The Magic Stick poster for a White Stripes/Greenhornes gig was certainly created by Jack, with its green-uniformed troop charging, bayonet fixed, behind a flapping red-and-white-striped flag. It was a house comfortably full of personal, home-made possessions.

The Soledad Brothers' Ben Swank was now a firm friend and house-mate, having moved from a similarly tough neighbourhood in Toledo, Ohio. Used to sharing his home with too many as a child, Jack also hated to be alone. Marcie Bolen and Meg were both frequent visitors, and he'd made the house one of Detroit's main crash-pads for fellow musicians. Though the identifying red-and-white-striped porch on *The White Stripes'* sleeve had sensibly returned to chipped white and grey-blue anonymity, by November visiting media were met by another arresting sight. Adding to his Auckland taxidermy purchases, Jack now collected stuffed, often mangy animal heads, left strewn on floors, then mounted on walls like a Scottish laird's trophies. These stripped and stitched beasts were his old upholstery skills turned transcendent. Sitting among "silent", "majestic" antelopes, elks, mountain goats, tigers and zebras, which he gave names like Poncheeda the pig and Aquinas (the Catholic philosopher-saint he would have studied if he'd become a priest), these glass-eyed natural wonders put him in his place. "No matter where I look, there are eyes staring at me," he explained to *NME*'s John Mulvey. They gave useful perspective to an ego which, though hobbled by self-doubt and criticism, he could feel the power of, and struggled to keep leashed. "It creeps me out," Meg confessed of a menagerie she'd dodged living with (although, showing solidarity as ever, she allowed two taxidermied animals in the sprawling home she'd moved into with Ko & the Knockouts' Ko Melina). The zebra sometimes joined them onstage.

Jack's favourite bands had been trooping into his red attic for months to record *Sympathetic Sounds Of Detroit*. "Now, people try and ascribe some sort of import," the Paybacks' Wendy Case told *Candy Coloured Blues* of the compilation, claiming Jack had just wanted friends to record their best songs on his equipment, in "a very innocent attempt to do something creatively interesting." Jack told Stevie Chick in London's *Evening Standard* that he'd made the album because it was "really difficult for bands here to get heard" in a city "totally beneath the media radar". When Sympathy released it on April 17, it was fortuitously ready to give sound and shape to a place where, Chick told his readers, "almost any night of the week . . . you'll come across garage bands thrashing out a blend of jagged R'n'B and raw punk-rock attitude that's swiftly become the city's sound-track." The Hentchmen, Von Bondies, Paybacks, Detroit Cobras and Dirtbombs, the Come Ons' gentler Sixties sound, Bantam Rooster's filthy

garage-punk shriek, the Soledad Brothers' slinkily sexy Chess blues, Ko &
the Knockouts' violent girl-group style, the funny, snotty Buzzards (a
Dirtys-Cobras team-up like a glam MC5) and Jack's latest protégés, the
jerkily abstract Whirlwind Heat, were all included. The White Stripes
cameoed with 'Red Death At 6.14', a series of guitar styles sketched
around the fate of a blue-fingered, devil-circled corpse.

"It was pretty laid-back," the Hentchmen's Tim Purrier says of taping
'Accusatory'. "We just went over to Jack's house and watched TV a little
bit. Went up and plugged into his amps and recorded a song of ours he
liked on his gear. That's what everyone did, pretty much." As with *White
Blood Cells*, Jack's producer credit signalled control more than interfer-
ence. "There wasn't any directing of us musically. Maybe, 'Try it one
more time.'" The Dirtbombs' 'I'm Through With White Girls', sung by
Mick Collins with a sandpaper sneer over harsh buzzes and jail-door clangs
of guitar, was still looser. "Mick told me that day, 'Oh yeah, we have to go
over to Jack's house and record a song,'" Jim Diamond remembers. "I
wrote it before we went over. We mixed all that album at my studio."

Jack's home made an impression on the musicians. "It seemed like, I
would say, an artist's house," Purrier feels, "with the painting and everything. It was a pretty big house for [what had been] just him and Meg."

"It was just a fucked up, little, cramped attic where he had an 8-track
reel-to-reel," Diamond says of the old rehearsal space, which replaced
Jack's packed living room for recording. "I remember the mics for the bass
amp fell off onto the floor. It was just a bunch of shit everywhere. The
whole house. It was this pretty trashed old house with junk everywhere,
that's what I remember."

Bands not on the album, such as the Witches and Outrageous Cherry,
probably suffered as it outlined the scene for major labels and media; the
first of many accidental divisions caused by Jack's benign patronage. The
heady, inspired enthusiasm of the Gold Dollar and Magic Stick wasn't
always tapeable, anyway. *Sympathetic Sounds Of Detroit* offered neither
Seattle's songwriting depth – Eddie Vedder, Billy Corgan and Courtney
Love alongside Cobain – or its smack-soured, sludgy depression. Bantam
Rooster's cheeky, careless, sometimes majestic sleaze, as on 2000's
Fuck All Y'All, typified hedonistic Detroiters high instead on booze and
vinyl.

In March, Dave Kaplan had taken the White Stripes to South By Southwest, an annual melee of gigs, next-big-things and networking in Austin,
Texas, which appalled Jack. The "feeding frenzy," Kaplan recalled to

Pollstar, was revelatory. "Just lawyers and labels, everyone trying to get a piece of them. At that point they had no manager . . . [or] lawyer." Jack's distaste was outweighed by the networking's worth when he was approached by Russell Warby, an agent at the major Agency Group's London office. "I first heard about the White Stripes from Nick Evans, a finely tuned antenna to all that was good coming from the US," Warby says, "who told me how they were touring with Sleater-Kinney. After that I asked people I trusted who saw them in the US to let me know what they thought. Broadly speaking, the reports were excellent. Subsequently, Nigel House at the Rough Trade shop enthusiastically supported *De Stijl*, so by the time I got to Austin, I was already certain that I wanted to work with them. That day, I was introduced through a succession of folks, including Scott Kannberg of Pavement, to Dave, who told me that Jack would be coming by shortly. We were introduced and the immediate impact of Jack was so impressive, he's tall and charismatic. I shook his hand and we spoke a little. I asked him if he had an agent in Europe, he said 'No', and I said, 'You do now!' – the cheek of me! I proposed coming to the UK at that time. I don't know how immediate their plans would have been otherwise. I wanted to get on with it. It felt that if they came then, there would be a very enthusiastic welcome awaiting them." Warby initially arranged a single low-key UK gig at the 100 Club for July.

Footage from a March 16 daytime gig at Austin's Fat Tuesday to chatting, milling festival-goers shows Jack respond by engaging with his guitar's potential more than the crowd. "The feel of electricity outside in the daytime is like artificial sunlight," he later complained to *Dazed & Confused*. "We're meant to be heard in a club where you're locked into a room and forced into experiencing something." But a broken guitar strap didn't distract him from doing his job, to further reward. Stevie Chick, a forlorn supporter of the band at *NME*, was trying to avoid an ill-advised tattoo when he gratefully heard a familiar sound. "I realised the White Stripes were playing across the road, at a party in a barbecue bar car park. When he did 'Hello Operator', he was everything I wanted him to be. He kept switching between a normal mic and a distorted one, it was just so exciting and chaotic. Everything was really professional at the time, and if a strap broke, it was a problem. But people made sure straps didn't break. When it happened with him, you wondered, 'What exciting thing's going to happen now?' They did 'Jolene', and there was nothing ironic about it, in the era when every shitty indie band did an ironic Britney Spears cover. It was a red-hot, searing experience. When we came back from South By

Southwest, we managed to get a review of that gig in *NME*. The live reviews editor was really excited and let us run it, helped by the power of Steve Gullick's photos. He jumped onstage to get them."

Chick's brief report noted two Americans far outside the Cass Corridor who'd already mutated the blues: "like Beck and Jon Spencer before them, the White Stripes have polished rock's barest elements till they sound fresh and new again. They can't lose." The April 21 *NME* then exhumed and ran Chick's *De Stijl* review. "Easing into its fourth decade," he wrote, "rock'n'roll seems to have picked up something of a middle-aged spread . . . 'back to basics', speaks the music . . . the musical equivalent of a tub full of diet pills." John Peel, meanwhile, renewed his support on his BBC Radio 1 and World Service shows, playing the band 19 times in heavy bursts between January and April, alternating *De Stijl* tracks with 'The Big Three Killed My Baby' and a Sup Pop Singles Club 7-inch, 'Party Of Special Things To Do', released the previous December. According to Peel's biography *Margrave Of The Marshes*, Jack himself sent his singles. 'Party Of Special Things to Do''s mix of Lewis Carroll, Hendrix distortion and psychedelic drift and its B-sides, blues jig 'China Pig' and suburban nightmare 'Ashtray Heart', were all songs by Peel's idol Captain Beefheart, confirming Jack and John's long-distance bond.

In May, Jack, Meg and Brendan Benson snuck into Room 286 of the Hotel Yorba to illicitly tape a live version of the song that made it infamous. There were "urine-soaked carpets", Meg said to *NME*, shuddering. Jack played acoustic guitar, with Meg on tambourine, cardboard box and backing vocals (she was used to making do; on an Auckland broadcast, she'd bashed a cardboard roll and box). Jack's voice is husky in places and necessarily, affectingly gentle. Needing to keep it down, he's at his most charming. Benson also recorded them playing Loretta Lynn's 'Rated X' there. *White Blood Cells* was originally meant to be country inspired, and driving back from Memphis after recording it, they'd parked up outside Lynn's mansion in Hurricane Mills, Tennessee. Jack was aghast when Meg flicked a cigarette out of the window on this sacred ground. The LP was dedicated to the woman he told *Mojo* was "the greatest female singer-songwriter of the 20th century", who he knew through an early fascination with the 1980 film of her life, *Coal Miner's Daughter*. 'Rated X' showed Lynn's straight-talking, salty feminism (whether she'd call it that or not), bemoaning the red-hot reputation of attractive women who raise their eyes at men after marriage. After his turns as Marlene Dietrich and Dolly Parton on previous B-sides, Jack leapt at this latest chance. "I love

135

putting myself from the female standpoint," he told the *Metro-Times'* Fred Mills. "Especially in my own songwriting . . . it's a great way to jump out of your own body and look at it from a different point of view." Played with a relaxed country swing new to them, Jack sighs, "Yeah, us women don't have a chance," as Meg enjoys strong backing vocals on music she loves. "Just let 'em talk, Meg," he cheekily concludes. The songs were released as a 7-inch single and CD B-sides in November, by which time the White Stripes were a phenomenon.

The band began their first major round of press in May. Their sibling ruse immediately bent under scrutiny, but somehow didn't break. "Well, we're brother and sister, of course," Jack had been able to begin an interview with *Bangsheet* the year before, even jumping on thin ice onstage in New Zealand by declaring, "And what a wonderful sister she is!" Now, May 11's *Entertainment Weekly* stated "the rumour is she's his ex-wife." In Detroit, where this was an open, eccentric secret, the *Metro-Times'* May 19 interview clearly explained: "They're both in their mid-20s formerly married to each other, and don't want to dwell on their relationship in print." Crowing over the *New Yorker* and *New York Times* both printing the legend, *Time*'s otherwise sympathetic June 16 report made great play of "the savvy sibling act that has duped the press." It was amazing how little difference all this would make, as Jack stuck to his guns.

He played a solo gig at the Garden Bowl bar, on Saturday, June 3. "It was packed, it was riveting," owner Dave Zainea tells me, as we sit facing the alcove where it happened. "One of the best shows I've ever seen. It had really grown for him, and I thought, 'My God, this guy's talented.'" The release of the White Stripes' third album was then celebrated in Detroit with three consecutive gigs, at Dave Kaplan's suggestion. "It seems like a pretty ballsy move for a local band," Jack told the *Metro-Times*, surprised at the approached venues' delight. When the White Stripes had sold out their only two Gold Dollar gigs of 2000 on consecutive nights, it had caused local amazement. Now, they were saying farewell to an old home they'd outgrown. "This may be the last time you'll be able to see this great Southwest Detroit duo in this intimate setting," Dave Yee's programme said of their June 7 gig, "as they continue to take the world by storm." Jack and Meg had wanted to accept red-and-white gifts as the entrance fee, an idea showing their unique status. "There are other bands on the bill," Jack realised, "that need to get paid money." On June 8 they played the Magic Bag, then on June 9 the Magic Stick, where the bar staff wore red and white, the Go supported and their friends sang their songs.

In New York a week later, the White Stripes proudly sold out a three-night run of gigs, when more than 40 major-label A&Rs sniffed round Jack, telling him how great he was. He wore a white T-shirt on which he'd scrawled "New York Confuses Me". *NME*'s John Mulvey also spoke to him on the phone then, having caught and reviewed the White Stripes at Hollywood's Troubadour in November, where he bought *De Stijl*. Jack used his first *NME* interview to emphasise his disbelief in gold rushes and gravy trains reaching Detroit. None of those A&Rs could be bothered coming to his town, and even if they did, it was just "'cause they're bored. It's not gonna last." Lyrical analysis drew this admission: "I've got a lot of chips on my shoulders about girls. I don't have many friends that are girls. I can't get along with them for very long." He came across as an agreeably odd, provincial Midwesterner, wary of Manhattan city slickers' cons. Canny brother Jack, though, continued to pull cons of his own with a poker face. "Brother-sister bands possess a perverse, cultish appeal," Victoria Segal's positive *White Blood Cells* review believed, in the same July 7 *NME* as Mulvey's piece.

"We hadn't been able to sell the first album for love or money," says Simon Keeler, then a product manager at Sympathy for the Record Industry's UK distributor Cargo, explaining this growing British interest. "When *De Stijl* came in and Peel played it, sales picked up more and more at Rough Trade's shops. But we couldn't get it into the major stores then, HMV and Virgin, because there was no press. Long Gone John wouldn't spend on it. So for *White Blood Cells* I tried a more thorough press campaign myself. Stevie Chick, John Mulvey and the live editor Andy Capper were already big supporters at *NME*, and Andy had an in at *The Guardian*." *NME* sub-editor Martin Horsfield may have been the first to spread the word, being a then-rare listener in the office to vital Stripes fan John Peel. "After Stevie's South By Southwest review in March," Keeler continues, "we were selling hundreds of *De Stijl*, but still hadn't hit 1,000 when in May I got about 100 of a three-track *White Blood Cells* promotional sampler with a beautiful sleeve. I sent it to a couple of people initially, including Peel. He immediately started playing it and said, 'When can I get the whole album to play?' So I badgered Sympathy to get it to him. And then we started to run out of records. I'd order on Thursday needing 150, and by the time they'd come from San Francisco on Tuesday I'd think, 'Shit, I should have got 500.' No UK labels were involved or chasing by June. But by the end of that month it was rolling freely of its own will, in every direction."

The White Stripes had sold 25,000 albums before *White Blood Cells* –
spectacular for Sympathy, but just an interesting ripple in the mainstream,
where all their early interviews were brief nods to a promising act. The star
of *Almost Famous*, Kate Hudson, fittingly wanted a gig ticket, and the eBay
value of 'Let's Shake Hands' had hit $100 (Italy Records' Dave Buick –
named a "local mogul" by *Entertainment Weekly* – had pressed it thinking
spare copies would be stacked in his wardrobe forever). None of that
meant as much to Jack and Meg as the video cassette they were posted of
five and six-year-olds singing 'Apple Blossom' in Kalamazoo, Michigan,
with the guitar-strumming schoolteacher who'd taught them. The White
Stripes' putative children's songs had found their way home. "I started
crying," Jack told the *Metro-Times*. "If it's gotten to that, how can you top
that?" Crying and raging were not privately uncommon, friends knew, for
this frustrated, tender young man, as he struggled to meet his desires.

On July 17, during a swing supported by the Von Bondies through the
Midwest and West Coast, where crowds often stayed modest, the White
Stripes made their US network TV debut on CBS' *Late Late Show With
Craig Kilborn*. *Time* heard Jack tell a friend it was their first time on TV. Few
knew of their Detroit and New Zealand dry runs. "The brother and sister
duo whose new album has made them the buzz of the alternative music
world," Kilborn introduced them to those Americans still up after 1 a.m.,
for low-wattage guests including an Irish comedian equally unknown
locally, Graham Norton, and actress Marlee Matlin. Though it wasn't much
of an occasion, the White Stripes rose mightily to it. With the Detroit flag
behind them, their uncompromised, exotic strangeness was reinforced in
this LA studio. You can hardly hear words in the possessed, gabbled screech
of their first ever song, 'Screwdriver' – what is wrong with this boy with
dyed-black hair lank and sweaty on his face? – till they resolve into a 1931
blues, 'Your Southern Can Is Mine', certainly making its TV debut. The
repeated, swung gut-punch of guitar is met with symbiotic faith by Meg till
Jack's raised finger stops her, then her watching eyes get lost in the moment
with him, as she's almost knocked off her stool matching his violent blows.
He's a punk channelling the Who through himself and his ex-wife, locked
together in distorted music. It makes no sense in the American mainstream,
a shocking thrill with no place to go.

The week after *NME* reviewed *White Blood Cells*, its July 14 issue
carried an ad with a picture of the LP sleeve. It listed three UK dates the
next month, starting: "Thurs July 26 100 Club (Sold Out)".

★   ★   ★

Bruce Brand picked the band up at Gatwick Airport on July 24. Sitting in the same vinyl-stuffed flat in a Victorian square in King's Cross, London, in which he lived then, he remembers the scene. "I went down on the train, thinking, 'There's only two of them.' Except there were three, with John Baker their Kiwi road manager, and they had a stack of merchandise virtually up to the ceiling on a barrow, and Meg had a suitcase bigger than my sofa. I was used to Medway louts being mouthy and arrogant, and they were nice as pie. Polite, and unassuming, which made a refreshing change. I offered to put them up here, but I had two cats at the time and they were allergic to them, so they stayed with my friends, a girl called Jacqui and a chap called Tim."

Brand was one of the scattered few who already knew about the band. A mainstay in the garage-rock scene of Kent's Medway towns and drummer with its charismatic leader Billy Childish's bands, one of those, Thee Headcoats, had stayed with Long Gone John in Long Beach in 2000. "He slung the first two White Stripes albums and some singles at us. I was just listening to the first album for the first time in years, trying to work out why it stood out to me then. And it's got songs, and it's got dynamics, and it's got feeling, it's not just trying to make a racket with garage and rock'n'roll." Brand's experience of the garage scene in Medway's run-down, cut-off working-class towns helped him understand Jack's Detroit sound. "After punk rock hit, we'd formed the Clock Rivets between 1977 and 1980, then we did the Milkshakes, which was more rooted in the early Sixties," he remembers. "Because punk rock took me back to my child-hood, and 'You Really Got Me' and the Who. But we'd gone as far as we could with punk. We thought, slow it down, and give it some nice atmosphere, and add some joy, rather than just energy. And that's what I picked up from the White Stripes." Like John Baker in Auckland, Brand had felt compelled to bring the band to Britain to play, but didn't know how to contact them until Dave Kaplan, also Thee Headcoats' US agent, rang him. He asked Brand to be the White Stripes' English support act with his band the Masonics, arrange their equipment, and hire a van to drive them.

Nearly 4,000 miles distant from Detroit's fervent rock'n'rock commu-nity, the wider world's musical currents were clearer. The UK's Top 10 albums in 2000 had been by the Beatles, Eminem, Moby, Robbie Williams, Craig David, Westlife, Whitney Houston, Coldplay, Tom Jones, Travis and David Gray. Oasis, down at 21, were the first post-Sixties name you could really call rock. On both sides of the Atlantic, the rap-rock hybrid of nu-metal bands such as Limp Bizkit were guitar music's ugly commercial rump. *NME*, with its own sales declining, picked Starsailor, Outkast, Elbow and the Avalanches as its hopes for 2001. By the end of January, all had been overtaken by a New York band, the Strokes. Their debut EP, *The Modern Age*, released by Rough Trade from a clear blue sky on January 29, was declared a "stunning single" from the latest American band "reinvigorating rock". *NME*'s interview with the Strokes that week placed them "along with At The Drive-In, Queens Of The Stone Age and . . . And You Will Know Us By The Trail Of Dead . . . at the forefront of the American rock renaissance." No mention of Detroit. When Stevie Chick filed his South By Southwest report on the White Stripes in March, he framed them as "a southern-fried cousin to the Strokes." The April 21 *NME* that ran his *De Stijl* review boldly declared on its cover: "We Love New York – Your Guide To The Most Rock'n'Roll City On Earth".

The band who *NME* would twin with the White Stripes as spearheads of an initially imaginary 'rock renaissance' were significantly different. From mostly wealthy, self-assured backgrounds and with model good looks – the first thing every girl I knew happily noticed – this four-piece were a much more normal proposition for success than Jack and Meg. Their city also had a massive music business. "In America there was really not a care in the world," bassist Nikolai Fraiture told me of a time when the World Trade Center's twin towers still stood, "and New York felt to us an epicentre of music and art." Their version of Ghetto Recorders was Gordon Raphael's TransporterRaum, an incense and amp-strewn concrete basement with classic analogue equipment recorded to computer, round the corner from the 2A bar where their friends worked, part of a Lower East Side scene like a far less dangerous or destitute Cass Corridor, shared by the Yeah Yeah Yeahs and Mooney Suzuki. In a comparable trajectory to the White Stripes, after forming in 1998 they had spent two years gigging to gain fans in Manhattan, then around the Northeast. Drummer Fabrizio Moretti also remembered a city with different horizons and energy to Detroit: "The universe was New York City to us. Thank God we were in New York. We were inherently driven to get to where we were supposed to go."

They were making young men's discoveries of a powerful past in parallel with Jack. "I grew up listening to the Stooges and the Velvet Underground," their producer Gordon Raphael, then around 40, told me. "I thought, 'I wanna produce this like *Raw Power*. This sounds like this heavy psychic vibe of a Lou Reed.' It really shocked me that they would be familiar with this vibration." Singer Julian Casablancas described his desired vibe to Raphael as time travel: "He said, 'Imagine if you took a spaceship into the future, and found a record from the far distant past that you never heard. What would that sound like?' The second thing he said was: 'We wanna sound like *nothing* that's happening now.' And what was happening now was Pro Tools, and massive drum sounds. He said, 'Why does it have to sound so blown out? Can't you just make it like a comfortable pair of jeans? Distressed, but not completely destroyed.'" The Velvet Underground's *Loaded* was the band's template (Television, too, as blatant-seeming as Jack's Zeppelin debt). "It was the craftsmanship of the songs," Moretti said of it. "This sad patina on them, even though they were all rocking. It seemed like they were striving to do something new at the time, and it was very exciting. It was new to us, though it was made 30 years ago."

The Strokes recorded their demo at rates Jack would approve ($300, with $150 of that owed), but Raphael saw no future for it in America. "The press in the United States was really trying to bury the electric guitar," he remembered. "*The New York Times* had a gravestone shaped like a guitar. 'Rock'n'roll is dead! We've got DJs and techno, and finally this boring 40-year-old monster is laid to rest.' Everybody in those days in New York was dressed like DJs." It took Britain's more febrile, opportunist, reactive music scene, able to send jolts of excitement through a small island via the national channels of *NME* and Radio 1, to flick the switch that revived rock's commercial corpse. Rough Trade, the recently revived indie label that in its original incarnation had signed the Smiths, was still run by Geoff Travis much like John Peel's show, on his own taste and instinct. After hearing the start of the Strokes' demo over the phone, he offered to release 1,000 copies in its raw state as *The Modern Age*. It had been recorded in three days in September 2000. On June 9, 2001, the Strokes made *NME*'s cover. They felt none of the pensiveness with which *White Blood Cells*' sleeve treated fame. "We felt like superstars," Fraiture told me. "I remember our publicist giving us a crash-course in the UK press. So it was like a game for us, it was fun." "We didn't know how we were going to do it," Moretti admitted. "After Geoff Travis, we had a chance. His stamp of approval opened so many fuckin' doors."

"Rough Trade's reaction wouldn't have happened in an office in New York City," Raphael believed. "Within 10 notes, that demo would have been in the bin. But a few people in England believed in it and this caused

New York to pay attention, when they came back and played the Bowery Ballroom in February 2001, after the glorious London experience. So there were record company limousines around the block, and I noticed they had a pile of contracts from every label in New York wanting to get them. And a year later, New York became a rock city. Down Ludlow Street, those same streets where all those people were in rave outfits, suddenly as far as the eye could see, there were boys with leather jackets carrying guitars."

In truth, after more than a year of high-profile gigs the White Stripes were already ahead of the Strokes in New York, and the wider US. But the interest raised there by *White Blood Cells'* release was still modest when they landed at Gatwick. Arriving in the slipstream of building British hype for the Strokes, with *NME* and the wider industry in the mood for a Stones to their Beatles, was significant. But without a UK label's professional roadies and PR pep-talks, Geoff Travis' clout, or the manager the Strokes also had, the madness that now began rested on Jack and Meg.

Bruce Brand leafs through his little black diary of those weeks, and remembers. Picking the White Stripes up from his friend Tim's on the 24th, they spoke to Source Records, a Farringdon indie label interested in signing them, one indication that word was out and possibilities were being weighed before their UK arrival. Another was Jack's request for a venue for a 'secret', tour-ending gig, much like their great night at Auckland's Pizza Pizza. "From the fact they did that, they obviously realised there was something going on," Brand agrees. "They looked at a place in Hackney about the size of this room, with the stage barely raised." Kingsland Road's On The Rocks helped its disqualification from Stripes legend that night with an unpleasantly rammed, disliked gig by A.R.E. Weapons, a New York band riding their city's Strokes-led fad into London.

"John Baker told me Jack wanted to play a secret show," Warby remembers. "Prior to them arriving we looked at all sorts of venues – Hoxton Hall, The Macbeth, Bethnal Green Working Men's Club. I even considered staging a show in my own small back garden in Kilburn. I still wish we'd done that. We'd started with one show, and the trip expanded," he adds of a tour prelude during which excitement built. "We were having to respond very quickly. The 100 Club sold out from photocopied leaflets which cost 47p handed out at the Strokes show at Heaven, and by word of mouth alone. The anticipation for it was enormous. By the time we advertised in the *NME*, London's Dingwalls was virtually sold out, too."

"As soon as a date was announced it would sell out," Simon Keeler confirms. "Then I'd told Russell Warby, 'John Peel wants them to do a session.'" Warby wondered if Peel was still relevant, an understandable doubt shared by then from large labels to *NME*. But the DJ retained Radio 1's highest percentage of young teenage listeners, and the ear and openness to push the band before anyone in Britain. His faith was about to be spectacularly repaid. "I said to Russell, 'If you don't do a Peel session, I think you'll lose your biggest supporter here,'" Keeler recalls. "And so I emailed Jack who said, 'I'm doing the Peel session, that sounds fantastic.' And Peel came back with the idea of a live session with an invited audience. Jack said, 'Just get people in that want to hear the record.'"

"Wednesday 25th July," reads Brand's next entry. "Delaware Rd W9. Brilliant John Peel session and dinner." Jack remembered their first meeting in an emotional tribute given to *Mojo* after Peel's death in 2004. "He looked us in the eye as if he was no more important than us. He was instantly our friend from the moment we met him. He bought us dinner and talked wildly about Gene Vincent. He complimented us when few cared. He did a session with Son House. He asked us for an encore. He sent out our music on waves to bedrooms and cars on the side of the road. He gave us to England, and England welcomed us because of him."

The dinner was part of Peel's happy routine with favoured bands before live sessions. After soundchecking at the BBC's Maida Vale Studio 4, Jack and Meg waited like expectant kids for the napping Peel to wake, then joined him at his usual Thai restaurant, where he was the only diner allowed a hot towel after meals; simple, ritual pleasures. Jack asked his 61-year-old host about gigs he'd seen. Peel regaled him with stories of Vincent, and the astonishing fact that Son House recorded a Peel session one July evening in 1970, as Jack was about to 31 years later. House had also played the 100 Club on his visit, where an outraged Peel had leapt up mid-set to offer refunds to chattering punters if they'd just leave, so the rest could listen. Jack had crossed the Atlantic to find his greatest blues hero a phantom step away. Peel, meanwhile, was unaware of others' interest in the band. "They're very sweet, aren't they?" he said to his producer as they walked to the studio. "We must make sure we mention their tour dates so they get a good audience."

Even regular Peel listeners who knew their records weren't prepared for what the White Stripes played. As on their US TV debut, Jack reacted to a wider audience by upping his music's dose. On the opening 'Let's Shake Hands' and 'When I Hear My Name', he mauls words with a parodic Southern accent and sulking, bratty screech, then lets them dissipate in breathy puffs. Hendrix is invoked with oscillating feedback on the latter song, where Jack's voice develops a Buddy Holly hitch. 'Jolene' is delicate and desperate. 'Death Letter', inspired by earlier talk of Son House, begins with the swampy sultriness of the blues' dreamed Delta, which duets with heavy guitar thunder. Peel's producer remembered that no one there could believe only two people were making this music, a reaction that would be endlessly repeated. Jack's ability to be two guitarists at once, in unison with Meg's simultaneous drum-cymbal blows, magnified by the coherent force of their pseudo-sibling bond, is the incomplete, rational answer. "I started to develop a subconscious style of playing lead and rhythm at the same time – back and forth, back and forth," Jack explained to *Guitar Player*'s Jimmy Leslie. Barely aware, he'd slip his pick beneath his finger, to flick almost instantly between playing with and without it. "Form follows function," Jack the Modernist believed, his body instinctively doing what was needed.

The high, hot, abstract lines of his 'Death Letter' solos, scribbled between Morse code marching beats and the letter's weird rustic mystery – 'What do you rekkin it read?' – anyway amounts to more, better guitar of this sort than indie circles had heard in decades. The John Bonham stomp Jack somehow gives to that guitar on 'Cannon' then bleeds into Son House's 'John The Revelator'. 'Who's that riding?' Jack nervously wonders before, alive to the crowd's murmurs, getting them to 'sing it with me'. When it starts to speed up this music moves, at the start of the digital age, like the trains on which those suffering and causing blues came and went.

The White Stripes' whole spectrum is in their three sets of three songs and encore that night. The manic children's song 'Astro' morphs into Screaming Lord Sutch's 1963 single 'Jack The Ripper', with its riff from TV's *Dragnet*. Played in tribute to foggy London town (rather than "Saucy" Jack's grim murders), it develops distortion in dialogue with Meg's drums. 'Hotel Yorba' shows its pop singalong potential, 'I'm Finding It Harder To Be A Gentleman' allows contemplation of Jack's lyrics, 'We're Going To Be Friends' reveals kindergarten innocence, and 'You're Pretty Good Looking (For A Girl)' is sweet Sixties British pop, rampagingly played. Jack singing 'I've got a feeling going now' with rising intensity on 'Screwdriver' shows the White Stripes' first, infectious trick still works. 'Boll Weevil', a surreal blues cover about a cotton-predating beetle eating the singer's Stetson, permits self-mythology – who was that tonight? 'You tell 'em Jackie White' – and beery accompaniment from the increasingly excited crowd.

But what John Peel remembered was a surprise encore added after they spoke: Gene Vincent's 'Baby Blue', sung with a curled-lip, Fifties hiccup Dexter Romweber would also have loved. "That's for you, John," Jack said. "Well," Peel concluded to his Radio 1 listeners, "anybody who ends their set with a Gene Vincent song wins the unstinting approval of this programme, that's for sure. Meg and Jack, the White Stripes, thanks very much. People will go away from here and their lives will never be quite the same again. It's been a magnificent night, thanks very much indeed." His wife Sheila reported his reaction to Jack's gesture in *Margrave Of The Marshes*: "He just welled up. You couldn't have prised the smile from his face with a crowbar."

The simplest answer to why Jack's life changed in the next 48 hours is to listen to that Peel session. Its fresh, unpredictable power cuts like a clean blade. It added to the fascination around the following night in Brand's diary: "Thursday 26th July 100 Club – White Stripes – Loaded late, I drove. Set up & s/check. Sold out. W/S 100 Club & Masonics (VG)."

"Other than Oasis, it was the only recent gig I could've sold out four or five times," the 100 Club's owner, Jeff Horton, said in *Candy Coloured Blues*. Jack was talkative when he arrived that day, wanting to know more about Son House's appearance on the stage he was about to tread, seeming "genuinely honoured" to be there. Originally a jazz club, then an R&B and punk hotbed, played by everyone from Louis Armstrong to the Stones to the Sex Pistols, this unchanged basement was steeped in Jack's sources. Its red walls, white insignia and faded black stage can't have hurt. "The 100 Club's history and reputation for being a place to see something very special, and indeed its colour scheme, made it an easy first choice," Warby says of booking it. "Jack and Meg appeared to appreciate it. I remember them arriving and being photographed on the stairs." Horton watched Jack set up with "two guitars, an amp [just bought in nearby Denmark Street], maybe an effects pedal, a kick-drum for Meg, and no backline [the usual crowd of amps, speakers and instruments at the stage's rear] – completely unheard of at the time."

"It was an iconic venue that no one really used at that point," Keeler remembers. "But I walked down the same shitty steps I'd been down before, and looked on the wall and saw the framed pictures of the Rolling Stones or whoever in '65 that looked torn out of an old *NME*. John Baker was running round like a headless chicken. There was an atmosphere of real excitement."

It was a blazingly hot week in England. Like most British venues, the

100 Club didn't bother with air-conditioning. With the crowd packed tight, sweat rained down its red walls. Short *Mojo* and *NME* features and Stevie Chick's phone interview with Jack in the *Standard* about Detroit's scene, plus LP reviews, was the total advance press. Still the familiar scent of hype hung in the air, with at least half a dozen PRs and some label representatives inside angling for work. "When they came to the UK, all of a sudden everyone from the *NME* was dead excited," says Chick. "I got tickets to the gig, and all the *NME* people were there."

"I really felt at the 100 Club that the audience were genuinely enthusiastic fans and friends," Warby says, "including all the labels that came along, even though many of them were very new to the band. Everybody wanted to experience this phenomenon at close quarters. It was intimate and special. This wasn't the industry looking on, this was the collective discovery of something thrilling." Keeler agrees. "Those sorts of shows are usually full of press people," he says. "I didn't feel it was. I think XL Records started going then, we bought 20 tickets for Cargo, and a few PR people came trying to get the press, but Jack didn't do press. I fielded calls all day. 'Blah blah wants to get in because he's a massive fan.' 'But it's sold out.' 'But you've got a guest-list.' 'I haven't.' And this was a concept that they couldn't understand. It wasn't like the Strokes, with 100 on the guest-list. It wasn't a showcase, it was a gig, just like ones my friends in Melbourne had seen months prior, and the one they saw in a grubby LA theatre months later. Maybe that was what shook up the British press. Maybe less is more works. It was mainly full of fans excited beyond all belief that they were going to see the White Stripes in front of them. The stage was only knee-high, with Meg with her drums on one side, and Jack with his ridiculous guitar on the other, and it looked fantastic. And the thing about them live is they were as tight as anything you could see." Beginning again with their first single, 'Let's Shake Hands', the White Stripes played a 45-minute set they'd honed in similar honest dives for four years. A moment's stunned silence. Then roaring applause. "We all thought it was astonishing," says Chick.

"I thought, 'They're really good. I reckon they're going to take off,'" Brand remembers. "I was standing there with my mouth open. It just had this weird energy that I couldn't describe – what's going on? There's just two of them, a girl playing the drums, a bloke playing the guitar, screaming his head off. But there was obviously some magnetic force going on, especially between them – because there were all these staccato stabs at weird times, and I thought, 'How do they know when to do that?' It had something going for it that I hadn't seen for such a long time. I had probably only subjected myself to generic garage bands over the previous 10 years. This was the first time I'd been surprised by something that was tangibly good, and I couldn't figure out what it was. And I still can't." Did it remind him of anything? "No. It was like a new experience. Considering what it is – just a noisy guitar and drum kit, and pretty basic for the most part. It was the sum of its parts, the way it was handled."

Not everyone was convinced, one PR telling anyone who would listen they should go home and hear some Howlin' Wolf. But following the Peel session, this gig powered a rising tide that swept the White Stripes along. Chick was asked as he left to write *NME*'s full-page review. "I wrote it immediately I got in," he remembers. "It's a bit hyperbolic. I have a memory of being in a slight alcoholic haze and hammering away at the keyboard, and being in such rapture for the band and what I'd just seen, and I poured it all onto the page." "White Noise, White Heat" was the headline in *NME*'s August 4 issue (published a week earlier). Chick wrote: "Tonight Jack White and his drumming sister/wife Meg (still not sure ourselves) tear apart the hype and expectation surrounding what is arguably the hottest 'underground' rock band in the States right now . . . tonight, we saw rock'n'roll born again; stripped back to its barest elements, dipped in dirt and sex and explosive passion, and sent reeling into the future . . . Jack White recalls the Jeff Buckley of his fabled early London shows. He's not yet swaggering (he's wordless between the songs all night), but there's an audacity to the way he tears between his two mics while slamming all manner of gorgeous, chaotic noise from his guitar . . . From a derelict corner of the United States of America this stunning resurrection of rock'n'roll is surging . . . Ask Jack White and he'll bashfully deny he's the future of rock'n'roll. Go make a liar of him."

The next day, with that review still unpublished and the media sea placid, Jack and Meg skipped their first scheduled interview, with *Dazed & Confused*. On this day off, they plotted moves months ahead. "I showed them Toe-Rag studios in Dalston," Brand remembers, "which they were aware of through their chums in the Hentchmen, and they were quite impressed with that." Its owner Liam Watson had already piled into the tour van to the 100 Club with his friend Brand. Jack kept his vintage analogue gear in mind for the future. "Then they wanted pizza," says Brand. "In Dalston then, we had to drive for about five miles to find somewhere in Leyton that even sold chicken nuggets! Which is all they'd eat, if they couldn't get pizza." At Brand's suggestion, they watched the Buff

Medways at the Dirty Water Club that night, a regular event at Tufnell Park's Dome venue above the Boston Arms. They picked it for their 'secret' gig on August 6.

"Bruce comes over and says, 'I want you to meet a friend of mine,'" recalls PJ Crittenden, still Dirty Water's booker, when we talk after the club's sold out Gories gig in 2015. "He says, 'Hi, I'm Jack, I'm in a band called the White Stripes, I wondered if I could play here.' He was shy. Very polite. A proper Southern gentleman type. I had the first two albums already from Rough Trade's shop in Notting Hill, friends of mine on internet newsgroups had told me to check them out. He had star quality. Even when he walked up to me, there was something about him. He was in his colours, black trousers and red top. They already had it all worked out. Even then, their first time in England, they were doing press. There was no management or organisation, it was them doing it, it was their plan. They knew what they were doing, they were very clever. I had no idea they'd been building in popularity, I didn't know John Peel had been playing them. Then the tickets sold out in an hour."

Saturday, July 28. At Bristol's 125-capacity, tiny Louisiana, the White Stripes started with a 10-minute 'Death Letter' and played for 90 minutes. On Sunday lunchtime, they left their West Country B&B and returned to the club, where *NME*'s James Oldham wanted to hear about their past. "Well, we'll try, anyway," Jack said brightly. Then he regaled the foreign press representative with his and Meg's childhood among eight siblings, and his half-joking desire to be a black man in the Thirties.

At Oxford's Point that night, the continuing heatwave became danger-ously unpleasant, with an 'Extreme Temperature Warning' on the wall, the venue's fan busted, and the PA struggling to cope. Brand called the airless, breathless place the Boiling Point. "After the Masonics played in a puddle, I went to the van and stripped right off and sat dripping for half an hour. When I tried to go back in, there was a physical heat-barrier between the door and the bar, and I couldn't bear to push my way through it." Uncomplaining Jack played on, sweat plastering his and Meg's hair to their smiling faces as another crowd capitulated. They were finishing gigs with 'Not The Marrying Kind'.

They returned to London for a larger gig at Camden's Dingwalls, where Whirlwind Heat bassist Steve Damstra was a face from home. "That was the best show in London," says Warby. "Jack thought that was special. There were clouds of steam rising from the audience, and condensation dripping from the ceiling." Then with Brand and John Baker up front in their van, they headed north: Nottingham's The Social on July 31, and the Manchester Roadhouse on August 1, where they tried out a more mellow set, to one punter's vocal annoyance. "Jack leaned out and grabbed him, saying, 'Are you fucking with me?'" Brand remembers. Such direct, physical anger would recur.

Brand had plenty of time to observe his new friends together. "Sometimes I got the impression they tolerated each other. They were like an old married couple – or ex-married couple. When people asked, I'd say they were an ex-brother and sister, because you weren't supposed to let on. There was some electricity there, but that's a positive force and a negative force. I never saw them overtly having a go at each other – the odd little jibe here and there maybe, that mild you could choose to ignore it. But apart from that, they were getting on with it." Years later, Jack told *The New York Times* he had to "grovel" to get Meg to do things, as she'd "completely controlled the White Stripes." So who was in charge? "Who'd you think?" Brand laughs. "Oh, Meg wore the trousers . . . I think she basically did as she was told."

He enjoyed their company as they passed nights on the road. "Jack's talkative, but not annoyingly. And he's got ambition and focus. He says he wants to do something, and he does it. Meg was nice, quiet and shy. Unaffected. She really liked the Bourbon. And I've got friends who are in touch with her who say she still does! But she was just the same when she was drinking. She said that she liked listening to music more than playing it."

Ewen Spencer, an English photographer who specialises in snatching images from sometimes suspicious youth subcultures, began a long relationship with the White Stripes on this tour, showing them sitting on leafy west English railway tracks that looked like the Deep South that summer, and in off-guard, offstage moments, Jack's usually pale skin flushed and wet with sweat. As Doug Coombe found in Detroit, Spencer's *NME* photos were an intriguing visual shortcut to the band's identity. "Whenever the Stripes weren't wearing their red-and-white clothes, Jack would say, 'The pictures have to stop now' . . . it was like, the charade is over, the curtain has been closed," he told the *Guardian*. Like Brand, he bonded with Meg. "I started smoking again because of [her]; we smoked together, just to kill the time while Jack was off indulging his creativity. She seemed wise beyond her years, a drummer with a lot of soul and a massive knowledge about music."

It was impractical for the White Stripes to orchestrate a media frenzy as they rattled up British motorways, Jack minus a mobile phone then as now. If anything, his wish to control his musical world tried to douse hysteria. Refusing an *NME* cover story, he and Meg stayed elusive. *Dazed & Confused*'s reporter Rowan Chernin, stood up in London, found neither label boss Long Gone John, their New York PR, tour manager John Baker or agent Russell Warby willing to be the conduit a local PR team were for the Strokes. Chernin finally hunted them down in Oxford, where Baker refused an interview. He found Meg on Magdalene Bridge, looking dreamily at swans passing beneath, and Jack scoffing a Big Mac. They reluctantly took questions in a quaint tea room. Even BBC Radio 4's *Today* programme found its insistent requests through Cargo's Simon Keeler knocked back, till Jack called from a payphone at Leeds' Rocket venue on August 2. With a tired Baker driving, they slept by the road towards Glasgow that hot night, snug in their van.

"The primary push for it taking off here was John Peel," Keeler recalls of the gathering storm back in London, "and I think the Peel session really kicked the label interest off. Long Gone John ignored most communications about the White Stripes, because he knew they were a big deal for him. So management companies were coming to us at Cargo. 'I need to speak to him, do you know who I manage? I manage Elton John . . .' It didn't matter. I had no authority. I'd get three or four calls a day, and it would be quite something. I spoke to people who you'd hear about on the *News At 10*. And I'd try to get hold of John Baker on the road, and his phone would cut out. In a way, it was a brilliant anti-marketing marketing coup. It's how it would have been in the Sixties, with the Who on their first jaunt up to Preston or wherever, and people saying, 'Where are they?' It added to the mystery of the White Stripes."

"Jack had a strong sense of what he wanted throughout, was charming and confident," Warby says. "Meg was enigmatic and watchful. Jack didn't want to do a load of press, wary of anything that wouldn't be invested in the White Stripes. But he was open to discussing suggestions that Simon and I made, even if he had initial reservations."

"I felt bad hassling Jack with my intermittent emails – and Jack did have email," Keeler remembers, "and telling him, 'This *Today* programme is a massive deal.' But it was. I think he knew what was happening. He's very astute and aware. But he didn't use it in a way that another artist would. Cool and shrewd sound wrong. But he played it with a very level head. 'That's happening – good.'"

After playing Glasgow's King Tut's (where half-Scots Jack hoped for red, white and black tartan gifts), the band flew to Ireland's Witness Festival. Then a final night in London, at the Dirty Water Club.

Now the controls to Jack's career slipped usefully from his grasp. *Today* ran their report on the morning of the gig, in the knowledge that *NME* had disobeyed Jack to put the White Stripes on their cover the next day. BBC employee Peel had already judged their session historic: "I've not been affected by anything as much as this since punk, perhaps even since I first heard Jimi Hendrix." *Today*'s Chris Jones, moved to pursue the band through hearing the Peel session, told his breakfast listeners that these unknowns loved old bluesmen, rock'n'rollers and Lonnie Donegan (they'd quizzed Peel on the skiffle king). "Not exactly the sort of music you'd expect to get Britain's rock music-loving teenagers queuing round the block to see," he noted. "But you'd be wrong." Hype? Jack hadn't even wanted to be interviewed. "We heard that in England you can suddenly become big for a couple of months," he explained, "and then everyone forgets about you." Speaking to millions, including the politicians who were *Today*'s staple interviews and the media who monitored their answers, Jones forthrightly hyped the White Stripes himself. Noting the Strokes June Top 20 hit 'Hard To Explain' and "scores more bands in Detroit playing a similar sort of music," he mistily compared 2001 to 1976, as punk hit: "Pop and rock in Britain is in a rut. It needs a kick up the backside . . . this new wave of underground bands from America playing their loud fusion of blues, punk and garage-rock look like the only ones capable of carrying that out."

"I flew back from Dublin with Jack, Meg and John," says Warby, "and while in the van called my office to see if I had any messages. I did – from every tabloid and broadsheet." The music industry and press begged to be let into the Tufnell Park Dome that night. "It was incredibly dingy," Chick fondly recalls.

" 'Yes, Kate Moss, you're on the list,' " PJ mock-wearily repeats. "John Peel was on the list and didn't come, Jarvis Cocker did. Jack said to me, 'If anyone turns up from *The Sun* they're not on the list because they're arseholes.' And then during the evening, I saw a guy wearing a really badly fitting suit. He went on the defensive and said, 'I'm from *The Sun*, but don't worry, we love the White Stripes.' "

"I was at the front thinking, 'Why are these photographers from *The Sun* pushing everyone out of the way?' " says Chick. "I spat bubblegum into their camera bags. Loads of people weren't watching the stage, they were watching the door, waiting for Kate Moss to arrive. The lights came on, and Jack had this acoustic guitar with brown paper on its body, and they did this version of 'Death Letter', which was astonishing." A *Sun* photo showed Meg looking almost bruised and hollow-eyed, as if purged by the pub's heat, staring at Jack with gloomy intensity, drumstick poised. Jack looked wide-eyed at the crowd of garage-rock diehards, supermodels and hacks, and thanked them. "I wouldn't have thought this was possible when I was upholstering chairs in Detroit."

"I saw Jack and Meg afterwards," says PJ. "They were pretty laid-back about it. It was as if they knew how it was going to go for them. They turned up at my gigs subsequently, in the audience. Other bands would email to get on the guest-list. Jack and Meg'd just turn up, heads down, and hold their money out to the girl on the door. Meg turned up subsequently much more than Jack did. She once said to me, 'The Dirty Water Club gig is my favourite one we ever did.' I expect she was just saying that. She was so lovely and nice."

"Jack took it all in his stride," Brand agrees. "I don't know what he was used to back home. But I get the impression they were bigger here first, and that allowed them to get bigger there. He was very verbose and confident. I reckon at the back of his mind he probably knew he was destined for bigger and better things, without shouting his mouth off about it – he was on the up-escalator and that was the only way it was going to be. But that's in retrospect."

The next morning, *NME*'s cover read: "DETROIT ROCKS! THE WHITE STRIPES THE SOUND OF NOW!" Inset at the top was a photo of Eminem in Australia, and at the bottom: "IS DETROIT THE NEW SEATTLE?" On August 8 came the tabloid deluge. "STRIPES ARE STARS", *The Sun*'s showbiz columnist Dominic Mohan declared, proving it with a photo of Kate Moss "and boyfriend" (the Kills' singer Jamie Hince). "BLUNK MUSIC," said Britain's second biggest-selling daily, the *Mirror*, fusing blues and punk to coin a term with mayfly longevity, and hedging a bet already feverishly taken: "The greatest band since the Sex Pistols or Hendrix . . . or just a load of old hype?" Showbiz reporters, not music critics, did the job, and the opinions of Peel, *NME* and *Today* were recycled, making the acclaim self-perpetuating. The broadsheets quickly followed, blanket coverage that couldn't be bought, and couldn't comprehend a band unknown only days before.

"Neil McCormick of the *Telegraph* phoned me up as part of the furore and said, 'It's flash in the pan nonsense, isn't it?'" Chick remembers. "Part of me thought, he's probably right, actually. This isn't something that's supposed to happen. It hit me like a ton of bricks when people liked them. I'd lost faith that bands like that could communicate to audiences the way they did. But there was nothing as exciting. It was that simple. Pour water on parched ground and it will respond."

Geoff Travis' Warner subsidiary Blanco Y Negro and the powerful independent Beggars Group's XL Recordings were the frontrunners jostling to sign them. "The idea of being on a bigger label scares us, because you hear so many horror stories about people being told what to do," Jack had said in *NME*. But he also reflected that being on an indie meant people who wanted his records couldn't always get them which, he'd later add, "makes me mad". Their music was only available on US import, and *Today* reported *White Blood Cells'* 12,000 copies almost gone. While the Strokes prepared to send their debut album, *Is This It*, to number two in the UK chart in August, Stripes sales stalled. So by early September they had signed to XL in the UK and by November V2 Records in the US, for a reputed £1 million and $1.5 million respectively. Long Gone John was hurt and dismayed, bitterly regretting their handshake deal (though Cargo had sold over 60,000 White Stripes albums when XL took over, sending $250,000 back to the US). But Jack had bided his time till his suitors were desperate, and struck a deal Orson Welles would applaud. "I didn't want money," Welles had said. "I wanted authority." Like his total control of the relatively cheap *Citizen Kane*, his Detroit pupil got just what he wanted. Talking to *Audioboom*'s Damian Abraham, Ben Blackwell remembered Jack's explanation to him. "Me and Meg talked about it. And we only wanted to make money if we earned it. We didn't want to make money because some label thought we'd sell a ton of records and we never did. And we were lucky. We never took an advance. We paid for all the recordings out of my pocket." The millions were mostly a music business mirage, *Billboard* confirmed, XL and V2 just licensing his recordings from his own label, Third Man Records. Having ensured he owned his first three albums when he signed with Sympathy, he now passed these on without having to compensate Long Gone John. Russell Warby was already booking a November tour of "colleges and ballrooms", when the White Stripes' records would get their real UK push. And Jack had parlayed hysteria into a deal which, even if the thought wasn't yet in his mind, founded his Third Man empire. It was around now that Ian Montone, already the White Stripes' lawyer, joined Dave Kaplan and Russell Warby in Jack's business inner circle in the rare double-role of manager, too. "What's a manager going to do except, when he gets an offer . . . call me up and ask me if I want to do it or not?"

Jack reasoned to *Pollstar*. Though he'd half-glimpsed Elvis in himself aged 19, there'd be no Colonel Parker.

On August 10, the White Stripes were back at work, playing a ballroom in Cleveland, Ohio. His New York PR told *NME* that Jack, "overwhelmed" by the UK response, would only be talking to "guitar magazines" now.

"I don't remember thinking or talking with Jack much about what had happened," Warby says. "My desire was to keep building the headline shows without getting ahead of ourselves. I don't know how it changed Dave Kaplan's plans in the US. But I think the reverberations from that week were felt all around the world."

How did Bruce Brand feel, when those 13 days in Britain and Ireland were over?

"It felt like the end of an era. The end of that volume. That's never going to happen quite like that again."

9

The Big Room

ON August 18, 2001, barely a week after a band it had nurtured became a transatlantic sensation, the Gold Dollar opened for the last time. The Hentchmen played, with Climax Divine and the Love Junkies. Neil Yee quit a scene narrower and larger than the one he'd imagined when his cramped, inspirational club opened, leaving town to travel the world.

"He told me he felt he'd done this, and it was time to do something else," says Matt Smith. "But my impression was that the local criminals had figured out there were these kids from the suburbs with money hanging out. There were crazed homeless guys running out of abandoned buildings, grabbing at girls. So some pretty scary people in that neighbourhood realised that there were people there that they could victimise. And I think Neil probably closed that place just in time to avoid there being a more severe incident. It was going in that direction, it was getting to that point where you didn't let your girlfriend walk to the car by herself after a gig there. He opened up this club that had been closed for years for a reason. Considering it was in a part of the Cass Corridor where people were just down there for drugs or prostitution, the Gold Dollar actually went pretty smoothly. But I think it was about to get pretty weird."

"I think I went to the last night," says the Go's John Krautner. "But if I can't remember, it must not have been that big of a deal. People get their kicks, lose their interest and then move onto the next thing."

The Garden Bowl, with the Magic Stick upstairs, fitted the new scene's drawing-power better. Jeff Payne, a scene veteran sipping whiskey at the Garden Bowl when we talk in 2015, remembers Jack sitting alone there around this time wearing a glittering jacket. Payne got his young son to sit with him, so he'd remember being in the orbit of someone soon to be a star. The Lager House, a great neighbourhood bar with a small back-room for gigs on a stretch of Michigan Avenue then almost as disreputable as the Gold Dollar's spot, became the intimate hangout of choice. Its location in historic, dilapidated Corktown was even closer to Jack and Meg's homes, and the White Stripes and Von Bondies were already among its regulars.

But the White Stripes were rarely there in 2001, when they played 117 shows. On their return from the UK they hit New York and the East Coast again, then spent September deep in the West and the South, building an American audience. The Greenhornes, who like their fellow Ohioans, the Soledad Brothers, were becoming important friends to Jack, were the support act. On September 11 they were in the Ozark mountains, set to play the Arkansas college town of Fayetteville, when, on a clear blue morning in New York, Al-Qaeda destroyed the World Trade Center, murdering thousands.

Some with tickets for the gig at JR's Lightbulb Club stayed at home, stunned. The White Stripes played as scheduled. Jack made no special comment onstage. "There was definitely thought on my end as to whether cancelling or proceeding would be in bad form," the club's co-owner, Wade Ogle, explains. "The decision to proceed as planned was likely a conversation between the band's agent and myself, coming down to 'we're all here, let's do it'. It was an intense hit'n'run-type show. I don't think I formally met Jack. I don't think the White Stripes even sound-checked. They descended down the stairs at showtime, played and quickly exited back up the stairs after playing. There was no hanging out with the public before or after the show." Ogle adds a snapshot of the level the band were at in American towns new to them, and the impact they made. "I think it was a $5 show, maybe $8, with a $500 guarantee. The show just about covered, so there were 100 people, maybe. For the most part, they were still way underground, with a buzz in those music circles. It was all happening at ground level – physically, with the band and audience face to face. Anyway, they were absolutely amazing. Super-intense. I remember thinking, 'This guy is really plugged into the source.' Really legit, passionate and talented. I also remember a few of us saying afterwards that they were going to be huge. Not punk rock, indie or cult band big but absolutely massive. Like when *Nevermind* came out."

The next month, the White Stripes not only chose ownership of music over an advance as they finalised their V2 deal, meaning they still needed cash. They also turned down a reported $1 million for their music to be used in a Gap Christmas ad, a valiant and costly stand for principles which, they soon realised, were no longer as firm among the rock communities in which they'd been raised. "When you come from where we are from and someone says we'll give you a million dollars to do a commercial, 10 years ago everyone would have said 'don't do that,'" Jack told *NME*. "But now, everyone says 'Do that' . . . people's opinions about selling out seem to have changed over the years." Their US PR told *Billboard* the million bucks was anyway, like the apparent millions in advances they'd never received, "way off the mark".

In early November, ahead of the White Stripes' European return, Dutch TV station VPRO filmed an evocative documentary showing a Detroit scene on the cusp of change. Mick Collins optimistically opined that if the White Stripes were its Beatles, "the Dirtbombs are the Rolling Stones", while the Paybacks' Wendy Case described a community that was finally "coalescing", with bands "helping each other and booking shows together". Filmed at 1203 Ferdinand, Jack reflected on their first UK trip. "We thought it was going to be a little tour," he said. "We got there and everything was sold out, and everyone wanted to do articles and photos. We'd heard so much about how England can make you popular and then they'll hate you six months later. We said, we don't want that attention. We'll just go and play shows. [*NME*] put us on the cover anyway. There's worse problems to have, I guess." He rationalised this success as if defending it to a hostile jury of his peers. "It just helps everyone else get a little bit of attention that they would never have gotten in the first place." Did he feel obligated to pay attention to other Detroit bands, his interviewer, Helmut Boeijen, perceptively asked. "It feels good to take another Detroit band on tour with us," Jack said. "They deserve it," Meg loyally put in. Now he was home, Jack could duck fame's chores like a naughty kid, as with the previous day's phone interviews. "I just had my roommate [Ben Swank] do 'em," he laughed.

He could forget all that on November 2, back onstage in Detroit for the first time since *White Blood Cells*' launch in June. Now the Gold Dollar was gone, and the White Stripes were playing in the Rivera Court at the Detroit Institute of Arts, beneath the factory-worker murals of the great Mexican artist Diego Rivera. Meg entered barefoot, and Jack walked on slowly waving Detroit's flag, a patriot honouring his home as it honoured him. Meg and the zebra head both peered at the fancy ceiling. Playing two sets in the round to 3,750 including family and friends, they began with 'Little Room', the *White Blood Cells* song that guiltily considers how success can separate you from its sources, and your community. After two hours, Jack's professional front broke into a boyish, 'Aw, shucks' grin at the warm applause, still very much one of his people. "We're all done," he said, pushing the sweaty hair back from his brow. "We can't believe this.

Thanks a lot." They finished with a remarkable, five-minute version of their first song, 'Screwdriver'. In its crucial moments Jack stands stock-still, he and Meg staring at each other, the prelude to the climax of this manic tune reduced to slow motion, its heartbeat barely moving. Then he walks with automaton stiffness to face the crowd, all the while matching Meg's single staccato beats over a low whine of feedback. Meg, moving lithely in a sleeveless white T-shirt and leaning over drums she fully commands, laughs at the fun. More than a warm-up for the long European tour that began that week, it was a special farewell.

NME printed weekly stories in their UK absence. An August 25 headline slyly asked, "Have The White Stripes Split Up?", relaying US reports of their divorce. "We're brother and sister," Jack calmly replied. "Someone started a rumour about how we used to be married and we played along with it. That was a bad idea; we get asked this all the time now." The October 20 *NME* asked him again if they'd been married, and his real name was John Gillis. "It's a lie," he lied. "My first name's actually John White. Jack's a nickname." His ID proved this, Meg added. His unusual decision to take her surname blurred the veracity of declaring her his sister. Maybe he'd realised it could. But even when the *Glorious Noise* website flourished their marriage certificate on May 23, 2002 (followed by proof of divorce), Jack insisted that the White Stripes story was the one he told. Facing down the world's press showed tough streaks of stubbornness and self-belief, pride in privacy, and bright faith that rock's public could still fall for outlandish characters in the new century. "If he tells you he's Bob Dylan," he said to *NME*'s John Mulvey in October 2001, referring him to another self-made myth who chose his own name, "he's Bob Dylan." Interviewers still try to break through this fiction told so long ago, but are always frustrated. In the band Jack invented, Meg will always be his sister.

'Hotel Yorba' was released in time for the November tour. The video for what became their first popular song in Britain was meant to be shot in the hotel where its live version had been recorded. With the establishment's then-customary hospitality, the unlikely young guests' return was cut short by hammer-wielding staff. They had to make do with standing in front of its forbidding brick walls for the single's sleeve, wearing bright red clothes on a bleak, snowy day. They walked past it in a video as warmly inviting as the song, with Dan Miller directing and his wife Tracee Mae Miller as the sweetheart Jack marries. Meg, drumming a cardboard box while stroking Jack's pet white rat, lounges then bounces on the apparent hotel bed Jack perches on, strumming. They grin at these games, having fond fun together. Meg's glamorous red film star dress, faraway gaze and pensively bitten lip added to her sex appeal in an indie world starved of women (except in Detroit's gender-neutral bacchanal). A scene with her roped to Jack, glumly trailing behind him and his bride in Detroit's Belle Isle wood, added another notch to the 'siblings'' mystique. "When you're a kid you have to drag your little sister around," Meg explained to *NME*'s Mulvey. Jack suggested it was an "inside joke" at his extrovert protectiveness of his shy "older sister". "It wasn't," gasped a man then as likely as a monk to discuss sex in public, "a *bondage* joke!" Pushed further about sex and relationships, Jack boldly declared: "If a girl goes out with me, she's going out with the band." Let Meg and Marcie pick the bones out of that.

When they returned to Britain ahead of 22 European dates, the nation was ready for them. With XL Records' backing and in-house PR, V2 newly aboard back in the US, all their albums generally available in the UK for the first time and a single to promote, the game had changed. "The next time was similar, but two notches up," says Bruce Brand, no longer required as driver but still a trusted friend. "They started getting more people involved, and it was a bit more professional." The Fender Twin amp and bass drum Russell Warby had bought on the last trip, sure at its start they'd need them again, were dug from storage. Brand spent two days painting red and white swirls on the drum. Jack and Meg stayed round the corner from his King's Cross flat, the budget now stretching to a Holiday Inn.

Jack popped round soon after touching down. "He said, 'I've written a song I want Holly [Golightly] to sing on," Brand remembers, "and he came running over and played 'It's True That We Love One Another'. I thought, 'What's that load of old cobblers?' He said, 'What's up, you don't like it?' 'I've heard you do better . . .' Anyway, we went to Toe-Rag and recorded it. It was like a test, to see how to record at Toe-Rag, and how it would come out." Golightly was former singer for Thee Headcoatees, an offshoot of Billy Childish and Brand's Headcoats, and a London garage-rock veteran of countless Dirty Water Club nights and quick Toe-Rag sessions. She was also a wryly witty chain-smoker and brief White Stripes labelmate on Sympathy, who once "took them out for some food and showed them the seaside", she recalled to *NME*. Now Jack turned up at her Bethnal Green door on the morning of Monday, November 5, clutching his new song on a scrap of paper. They taped it at Toe-Rag in two hours that evening, when she got back from work. "I'd been recording there for so many years prior to those kids rolling into town, and continued to do so after that," Golightly tells me. "It was simply a fun thing to do at the time, since I lived just two streets away." The first White Stripes music for a US major label is an even scrappier Scouts-style singalong than 'Hotel Yorba', made from piano, tambourine and ragged handclaps. But as a cheeky chess-move in the band's mythic games, it's priceless. In this garage-rock soap opera, Holly asks Meg whether stingy, rude, reserved Jack really loves her. 'You know, I don't care 'cause Jack really bugs me,' Meg replies. With Meg as yawning peacemaker in their squabbles, Holly admits she loves Jack 'like a little brother', before denying his bold request for some 'English lovin'' due to the chance of 'one in the oven'. He finds Holly's pert suggestion to 'go off and love yourself' equally impractical, as then 'there won't be anything left/ For anybody else.' Released on *Elephant* more than a year later, it ends with approving studio chat. "Jolly good," says Golightly. "Cup o' tea then, Bruce. Let's celebrate!"

The White Stripes recorded their UK TV debut for *Later . . . With Jools Holland* the next day, for broadcast that Friday. Holland introduced them as "the brother and sister team that are the White Stripes", and you'd never have doubted it watching them. During 'Hotel Yorba' Meg looks at the ceiling again, plainly a tactic to stay in her own dreamy head and not be bothered by the crowd and cameras. She's similarly relaxed watching Jack, their intuitive reading of each other charmingly visible and complete. She smiles sweetly at his solo on 'Let's Shake Hands', during which, just-snapped string hanging from his Airline guitar, he retunes into a Dick Dale twang, matching the pre-Beatles shiver and shake of his voice. They look happy doing this work together.

Thursday must have been even more comfortable, as their second Peel session was among those broadcast from the DJ's book-lined Suffolk cottage study. His wife Sheila cooked dinner for all before Peel arrived home to renew a friendship based on music more than publicity. After sessions at cosy, welcoming 'Peel Acres', red wine and music always flowed. "He gave me the Sex Pistols 'Anarchy In The UK', the promo version of it," Jack recalled to Canadian interviewer Nardwuar. "That was a really nice present to give me."

They slipped across the English Channel the next day for the Les Inrockuptibles festival, making their French debut at Paris' Belle Époque theatre venue La Cigale. Their first B-side, Marlene Dietrich's 'Look Me Over Closely', often played on this tour, fitted the old Europe ambience. Then they acquiesced to sessions for XFM on November 10 and Radio 1's

Lamacq Evening Session on November 13. Both had begged unsuccessfully for the band's time on their July tour, when a luckless Lamacq assistant had suggested to Simon Keeler, "Can just two of them come down?" Steve Lamacq himself had, though, followed Peel in playing them early, helping build the subterranean pressure that had burst its banks that summer. He was rewarded with a cover of Burt Bacharach and Hal David's 'I Just Don't Know What To Do With Myself', a 1964 hit for Dusty Springfield, suggested by Meg. Jack's voice begins at its most deliberately feminine, high and dainty, his guitar in period character, the arrangement spare. Spurning rubies and parties when he can't be with his lover, he switches to roaring, masculine desperation for a fuzzed-up rock chorus, his repeated pleading cracked and wild. His old-fashioned views of women are again blurred by androgyny, as he lets his gender bifurcate. Adding secretly lesbian Dusty to Marlene, Dolly Parton and Loretta Lynn in his sonic dressing-up box, some in gay music subcultures must have noted Jack. He could do a spine-chilling version of Judy Garland's 'Over The Rainbow', if he chose. Just as 'Jolene' had been New Zealand's point of connection a year before, this performance gained unexpected life. First reused as a B-side to 'Fell In Love With A Girl', it was also included on *Elephant*.

They began their second UK tour on November 11 at Brighton's beachfront Concorde 2, almost level with the dark English Channel rolling in. With the winter chill in stark contrast to their first visit, both White Stripes soon caught colds. London's 500-capacity Dingwalls had been the summer's biggest gig, but on November 21 the city's 2,000-capacity Astoria was sold out. This former cinema from the Twenties, much mourned since its 2009 demolition, was where I first saw the White Stripes. Jack sarcastically congratulated the crowd for being "very good at standing still", but he misread the mood. No musical detail has stayed with me. Just the shock. I was standing in the balcony, its seats softly lit by rows of red lamps, and I can't even recall Jack and Meg's faces – just two red-dressed figures on a stage whose bright light matched the massive volume, seeming louder in proportion to its improbable source. Just two people, as disconcerting as Dr Who's TARDIS. There was a tightness and concision to everything, from the clothes to the music. It felt both new, and punk to its bones.

It was around now that one of the band's Auckland hosts, Amber Easby, informed John Baker that she had moved to Britain. Invited to sell the tour merchandise, she was startled by how things had changed. "At the end of the show, I was swarmed by maybe 1,000 people," she told Radio New Zealand. "The table was being pushed back to the wall with me behind it, with people waving money at me. I remember sitting on the end of Jack's bed at the end of the night overwhelmed, I didn't know what to do with the volume we'd sold." She was soon taken on as merchandise manager, a job which, like so many of Jack's early adopters, she's kept. These days, she has a truck for her wares. Stevie Chick was among the Astoria customers. "I remember people pouring out into the street from that wonderful, so lamented venue, and everyone was buzzing," he says. "It was a genuine groundswell. It felt like, this is actually happening, there's a hysteria to this. It's what was needed."

By November 22, 'Hotel Yorba' was at number 26, their first chart hit anywhere, and Jack was striding into west London's BBC TV Centre to perform on *Top Of The Pops*. He hung nervously around the Star Bar, where he hardly seemed one, hoping to shake Paul McCartney's hand. "He said hi to all the girls," Jack complained sadly. "But not to me." He and Meg looked like aliens from a different pop planet next to Westlife and Jennifer Lopez. But whenever they played they seized their moment. Even with only his vocal live, Jack's wide-eyed, tousle-haired face could still bring out the simple innocence of 'childish thoughts like these', and as he moved sharply to the mic facing Meg, who sang along though her mic was dead, Britain's general public saw their bond.

From November 23 to December 4, the White Stripes introduced themselves to German, Belgian, Dutch and Italian clubland and a Spanish festival, and returned to France where, at the nautical-themed Marins d'Eau Douce club outside Toulouse, Jack sang part of Dylan's 'Isis' a cappella, and ended standing on Meg's bass drum, thrashing chords. On December 6, they finished this firming of their European beachhead at north London's Forum. "Richard Branson was backstage," the Dirty Water Club's PJ Crittenden remembers, "with Meg, Holly Golightly, Bruce Brand and Russell Warby. They were all deciding, 'The beer's run out, where shall we go now?' Richard Branson said, 'Err, I'm actually a bit hungry, is there somewhere we could eat?' So we got two taxis down to the Marathon kebab shop on Chalk Farm Road. We walked in and no one noticed Jack and Meg, it was, 'Richard Branson's walking in.' And in the back-room where we could all sit and eat, this guy who performed there regularly, Daniel Jeanrenaud, he goes into overdrive." This bequiffed, battered French rocker, then 41, had formed the Kingsnakes with three former Flamin' Groovies in San Francisco in the Eighties, reformed the band with the young Manu Chao in Paris, leant an approving Chuck Berry his guitar, and toured with BB King, Bo Diddley and Link Wray. Misadventures and excess found him in the midst of 11 years sleeping above the Marathon, and playing from midnight till four in its notorious back-room. "Marathon was the French Foreign Legion of rock'n'roll," Jeanrenaud recalled to *Vice*'s JS Rafaeli. "It's where guitar players go to lose their identity. I divided my time between freebasing and jamming with Jack White." At a moment when Jack was in love with London and still able to experience it with little hassle, it was a fortuitous night. He enjoyed an ambience akin to his grimier Detroit haunts enough to return on June 13, 2002 with Meg and Brendan Benson after the latter's Camden Monarch gig, borrowing Jeanrenaud's guitar to duet on "Sixties blues tracks", the Frenchman recalled. Finally on that first night, the party had to end. "Meg was so drunk she was practically face-down in the food," PJ says, "so we had to take her to the taxis and take her home. Fun times."

"Scenes don't mean anything to me," Jack had told Robin Bresnark, reporting for the *Metro-Times* on the summer UK tour's impact. "But we'd love to come back with the Detroit Cobras and the Von Bondies, and I'd be really glad if they did well over here." He was true to his word, making the Von Bondies (and of course his girlfriend Marcie Bolen) that winter's European support act. The Cobras toured a day ahead of them with Detroit's original two-piece, Bantam Rooster. Dave Kaplan ended up booking all these bands and the Electric Six and Dirtbombs, as well as kindred spirits Denmark's Raveonettes and London's Kills, allowing concerted effort. Both Jack and Andy Gershon, the new V2 president who had made the Stripes his first big signing following their UK success, meanwhile, claimed their peers were a key factor in the deal. "I've worked with so many bands and done so many 45s and things," Jack had mused to *Billboard*. "It'd be nice if all this stuff that I'm involved with would all go through one thing, and [we could] see how available we could make it to people." Gershon told the trade paper that Jack's prolific output as musician and producer made him an "amazing resource. There's nothing better than someone who recognizes . . . and gives back to the community that he came from." V2's contract gave them the option to distribute any act Jack released on Third Man Records. Labels and bands previously anointed by the then unknown Jack's hand also benefited. "Jack recorded half of the records or played on them," Italy Records' Dave Buick told VPRO of his 7-inch catalogue, "so those all sell now, too. It's amazing."

The superstition that there was something in Detroit's water now caused a shorter, smaller version of Seattle's gold rush, with *Sympathetic Sounds Of Detroit* as a guide to the territory. Rough Trade and Blanco Y Negro boss Geoff Travis, who had eagerly tracked the White Stripes across five US gigs in the months before the 100 Club, was a Detroit Cobras and Dirtbombs fan, too. When his Blanco Y Negro offer for the Stripes was still on the table, Bresnark asked if he would sign other Detroit bands if that bid failed. "Only if I loved them as much," he answered. "But I think there's a lot of A&R people over here thinking just that." Chrysalis Music A&R Polly Comber told Bresnark she'd definitely chase others on the scene, if she couldn't get the main prize. "There could be a lot of money spent in the next few years on Detroit bands. People will certainly be going over there." The Cobras' Rachel Nagy, though, always a loose cannon at the Gold Dollar, had given this pre-emptive, accurate warning to the *New York Press* in July. "This whole idea that there's going to be a Detroit explosion . . . it's gonna be a pop, a fizzle, and that's it. The well is not very deep." She also gave a clue to brewing jealousies. "I love Jack. People are always saying, 'Man, they aren't that good. They shouldn't be making it this big. It doesn't make any sense.' I can't think of a single person I would rather see it happen to."

The Dirtbombs, led by teenage Jack's hero Mick Collins, with his first album's co-producer Jim Diamond on bass and nephew Ben Blackwell as co-drummer, had their classic Detroit statement *Ultraglide In Black* praised in *NME* days before the White Stripes' UK debut. The album covered great soul tunes in garage-punk style, praised Ann Arbor radical and MC5 collaborator John Sinclair's White Panthers in the sleeve notes, and pictured Mount Rushmore with Motor City geniuses Smokey Robinson and Marvin Gaye replacing dead presidents. "We're essentially a dance band," Collins told *NME* in November, when they headlined sticky-floored London rock dive the Garage.

The Von Bondies, singled out by Jack's relationship with Bolen as well as *Lack Of Communication*'s intrinsic quality, were the prime beneficiaries. If a crowd or label wanted a Detroit double-shot, they were right there sharing the White Stripes' European stages, and even their tour bus (a particularly generous, cost-saving gesture by Jack). *NME*'s John Robinson dismissed them as "a pretty average garage-rock band" at the tour's Brighton start. They seemed dazed by the attention. "We never sell out in Detroit," Jason Stollsteimer told *NME*. "Detroit does not appreciate its artists . . . [but] this is a golden age for Detroit music right now. And we know how lucky we are to be a part of it." Returning in May 2002, they and the Dirtbombs supported the White Stripes at Shepherd's Bush Empire for a Q-sponsored televised show. Simon Keeler, still distributing these bands at Cargo though the White Stripes were lost to XL, relished the collateral victories Jack's patronage allowed. "Seeing Mick Collins sing 'Ode To A Black Man' on the telly," he smiles, "I thought, 'I've done this now.'"

Bolen had been at *Top Of The Pops* with Jack for 'Fell In Love With A Girl', also eager to meet McCartney. Stollsteimer felt slighted, arguing her place was at the soundcheck for the Von Bondies' first Peel session that night. Jack was in turn enraged by what he saw as Stollsteimer's verbal spitefulness to Bolen. The band's manager Alex Hannaford told *Kerrang!*'s Stevie Chick that Jack asked him to "keep an eye" on their singer. "Those shows were incredibly important," bassist Carrie Smith would concede to *Spin*'s Chris Handyside of their Jack-sponsored European tour. "We got so much exposure and press." But, she added, they then tried to escape their role as "just a baby band of the Stripes". Such hairline cracks in unity would spread.

It also became increasingly apparent that while the White Stripes could hardly have existed without their city and scene, Jack in particular was an anomaly there. He knew it, but didn't want to face the implications. Interviewing Iggy Pop for *Mojo*, he asked the older man if, when starting out, he ever felt "things were getting in the way, like the attitude of everyone was becoming lackadaisical, or there was too much partying going on and you'd much rather get back to writing." Iggy averred that he had adopted an if-you-can't-beat-'em-join-'em approach. Jack just kept adjacent to the carnage. "Jack hung out in the bowling alley, mostly," the Majestic's owner Dave Zainea says of his many nights among his friends there at the Garden Bowl. "He wasn't a big drinker. He wasn't a partier at all. That's why you could see he was driven – this guy's going to make it. That was Jack's path, he recognised that he was good, and honed his career and craft, and God bless him. I'm glad he's doing well, man."

Matt Smith doesn't believe being the only sober man at the bar cut Jack off from his peers. "Jack was very social with a lot of people, he had a lot of friends, and they were all very supportive of the White Stripes, too. He had a lot of support from his friends through the whole thing." A hilarious video shot in 2001 for 'You Got Me Down' by one of *Sympathetic Sounds Of Detroit*'s most obscure bands, the Buzzards, shows how joyous that scene could be. Singer Joe Burdick's attitude as he stumbles, John

Belushi–like, through a fantasy city resembling a giant dive–bar frequented by feminist go–go dancers, is made communal when a dozen friends on a sofa bounce and sway to the song. Ben Blackwell is there, and Meg, drink in hand and having a ball. Jack, clinging to a cigarette, starts slightly, self-consciously apart, but finally lets himself go, a sloppy smirk spreading across his face. He had been all but friendless before the Gold Dollar's denizens took him in. He didn't want to let them go.

But his doubts were growing. "Detroit has a history of blowing it," he'd told *NME*'s John Mulvey before the second UK trip. "I don't think they would shun success or anything, but they won't do what they have to do to get to that position." A year later, he complained to *Mojo* that bands he knew had enough "interest and creativity" to make fine records, but something "just stops them". "They're almost intentionally doing it to themselves," he said, blaming a "record collector mentality" that flinched at loss of cool if "more than a hundred people are into you". He was blunter to Barney Hoskyns, after the contradictions of his place in the scene had forced him from it: "The problem that I started to not like was that a lot of them were aspiring to idols that they thought were purposely not succeeding."

Matt Smith perceived similar conservatism when he was producing Jack in the Go. "After we'd record, they would hang out at the bar with all these guys from other garage-rock bands, and they were getting a lot of negativity from the scene about things we were doing that were quite outside a garage, soul aesthetic. There was pressure to conform coming from the scene, which ultimately caused real problems for them." Was the Go's apparent breakout from a tight-knit scene when they signed to Sub Pop, multiplied a hundredfold in the White Stripes' case, resented? "There's that. And there's also this Detroit thing. Detroit has a really weird relationship with musicians. It's not a nurturing place for them. You become a musician here because you've dropped out of society." The propulsion immortalised in the Animals' 'We've Gotta Get Out Of This Place', the rocket-fuel need for more, which Jack burned with even as he tried not to leave, is often replaced in his city, Smith believes, by stasis and falling back. "Speaking as someone who's stayed, I think it's normal for someone in a rock band to say, 'I wanna get *out* of here' – to want to get out of something. And I think a lot of bands in Detroit don't become as successful because they don't have that desire. There's a pressure holding them back. They don't want to fit into society, but they don't want to get too far out there, they pull back a bit, and have some bit of normality in their lives, and glamorise their idea of what it's like to be normal. I mean, Iggy Pop wanted to get out of this place. But when I was coming up playing music, I ran into guys from the Stooges and the MC5 who'd stuck around. I don't know if that turned out to be a good thing for Rob Tyner or Fred Smith [the MC5 founders died in the city]."

"I don't think people were intentionally trying to not be successful," argues the Hentchmen's Tim Purrier. "In reality, being successful is pretty hard. But there's definitely that underdog thing, and we're a fine example. We loved all these bands that no one had heard of, and we end up being a band that most people haven't heard of."

"I think Jack was a lot more ambitious than a lot of people," the Gories' Dan Kroha considers. "But I don't think anybody was purposely not succeeding. I think people just like to party. They just like to party their fucking asses off, you know. And they did, too, man. And, I don't know. I remember Johnny Hentch saying Jack, that's all he talked about was music. That's all. That's it. That's all he cared about."

So he was driven in a different way to those around him?

"Yeah."

"I think if you're putting up with all the bullshit of being in an original band, you have hopes of succeeding," Dave Feeny says, considering Jack's suspicions. "But having worked with Jack and having Kid Rock at my Tempermill studio, there's a completely different level of focus and drive that 99 per cent of bands just don't have."

Looking at Jack in that Dutch documentary in November 2001, when he's still almost unknown in the US but already doing better than his friends, he looks bashful and boyish, a kid trying to do the right thing. And he did, honouring the ethics he perceived in the musical community that raised him. Maybe he overestimated that scene's nobility, and maybe he was fooling himself about his own. But his actions, as Brendan Benson, Blanche, Whirlwind Heat, the Soledad Brothers, the Clone Defects, the Hentchmen and the Go joined high-profile White Stripes tours over the next year, were rare. The Beatles didn't reach back to Liverpool for Gerry & the Pacemakers.

There was something, though, that his idealism tried to suppress, which leaked out in those disappointed comments about Detroit. He had felt at the back of a line of siblings at home, been bullied in high school and doubted what was inside his head would ever truly be understood or accepted. And yet, as he'd shown when asked to compromise in the Go or negotiate with major labels, when he gambled his future on a band that at first seemed absurd, played the blues in Mexicantown or painted his house there in that band's bright colours like a target, he couldn't be told he was wrong. He had the inner nerves and sweetness of a picked-on kid, and the bullying confidence of champion athletes and war-winning generals. This was the endless battle he told Jim Jarmusch he fought with "what's good and bad about ego". Catholic-raised Jack may have thought of Jacob wrestling in the dark with God. Christ's moral grappling on the mountain with Satan certainly occupied his thoughts later. There was an almost monstrous creative energy in him. For now, he kept it in check, dutifully sharing it with a community of 50 or so lesser musicians who were his friends, though some of their values now chafed like chains.

Interviewed for *NME*'s Christmas issue, Jack loyally declared *Lack Of Communication* his album of the year. "Von Bondies are the best rock'n'roll band in Detroit, no doubt. I love 'em." The Greenhornes and the Detroit Cobras' *Life, Love And Leaving* – Rachel Nagy being his city's "best singer" – got mentions, too. Meg chipped in with her hangover cure for the festive season, recommending repeated doses of sleep, water and aspirins. "And then when you're finally all right," she advised in languid Blanche DuBois mode, "you can get up. About three, usually." Jack reflected on the year that had transformed their lives with deliberate, protective modesty for John Mulvey. He'd licensed the White Stripes' albums instead of signing for a weighty advance to deflect "any pressure on us", he said, instead "keeping it safe".

His efforts in the four years leading to this point had been cautious but concerted, doing just enough. They perhaps reflected the insular, low self-esteem of the place he was from. He had contacted Dave Kaplan so the White Stripes could tour the US more solidly, and touted his band to indie labels, settling on Sympathy because they allowed him control. Then he let others enable his ambitions. John Baker had to not only concoct their first foreign tour, but personally send plane tickets at great expense before Jack would go. Russell Warby proposed the UK tour that changed everything. John Peel, Simon Keeler and the journalists and record-shop owners who provided the conditions for that tour to succeed weren't pushed by Jack. The White Stripes' work made them yearn to transmit its excitement, volunteering vital, extra responsibilities. Jack's minimal interviews, with telling photos, fanned the flames without burning them out. There was a passive mastery to his actions. He trusted his success so long as it was tied to his music, which he knew was honest. That wasn't bad ego.

"We're sure to disappoint with the next album," he anyway concluded

Jack White in 1998, the year the White Stripes recorded their first 7-inch single. He kept a copy in his bathroom, barely believing it was real. REX/SHUTTERSTOCK

Jack (left) in Goober & the Peas. His first professional band, joined when he was 19 and his surname was still Gillis, taught him that country music could be "beautiful".

Jack with the Hentchmen in 1998, when upholstery and four bands occupied his time.

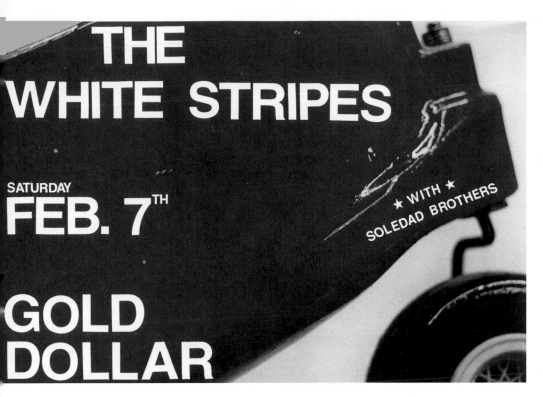

THE
WHITE STRIPES

SATURDAY
FEB. 7TH

★ WITH ★
SOLEDAD BROTHERS

GOLD
DOLLAR

flyer for the White Stripes' first Detroit headline gig. The Gold Dollar club was their second home in the Nineties.

Dan Miller and Jack take turns fronting country rock band Two-Star Tabernacle's last gig, at Paycheck's, Hamtramck
n March 12, 1999.

Orson Welles in *Citizen Kane*, which he directed, starred in and co-wrote aged 24. Jack kept similar control of his music, and shared his favourite director's talent for showmanship and sleight of hand. ARCHIVE PHOTOS/GETTY IMAGES

The great Mississippi bluesman Son House, who died in Detroit in 1988. Five years later, Jack heard House's song 'Grinnin' In Your Face', and felt his life "released". APIC/GETTY IMAGES

The Flat Duo Jets. Dexter Romweber's guitar-drums duo were another key early influence. "I had to reassess what backwards meant," Jack said, recalling their raw rebooting of Fifties rock 'n' roll. STEVE EICHNER/WIREIMAGE

The Gories. Prophets without honour in Eighties Detroit, these ragged pioneers of its garage-rock revival were idolised by Jack.

The White Stripes play Paycheck's on March 13, 1999. Meg had just narrowly decided to continue with the band, after separating from husband Jack.

At London's Forum in December 2001: the Stripes reap the rewards of that summer's triumphant UK tour. BRIAN RASIC/GETTY IMAGES

Black, white and red all over: the White Stripes' colour-coded style made them memorably photogenic.
TIM RONEY/GETTY IMAGES

Jack and Meg begin to accept their growing stardom, at 2002's MTV Video Music Awards. KEVIN KANE/WIREIMAGE

"I can stick it in from here..." One of Jack's biggest heroes, Iggy Pop, is all over him in 2003. MICK HUTSON/REDFERNS

Jack at John Peel's funeral, at St Edmundsbury Cathedral, Bury St Edmunds on November 12, 2004. The DJ was a constant supporter and friend. REX/SHUTTERSTOCK

Jack and Loretta Lynn share one of two Grammys in 2005 for *Van Lear Rose*, the comeback album he produced for the country great when she was 68. ROBYN BECK/AFP/GETTY IMAGES

The Pyramid Stage, Glastonbury, 2005. The White Stripes' headline set was a thrillingly improvised peak for them.
BRIAN RASIC/GETTY IMAGES

to Mulvey. "It's not gonna be accepted like this one is, I know it. It doesn't matter what we do. Oh well."

For three solid months at 2002's start, the White Stripes pressed home their impact abroad. From January 11 to February 3, they built their Australasian return around the continent's touring Big Day Out festival. Headliners the Prodigy, New Order, Garbage and Basement Jaxx confirmed rock's mainstream eclipse. Auckland's Radio bFM continued to push the White Stripes, but when the festival reached the city's Ericsson Stadium they were a side-stage attraction, while System Of A Down played nu-metal to the main stage moshpit as grey rain fell. Recognised as festival highlights, Jack and Meg's profile anyway rose. On January 29 or 30, soundchecking before a gig at Melbourne's Corner Hotel, Jack secured a more important prize, as he stumbled on an ominous, seven-note riff. "I thought, 'Oh, this is really cool,'" he recalled in *It Might Get Loud*. Ben Swank, brought along for the tour ride, dismissed it as "all right". Undeterred by the first review of 'Seven Nation Army''s core element, Jack dug in his heels. "You think, 'God, there's something to this. I'm gonna get there.' You've gotta have some imagination. So I kept at it." Still, he briefly put the riff aside, thinking he could save it for "a James Bond theme, or some spy movie."

White Blood Cells' second single, 'Fell In Love With A Girl', would prove equally vital. Released in the UK on February 25 where it reached number 21, Jack preceded a month's touring of France, Germany and Scandinavia with a return to *Top Of The Pops* on February 21. A song under two minutes long became a means to explore other music in the minute of pop time remaining, and consider its subject more fully. Taking the mic and stepping towards the crowd in the unpredictable preacher mode seen at early Gold Dollar gigs, with only Meg's martial beat behind him, he ruptured the show's rigid format. "People say when you're in love, don't talk with the person you're with," he begins. "I say forget it. I say stick with it. And don't mind what other people say. Right? Right . . ." With the camera close on his wide-eyed, wild-haired face, he slips into Cole Porter's 1928 sex song 'Let's Do It, Let's Fall In Love' (with a line surreally amended to "even educated trees do it"), merged with Charley Patton's 1929 'Shake It And Break It (But Don't Let It Fall Mama)'. Meg's tongue slips over her lip in pleasure at her idiot ex's chutzpah. Then they slam back into the single, Jack jolting back from the final chord. He'd wanted Billy Childish to paint onstage too, in an honourable acknowledgement of England's garage-rock scene. The producer baulked, so Jack wrote Childish's name on his arm instead. "Jack wanted to do a duet with Billy at some point," Bruce Brand recalls. "And Jack being Jack, he wanted it to be one of his songs, and Billy being Billy, he wanted it to be one of his. So obviously that didn't happen. Neither are sidemen, or team players."

'Fell In Love With A Girl''s video showed the first real benefit of major label backing. Jack had asked for the director of Beck's 'Devil's Haircut' video, but by happy accident got the Frenchman behind Beck's 'Deadweight', Michel Gondry, whose penchant for dreamy, emotional fantasy would peak with *Eternal Sunshine Of The Spotless Mind* (2004). "There's something charming and naive about their use of black, red and white imagery," Gondry told MTV.com's Gil Kaufman. "I made a parallel between that and the basicness of the colour of Lego blocks." Gondry dramatised his intentions by bringing a Lego sculpture of Jack's head to dinner with the White Stripes. "You couldn't argue with that," Jack conceded. Gondry, an inventor's grandson whose childhood Lego obsession had led him to build a zoetrope cartoon viewer from it, was a kindred spirit. First filming Jack and Meg in heavily contrasting red and black makeup in the streets of London and against a blue screen, 25 pixellated images per second of screen time were printed, each then built as Lego models and filmed by 15 animators. Digital pixellation served handmade art in a process that took over six weeks. "I wanted it to feel like a children's programme," Gondry explained, "which is why I didn't make it too slick." Adding yellow cymbals and guitar straps and blue sky to the White Stripes' core colours, the director had found a perfect metaphor for the band's innocent qualities. Lego Jack and Meg run up and down steps as if in a kids' adventure show, the jerky shift from one built image to the next maintaining brightly coloured motion at the song's pell-mell pace. With actual pixellated footage briefly slipped into the animation, there's a hint of sensual reality to the red-lipped White Stripes. Lego Meg's drumming meanwhile captures Jack's childish ideal of her role, with her featureless, ponytailed face, and stickless white hands flailing at toy cymbals.

MTV soon had this suitably original, carefully naive shortcut to the band's world on heavy rotation. Jack discovered its impact back among the Gillises. "I have like 20 nieces and nephews," he told *Nashville Scene*'s D. Patrick Rodgers. "I remember being at my brother's house and my nieces and nephews were watching this video on MTV and loving it and saying, 'Play it again! We want to see it again!'" The more usual Gillis reaction to his latest 45 was, he recalled, "'Oh, that's nice. Whatever.'" His school friend and teenage bandmate Dominic Suchyta also saw it. "The first tune Jack and I had ever learned to play was 'Can't Explain' by the Who," he recalled to *Detroit Free Press*. "It was weird when I saw the White Stripes on MTV . . . it was really familiar. It was Jack."

The video finally gave the band American success more than a year after *White Blood Cells'* release, as the single also picked up substantial radio play from April into June. Jack reacted suspiciously to hearing one of his songs on mainstream US stations. "I just laughed," he told *Rolling Stone*'s Neil Strauss. "It would be Staind, P.O.D., then us and then Incubus. Half of your brain is going, 'What is going on? This is pointless.'" The other half hoped for real change, as the success of the Stripes, Strokes and Hives helped return 'realism' to music. No sense of personal triumph was permitted. He distrusted this victory too much to embrace it, due in part to disbelief. "It didn't make sense to even me or Meg when the White Stripes broke into the mainstream," he recalled to *Nashville Scene*. "We had already done three albums, and we had already made up our mind that obviously we're doing some very strange thing that has its own tiny little world of 100 people in every town that might be interested in it." Their Fayetteville crowd on 9/11 confirms that figure.

Proof of the band's rising American status came on their return from Europe. They had first been scheduled to play on *The Late Show With David Letterman* in October 2001, in the wake of their UK breakthrough, then been bumped from bookings an insulting nine times. They finally took the stage on March 18 at New York's Ed Sullivan Theater, where the Beatles had transfixed America in 1964. Jack got Letterman to hold up *White Blood Cells'* vinyl LP with surreal difficulty, six months after anthrax-poisoned letters were posted to media outlets in 9/11's paranoid wake. "It had to be checked for anthrax before he held it," Jack explained. Satisfied their album wasn't a terrorist device, Letterman introduced "a wonderful rock'n'roll band from the great city of Detroit". The zebra head was joined onstage by the Peppermint Triple Tremelo, an invention of mysterious purpose first seen in *De Stijl*'s inner sleeve, which explained that it was a red cabinet "designed and constructed by Jack White with electrical wiring by Johnny Walker", containing three varieties of Leslie revolving speakers, with the band's peppermint symbol set on one speaker to spin "at both slow and fast speeds". It spins behind Jack as he sings 'Fell In Love With A Girl' with extra bratty, breathless intensity, head maniacally bobbing as Paul McCartney's once did here. Meg swings her body to the beat, tongue absently over her lip again with millions watching. Then Jack moves to the mic-stand facing her and sings 'Little Room' in an echoing, lift-shaft voice. Standing in CBS TV's big room, the song's sadness at success' inevitable, distancing course has found its moment. Jack finishes by mock didactically wagging his finger at the main song's harsh lesson of love, then yanks his guitar to a dead stop. On network TV in 2002, realism's the right word.

Brendan Benson was the regular support act for another swing through the eastern USA in March and early April. Beaten up by the music business out in LA, Benson had been contemplating life as a painter back in Detroit when Jack steadied his nerve. "I walked into this tiny bar without knowing who was playing," Benson recalled to *NME*. "I was having trouble writing, being too self-conscious, and seeing Jack, who is just so straight from the heart, was a revelation." His 2002 album *Lapalco* was like nothing else being made in Detroit, including McCartneyesque sonic filigrees for their own sake in breezy yet crafted, Seventies-style pop. His persona in songs such as 'My Life In The D' (D meaning Detroit, where that life was 'a tragicomedy') was as a mild-mannered, literate loser in love. Hints at deeper discomfort in his own skin were dropped amidst the creamy harmonies of 'Metarie' when he declared, 'I'd like to move out of this place/ To change my name, maybe get a new face.' Jack knew the feeling, and their relationship, though at first reverential on Benson's side, would prove significant.

George Roca and Nichol Lovett's documentary *Nobody Knows How To Talk To Children* caught the White Stripes' four-night stand from June 5 to 8 at their favoured New York venue, the Bowery Ballroom, as the city's celebrities anointed their stardom. Bette Midler danced in the balcony, and Macauley Culkin and Drew Barrymore joined the Strokes' backstage partying. Sheryl Crow was there – "Bob Dylan's ex-girlfriend" to Jack – and Cameron Diaz asked to be. "If Kirsten Dunst comes to the show I'm gonna retire," Jack sighs in the film. The watchful crowds and stock-still celebrities there to be seen, not thrill as Jack plays his guitar with his teeth like Charley Patton during a 10-minute 'Stop Breaking Down', are an otherwise resented new audience. "They're being fucking lame, don't you think?" Jack snaps backstage, as the crowd cheer for more. "How do we get the tickets to the kids with all the records?" A barrier is rising in his mind between old friends and fans, and most others fame brings his way. Backstage vignettes of boredom and subtle revelation are caught: Jack and Brendan Benson singing Benson's 'Folk Singer' and Queen's 'Crazy Little

Thing Called Love'; Jack carefully reading his reviews, lying arms crossed like Nosferatu as Whirlwind Heat's support set bleeds through the walls, and seeing *White Blood Cells* in a shop window. Back at the hotel, John Baker faces down a drunk threatening violence in the lobby, and Jack dozes in a corridor, locked out of his room, while others watch porn on TV. Dave Kaplan's expedition to a 'Brooklyn-style' pizza joint after a show bruisingly backfires. The sound of sneering laughter from black locals in nearby booths burns Jack, a pale-faced rock star as alien here as he was in Mexicantown, his old bullied humiliations returning. He stands up angrily and leaves. His attempt to be normal in New York has failed. This is *vérité* Jack, losing his temper, joking in daft accents, swearing (as he wouldn't in interviews), sharp-witted and sharp-edged, being friendly yet ruling the mood of a group where he's the most important person, his persona's artful masks nearly stripped, his image for once uncontrolled.

The Meg the film captures is even more startling. Her shy, murmuring public face is replaced by the drunkenly chatty, funny, flirty woman her close Detroit friends love. She's delighted at the guard who's swept the stage so her hippieish bare feet won't step on cigarettes, and berates her drumming performance, caring about it more than Jack ever thought. "I was not in the zone tonight," she says miserably. "I was playing horrible." She's remarkably soft and intimate with Jack, swapping urgent whispers in ears as she clutches his arm and insists: "I am not drunk." "One guy said I'm really Meg's husband and brother," Jack said earlier, and that's how they look. Seeing the camera, she winks. "We're having a secret confidence," she explains. "It's something that you don't want to know about. Because it would be too weird and scandalous for you to know about. You're trying to steal his soul, I know." She enjoys the booze-buzzed backstage whirl, where the Strokes' Julian Casablancas gives her many goodbye kisses, and makes long phone calls in a hotel room filled with people. She is unfazed by but alert to her new situation, complaining, "There is no integrity involved in this whole experience." Eyeing the directors, she states: "I have visions of Dylan's *Don't Look Back*, and I realise how completely uncool we are. We're not Dylan. We can't do it."

Rather than D.A. Pennebaker's beautiful record of Dylan's abrasively brilliant 1965 UK tour, this is more like *Cocksucker Blues*, the uncomfortably revealing 1972 Rolling Stones documentary barred from release by its subjects, which Jack had watched on bootleg at 1203 Ferdinand. He had allowed *Nobody Knows How To Talk To Children* so long as Third Man retained its rights, its makers wore white lab coats as they filmed and they didn't interfere with the musicians. Amateurish, barely audible sound and fuzzy footage made Jack force it into bootleg purgatory after one, unsanctioned screening at 2004's Dallas Film Festival. There were plenty more reasons to keep its raw revelations quiet.

On April 14, the White Stripes, nearly home, played East Lansing's Union Ballroom. Their new, big audience in the college town greeted them with a moshpit, stage diving and moments of violence. Jack left his guitar feedbacking onstage. The next day, they were sitting in Hamtramck's Norwalk Bar, talking to a journalist. Wearing a black suit and bowler hat though it was 80 degrees outside, Jack vainly searched on the jukebox for Don Ho's 'Tiny Bubbles', a 1966 Hawaiian lounge tune with a hypnotic snare beat he used to enjoy with Meg, after his upholstery shifts nearby. "Did ya just come from a wedding?" asked the barman. Soon, they had gone again.

10

Elephant

BETWEEN April 24 and May 13, the White Stripes returned to Toe-Rag Studios, and recorded *Elephant*. "They were staying opposite here at the Holiday Inn again," Bruce Brand remembers as we sit in his King's Cross flat. "I'd drive them to the studio to save them the 15 quid each way in taxi fares. They might have taken a taxi back." Toe-Rag's owner-producer Liam Watson, whose band the Masonics had been bottom of the White Stripes' 100 Club bill, charged his usual rate of £30 an hour, for a total cost of less than £4,000. Entered from a concrete alley in Glyn Road, Homerton, in London's then pre-gentrified East End, the warped yellow-and-black lino squares of Toe-Rag's tiny studio floor and white tiled, sound-proofed walls, also bent in places, were an effective, cramped recording space. Perhaps more important was the control room, with its REDD 17 valve mixing desk from Abbey Road, and Studer 8-track tape ("the Rolls-Royce of tape machines", Watson believed).

Watson started salvaging vintage gear after major studios converted to digital in the Eighties, and junked their analogue history. Beginning at Toe-Rag's original location in Shoreditch between 1991 and 1998, his collection included Decca Records equipment used on Sixties Stones sessions. Seventies porn magazines and framed pictures from skips added to Toe-Rag's ambience. The studio was an extension of Watson's enthusiasms as a musician, and promoter of the Frat Shack garage-rock nights in the Rails bar near Euston Station in the early Nineties, a minor parallel to Detroit's simultaneous scene. Joe Meek and George Martin were his British producing ideals, and he sometimes wore a white lab coat like Abbey Road's early Sixties engineers, who dressed like lofty, austere scientists ready to experiment on rock band specimens. Though mild-mannered and wired on nothing stronger than tea, Watson's efficient pursuit of old values of excellence made him a kindred spirit to Jack. "You're looking for performances," he told *Sound On Sound*'s Daniel James. "You know when the feel's right . . . I'll take as long as is needed, and no longer." It was 'hands-on' in comparison to digital processes, a matter of physically aligned tape, and mic placement to find the right sound in a room: "You don't need to fuck around on a mixing desk in order to make it sound good." A regular early user of Toe-Rag, Max Decharme, remembered Watson's mantra to *Mojo*: "Have a good time, lads, but don't go too far."

Watson assessed his job to *Sound On Sound*. "I totally consider myself a producer . . . I wouldn't engineer for somebody – there's no way I would be an engineer . . . When I make a record with somebody, it will usually end up sounding a certain way, because of the things I do. And if that isn't record production, I don't know what is. No one tells me what to do, but I will ask them what they want." He was speaking after *Elephant*'s release, when its inner sleeve credited him with engineering, recording and co-mixing, and Jack as producer. Watson didn't dispute this, but his words suggest a similar grey area to Stuart Sikes' memory of Jack not advising him on *White Blood Cells*' sound. Since Jack's grudging acknowledgement of Jim Diamond as *The White Stripes*' co-producer, when he provided an identifiable sound at Ghetto much as Toe-Rag did, Jack's need for ultimate control meant no one else's contribution could ever count as producing. "I should think because we never had to talk about anything they were completely compatible with the way I do things," Watson said, explaining their roles to *Hot Press*' Peter Murphy.

"No computers were used during the writing, recording, mixing or mastering of this record," *Elephant*'s sleeve also sternly declared, and Jack typically told *Sonic* that "digital recording devices are the devil's handiwork. They hollow out the talent of people and make them sound like mumbling robots." Toe-Rag's proximity to reporters in London, still more fascinated by the White Stripes than Americans, made it the story on the album's release. But its analogue arsenal was only a variation on the White Stripes' previous work at Ghetto and Easley-McCain. The idea that Toe-Rag was eccentrically frozen in 1963 was also a regularly repeated exaggeration. "Rubbish," Watson retorted in *Candy Coloured Blues*. "I did a bit of a custom job [on *Elephant*]. But this desk is from 1981 or something," he noted, glancing around his studio. Digital recording was available there, the Studer on which *Elephant* was taped was from the early Seventies, and the rare RC quarter-inch reel-to-reel on which it was mixed, though using mid-Sixties electronics, was from 1979. The studio's atmosphere and restrictions were more important to Jack than carbon-dating its gear. "Toe-Rag is the absolute opposite of paradise," he approvingly told *Sonic*. "It is cramped, almost claustrophobically small, and it is uncomfortable, it is cold and it is damp." The barely working "wicked little radiator, which stands in the corner and glows threateningly" added to its appeal. Though a step down from Easley-McCain's half-used, 24-track professionalism, Jack also viewed *Elephant* as a period of release, after *White Blood Cells'* austere rules on what the White Stripes could play. "This time our limitations were we're going to another country, we want to finish it in 10 days, and we're going to work only on an 8-track," he told *NME*'s James Oldham. They'd "relaxed a little bit", he believed. *White Blood Cells* took three days, after all.

"This album is dedicated to, and is for, and about the death of the sweetheart," Jack wrote in his latest poetic liner notes. In *The White Stripes* he'd pondered his loneliness and longing for childhood, dedicating it to Son House. *De Stijl* was dedicated to an aesthetic ideal, and *White Blood Cells* to Loretta Lynn, its prose-poem leaving its makers on fame's daunting edge. Jack made *Elephant* about a social vision. In forcefully impassioned language, he mourned "the sweetheart's loss in a disgusting world" of bad manners, easy laughs, selfishness, debauchery and exploitation. "You're having fun, right?" he asked bitterly. "Break the rules, rebel, break them hard, help yourself." The notes' last paragraph sought solace in nostalgic dreams, sinking into sense-memories and imaginings where courtesy, honesty and comfort thrived in quiet Detroit streets, whose clotheslines, heating vents and attics sat among small natural wonders. It sounded like a fantasy of an America Jack never knew and that never was, the Eisenhower suburban dream that rock'n'roll helped awaken, not the broken Detroit of his youth. It hinted at Orson Welles' second masterpiece, *The Magnificent Ambersons* (1942), an aching elegy for a Midwest family's golden early 20th century, whose darker last reel was cut and lost. Jack's words were also a warmly sensual version of Dylan's 1993 *World Gone Wrong* liner notes, which set the modern "egotistical degraded existentialist Dionysian idiot" against "America when Mother was the queen of Her heart". The most reliable affection in Jack's tribute to sweethearts came from "motherly intervention". Ringing your parents was more important here than staying out late, and when his world crashed soon afterwards, he'd name his mother as his only rock. Romance was another realm of struggle and work, the one he found most difficult and troubling. "What is the correct way to act?" he wondered. "What is your mind telling you? What's your body telling you to do?" In a TV interview with his friend Conan O'Brien a decade later, he was still pondering what was "biological" between men and women, and the thoughts and actions that divided them. No wonder he found it hard to be a gentleman.

Jack's initial intention had been to emphasise his music's quieter, sensitive side. A couple of days into recording, he instead restated the White Stripes' roots in blues, after banning the sound from *White Blood Cells*. 'Ball And Biscuit', the descriptive nickname for the flat disc top and sphere of the STC 4021 mic designed for BBC Radio in the Thirties (Toe-Rag had one, of course) became the title of their mightiest blues statement yet. Written in the studio, its lyrics were sultry, drawling boasts and come-ons that Jack assured *Mojo* he'd never say in real life: "My whole vision of the song was a girl passing me by and me thinking these things." It sounded convincing enough to make obsolete his 2001 assurance to John Mulvey that he didn't write about sex. As with 'It's True That We Love One Another', he also added his mythology to that of the blues, declaring himself both third man and seventh son.

More to the point, Jack spoke about the song to *Sonic* as if he'd been ambushed, even possessed, by his guitar. "All was peaceful and calm when, suddenly, it was as if the Devil got into me and I could not hear anything except guitars. Fat, dirty, ear-destroying guitar sounds." His instrument roared off the leash and spoke for him in wordless statements standing in for choruses, redoubling in stormy power after each verse. This was extreme 20th century music, electricity's early magical potency invoked as high guitar lines pranced and taunted like gremlins on a telegraph wire, and pushed into still thinner-aired, squealing extremes. Deeper tones were tossed down like depth charges. Chords rattled and cracked into feedback. The slow, hitching verses were footnotes to Jack's intentions. "Just stick around," he muttered as its seven minutes wound down, "you'll figure it out." Beneath the guitars, it was the most basic blues tune. This was why hearing him had reminded John Peel of Hendrix. Watson responded to the hard, bulleting crunch of Meg's downbeat by "playing around with compressors and making it sound stupid", he described in *Candy Coloured Blues*, playing the result at huge volume to the band's gleeful approval. Soloing on such a scale broke previous, hair-shirt constraints. "It was a little present to myself," Jack told *Total Guitar*. "I let myself go." He'd been missing his difficult months as the Go's lead guitarist, when soloing was his sole responsibility. "I was just thinking about those days, I guess."

Then there was the guitar sound the whole world got to hear. "After driving them to the studio, I'd hang around for an hour, make a cup of tea, and hear snippets," Bruce Brand remembers. "I heard them recording

'Seven Nation Army'. I thought, 'Wow, that sounds good! Cor, it's like John Barry.' It had a really weird sound to it, which isn't present on the record. It still sounds good, but it doesn't sound half as spooky as it did live in the studio. I thought, 'Cor, I can't wait to hear that.'" John Barry's wordless theme for *On Her Majesty's Secret Service*, with its pulse of bass and synth ominously stalking beneath dark, doomy brass, is his most satisfying Bond work. 'Seven Nation Army''s repeated, threatening riff is its kissing cousin. Its seven notes are played on Jack's Kay Hollowbody guitar through the DigiTech Whammy pedal's low-octave setting. That makes this bassless band's defining moment sound like the instrument their brief bassist, Steve Nawara, believes Jack always missed.

The riff repeats twice in 'Seven Nation Army''s opening seconds, then Meg joins in as if flatly hammering at the door, sounding very close. It's an alienated, barren backdrop in which Jack wearily murmurs before becoming sarcastic, then defiant, as his rage reaches boiling point. The lyrics, written during recording, find him preparing to retaliate against conspirators he feels closing in. You can picture him in the corner of a Detroit bar among laughing hangers-on and distrusted friends, as his mind races behind watching, warning eyes. He can't sleep, obsessing over his worries aloud, smoking nervously. Then the singing stops and, like a barstool tumbling over as the fighting starts, the riff becomes higher and aggressively full, thrusting his tormentors away.

"I've always tried to stay away from [songs about anger]," he told Jim Jarmusch in *Interview*, "but it came out a couple of times on this record. 'Seven Nation Army' is about this character who is involved in the realm of gossip with his friends and family and is so enraged by it that he wants to leave town." He confirmed to *Mojo* that "the song's about gossip. It's about me, Meg and the people we're dating." The second verse describes the chatter making his business known to all, and gives fair warning what'll happen if word gets back to him. The riff serving as tune and chorus is more fully violent the second time, layered over its 'bass' line and lashing out, then expanding and evaporating into feedback. The second verse ends with Jack feeling homeless, the third finds him in 'Wichita/ Far from this opera for ever more', sweating at honest toil, blood steaming off him as he burns his mind blank, before accepting he must return home. After the riff's brief, brutal reprise, 'Seven Nation Army' shudders to a halt, exhausted.

Elephant otherwise comprises a startling variety of songs of often anti-romance. 'There's No Home For You Here' is a kiss-off of

Dylanesque viciousness, as Jack ponders how to throw out a girlfriend he's grown to loathe so badly he can only view her at breakfast through the kitchen mirror. The news she's outstayed her welcome is relayed in hypnotic murmurs, precisely articulated verses, rapped out rage, and a chorus of manic multiple Jacks screaming the title in her ear. This extreme choral terror was achieved by layering his voice at various points across its wide spectrum during 15 takes, Watson recalled, naming "the one with the Queen harmonies" his favourite to *NME*. Jack had wanted to see how far an 8-track recorder could be pushed, deciding on reflection they'd gone "too far", almost breaking the box in which the White Stripes worked.

After Jack took the woman's part on 'I Just Don't Know What To Do With Myself', Meg, who'd recently been singing 'Rated X' live, took her first lead vocal on the swampy Southern Gothic of 'In The Cold, Cold Night', which Jack wrote with her in mind. Over impish acoustic guitar skips, cymbal tishes and a low organ hum, Meg, starting to feel 'like a full-grown woman', invites her lover to creep back across her cabin floor and provide 'the fuel to make my fire bright'. In this sex song, desire's flames flicker and culmination is coolly suspended, and Meg's slightly flawed, slightly husky voice feels just right. Her love of songs like this lets her sing them, and her stepping to the front makes the White Stripes more of a band. Jack had a mix of Mazzy Star and Peggy Lee in mind (the erotic shiver of the latter's 'Fever' is surely present). When he played it to Meg in the attic where their group began, she laughed happily. This contrasted with her itch to punch him for 'Girl, You Have No Faith In Medicine''s intemperate, near-misogynist rant.

Jack mostly explores male pathologies. 'I Want To Be The Boy To Break Your Mother's Heart' is mid-Sixties pop built from piano and slide, as he anachronistically pines for his girlfriend's mother's approving love. Oedipal at one remove, it pales next to 'You've Got Her In Your Pocket'. Jack's acoustic guitar and voice are at their most gorgeously McCartneyesque here, the sense of yearning great. The singer's secret need to possess the object of his affection in the manner of John Fowles' *The Collector* (in which a girl is imprisoned like a pinned butterfly) is offset by its impossibility, the music making us sympathise as the girl slips through his despairing clutches. A song about a sad, needy boy that suggests something nastier, Jack said it was Meg's favourite. 'The Hardest Button To Button', meanwhile, is an *Eraserhead*-style domestic dystopia, with Jack as a hillbilly outsider silencing his new baby's earthquake roar by voodoo methods. 'Seven

Nation Army''s threatening 'bass' pulse, here resembling an Eighties synth, sits under grunge guitar in an arrangement of simple density, spacious yet claustrophobic. 'I had opinions/ That didn't matter,' Jack sings through a mic giving distancing, radio-wave distortion. It was about "the odd man out in the family", which he still thought he was. Alienated individuality was also behind 'Black Math''s sludgy then racing punk guitars. It asked if 'the fingers or the brain' should be taught, and championed the graft of personal learning over rote education. Jack had been thinking of a day at Cass Tech when he handed his books back to his maths teacher, declaring: "I refuse to learn from you any more."

Guitars rule the rest of *Elephant*. 'Little Acorns' begins with silent movie-style piano accompaniment to the stentorian tones of Detroit TV news anchor Mort Crim offering an absurd homily about a squirrel, a happy accident resulting when Jack recorded the piano on a tape supplied by a Gillis brother who worked in radio ad distribution. The song then switches into Jack's own unsolicited lifestyle advice to a girl whose 'problems hide in your curls'. 'Hypnotize' is two minutes of straight punk rock written with the Hentchmen in mind, with a great, burrowing fuzz riff, which revs Meg up, and lyrics about another obsessed boy wanting to hold a girl's hand till the circulation stops. 'The Air Near My Fingers' is the most intriguing of this sequence of minor songs, with Jack in the rare role of a boy refusing to take a manly stand and dodging school's discipline, and music distinguished by jaunty, prog-folk organ solos. This leads into an Iggy whoop at the start of the aggressive 'Girl, You Have No Faith In Medicine'. Then 'It's True That We Love One Another' forms a perfect coda, letting the light and humour back in. Harking back to *The White Stripes* in its brutal sonic power, *Elephant* added songwriting sophistication to its varied extremity. It was Jack's favourite White Stripes LP since their debut over four years before.

The White Stripes played two gigs during the more than two weeks they booked at Toe-Rag, only 10 days of which were spent recording, just as Jack planned. Their Shepherd's Bush Empire show with the Von Bondies and Dirtbombs on May 2 was followed by them headlining the same bill in front of 5,000 at Dublin Castle for the first day of the city's Green Energy Festival on May 4. According to one report, only 70 bothered to watch the Dirtbombs. Two big homecoming gigs followed on May 22 and 23 at the 1,700-capacity Royal Oak Music Theatre, a former Twenties cinema with ornate decorative touches, and part of a genteel block including a salon, gallery and estate agents when I visit it in 2014. It was round the corner from Meg's old workplace at Memphis Smoke where she and Jack used to meet for dates, and the supporting acts over the two nights were Gold Dollar regulars the Detroit Cobras, Clone Defects, Buzzards and Whirlwind Heat. Jack's family hand-jived to 'Hotel Yorba' in the balcony as the White Stripes played in front of a giant Stars and Stripes discovered backstage. 'Home' and 'mother' were words Jack kept repeating in the songs he'd just recorded, and he was briefly back with both. "It doesn't feel like the White Stripes have a home anymore," he nevertheless told *Mojo*, with gloomy foreboding.

Brendan Benson and Whirlwind Heat were the support acts again for North American dates in May and June, when Meg read Mötley Crüe's salacious rock beast memoir *The Dirt* on the tour bus. Jack chose Loretta Lynn's more stoic autobiography *Coal Miner's Daughter* for his lesson in stardom's high reaches. On June 1, the White Stripes saw the 21st century version for themselves at the MTV Movie Awards, in Los Angeles' Shrine Auditorium. They ran down the red carpet, ducking their heads, and dodging the cameras and yelled interview requests. Backstage, a corridor was cleared for the passage of Eminem and his entourage, his head also bowed by his fearful discomfort with fame, Sharon Osbourne heckling as he passed. These two sides of Detroit's musical resurgence were, along with Kelly Osbourne, the night's only performers. "We've slipped into some other dimension," Meg shuddered. "I can't even fathom why they asked us to perform here," Jack told *Rolling Stone*'s Neil Strauss. "We've never aspired to this level of attention. Look at the money they spent," he added with distaste. But again, they broke through televised music's mundanity. Perhaps a hundred White Stripes Fan Club members charged down the aisles and fanned out around the stage, dressed in replicant red-and-white rather like the army of Slim Shadies in Eminem's 'The Real Slim Shady' video. Laughing, dancing and pogoing to 'Fell In Love With A Girl', they turned the slick MTV event into a bright fantasy of a Sixties TV show. The White Stripes, introduced by Jack Black, again improvise freely around their short hit. Seeming to change his mind mid-performance in front of millions, Jack swerves from 'I Think I Smell A Rat''s flamenco flourish into 'Dead Leaves And The Dirty Ground', building its fuzzed-up power as Meg watches carefully, then smashing back into 'Fell In Love With A Girl'. An MTV helicopter maintained their record of never missing a gig, zooming them to that night's club show in Pomona, California. There, Jack again confessed to feeling alienated by this rush of success and new, untrusted fans.

"I'm too lost in some other thought," he told Strauss of his churning mind onstage. "I'm scared of actually enjoying things."

The show was televised on June 6. "I remember a lot of us who were on the scene were all down in the Garden Bowl, drinking beer and eating pizzas," Doug Coombe remembers. "And we looked up and were like, 'Oh my God!' I think that was the moment when we were all like, 'They are going to be huge.' I think we were all happy, but it was like, 'Holy cow. They're rock stars . . .'" Three years earlier he'd seen them playing for free upstairs at the Magic Stick to almost no one. "But the beautiful thing was, you still always saw them around town, they were still cool and super-nice and approachable."

Jack had often claimed that a two-piece band could never play arenas, setting a natural lid on their success. In the early evening of June 29, they cleared a higher hurdle, holding a crowd of 40,000 at the Glastonbury Festival's main Pyramid Stage. The weather was grey and cool after rain, and the White Stripes were specks against a plain backdrop. But the big screens and BBC TV coverage kept the near-Noh theatricality of Jack's face in close-up. Meg, eyes shut, looks blissed out in contemplation of his lachrymose verses in 'Jolene'. There's a choppy, echoing preview of 'Ball And Biscuit', and blues seizes the centre of this biggest stage. Jack pauses to plug in his Kay Hollowbody, then Son House's 'Death Letter' runs into Blind Willie Johnson's 1927 'Motherless Children' over 7½ minutes. 'Nobody'll treat you like your mother will – oh, but mother is dead!' Jack cries. Singing in a foppish, melodramatic English accent, he spins round playing slide, strums his guitar like a banjo and picks it lying on the floor. "Does anyone know the name of the person next to them at this point?" he wonders, searching for individual connection in the vast mass. "I want everyone to go home and hug their mothers tonight. And Meg would like the same." The maternal relationship, rarely broached in rock'n'roll, was much on his mind. Then he orates Welles' words in 'The Union Forever' a cappella, with a shit-eating, shark's grin more Jack Nicholson than Jack White, ready to sell us snake oil or maybe a bridge. Meg, eyebrows expressively raised, doesn't falter as she sings 'Rated X', and grins at Eddie Cochran's 'Baby Blue' from that first Peel session, showing no nerves, instead having a ball. Another blues, 'Boll Weevil', allows a singalong as the clouds close in, and expresses the other concern haunting *Elephant*: 'I'm looking for a home'. Given a live opportunity, it was plain by now that the White Stripes couldn't miss. Other huge festivals, including Denmark's Roskilde, Japan's Fuji Rock, and the UK's Reading and Leeds, got similar treatment that summer.

On July 14 in Rushmor Records in Milwaukee, Wisconsin before another Midwest show, Meg was asked by a fellow browser to stay put while she found a White Stripes-loving friend in town. Meg patiently waited for the fan, then signed a pound note left in her purse from Glastonbury. Stardom could be nice.

It was also relative. Continued promotion of *White Blood Cells* into 2003, two years after its release and a year after recording *Elephant*, eventually nudged its sales past 1 million, including 700,000 in the US. This was little more than cult success in the days before free online music slashed sales, but continued a modest rock resurgence. Swedish uniformed garage act the Hives' *Your New Favourite Band*, released between White Stripes UK tours on October 22, 2001, soon sold 100,000 in Britain, where the Strokes' *Is This It* was pushed by two Top 30 singles to number two in the album chart, and sold 300,000. In August 2002 Australia's the Vines sold 100,000 and just missed the UK Top 10, the White Stripes' old New Zealand support act the Datsuns did well, and raw, romantic London band the Libertines started to stir. Inspired by the Strokes and blurring William Blake with Tony Hancock, they fuelled a further generation of often working-class rock'n'roll.

Julian Casablancas' narcotised shrug of a voice hinted at the weary creative stasis that made his band fall into irrelevance with subsequent albums. But *Is This It* eventually sold 1 million in the US, and they and the Stripes led rock's rearguard action in 2002. As the Strokes partied backstage during the Stripes' Bowery Ballroom run, a plan was hatched to co-headline major gigs. "We wanted to show there's no competition or rivalry between us and we're friends," Jack explained to *NME*'s James Oldham. "We didn't want it to turn into some stupid Blur versus Oasis thing." At Clutch Cargo's in Pontiac on August 8, the 800-capacity former church where 1997's Demolition Doll Rods and Cramps gig had given Jason Stollsteimer, Marcie Bolen and Ben Blackwell visions of a Detroit rock'n'roll future, Jack and Meg hung out with old friends. Casablancas was on crutches when the Strokes played, then '76 Trombones' from Broadway classic *The Music Man* introduced the White Stripes. As they had at Glastonbury, they played 'Ball And Biscuit', and the plantation work song 'Pick A Bale Of Cotton'. Afterwards Meg and her housemate, Ko & the Knockouts' Ko Melina, DJed at the Magic Stick, playing Led Zeppelin's 'Black Dog', the Beatles' 'Tomorrow Never Knows', the Archies' 'Sugar Sugar' and a favourite from Meg's innocent, music-soaked childhood, Shirley Ellis' 'The Clapping Song'. While the other Strokes drank and flirted at the bar, Jack hoisted Casablancas, his busted leg's hindrance multiplied by booze, up the stairs from the Garden Bowl. The New Yorkers gave out of state stardust to the Detroit scene's epicentre.

The following night's 6,000-capacity, riverside double bill in Detroit's Chene Park was the White Stripes' biggest hometown show yet, watched by many who'd never bothered to before. "So many times, when someone breaks from Detroit, it has nothing to do with people here," Doug Coombe wryly notes. The bill was reversed on August 14 and 15 at New York's Irving Plaza and Radio City Music Hall. The White Stripes played to 6,000 without a soundcheck at the latter, their most prestigious US show so far. Hundreds milled in 51st Street afterwards as the bands chatted to them from second-floor windows, Meg waving to the boys, Jack throwing down a red T-shirt and the Strokes' Fabrizio Moretti pretending to jump. These old-style showbiz scenes only lacked a ticker-tape parade.

A more personally important night for Jack came on August 11 when he joined Beck for his acoustic gig at Ann Arbor's Michigan Theater. They covered Sixties TV's *Get Smart* star Barbara Feldon's single '99', Jack took the guitar for Beck's 'Cool Brains', and they both played Robert Johnson's 'Last Fair Deal Gone Down'. Five years older and further down fame's line than Jack, Beck Hansen had also become obsessed with acoustic blues and folk as a teenager in a hostile Latino neighbourhood, and been sustained by insular bohemian scenes (New York's anti-folk movement, and the Silver Lake neighbourhood's coffee bars in his native LA). When he added the hip-hop Jack decried to the self-sampled slide guitar of his 1994 hit 'Loser', and further fused forms on the 1996 album *Odelay*, the slightly built, machismo-free Beck's success became a comfort in Jack Gillis' schooldays. Now he needed him again. "In my circle of family and friends it seems I never have anyone to talk to about what I'm going through," he recalled to *Mojo*'s Will Hodgkinson of stardom's "scary" path. "When I first met Beck I just wanted to grab him . . . I just wanted his advice so badly." Beck was soon another unlikely face at the Magic Stick bar, and he and Jack stayed friends and collaborators.

The White Stripes returned to London in September for vocal re-recording and remixes on a couple of *Elephant* tracks. They were closely watched now, by the rock press at least, as they shopped in posh West End department stores Liberty and Selfridges (Meg loved English shoes), and saw gigs by Mudhoney, the Datsuns, and a Von Bondies/

Greenhornes double bill. They returned to *Top Of The Pops* as a third single, 'Dead Leaves And The Dirty Ground', hit number 25 to help *White Blood Cells'* sales keep ticking. 'Yeah, it's a stick-up,' Jack warns the audience in an unstable voice. 'Let's not make it a murder.' Meg mimes listening with exaggerated interest, and they end by bowing till their heads almost touch, like twins sinking into each other. Michel Gondry's video for this song was less groundbreaking than 'Fell In Love With A Girl', but found more drama and pathos. Jack is a Pop Art Reggie Perrin in black bowler hat, suit and red shirt, heaving private sighs as he trudges down his suburban London street. He discovers his records smashed in the front garden, the cat in the fridge and evidence of anarchy everywhere. Gondry runs parallel ghost-images over him, of he and Meg as playful young lovers setting up their happy house, her poking fun as he shaves suggesting intimacies from their real marriage, and the havoc when her friends slip in while he's out. 'If you're thinking of the Holy Ghost . . .' the song goes, while phantom-Meg packs her bag and steps over Jack as he cowers in bed, broken. He convinces simmering with rage, too, face set as he ponders the 'rock'n'roll' partiers who despoiled his ordered life.

'We're Going To Be Friends' was also released to the US media as a promotional single in late 2002. In its simple, cheap video, Jack is a pensively introspective, strumming troubadour on a couch on a night-time lawn opposite a house that could be his own. Meg lies stretched out behind him, a sleeping beauty. Jack nudges her when the song ends, and she blinks awake like a cat. In 2004, the song found a second life in the credits of Jared Hess' eccentric comedy about extreme teenage dysfunction, *Napoleon Dynamite*. The White Stripes gave permission as soon as they saw this queasily awkward film.

Beck was not the only hero the band met as their profile rose at 2002's end. At the Quart Festival in Kristiansand, Norway, they were among those dancing and watching at the side of the stage as David Bowie, whose 'Moonage Daydream' had given the White Stripes life, ranged across his career. On September 13 and 14, their productive London visit found them at the Royal Festival Hall with, Jack said from the stage, "the great honour for us to be asked to fill the shoes of the Yardbirds." With the Greenhornes' Jack Lawrence on bass, this was part of a Jeff Beck show leafing through his back-pages, watched by another ex-Yardbird, Jimmy Page, on its first night. A black Yardbirds logo was added to Meg's peppermint-striped drums, and in this new context she added simply effective fills few knew she could play. Jeff Beck's high, rasping tone, his impatience with effects as he wrestled sound from his instrument and amps straight through his fingers, was Jack's way, too. "Jack White shook me," Beck later admitted to the *Daily Telegraph*. "The White Stripes in full flood, it was like Zeppelin." But the younger man watched and tried to learn as Beck plugged in and slashed through a chord's overtones in ways he couldn't yet grasp. "It was the most fantastic thing I have done," Jack said of being a Yardbird. Experiencing music with respected elders was valued higher than his own achievements. When the Stripes supported the Rolling Stones on October 16 at Toronto's Air Canada Center and October 20 at Columbus, Ohio's Nationwide Arena, he was again reverent, relishing the "bizarre" experience of chatting with the Stones backstage. Picking momentarily hip support acts was standard, shoddy Stones practice, a form of inter-generational leeching. For Midwest and Canadian gigs, the White Stripes were 2002's obvious pick. But hearing that the Stones had actually watched their set, unlike when they'd roped in the Strokes, made Jack feel a more genuine connection. Punk rock's desire to kill your fathers was the opposite of his. He found touching music's past essential and natural. "I jumped in this running river," he told Conan O'Brien years later. "I just jumped into it."

The river ran both ways. In between shows with the Strokes in August, Jack activated Third Man Records' option to record other acts, producing Whirlwind Heat's *Do Rabbits Wonder?* in four days at Brendan Benson's home studio. The album's jerky post-punk collages, ray-gun synth effects, frenetic extremes and cut-up lyrics made it hard to like. When V2 and XL released *Do Rabbits Wonder?* in *Elephant*'s wake on April 15, 2003, these weren't the protégés they'd hoped for from impresario Jack. But they were friends from Michigan he liked having around, letting singer Dave Swanson film *Elephant*'s making for hazy future use, and later document the second Raconteurs album. Whirlwind Heat also shared his reasons for making music. "It was this friendship thing of being creative with each other and having ideas about music . . . just that whole ethic of doing stuff and not being lazy, working hard at what you do," Swanson remembered to *Leeds Music Scene*'s Cathy Simpson. In 2007, when the major-label distribution was long gone and his band was winding down, Swanson looked back with pride. "We have always done what we liked and thought was right," he told *Turn It Down*'s Rich Tupica. "We have done a whole lot for a band that sounds like ours." Jack's generosity recognised and enabled that. It was a template for Third Man's future.

The White Stripes maintained their own momentum with growing assurance. Back at Radio City Music Hall on August 29, Jack, wearing a Twenties-style white suit and fedora, red shirt and rose, was accompanied by a beaming Meg to the MTV Music Awards. They no longer raced down the red carpet. Republican presidential candidate John McCain introduced them on *Saturday Night Live* on October 19, playing 'Dead Leaves And The Dirty Ground' and 'We're Going To Be Friends'. And on October 1, they accepted Nissan's sponsorship of a free, 'guerrilla' lunchtime gig in New York's Union Square. This tie-up with not only a corporation, but the car industry Jack partly blamed for Detroit's desolation, seemed to contradict their refusal of Gap's money. Having ensured no sponsor's logo sullied his stage, Jack simply saw playing to the 9,000 students, office workers and passers-by who paused to watch as an opportunity. It was hard to argue when the White Stripes overran, the power was pulled and they played on unamplified, Jack leaning over the crowd as he conducted their singing of 'Boll Weevil', 'Farmer John' and 'Louie Louie'. This really was folk music.

Such special occasions were exceptions in the autumn and winter of 2002. Two years of relentless touring all but stopped then, while Jack went to work in the movies.

11

The Folk Singer

THE Greys pub, Brighton, August 3, 2015. A few dozen sit packed around Tim Eriksen, formerly of folk-punks Cordelia's Dad, as he visibly gathers strength to sing songs from his native Massachusetts and the American South with gravity that looks exhausting. "A lot of these songs are like water," he says of their endurance. "They find a crevice and work their way in." He picks up a hand-built Tennessee banjo to sing of a woman murdered in 1810, then a young Brighton woman leads the harmonies on words written by a proud Southern girl to a Northern suitor at the Civil War's height in 1863, filling the pub with images of a 'crimson tide' and 'boys in grey'. Eriksen explains how that war still lives in Southern bars where it's unwise to pass a $5 bill with its Abraham Lincoln side up. His passion is shape-note music, where four notes are written as shapes in a simplified score, performed a cappella by four sides of singers forming a hollow square. This stark, intense community music took the name of its 1844 songbook *The Sacred Harp*. In 2002, Eriksen's expertise made him an on-set adviser to Anthony Minghella's film of Charles Frazier's epic Civil War novel *Cold Mountain*. 'Wayfaring Stranger', introduced tonight as being "a comfort to many of the sides in the Civil War – there were sides that got forgotten about", was among Jack White's songs on the film's soundtrack. He also had a supporting part as Georgia, an itinerant musician who falls for Renée Zellweger's Ruby. As the pub clears out around midnight, Eriksen remembers the weeks they spent together.

"[Writer-director] Anthony [Minghella] really was very focused on the music," he explains, "and it was hearing the Sacred Harp songs that opened the floodgates for him creatively. T Bone Burnett was brought in to produce the soundtrack close on the heels of his work on *O Brother, Where Art Thou?*. They tried out a number of people for Jack's part. One was Justin Timberlake, who grew up in Kentucky singing some of that stuff in church. Ryan Adams was another guy they spoke to, through his New York lawyer. They wound up settling on Jack because they wanted somebody cool that wasn't yet totally discovered, could do his own singing, and had a connection to older forms." Burnett's wife, the singer Sam Phillips, suggested him. "Of all the young singers out there, he has done the most homework," Burnett told *No Depression*'s Lloyd Sachs. "It's not easy to do those songs, to make them new. You have to really metabolize them somehow. They have to mean something to you. Like all storytelling, you have to believe them."

For Jack, his dream while recording *White Blood Cells* of recording a soundtrack like *O Brother, Where Art Thou?* had come true. "I had no idea that [Burnett] even knew of the White Stripes or our love for old American folk music," he told *Sonic*'s Lennart Persson. "It felt like a huge compliment. The invitation completely shook me up and if my role had not been firmly rooted in the music, I would certainly not have taken it." The songs picked for him included 'Sittin' On Top Of The World', which had introduced him to the blues, while he'd played 'Wayfaring Stranger' with Two-Star Tabernacle. "So I just felt this huge calling, that the part was for me," he told *The Guardian*'s Keith Cameron. He emphasised to *Q* that *Cold Mountain*'s lure was "getting the chance to expose American folk music, which doesn't get heard"; not, he added to *Comingsoon!*, "a step in a direction to more fame or celebrity."

Jack's character Georgia is one of a trio of Confederate deserter-troubadours wandering the war-ruined South, led by Brendan Gleeson as the roguish dad of Zellweger's Ruby. In a plot that echoes both *The Odyssey* and *Gone With The Wind*, and outdoes the latter's virtual elision of slavery's real part in its Southern heroes' lives, Confederate soldier Inman (Jude Law) struggles to return to Ada (Nicole Kidman), who maintains her Tara-like home with the help of tough, eccentric Ruby, as local villains led by Ray Winstone circle.

Minghella's follow-up to 1999's *The Talented Mr. Ripley* (and 1996's Oscar-winning *The English Patient*) is ripely beautiful to a fault, with a cast also including Philip Seymour Hoffman, and Donald Sutherland as Ada's preacher father. Jack shyly reminded Sutherland that they had shared a set before, on *The Rosary Murders*. Wearing blue-checked trousers and a sort of over-sized pillbox hat, with long hair, a kind smile and the drawled accent of his beloved South, Jack boyishly convinces in a role with little dialogue. Still, acting with such stars felt "completely unreal", making him "weak in the knees" mid-scene. Minghella was anyway impressed by his novice actor's ability to blend into the past. "Jack fit [easily] into the fabric of this movie," he said. As Jack had hoped, the whole film was anyway rooted in music. Minghella worked on the score with composer Gabriel Yared, and saw the soundtrack's 19th century songs as "time travel". Faced with death, Gleeson's singing almost changes the mind of Winstone's killer, waking memories of a kinder, moral self. Minghella took the rare step of recording the music before filming started, so it could be played on-set.

The session was at Nashville's Sound Emporium in the third week of June, shortly before the White Stripes' Glastonbury show. "It took four days to do the basic stuff," Eriksen remembers. "He showed up after a day or two. I met him first in the hotel elevator. I didn't know his band, so I asked him about it. And he said, 'Well, it's kind of like Robert Johnson, only not lame.' I said, 'Oh, you mean like Pussy Galore?' And that was a blank slate for him – he didn't know that mid-Nineties experimentation with something like blues in a more raw form. I asked him how it was going musically, and he'd had a bunch of car commercial offers and he had turned them down, smartly. And he'd had a White Stripes song in another, small film that Brendan [Gleeson] was in and had had to sing, so they bonded over that."

The movie's musicians were as daunting as its cast to Jack. "There were so many amazing string musicians there, people who built their own instruments," he told *Sonic*. "I did not once dare to touch my guitar – I only sang." Eriksen saw his nerves. "It was an interesting moment. He was really green and really intimidated. He showed up in his red shirt and his black bowler hat, and he was just sweating bullets. Here's [bluegrass masters] Mike Compton and Norman and Nancy Blake, and T Bone, and he'd never done anything like that before. So he was, I think, anxious to prove himself. I remember *People* or *Time* had done a piece on the *O Brother* phenomenon that week, when they sold another 80,000 copies. The guys involved in it were talking about how it kept snowballing. And Jack showed me a copy of *Rolling Stone*, saying, 'Look, here's my record. We sold 8,000 copies last week!'"

Bluegrass' most revered living player, Ralph Stanley, then 75, arranged Jack's version of 'Great High Mountain', and led 40 singers in a vocal call and response on June 19. How did Jack interact with him?

"With Ralph?" Eriksen chokes. "Ralph doesn't really interact a whole lot. He was cool. Jack was really just nerve-wracked by the whole thing."

Eriksen, steeped in American folk forms before and beyond blues, gave Jack the wider sense of their nation's music he needed. "He exhibited a real reverence for the people involved in the film and some of the older music," he recalls. "He obviously didn't know Sacred Harp, no one did.

191

But he had studied up on the songs he had to sing. Stylistically, it was a funny match. 'Wayfaring Stranger', for example, wasn't the best version there ever was, but there was something about his take that was of the moment. He was self-conscious about stuff, and I worked with him a little bit on the style of 'Great High Mountain'. We sang that together, and they largely mixed me out of it on the CD. In the film, they captured a bunch of it live on-set, with Jack on mandolin. I don't think his knowledge went back beyond the recorded music era. But he was interested in everything. I'd organised Sacred Harp singing on Sand Mountain, Alabama, a two and a half hour drive south of Nashville, on the final day of that week. Jack was keen to come down, but couldn't. I gave him Sacred Harp recordings, of this music that implies stories about the time and place that are not the usual stories, about community and participation in something vibrant, and he told a journalist he was into that music now. I don't think it lasted very long, but he was fascinated with it."

These sessions just before meeting Jeff Beck and the Stones confirmed Jack's deference to elders. "He definitely had that," Eriksen agrees, "which not all rock'n'roll people do. If there was ever anything interesting about the folk revival, it was the idea of listening to old people. In a late night moment of hanging out a few months before he died, [country great] Charlie Louvin said to me, 'Of all these guys saying, 'The Louvin Brothers, oh the Louvin Brothers,' not one of these motherfuckers ever asked me to open for them.' Charlie Louvin at the end of his life was playing for 20 people in empty bars. Jack put his money where his mouth was in that way, and within a year went on to produce Loretta Lynn. So I respected that. He was ambitious, and he was self-conscious, which is common and understandable, being a budding rock star when that still wasn't inevitable. But I thought, 'Okay, if there's gotta be rock stars, I like the way he's doing it.' He was playing it positive. He was playing it to the credit of the people he learned from, rather than in fear of them. I know other people that have achieved a degree of fame who seem to live in mortal terror of being found out, and wipe out their tracks. Jack didn't have that negativity."

Was it like he was trying on the trappings of a successful musician till they fit?

"It was totally that. The fact that he wanted to show me that he had sold 8,000 copies that week, that he belonged in the room, and he wasn't just eye-candy. He seemed to me very conscious of being on the stage and wanting to play it right. I got a pretty strong sense from Jack that he was engaged in strategising for aesthetic and practical reasons, but also to do the right thing. He was interested in using whatever he was doing to bring attention to people he genuinely respected. What he did with Loretta didn't make him look bad, but at the same time he was able to do something really interesting aesthetically. I got the sense that he was very well-versed in the literature about the people he really liked, and that he had a romantic sense of music and rock'n'roll and blues. Like with Loretta, there was a literary understanding of it, it wasn't just, 'I like this music so I'm going to record it,' it was something about the lyricism and the romance of a certain story about a certain person."

Cold Mountain's shoot began in mid-July, with Transylvania's Carpathian mountains and surrounding fields, which were still harvested by hand, mostly standing in for the Appalachians. Jack worked for six weeks there. "It is weird to be sharing a cigarette with Nicole Kidman in the middle of Transylvania," he reported to Radio 1.

"I was there for the first three weeks of Jack's stay," Eriksen remembers. "The first thing they filmed was a battle scene in a crater. It was unbelievably hot and rainy the whole time. The Romanian army extras were all ready to fuck off back to base because they weren't getting paid, and were being forced to wear period woollen clothing in unbelievable heat and the mud. That was filmed outside Bucharest. The next scenes were at four sites around a beautiful little Transylvanian city, Brasov, all guarded by Romanian soldiers with AK-47s to keep journalists away. We stayed in Poiana Brasov, a very little ski resort, and it was summer, so there wasn't a whole lot going on there." The temperature there dropped to -25. "It was raining all the time and it was really hard to film the outdoor stuff. Nicole Kidman, Jude Law and Renée Zellweger were all staying at this little ski chalet, and I was staying with my family and the plebs at a hotel a quarter-mile away. I connected more with Jack there because I'd said that I could only do the film if I could bring my wife [the late Minja Lausevic, like Eriksen an ethnomusicologist] and my son Luca, who was six months old when they asked me. And my wife, who was a pretty exceptional person, really hit it off with Anthony, and he really bonded with Luca, who got cast as Renée and Jack's baby in the final scene where they gather round the Easter table in a beautiful house they built. We'd already spent quite a bit of time with Jack in the Nashville studio and the hotel. Now we hung out on-set for a whole afternoon so that Luca wouldn't freak out with him, then it took two or three days to shoot that last scene. I also had to watch *Tree of the Wooden Clogs* [Ermanno Olmi's closely observed, quietly beautiful, three-hour-long, 1978 portrait of Lombardy peasants' struggles with their land and landlords at the 20th century's start] with Jack and Renée, because Anthony wanted us to see its very intense presentation of peasant life."

Jack's on-set romance with Zellweger was his most clichéd Hollywood move. Rain-bound isolation and their roles' closeness both worked their spell. When his Georgia plays mandolin and sings 'Wayfaring Stranger' to her Ruby, she has a faraway, serious, increasingly sultry look, lost in him. "She's an original," he says, hooked. "Well," Ruby sniffs, "I know [Georgia's] supposed to be the ugliest state." He runs to save her later, a quick shadow in the snow, is shot and slung over a horse, face bloody, and ends wedded to her in a rustic idyll. "He's a sly film presence," Minghella observed. "There's no dialogue, but there's no doubt when you leave [his first scene with Zellweger] that Ruby and Georgia have made a connection. They barely have eye-contact, but it's right there."

Eriksen saw the real thing's start. "It was right at the time when they were just checking each other out – he was showing her guitar chords in the chalet, and she was like, 'Mm-mm!' Then they had a crazy party where Nicole [Kidman] was chasing a bear, and somewhere I have video of Renée and Jack flirting there." They bonded over a human skull Jack bought in a junk shop. "She told me you can tell if it's a man or a woman by the teeth," he told Q. "That impressed me. You think you're going to be surrounded by Hollywood arseholes, but she knows a lot about skulls."

He insensitively rang Marcie Bolen back in Detroit to tell her all about his new film star friend's wisdom. Bolen's similarity to him had partly been just such odd, isolating intellect. "I was not very social," she said of growing up, in Chris Handyside's *Fell In Love With A Band*. "I'm more mechanical. I like facts and mathematical skills . . . I wasn't on the same wavelength as most people. I didn't know how to communicate with them." Her relationship with Jack already badly faltering as he vanished into his band's success, and "we didn't see each other and we were fighting a lot", as she told *NME*'s Mark Beaumont, neared its end as he filmed in Europe. "There was a year when we were on and off here and there," she recalled. "We kinda split up but were staying friends. Then he'd gotten a new girlfriend . . . Things just kinda blew up and we said, 'Right, we can't talk for a while.'" Movie star lovers had advantages that took Jack out of her league. "She was able to fly around and go see him," she told *NME*. "I didn't really have the money to fly wherever he is." As her bandmate

Cassie Smith noted, "He's probably reached a level of celebrity that's more in tune to her than to where we are."

Back at the Greys, Eriksen tells his audience that the rock'n'roll-prefiguring, charismatic 19th century preacher "Crazy" Lorenzo Dow "wasn't above lying to get to the truth". That's just how Jack sometimes speaks of his art and public persona, with its deceptive threads in plain view. In Eriksen's weeks with him, he noted a natural and sympathetic double life.

"He seemed to be clearly on the ball and engaged in creating himself as he wanted to be," he says. "Not everybody is. Kurt Cobain was another person I knew a bit who seemed not to be able to quite navigate that. It's a funny world, where you have to play so many different roles – doing exactly what you want at the same time as positioning yourself. My sense is that he's very savvy about that, and that he would probably go to the mat for something that he thought was important.

"Jack seemed to have an ability to be himself," he concludes, "and at the same time to be conscious of how it played in the broader scheme of things, without being a 'player'. He was able to talk about what was interesting about what he was doing, while also being interested in what was going on around him. He was very self-conscious and nervous during that initial period, but not uncomfortably so. I think cute is an obnoxious term, but . . . he was sweet and smart in my interactions with him, and genuine and able to figure out how things read. I liked the way he was. And here's a greater test of things. I liked the way he was with my son. He was cool. He was cool with my son."

Eriksen had left by the time Meg flew in at the shoot's end on November 23, to play a White Stripes concert for cast and crew at Brasov's five-star Aro Palace Hotel. Romanian folk-dancers, given a copy of *White Blood Cells* by a crew-member, surprised them by dancing to 'Fell In Love With A Girl' and 'I Think I Smell A Rat' in full local costume. "We stood up there and played 'Isis' and 'One More Cup Of Coffee' with T Bone, who had played both of them with [their writer] Dylan on [1976's] Rolling Thunder Revue tour," Jack told *Sonic*. "That was definitely the high point of the film project for me."

As had happened with *Elephant*, Jack's work on *Cold Mountain* was set aside for a year. In the summer of 2003, he'd follow it with a more confident leap into American traditions outside rock'n'roll, when he produced *Van Lear Rose* for Loretta Lynn in Nashville. Watching the 1980 film of Lynn's life, *Coal Miner's Daughter*, had made a profound early impression, by some accounts making him rush out to buy his first guitar (probably in 1989, aged 14).

British director Michael Apted takes an outsider's, anthropological approach to Lynn's childhood in Butcher Holler, in the bleakly beautiful mining country of the Kentucky Appalachians. Though it's 1948 when 13-year-old Loretta Webb (Sissy Spacek) marries 19-year-old Oliver "Doo" Lynn (Tommy Lee Jones), the film showed Jack a physically primitive and primal South barely changed from a century before. A moonshiner is hunted and shot in shadowy woods as Lynn sings 'In The Pines', a spectral folk song of dangerous jealousy perhaps dating back to *Cold Mountain*'s Civil War Appalachians. Jack would hear it again when Kurt Cobain made it a lacerating blues on Nirvana's *MTV Unplugged In New York*. The Webbs sing and dance together in their cabin to Bill Monroe's 'Blue Moon Of Kentucky' on the radio's *Grand Ole Opry*, a folk response to technology; Jack called his own musical family hillbillies, and the Webbs surely seemed more like them than the Mexicantown outside his door. Watching Lynn's bare, killingly tough early life, with radio the only media distraction from music-making, the man who wished he'd been a Thirties black man might as well have been a coal miner's son.

The film began Jack's fascination with the South, which grew when he spent time there preparing for *Cold Mountain*. It also shows a music career gradually building due to Doo and Lynn's grinding effort, followed by a rush of success. This becomes another sort of numb grind as fans snatch at Lynn's hair for keepsakes, pills dull the pain on a tour bus that rolls on forever, she forgets the words of her once-heartfelt songs and finally cries, broken, to thousands of silent fans out in the dark: "Things is moving too fast in my life . . . my life's running me." Among all the films and books young Jack found to help imagine a musician's life – after seeing the Stones' *Cocksucker Blues*, going on the 21st century road proved a dull letdown – this was an inspirational yet sobering tale. It also helped make Lynn one of his major heroes, and an unlikely strand in the White Stripes' DNA. "Meg wants us to be like Emmylou Harris and Loretta Lynn," he'd told an Auckland interviewer in 2000. But his time with Goober & the Peas had deepened his own taste for country – Lynn most of all. "She wrote her own songs in a time when no [other country women] did," he told Jaan Uhelszki in *Mojo*, "tackled subject matter that everyone else was afraid to touch. She was not a fake product of the Nashville system." On becoming the Country Music Association's 1972 Entertainer of the Year, she ignored that system's orders not to kiss black country star Charley

Pride on national TV. Then there was 1975's pro-birth control hit 'The Pill'. "She was writing songs for all the women of the world as well as herself," Jack added to Uhelszki of his favourite song by her, 'Fist City', in which a love rival is directly disposed of. "This song tells it all about Miss Loretta's attitude, and it makes you want to do whatever she says."

As with so many of the turns in the first part of his career, Loretta Lynn came to him. When *White Blood Cells* gained mainstream US success, her manager Nancy Russell, noticing its dedication to Lynn and the White Stripes' cover of 'Rated X', handed the 'Hotel Yorba' CD it was a B-side of to Lynn. "He done that song just like me," she noted approvingly to the *Metro-Times'* Fred Mills. Russell "put the whole thing together", Lynn later claimed. Lynn wrote a letter of thanks, then invited Jack and Meg to Hurricane Mills, her home 65 miles west of Nashville. The mansion Jack had seen in *Coal Miner's Daughter*, and which he and Meg stopped at in homage when driving home through Tennessee after making *White Blood Cells*, was abandoned after Doo's death in 1996. That blow had left Lynn's mind temporarily "stopped somewhere along the line", she told Mills. She now lived in the smaller house built by Doo in the film's closing scenes, its large windows overlooking lush Tennessee countryside, with her personally tended vegetable patch in front and homely artefacts inside. These included antebellum dolls, a portrait of Lynn from a fan in jail and a rug from one of the many Native Americans she'd put through school, honouring her Cherokee ancestry. She kept Jack and Meg fed with chicken and dumplings and biscuits and gravy, then offered them the pick of boxes of her vinyl LPs; they demurred, saying they already owned them. Wasting no time, she also pulled out 'Van Lear Rose', a stirring tribute to her mother Clary (who grew up near Van Lear, Kentucky). Jack asked to demo it. "I dreamt of working with her," he told *The Independent On Sunday*'s Jancee Dunn. The straight-talking Lynn found Meg (more bashful than ever with her hero, as Lynn was at a similar age) worryingly quiet. "She didn't talk," she recalled to the *New York Times* years later. "She just kind of gazed into space. She didn't seem like she wanted to be there." Still, Lynn gave Meg one of her old, knee-length red stage dresses as a parting gift.

On April 19, 2003, at New York's Hammerstein Ballroom, Lynn accepted the White Stripes' invitation to support them. Jack briefly practised with her in their purple tour bus, then guested on 'Fist City' and in her old duet partner Conway Twitty's role on 'Louisiana Woman, Mississippi Man'. Lynn appeared when the White Stripes played to trade verses on 'Rated X' with Jack and Meg. The latter wore the old dress of Lynn who, white-gowned earlier, was now red-blazered, with Jack in a country star's white-tasselled red Nudie suit, which he'd debuted on *Elephant*'s sleeve. Lynn had entered their colour-coded world. "Miss Loretta, you are the most gorgeous thing to ever come out of the South," Jack the gentleman flirted. "I'm looking for a girlfriend, you know." "Well," Lynn replied, unfazed, "I'm lookin' for a boyfriend." Blanche's Dave Feeny, whose band opened that night, observed the relationship. "She didn't really know what to make of Jack," he says, "but could see that he was adored by the crowd and I think that influenced her. I think they had a little innocent crush on each other, definitely some mutual respect, and I know Loretta enjoyed the attention." Lynn knew that Jack wasn't some young dilettante. She could see that, like her, he put the time in. "I haven't seen anybody work as hard onstage," she told Jancee Dunn. "He come off just wet. And Meg's a funny little girl, but man, can she play them drums."

Before that first meeting in New York was over, Lynn "was telling him I was getting ready to go in and do an album myself," she recalled to *CMT News*. "He said, 'Well, could I go in and produce it?' I said, 'Why not?'" Feeny remembered a less certain scenario to *NME*. "She was pretty hesitant and they went round and round about it. I'm not sure she trusted his intentions at first, but she finally realised he was very serious about it and agreed to do it."

On the first weekend of June, just before a White Stripes US tour, Jack visited Hurricane Mills again, to test this more substantial collaboration. Lynn wrote new songs and dug out old ones, demoing them on guitar in her home studio in anticipation. "I've a funny feeling that I've got a couple he might even want to do himself," she told the *Metro-Times*' Fred Mills, sounding eager at the prospect. "I run across one called 'Portland, Oregon, And A Sloe Gin Fizz.' It's a little uptempo thing, and I think he'll like that one." Jack said later to Conan O'Brien that, comfortable with working with women, he didn't notice his collaborator was 68. "He's 27, and it's hard to make yourself work with somebody who's so much younger," Lynn confessed to Mills. She eventually concluded to *NME* that "there's so much of an old soul in him. You heard of people born like that?" Considering their continuing, flirtatious relationship to *Uncut*'s Jaan Uhelszki in 2016, she mused: "We're like brothers and sisters." A likely and familiar story.

A lovely photo by Statia Molewski shows the pair dancing in their New

York stage outfits, the taller Jack looking down at Lynn with affectionate delight. But the diffidence he'd shown with Ralph Stanley had already vanished. This collaboration formed the template for much future work with older musicians. "I don't try to just bombard them with compliments," he told Mills, instead seeing if "our own personalities can be comfortable with each other." After producing the similarly iconoclastic rockabilly and country star Wanda Jackson's *The Party Ain't Over* (Jackson was 71 during its 2009 making), he explained his method with her and Lynn to *The Word*'s Dorian Lynskey. "I was not trying to manipulate them but to get them into zones where they were uncomfortable and something new can happen . . . That's the mark of a good artist: when a challenge is put in front of them, they rise to it." The cold-blooded mutual cash-ins of Sinatra's Nineties *Duets* albums, or a guest-spot offered to Jack with Jerry Lee Lewis in the 2010s, repulsed him. He wanted to make art with his heroes, not hand them a buck, or bow his head.

As Tim Eriksen guessed, Jack also felt he was tapping an American source, a Southern folk artist he already felt he knew from a film he'd watched as a boy, who had lived in a lost country he longed for. "She's so country," he told the *Metro-Times*' Mills, "and the storytelling is just like poetry that's coming out of her. From her telling a joke or telling some anecdote to the stories she tells in her songs, it's completely American."

Dave Feeny joined the *Van Lear Rose* sessions at the start, playing pedal steel, slide guitar and dobro, and sometimes engineering. "I got a call from Jack I think on a Wednesday," he remembers, "and he asked if I wanted to come to Nashville to do demos with Loretta that Friday. So we were there the first day, just setting up and running through some of the songs, when Loretta came out. We were in the middle of a take and the way that the little studio was set up, I was the only one she could see through the glass door as she peeked in. My brain melted and my hands ceased to function, I screwed up the whole band. Jack stopped us and was looking at me from the other direction. I just pointed to the window!"

The demos turned into the album's first session. *Van Lear Rose* was recorded in Eric McConnell's East Nashville home studio in two periods totalling 12 days, his dogs wandering in and out as he taped on 8-track. The Greenhornes' bassist Jack Lawrence and drummer Patrick Keeler completed the quartet Lynn dubbed the Do Whaters because, she told *CMT News*, "they got in there and did whatever we needed them to". Blanche's Dan Miller added acoustic guitar, and *Cold Mountain* veteran Dirk Powell linked the two projects on fiddle, bowed bass and banjo.

"It was fantastic," says Feeny of Lynn's studio work with Jack. "There were a few demos beforehand that Jack had, but Loretta also had a bunch of grocery bags filled with legal pads, all of which were full of songs she had written. We started leafing through and she would say, 'Oh that's one I wrote for Elvis,' she would just start singing it and 10 minutes later we were running through it in the studio, and 20 minutes later it was done. I remember sitting back and listening to the playback thinking, did that just happen? I know this will sound a little over the top, but it was magical, everything fell together very organically. I sat in the engineer's chair while we were doing vocals, and I never heard Loretta sing a wrong note. She just wanted to hear drums in the headphones, she'd get her first note from Jack standing next to her playing guitar, and she would go from there."

Feeny, a prolific and experienced producer at his own Tempermill Studios in Detroit, observed Jack's qualities in the role. "He works fast, he'd have an idea for something and then we'd just run with it. He was always receptive to everyone's input – if we had an idea for a change or an intro, he'd be happy to try it. He's also a huge music fan and did his homework. I was always surprised that he'd ask questions about something from Loretta's early career like 'You Ain't Woman Enough', and have her use that as a reference for another song."

As with Jack's own sessions, most songs were first takes. He also maintained a White Stripes policy, which he explained to *Mojo* as "treating each song like the A–side of a 45", rather than giving LPs a "gigantic blur" of unified sound. "I wanted to present each song the best way possible and bring out [its] character," he told *CMT News'* Bill Conger of *Van Lear Rose*. Adoring Lynn's voice, he puts it front and centre, catching her swallow and breathe over 'Trouble On The Line''s steel guitar and brushed drums, and the bare, close acoustic guitar on 'Miss Being Mrs', a forlorn lament for life with Doo. Most imaginatively, on 'Little Red Shoes' Jack tapes Lynn telling a breathless story about her near-death, deep poverty and loving family in Depression-era Kentucky over looping, ambient steel guitar (music written by Jack and engineered by Brendan Benson). 'Van Lear Rose', 'High On A Mountain Top' and the fine, funny 'Story Of My Life' are also heavily autobiographical, drawing on bluegrass tales and traditions. But this isn't just the back-to-basics move Dolly Parton was then engaged in. 'Have Mercy', the song Lynn wrote for Elvis, purrs with a powerful rockabilly engine as she adopts a Presley vocal tremble, Jack adding Sun Records echo and slashing guitar. 'Portland,

ack in 2006. Family life and other projects were starting to distract him from the White Stripes. BRYAN BEDDER/GETTY IMAGES

The Raconteurs (Jack, Patrick Keeler, Jack Lawrence and Brendan Benson) in 2006, the year their first recording, 'Steady, As She Goes', became Jack's second-biggest hit. JASON SQUIRES/WIREIMAGE FOR MTV.COM

The Raconteurs live. Playing with his new gang made Jack a better guitarist, and a better folk singer. TIM MOSENFELDER/GETTY IMAGES

Dapper at 2007's Grammys, where the Raconteurs were nominated twice. LESTER COHEN/WIREIMAGE

Meg looks pensive and tired during the White Stripes' 2007 Canadian tour. Her growing discomfort meant the band effectively ended soon afterwards. DOUGLAS MASON/GETTY IMAGES

"It's called Ka-ra-teh": Jack as Elvis, showing John C. Reilly how to be King in the spoof biopic *Walk Hard: The Dewey Cox Story*.
COL PICS/EVERETT/REX/SHUTTERSTOCK

Jack in Gatsby mode in 2008 with his second wife, model and singer Karen Elson. MICHAEL LOCCISANO/FILMMAGIC

With Jimmy Page and The Edge at the premiere of *It Might Get Loud*, a revealing documentary on the three guitarists. Jack probably won the unspoken duel. MALCOLM TAYLOR/GETTY IMAGES

With Alicia Keys, performing the unconventional theme song to the misbegotten Bond film, *Quantum Of Solace.*
MGM/EVERETT/REX/SHUTTERSTOCK

The Dead Weather in 2009. Alison Mosshart astride the monitors and Jack happy drumming at the back, for the first time since Goober & the Peas. JAY WEST/WIREIMAGE

Jack at the White House with Karen Elson on June 2, 2010.
President Obama watched him perform 'Mother Nature's Son',
on a night honouring Paul McCartney. Eight days later,
Jack and Elson announced their divorce. TRACY A WOODWARD/
THE WASHINGTON POST VIA GETTY IMAGES

Glastonbury 2010. The Dead Weather let Jack indulge his
drumming, then move upfront when he felt like it.
TABATHA FIREMAN/REDFERNS

With marriage and the White Stripes behind him, Jack, 36, began his solo career in 2012. Blue was now the colour.
JIM DYSON/REDFERNS VIA GETTY IMAGES

With Ruby Amanfu, one of a loyal musical community Jack gathered around him in Nashville for prolific, impromptu recordings.
KEVIN WINTER/WIREIMAGE

Delighted to be honoured by his adopted hometown at Nashville's Music City Walk of Fame in 2015. TERRY WYATT/GETTY IMAGES

Inside Third Man Records, Nashville: HQ to a creative empire of limitless ambition.

Jack with his favourite object, a vinyl LP. His role in the format's resurgence typifies a life built on stubborn, unfashionable values. It's made him an anomalous star in a digital century he's often despised.

Oregon' is a duet, at Lynn's insistence, with psychedelic organ and tabla-style drums that swirl into focus, then burst into mid-Sixties pop, guitars blasting like brass as Jack and Loretta eye each other over pitchers of sloe gin, and have a shameless one-night stand. This high-rolling fun is bettered by 'Mrs. Leroy Brown', in which Lynn is another scorned woman striking back, emptying her errant husband's bank account and ploughing a giant limo into a smoke-thick honky-tonk, to batter the floozie on his lap. 'Come on, Jack, we're out of here,' she commands, job done. Jack laughingly assents, everyone having a blast. His croaking, sandpaper vocals throughout *Van Lear Rose*, though, sound like he's been sleeping in a honky-tonk himself. He noticed, and quit smoking.

After the sessions were split in two when Jack crashed his car on July 9, 2003, Liam Watson was asked to mix *Van Lear Rose*. *White Blood Cells'* engineer Stuart Sikes eventually got the job, back in Memphis' Easley-McCain studio. "I think Loretta's manager was into me mixing it," Sikes recalls. "That one was as fast as *White Blood Cells*. We mixed it in probably two days. I just remember Jack wanting a lot of low-end. And I remember Loretta asking us, 'Boys, is ma voice in toon?' And I've got a Grammy in my living room." When it was finally released on April 27, 2004, *Van Lear Rose* hit number 24 in *Billboard* (Lynn's biggest mainstream success) and number two in its country chart, and Jack found himself sharing 2005's Grammys for Best Country Album and Best Country Collaboration With Vocals (for 'Portland, Oregon'). His confidence in Lynn's essential instincts and untapped versatility had resulted in his finest hour as a producer.

Jack's absorption in country's Southern roots and the world of *Coal Miner's Daughter* nearly went a step further in 2004, when he plotted to repeat the Fifties tactic the film shows forging Lynn's success, and place himself in scenes he watched in his teens. "I saw Jack at a gig he did in Detroit at the Fox Theatre that year," Tim Eriksen remembers. "And he said that he and Loretta were talking about doing a promotional tour in, I think, a Lincoln Continental, some old beater, that Loretta went around in to radio stations when she made her first recordings and said, 'Here, you gotta play my single.' Jack was talking to Loretta about just the two of them going around and showing up at the country stations and saying, 'Here, you gotta play this record.' I'm surprised he didn't do it. It was such a good idea."

This was all to come when the White Stripes ended 2002 with 'Candy Cane Children', a Christmas 7-inch released on December 16 as a "present to the fans", XL said. The song was from the band's pre-history for most, first released on 1998's Detroit Christmas compilation 7-inch *Surprise Package Volume 2*. In the simple vein of those early singles that barely left Detroit, its toreador, tempo-switching riff feints at Meg's drums. Jack addresses a boy and girl both named Candy Cane, sourly explaining Christmas as the climax to '364 days of tears', and wearily concluding that if 'you think it might be fun to make a stand/ Think again, man.' Some of the band's growing tribe of fans soon named themselves Candy Cane Children. The B-side gave them a less jaundiced gift. "In the spirit of the season," Meg announces, "Jack is going to read you a passage from the Gospel of Matthew." A TV or radio murmurs from the next room as he gives earnest drama to the story of the three wise men discovering and worshipping Jesus, and not betraying him to Herod. Meg then haltingly sings 'Silent Night', Jack feeding her misremembered words as she stumbles. "Good job," he tells her anyway, as his family rarely had to him.

Back in Detroit on December 20, a black-garbed Jack sang Christmas songs and Elvis' 'One Night' as Ben Swank played drums during a benefit gig across two stages at the C Pop gallery, handily opposite the Majestic. Meg was there too with her first steady boyfriend since Jack, Swank's Soledad Brothers bandmate Henry Oliver, and her housemate Ko Melina. So was Marcie Bolen. Jack and Brendan Benson cadged cigarettes, and all seemed well at the end of Detroit garage-rock's big year, which had continued in parallel to the White Stripes' success. In June, Sire Records' Seymour Stein, whose previous signing from the area was Madonna, had put the Von Bondies to work on *Lack Of Communication*'s follow-up in San Francisco, with ex-Talking Head Jerry Harrison producing. In November, the Dirtbombs, Von Bondies and Electric Six all played New York's Bowery Ballroom with kindred spirits the Kills and the Datsuns. "We have equal love for the Jackson 5 and the MC5," the Go's Bobby Harlow announced to *NME* as they played three London gigs the same month. A career capsized by Jack's sacking and Sub Pop's refusal of a free jazz-influenced second album had been revived by a sympathetic UK label, Lizard King, who released a self-titled LP in 2003.

The Electric Six also crossed the Atlantic in November, when guitarist Surge Joebot considered the lack of career alternatives to rock'n'roll back home. "There is a drugs trade," he advised *NME*, "but you can only do that so much." In January 6, 2003, they released a bigger UK hit than the White Stripes ever managed, the garage-glam-funk novelty 'Danger! High

Voltage'. 'Fire in the disco!' Dick Valentine howled, donning a glowing, bulbous codpiece in the video for emphasis. Combining giddy hedonism and swirling, Roxy Music-inspired sax solos with slickly addictive, sleazy silliness – pure Gold Dollar – it hit number two. The song had first been released back in autumn 2001, when the Electric Six were still the Wildbunch. Their signing and push by the White Stripes' UK label, XL, had a great deal to do with the presence of a familiar-sounding, high-pitched second vocalist, credited as John S. O'Weary. "I couldn't believe Jack was singing on that record," its co-writer, Steve Nawara, laughs. "I thought it was so hilarious. He was a hard, very minimalist rocker, but, 'We have this disco song we want you to sing on.' That's why his name on the record is John S. O'Weary. John So Weary of playing this fucking disco song!"

To Nawara, this was still a golden time, fulfilling all the promise he'd felt when he found his tribe at the Gold Dollar. "We all knew that the world should be sharing this stuff, because the music was so good. But at the time, the music that was coming out was not very attentive to rock'n'roll. It seemed like no one wanted us, so why bother? And so the fact that every-body started getting popular and famous and making money was just the most dumbfounding thing. We couldn't believe it. When that all happened, to be honest with you, it kind of gave me faith in the universe again. I couldn't believe that people were listening to rock'n'roll again, and to me it was an inspiring time. I was proud to be a human being at that point, because it was no longer Britney Spears. 'Okay, we wanna hear some rock'n'roll. We wanna hear something with some truth to it.' To me it was a very empowering time. I was very proud of it, and I still am to this day."

A cloud passed across this sunny vista, though few noticed at the time. In December 2002, according to later reports in *Spin* and other publications and the Von Bondies' then-manager Alex Hannaford, Jason Stollsteimer filed a police complaint that Jack had come to his door, barged in yelling, and allegedly assaulted him. He was apparently incensed by what he saw as Stollsteimer's ungrateful sniping at his contribution to *Lack Of Communication*, as when he told Germany's *guesteliste.de* that as producer, Jack "sat in the studio and made sure we didn't kill each other. That's it." No police charges were filed, and the press weren't told. The bad blood festered.

The rest of the winter was spent preparing *Elephant* for release. Bruce Brand, a graphic designer going by the name of Arthole when not drum-ming, was put to work. In contrast to his treatment of perceived enemies, he found Jack generous to friends. "I was working on the sleeve with a clapped-out old Apple," Brand recalls. "And he asked me, 'How's it coming along?' I said, 'All right, but it takes half an hour to open that big picture you sent . . .' He said, 'Hmm, sounds like you could do with a new computer.' Two days later, the doorbell went, and I finished it off on that," he says, pointing to an old computer on his floor. "It's probably still in there somewhere. I've got all the artwork I've done for 'em, *Elephant* and loads of singles. Jack sent me a scan of the back of a Seventies blues compilation [one of the Document records he'd obsessed over as a teenager] and said, 'I want it to look like that.' So I meticulously traced the typeface, and I knew he likes his threes, so I did the Es as red backward 3s. He supplied the pictures, and I did layout. There were six versions of the sleeve – he changed the colours on 'em, for LP and for CD in the UK, US and the rest of the world. That looked great," he says, picking an LP from his shelf, "it looked like ox-blood. But he saved in the wrong format so it went grey . . . He was always very specific in his requests. When we did *Get Behind Me Satan* later, he was very meticulous. He had a little jazz beard, and he said, 'Could you turn it upside-down?' And then he wanted the dirt removed from his fingernails. I thought, is he looking through a microscope?"

Jack called *Elephant* the band's "English" album. Holly Golightly's presence was one way of "paying respects" to the country of John Peel, Toe-Rag and their first great success. He holds a cricket bat on the sleeve, a sport Peel recommended (Jack remained hazy on its rules, but Ben Blackwell loved watching it during Australian Dirtbombs tours). Cricket and the Queen also got lyrical nods. More importantly, the album's name met its 'death of a sweetheart' theme. "Elephants . . . become very emotional if they come across the dead bones of another elephant," Jack told *NME*, "and try to bury them." This tender sentiment in the animal world touched him. Elephants also matched his and Meg's personalities – "majesty and regalness, and innocence and subtlety". They're dressed as "dying country stars" on the sleeve to mourn the music's modern "dishonesty", Jack in a red-and-white Nudie suit and Meg in a white dress (funeral-black on the US LP), faces pale as ghosts; on one inner sleeve photo, they twirl, dancing together, while another shows only Meg's blood-drained feet. Every visual element, from the tusk-like cricket bat to the trunk they sit on, keeps inside these latest boxes. Dirtbombs co-drummer Pat Pantano took the photos in Detroit in late December, while Jack's Elvis Christmas CD played. Blanche's Tracee Mae Miller did the makeup and hair. *Elephant* was wholly made by musicians, then handed to a major label.

The White Stripes returned to the stage in England first, on February 7 at London's Electric Cinema after an XL Records promotional film, playing Zeppelin's 'In My Time Of Dying', 'Black Jack Davey', 'You've Got Her In Your Pocket' ("A new song from a record that Miss Meg White and I will release this year"), 'In The Cold, Cold Night' and 'Hotel Yorba' ("a song that was a hit on this island many years ago"). In early March, Meg slipped on melting ice outside a New York club, fracturing her wrist in two places, forcing the postponement of *Top Of The Pops*, an Austin, Texas showcase and a Peel session. V2's New York lawyers forced Peel to cease and desist playing the album when he got it in January. His enthusiastic support of their previous releases, of course, was one reason they were on V2. On March 16 Meg, though winged, joined a press tour of Australasia and Japan. Journalists worldwide were only sent *Elephant* on vinyl (I remember my pleasure when the postman slipped it under my door, and at Jack's reasoning that only those with record players should write about it). It was still leaked online in February, forcing its release a week early on March 31.

These were all details as, at the moment of greatest expectation, Jack pulled out his ace. Neither XL nor V2 wanted 'Seven Nation Army' as a single. Jack, as his contract allowed, insisted. Released on March 7 in the US and April 21 in the UK (but to radio weeks earlier), it was, like Outkast's 'Hey Ya' the same year and only a few this century, a natural hit. Unlike 'Fell In Love With A Girl', the video – kaleidoscopic red, black and white triangles and Ray Harryhausen-style skeleton regiments super-imposed over Jack and Meg – was barely a factor. The riff, and the song's simmering defiance, conquered all. It hit number seven in the UK, four in Germany, three in Italy, and only 76 in the US (their first entry in *Billboard*'s Top 100). "It's very hard to write a mainstream, appealing song without a chorus," Jack noted proudly to Brian McCollum.

And then it kept going. The riff worked equally well pounding out as London strippers plied their trade in seedy East End clubs, at high-end hotel receptions, and from the stands and TV screens as fans of every major sport sang the riff, or added lyrics to praise or bait their team or foes. Supporters of Belgian football's Club Brugge were the first, after hearing it en route to a 2003 Champions League game at AC Milan's San Siro stadium, chanting it as their underdog team somehow won. By 2006, Italy's foot-ballers and fans were singing it to countless millions as they won the World

Cup; cup-winners Alessandro Del Piero and Marco Materazzi then sang it onstage with the Stones in Milan. "Even the President of Italy sang the song," Jack told Pamela Des Barres. "I wanted to fly there and see it, because it was a chant in the streets of Italy." A friend of his saw passengers on a passing cruise-ship trade the riff with sunbathers on a Mediterranean beach. "I didn't get to see any of that," Jack sighed. The chant crossed back to America, sung by baseball crowds oblivious that its writer was in the stadium. He didn't see his song's fame in terms of sales, but a more ancient process. "Nothing is more beautiful than when people embrace a melody and allow it to enter the pantheon of folk music," he said. "As a songwriter it is something impossible to plan . . . I love that most people who are chanting it have no idea where it came from. That's folk music."

In 2003, 'Seven Nation Army' helped *Elephant* pick up unstoppable speed. In its first week, the album sold 126,000 US copies and hit number six; in the UK, it sold almost 65,000, going straight in on April 6 as the White Stripes' first number one.

On April 7, *Elephant*'s originally intended release date, XL hired a coach to take music journalists from London to review the first night of the White Stripes' world tour, at Wolverhampton Civic Hall. Champagne was popped and passed round as we entered the West Midlands in a mood of heady celebration. Whirlwind Heat were on the bill. So were Jack's former, forgiven employers. "We got talking," the Go's John Krautner remembers, "and Jack invited us to open up for him with four big shows, and he was playing 2,000–4,000-capacity theatres at that time, and they were filled. And I gotta say, that was pretty cool of Jack. And if Jack was letting us do that at that point, then maybe it's all water under the bridge."

I scribbled this inside the Civic Hall during the gig's opening songs, for the next morning's *Independent*: "The media uncertainty [around their relationship], like the raw-boned blues howl of their music, recalls rock's first days, when alarming records appeared from nowhere, and their makers were alien unknowns . . . Meg is in white, Jack is in red, and, to a roaring welcome reserved for heroes, they act out their relationship with each other and their music in a mood of high-octane drama . . . It is the taunting way Meg thrusts her chin at her possible ex-husband as she slams the drums, while he shoves himself close and pulls blues squalls from his guitar, that makes the spectacle so human and raw . . . In the new single 'Seven Nation Army', with a single guitar Jack drags up a series of sounds that strip all rock's embellishment. A bass riff tunnels through its tune, followed by a thunderous bull-roar. Finally, the tension coiled in all the

White Stripes' playing is unleashed, as Jack howls arcane words about the Queen of England and hounds of hell. By the end, his face is masked by a curtain of sweat-drenched hair. And his amped, echoing notes make this Midlands hall seem like the temporary, unexpected resting place of the sexual, spectral sound that rock'n'roll was when the world first fell in love with it." The only person who didn't get drunk that night would have been Jack. *Elephant* went on to sell 5.5 million copies.

After five UK gigs, the White Stripes paused for breath back in Detroit. They played the Scottish Rite Theatre on April 15 and the main stage in the same Masonic Temple building the next night. The same week, they'd play with Loretta Lynn for the first time in New York. For now they were two blocks from the Gold Dollar, already a ruin from another age. At the Scottish Rite, they were watched as always by friends, family and fellow musicians. "Thank you, Detroit," Jack, in a torn, Frankenstein-stitched red shirt, said at the end. "This will always be home, no matter what."

"Doesn't matter if you took the helicopter, or climbed up and got all bloody from it," Jack told Conan O'Brien, remembering the view from the summit years later. "The rewards up there are fleeting. And you can't hold on to it. Other people won't let you hang on."

12

Satan

DECEMBER 2014. Driving into Detroit's East Side along Van Dyke Avenue on a weekday afternoon, the devastation is frightening. Most of the houses are burned out and rotting, whole blocks and streets gone. I'm used to this further downtown. I'm not used to the people still standing around in a neighbourhood that looks abandoned, sitting on busted sofas on shattered porches, barely moving. I can see straight through a grim, torn-roofed, windowless shell's billowing, filthy curtains to its empty back doorframe, and there is someone moving inside a place that's not a home. A living, suffering human being couldn't look more like a ghost. George A. Romero made his apocalyptic zombie films attacking American capitalist and racist norms in Pittsburgh, a declining industrial city on the other side of Lake Erie. Much later, I make the link between the living ghost behind the curtain and his shambling, vengeful horrors. At the time, I feel visceral shock at dropping into a world where people move near me in a nightmare. Their lives look dangerous and exhausting. Detroit's pride is its great people and music, but leaving mostly black citizens to such poverty is its country's terrible shame. "These used to be streets," my cabbie Magic Mike says, pointing at scrub fields. "I never come here."

Turning into Seminole Street, it's just the same at first. Then the neighbourhood and buildings remake themselves as prosperity returns, and the landscape transforms into a sedate, tree-lined avenue with archaic street lamps. It could be Cheltenham, or some other prosperous English country town. Signs warn of the private security patrols. "I ain't never seen places like this before," Magic Mike says. The contrast is as shocking as the ghetto we left two minutes ago. We're in Indian Village (the next street is Iroquois), where Detroit's industrial pioneers, lawyers and judges built their mansions between 1894 and the 1910s. Henry Leland, the machinist who founded Lincoln and Cadillac, lived in mock-Tudor splendour at 1052 Seminole. Jack bought 1731 for $524,000 on March 28, 2003, the

208

week before the White Stripes' world tour began in Wolverhampton. It had been built for 19th century lawyer, acting mayor and police chief Ralph Phelps by C. Howard Crane, architect of the Fox Theatre, where Jack was a busboy.

It's a wide, white, simply Georgian-style mansion, far from the grandest on the street, with a substantial lawn, and trees shielding its grounds from view. The gates' black ironwork, like the white double-pillars leading to the black door, white walls, red-tiled roof and black-shuttered windows, match Jack's colour requirements. He reportedly spent $200,000 renovating its four-bedroom, five-bathroom interior, including an especially monomaniacal laundry room with a red-legged white sink, and small red squares studding its black and white tiles. With its provenance, panelled walls, grand staircase, chandeliers and walk-in safe, Jack had bought a life in the wealthy, stylish city past he mourned. "The architecture of Detroit is so incredible," he told *The Tennessean*'s Brian McCollum, "because you had the car money at the right time. I loved the architecture of that home. It just breathes so nicely."

His ex-wife loyally moved to a more Gothic property a block south on Seminole, from the previous rambling old place she'd shared with Ko Melina. "The last time me and Holly Golightly toured America, we stayed with Meg," Bruce Brand recalls. "I spent most of my time playing pinball – because there wasn't any room in the pool. It was a big old house, with three or four people living there." Troy Gregory also visited. "It was big, but not tricked-out. It was a home, with one of her girlfriends there with her. Walking through to the big basement where we jammed was like a Hammer film." Such homes recall the mysterious Detroit mansion of Tom Hiddleston's vampire rock star in *Only Lovers Left Alive*, with its drug dealers and fans haunting the shady street outside, not 1203 Ferdinand, where Hiddleston drives in dreamy homage.

But as we started up Seminole, I thought, did Jack really move here? He was next to a neighbourhood much worse than his Mexicantown home. "The cowardly thing would have been to move to a nice house in the suburbs," he explained to *Mojo*'s Andrew Male. "But you don't get points for that." The nightmare on his doorstep meant he was loyal to his peers. "My mistake is, I continued living where I'm from, Detroit, after I got successful," he later reflected to Stevie Chick. That mistake chased him down in 2003.

There had been 41 White Stripes gigs since Loretta Lynn played with them in New York on April 19, the US *Elephant* tour broken with a May swing through Europe. A photo-shoot with Iggy Pop straight after the Stooges' reunion gig at the Coachella festival in Indio, California on April 27 was one giddy highlight, as Iggy wrestled his young admirer to the ground, muttering, "I can stick it in from here . . ." In a more polite inversion of status, the Stooges' brutal guitar genius Ron Asheton asked to be introduced to Jack. During a week off in Detroit, he took Renée Zellweger to the Magic Stick on the Fourth of July to celebrate the opening of Dave Buick's shop, Young Soul Rebels Records and Tapes. Honouring the man who started the Stripes' vinyl career while squiring a Hollywood lover, Jack, wearing a white silk shirt, wound back time by creating a new band for the night, the Science Farm, with Ben Blackwell and Brian Muldoon. Marcie Bolen made small talk in the crowd with her replacement. "She was really cool," Bolen told *NME*'s Mark Beaumont. "Then Jack had a birthday party, and she put everything together." Zellweger was with him as he turned 28. "27 is the year of rock'n'roll death," Jack recalled to *NME*. "Just before midnight we were sitting around and my friends were saying, 'You've only got about 10 minutes to go, Jack, don't leave the house.' And then we went to bed, woke up and the first thing I did was get in that accident."

Jack had only made it three blocks from his new home on July 9, with Zellweger in his Ford Thunderbird's passenger seat, when a car crash totalled his summer. "This 75 to 80-year-old woman drove right out in the middle of the street," he told *NME*. "There was nothing I could do to get away from it." He got out, checking Zellweger and the other driver were okay. He felt no pain. But his car's airbag had crushed his left index finger against the wheel. "I looked down and saw my finger was just destroyed." He ran back to his house and grabbed his guitar, to see if he could still play. He announced the answer on the White Stripes' website, with lower-case, gonzo urgency: "Hello candy cane children, I broke my finger, three breaks, car wreck, horrible left turn in front of me, no chance of escape, air bag, the air near my fingers, devil in my left hand, doctors say no way, lots of pain, typing with one finger, made it through year of rock'n'roll death, got off with just a warning." *NME* received a more detailed diagnosis. "It was a multiple fracture which means it didn't actually go through the skin but it shattered inside the finger. I can't do anything creative. I can't even tie my shoes." A hospital check-up revealed his finger's ruined bones between its knuckle and first joint were pushing apart instead of healing, needing the permanent insertion of three metal screws. White Stripes music played during the operation, which Jack had filmed and put online. "I always watch surgery documentaries on TV," he enthused to *NME*.

Dylan's fabled motorbike spill near his home in 1966 had stopped a punishing schedule that could have killed him. He vanished for more than a year, his music much changed on his return, and didn't tour again till 1974. Jack's crash at his own commercial peak had more prosaic effects, at first.

The video for *Elephant*'s second single, 'I Just Don't Know What To Do With Myself', was shot without the band. Sofia Coppola's two-line pitch for a black-and-white film of Kate Moss pole-dancing made Jack optimistically picture a metaphor for a lost woman letting herself be exploited, not the slick "underwear ad" starring their Dirty Water gig's star ligger the director presented. "We've insulted Burt Bacharach," he shuddered to *Q*'s John Harris, and barred the video's US use (though it probably helped the single chart at 13 on its September 1 UK release). 'The Hardest Button To Button''s video was shot soon afterwards with Jack's hand in a black cast. Michel Gondry returned to direct Meg's stop-motion, blinking movement across Manhattan playing 32 consecutively filmed bass drums. Though it reached 25 in the UK on its December 9 release, it wasn't much of a single, and the animation didn't compare with 'Fell In Love With A Girl'. Bruce Brand's sleeve homage to Saul Bass' Sixties film posters, and the B-side's echoing, tense, slide guitar take on the Soledad Brothers' 'St. Ides of March' added more, as a mostly acoustic, pensive cover of Blanche's 'Who's To Say' did to 'I Just Don't Know What To Do With Myself'. Jack played guitar on Blanche's original, too, an opiated, Velvet Underground take on country.

The White Stripes' place on the bills of Scotland's T in the Park festival on July 12 and Ireland's Witness festival the next day had been cancelled immediately, costing the band £200,000, *NME* believed. The first 18 dates of their tour's next US leg were postponed and, finally and reluctantly, second headlining slots below Blur at the Reading and Leeds festivals on August 23 and 24 were scrapped.

At Reading, the Detroit festival presence pioneered by Meg's missing band saw her drum on Brendan Benson's 'Jet Lag', and the Electric Six play a jammed main tent where hundreds pressed from outside to hear their recent, second UK Top 5 hit, 'Gay Bar'. On September 2, following a familiar path, the Soledad Brothers played the 100 Club, and sang Son House's 'Death Letter'. Twenty-three Detroit bands were at South By Southwest. "The White Stripes opened up the whole world to Detroit," the Electric Six's bassist Steve Nawara says of that heady summer, "and the next thing you know all of our buddies were hanging out in England at the Columbia Hotel. It was exactly what I wanted ever since I was 12 and was dreaming of being Jimi Hendrix and Led Zeppelin and the Beatles. So to have that opportunity had a very dream-like quality to it." In the sense that he might wake up? "Yes. And I don't think I actually ever did. Because even though we were touring all the time, and getting gold records, and going on *Top Of The Pops*, it was still the music that I was really after. So if you ever do have to wake up, then what the hell are you going to wake up to anyway?"

As his friends worked and partied in Europe, Jack wore his black cast for six weeks, unable to move his left wrist at all, or play guitar for a "terrible, horrible" two months. When he gratefully held it again to finish *Van Lear Rose* in Nashville in September, "C to D minor, chords like that" were unreachable. His injured finger was deeply scarred, with fluid above the knuckle and swelling below. It no longer bent 90 degrees, permanently restricting his playing. In his lost months, he was seen by paparazzi with his good hand in Zellweger's as they dined with Meg and Beck in New York. He visited California. He also hung around a Detroit that was darkening to him.

"A lot of people were excited that, 'We can possibly do something with ourselves musically,'" the Hentchmen's Tim Purrier says of its early boom-time. "There was some optimism that they weren't just playing in a band for nothing. That they might make some kind of career." To Dave Feeny, there was "both a lot of bandwagon-jumping and sour grapes. The White Stripes' success certainly carried over to groups like the Paybacks, Hentchmen, Blanche, the Dirtbombs, Electric Six, the Waxwings, Detroit Cobras, the Sights and Brendan Benson."

"When the White Stripes started getting super-big, I actually photographed them less," Doug Coombe remembers of their changing status in Detroit. "I just wanted to let 'em be. Eminem and J Dilla blew up around the same time, so there was a lot of excitement about music from our city finally being recognised. But I was leery, because I'd seen what happened in Seattle. Like [Ann Arbor's] Big Chief, who signed to Sub Pop in the early Nineties, then signed to Capitol then broke up. It creates its own pressures."

"I remember Seymour Stein sniffing around," says Dan Kroha. "The Doll Rods were almost old hat already. So we missed out on all that excitement. And I was also cynical of it. There was a time when people *really* wanted to be hanging out with Jack and Meg, and were really vying to and making a big deal of, 'Last night I was with Jack and Meg, and blah blah blah.' I was just like, 'No, man, I don't want any part of that.' So I really stepped back. And when people came to town doing articles about Detroit, I fucking stayed away. I didn't talk about it."

"We were going to Europe and seeing huge posters next to McDonald's saying, 'The White Stripes are coming'," Troy Gregory recalls. "It's nice to see that with anybody from the neighbourhood. Like when we were kids and my dad would point out, 'The Supremes lived over there. That singer was a hooker on that corner . . .' It's good, because you're always told in a working-class town that you're wasting your time to have aspirations, that you're worthless and musician's a stupid job, don't even try. Then you had people coming in from England, Germany and Italy, wanting to see the Gold Dollar and the Magic Stick, asking, 'Where's the Hotel Yorba?' and interviewing bands Jack told them about, to help his friends. So people were very happy for them. But then problems started with finance. 'Oh, I played on that, so I should get this much money.' A lot of people became very jealous, and felt they were owed things."

"I was jealous," Dan Kroha admits. "I never held it against Jack, and it never caused me to be mean or snobbish to him, but yeah I was jealous, because those guys started off opening up for the Doll Rods. And I think the Doll Rods had a chance of making it, and we worked really hard. But I know how the music business is."

"Now even the parties afterwards were packed like the clubs," Gregory says of the scene as it heated up, "and you'd have people going, [thuggish voice] 'I fucking hate so-and-so, their band sucks.' I remember a fight at one of the parties because someone fucked somebody's girlfriend. Someone got their window busted out, all of this type of shit. It never seemed like cocaine was around much. But all of a sudden, it was everywhere. And that leads to really poor judgement. So there was more, 'Well, fuck those guys,' and people were taking sides. Even members of the Electric Six quit or were fired."

"There was resentment," Nawara says of his band's return from European conquest. "There was also a very strong punk ethic. So it was, [sneering] 'Oh, you sell-out.' Meanwhile, everyone was jealous of you! It created divisions among our little group, that was so closely knit before. But not enough to destroy it. I'm still friends with everyone. I don't remember the hate that much."

When Eminem got fame and money, he bought a regular house in a regular street. The neighbours gawping at him in the bathroom and knocking on his door to fight forced his retreat into a gated community. Now Jack stood at the Magic Stick's bar, wishing nothing had changed in the small community that first accepted him. "At this very moment there are probably Detroit bands talking rubbish about us," he'd worried to Sweden's *Sonic* in May. "We all used to be sitting in the same boat, but now Meg and I are sitting in our own little boat. It can be difficult to relate to others who are still in the same position we were in a year ago." He said he sometimes dreaded depressing others with their latest success. "Instead I hope that our friends find inspiration in what we've done, to give them new hope. We have," he added plaintively, "worked hard."

"Jack was just another really good musician around town," Gregory says. "But now he's going out to the bar, and people come up who just want to be his friend because he's famous, or rich, and what can they get out of him? And even other friends, because everyone else is still broke, are going, 'You're making all this money. How come you're not buying the drinks?' I don't think he had enough people who just said, 'Good job, man,' and left it at that. It was somebody getting in his face saying, 'I want to talk to you about my band, you should sign them.' Or resentful guys going, 'Why didn't you get us to open for you? Why'd you get the Strokes?' People hating on him stupidly, or wanting to be his best friend."

"The White Stripes made people buy those other bands' records," Simon Keeler says, listing their impact when he worked at UK distributors Cargo. "Before them, we sold 500 of the Dirtbombs' first album. We sold 5,000 of the next one. We'd sold 1,300 of the Von Bondies' *Lack Of Communication* on Sympathy, then we licensed it and sold 30,000, giving the band £20,000. I couldn't sell [Alabaman two-piece] the Immortal Lee County Killers records, but once the White Stripes happened, they came over and did a Peel session. It also facilitated me putting out the 5.6.7.8's, and distributing the first Electric Six single. It greased the path that Jack left behind him, and people slipped in easy. I don't think a lot of them actually fucking realised that. But anyone who thinks otherwise can get back to putting out their records that won't sell 400 copies. Anyone who's bitter, saying, 'Why didn't we sell 50,000?' – I'm talking about the Von Bondies primarily – your records aren't that great, mate, and you did pretty good. What people don't see is Jack's eye, the effort that he puts into everything. People should take inspiration from that, not say, 'Why isn't it happening to me?'"

"If you're working in a job you don't like, and see something can come out of [music] from some other cat you know, it changes the perspective," counters Gregory. "It shows even moreso a desperation. You've got people just scraping to get by, and so they get jealous when people come through going, 'Oh, did ya ever hear of Jack White?' It's like a friend winning the lottery. And it's not necessarily just greed. It's a survival thing. You and all your buddies only have 25 bucks between you, and you've got to go to work in the morning and your car's a piece of shit, and suddenly one of your buddies is selling millions. Very hard, from a working-class background. And other bands felt they didn't get their payoff from it. Jack's getting more and more popular, and it just baffled them. And I'm sure he took a lot of his buddies with him for a while, until they started expecting it, or got weird about his success. 'How dare you be brilliant?' I've seen that reaction to other friends that succeeded.

"You have the desperation to do this, to work in some shitty-ass job so you can go out and play," Gregory concludes, "but then a lot of bands saw, 'You can get really big – I want that shot.' Instead of, 'Let's get together and create something off the cuff,' it was, 'Let's get together and create something that's gonna fucking sell.'" The careless creative spark that had flickered and caught in Zoot's and the Gold Dollar, luring Gregory back to Detroit, dimmed for him. "I stopped following other groups, and went touring with the Dirtbombs."

When Jack stood at the bar now, he unbalanced it. By Gregory's estimation, to local strugglers he was a sudden glimpse of escape to claw and clamber at, like the last helicopter out of Saigon. That was by no means true of all the 50 to 100 at the scene's core. But with the hangers-on too, they must have sometimes seemed claustrophobically demanding to a man who had anyway lost faith in their values. Jack was an international rock star returning home to petty small-town problems.

He mentioned one to *NME*'s John Mulvey in September. "Everyone's been a really good family," he claimed, "except for the Von Bondies . . . The singer has really gone off the deep end. He's very mean-spirited . . . I don't speak to them. When you get burned constantly, there's no point in forgiveness any more."

The White Stripes restarted the *Elephant* world tour on September 13 with their biggest headline show to date, playing to 8,500 at Berkeley's outdoor, century-old Greek Amphitheatre. For once they soundchecked thoroughly, Jack testing a finger that would need physical therapy during

2003's remaining 46 gigs. *NME*'s Mulvey noted simplified early songs that night, Jack trusting his capacities more as it went on. He read Johnny Cash's 'I Got Stripes' lyric to mark Cash's death the day before, and the incrementally expanding stage-show now fired red-and-white striped strobes during 'Seven Nation Army'. The tour bus, with Meg's new Miniature Pinscher puppy Chester on board, drove almost 1,000 miles to their next gig in Vancouver. They continued through the US, New Zealand (including a secret gig at Auckland's Freeman's Bay Primary school) and Australia (where a televised, thrilling, blues-heavy set at Sydney's Livid Festival on October 18 showed the cloud of long, frizzed hair that a beefed-up, sombrely black-shirted Jack had grown while away, and Meg's Sixties Loretta Lynn bouffant). In Japan, Jack bought traditional Japanese folk CDs, and Meg drank sakes and beer into the night. But in Tokyo, *Q*'s John Harris found Jack with black rings under his eyes, and gently trembling hands. "I want to go home right now," he said, then laughed mirthlessly. The next stop was Rio. A further month of gigs lay between Jack and Detroit.

The White Stripes returned on November 28 and 29 to the city's Masonic Hall, where they'd begun their fractured US tour in April. The next night in Cleveland they finally, briefly reached the end of the road. On December 7, Jack wore a garish gangster's maroon pinstriped suit and fedora to *Cold Mountain*'s premiere in Westwood, California. At UCLA's Royce Hall the next night, T Bone Burnett oversaw singers led by Jack and Alison Krauss and readers including Anthony Minghella and Nicole Kidman in *Words And Music From Cold Mountain*. Backed by soft, slow mandolin, fiddle and banjo, Jack opened with 'Wayfaring Stranger'. Wearing a brown, wide-lapelled suit, he was still and seemed hunched, with a pinched, weary voice, as if acting the part of a dying hillbilly star. Jack's five songs on the soundtrack album, released on December 16, included one he'd written, 'Never Far Away'. A session in Hollywood's Capitol Studios had let him add acoustic guitar to his first nervous Nashville go, which Norman Blake's mandolin and Nancy Blake's cello now wove beneath. His lyric traced Jude Law's wounded soldier's mystic odyssey towards Kidman's Ada, the vocal delicate like McCartney singing a Seventies West Coast ballad. Perhaps helped by Burnett's production, this was a mature, limpidly affecting Jack.

On December 13, he was at the Magic Stick for the launch of Blanche's debut album, *If You Can't Trust The Doctors . . .* Brendan Benson, who like Jack had guested on the track 'Who's To Say', opened for them with Chris

Plum. The Von Bondies were there too, after their own eventful, lower-key year. They'd been bottom of the bill for the Stooges' Detroit area return at Clarkston's Energy Music Theatre on August 25; when the White Stripes played Coachella's main stage in April, they were in the humid Mojave tent, watched by Jack from the third row, Jason Stollsteimer claimed. They'd finished their major label debut, *Pawn Shoppe Heart*, and tomorrow was to be packed with press interviews and photos. Jack was talking intently with his recent ex, Marcie Bolen. She gave him a stuffed baby duck as a peace offering – he refused the well-meant gift, the sort of 'comedy taxidermy' he loathed. Already seething, he spied Stollsteimer, who he'd attacked a year before, standing stage-right in the packed crowd as Benson played. "He was pissed, and I was like, 'Oh man, something's going to go down,'" Bolen recalled in Steve Miller's *Detroit Rock City*. "I just knew he was in such a bad mood, and I was going over to Jason, 'Stop. Don't do it.' Jack was yelling at him and I was hitting him on the back, 'Don't, don't, don't, don't.'"

According to the police report that followed, Stollsteimer told Jack, "I have nothing to say to you." Then Jack boiled over. He spat at the man he saw as his nemesis, and punched him to the ground, hitting him up to seven times. The photo taken immediately afterwards shows Stollsteimer's eye purple and swollen shut, and his face caked with blood. His fellow Von Bondies helped drag Jack off, tended to their singer's wounds with ice and towels, and took him to the Detroit Receiving Hospital two blocks away. According to Stollsteimer, he was later operated on for permanent damage to a torn retina. In the crowd watching Benson, many saw nothing. The Von Bondies' press schedule was scrapped.

The next day, Jack's mug-shot was taken at the 13th Police Precinct. He hired Wally Piszcatowski, Eminem's lawyer on a concealed weapon charge in 2001, whose statement to the press emphasised Jack's position as "a positive spokesperson for the city of Detroit . . . he's helped a lot of people in this community and that should not be forgotten." Claiming self-defence, Jack was charged with aggravated assault, and faced a possible though unlikely year's jail. "He probably would have continued [the] beating had several of the bystanders not pulled him off," Wayne County prosecutor Mike Duggan told reporters. "We concluded that Mr. White did, in fact, bruise his hand on Mr. Stollsteimer's face, but that does not constitute a valid charge. All of the witnesses indicated that Mr. Stollsteimer did not provoke and did not even attempt to fight back. It was not a fight in which blows were exchanged." Jack blamed one witness in particular for that account. "He's like, 'You didn't stick up for me. You told the lawyer that, what I did,'" Bolen recalled to Steve Miller. "I'm like, 'I just said what I saw.' . . . He's like, 'Fuck you. You should have stood up for me. That guy never stuck up for you.'"

On New Year's Eve, the White Stripes headlined a double bill with the Flaming Lips at Chicago's Avalon Ballroom. "I'm glad to be here with friends tonight," Jack told the Lips' singer Wayne Coyne. "Thank you." Coyne hugged him. "We're gonna play a song together real quick," Jack continued, as Coyne pointed meaningfully to his watch and 2003 ticked down. "A song about friendship . . . the year has been long, it's been good and bad, but we're all still friends, right?" he asked the audience, his arms held out beseechingly. Streamers started to trail over him as the Stripes and Lips played 'We're Going To Be Friends'. Then Jack spent 2004's first seconds playing 'Seven Nation Army', as red, black and white balloons and confetti dropped on the roaring crowd. "Happy New Year!" he wished, optimistically.

On January 14 he pleaded not guilty to 36th District Court Judge Donna Robinson Milhouse, and posted a $5,000 bail bond without travel restrictions, permitting an important UK tour to start five days later. The charge hung over him till March 9, when Jack, in a black pin-stripe suit and fedora and with auburn hair nearer his natural brown, told the same court's Judge Paula G. Humphries that a "tussle" resulted in Stollsteimer's face falling on the fist Jack had injured in his car crash, then being punched "a couple of times". He pled down from aggravated assault, to guilty to assault and battery, paid $750 in fines and costs and agreed to anger management classes. Afterwards, he read a note plucked from his fedora to the waiting press. "I regret allowing myself to be provoked to the point of getting into a fist-fight, but I was raised to believe that honour and integrity mean something. And that these principles are worth defending. And that's how I live my life." This high-mindedness was hard to equate with Stollsteimer's bruised face. Later that evening, while Jack and his circle brooded at the Bronx Bar, the Von Bondies launched *Pawn Shoppe Heart* at the Magic Stick.

Jack waited till July to give a 700-word defence of his actions, typed with all-lower case urgency. He claimed he'd been "completely exploited" for "recognition and fame". He said Stollsteimer "grabbed me to pull me down and pulled out a good deal of my hair", making Jack "hit him to get him off of me. Then he landed on my hand, which became cut on the broken glass." He sneered at the infamous photo Stollsteimer had "insisted" on, and blamed the "permanent damage" to his eye on a teenage contact lens accident mentioned when they'd toured together. Stollsteimer had "played the victim" at Jack's expense, the culmination of "almost two years" of "spreading lies and gossip", with "perfect timing" for *Pawn Shoppe Heart*'s release. He listed all he'd done for the Von Bondies – producing *Lack Of Communication* for free, playing and singing on it uncredited, paying for plane tickets and food on high-profile world tours. He didn't mention the guitarist had been his girlfriend. Still the generosity was true, and typical. "Violence is a ridiculous notion," Jack concluded. "And I would never walk up to someone with the intent to inflict pain on them. But I'm not going to let someone do the same to me without protecting myself."

Jack's version sounded paranoid in places. His memory of the melee might be honest, but wasn't recognised by witnesses. Far from benefiting *Pawn Shoppe Heart*'s press campaign, the beating cancelled it (with some interviews rescheduled). No one made him punch, and keep punching. It's true that many who dealt with Stollsteimer in those days found him "horrible . . . greedy and unpleasant", in the words of one label person who was asked to exploit that brutal photo. The 25-year-old from Ypsilanti who felt a Detroit outsider could be foolish and aggravating.

Stollsteimer claimed to *NME* that "I got rid of all my anger problems when I was a kid, and I'd rather stare someone down than fight them." Jack, though, was different. Recalling an incident at the Dirty Water Club in 2002, he admitted to *Mojo*'s Andrew Male that "sometimes there's a voice inside of me that says, 'This element needs to be removed.'" "I know the person he punched that night," Dirty Water's PJ Crittenden says, "a German called Clement. I think it was a case of the guy dancing too vigorously, and he bumped into a woman, and Jack defended the woman's honour. The guy didn't do it on purpose. Jack went a bit over the top, but Clement didn't care." A *Metro-Times* editorial was less forgiving, claiming: "This is hardly the first time White's temper has gotten the best of him. Whispers about White's violent outbursts have been in circulation around the incestuous Detroit rock scene for quite some time, though you'd be hard-pressed to get aspiring musicians to go on the record about it." The paper cited an "altercation" with the Sights' drummer Dave Shettler in the Garden Bowl in 2001 (the Sights' singer Eddie Baranek would try, like Stollsteimer, to distance himself from Jack's patronage with negative interviews during 2003), while Jack "reportedly . . . kicked" the Datsuns' Dolf de Borst in England. More positively, the paper had reported Jack being punched in October 2002 when foiling a purse-snatcher outside the Lager House.

In the USA's then-murder capital, all had seen worse. "I wish it didn't happen, because I like Jack and Jason," Dave Zainea says, sitting in the Garden Bowl in 2015. "I don't like any violence, especially in my own club. I don't think it's that big a deal. Jack grew up in Detroit, I grew up in Detroit. Sometimes you get in fist-fights." John Krautner agrees. "Normally something like that would have been tucked under the rug. People get punched in the face all the time in Detroit. Usually it's their own fault," he laughs, "and I think in this case it was too. But Jack was on MTV. Suddenly it was like a celebrity punched out some local guy!" Jim Diamond alone sounds disgusted. "It was completely idiotic and unnecessary. Jason's not a threatening person in any way."

Back then, Blanche's Dan Miller, one of Jack's first and most fervent supporters, told *NME*'s John Mulvey that Stollsteimer had already been "a dead man walking" in Detroit. The *Metro-Times*' music editor Brian Smith (likely its editorial's writer) told his predecessor Chris Handyside that "there is unbelievable resentment towards, of all people, Jason . . . you go to clubs and overhear snickers about what a pussy the guy is." Stollsteimer later said "almost every Detroit musician turned their back on us." Jack was the winner to side with in a scene whose idealism had been tarnished.

The red rage Bolen saw consume him seemed the culmination of something more than loathing Stollsteimer. "I was driving myself mad trying to figure out what it is I'm doing wrong, because it really feels like I'm doing the right thing," Jack told Andrew Male of his good intentions to peers. "It's almost like you're supposed to be more selfish in this game . . . to get what you want." He'd pictured his response if pushed too far in the White Stripes' first song, 'Screwdriver'; he wouldn't 'stand there grinning'. In 'I Think I Smell A Rat', he'd fantasised wielding a baseball bat. 'Seven Nation Army' was in part a disavowal of local resentments and jealousies, Dylan's 'Positively Fourth Street' relocated to Cass. Now the old, boyish Jack, talking giddily and beaming innocently, seemed a long way from the beefy 28-year-old bulling towards Stollsteimer with blood in his eyes. The most wrenching change since his breakdown and refashioning at 19 had begun.

Between court dates, the White Stripes began their UK return on January 19 at Liverpool's atmospheric Royal Court Theatre, playing their biggest British shows yet at London's Alexandra Palace over the next two nights.

Elephant had pushed them into the arenas they used to fear, and the Meg wannabes in red and white at Wolverhampton six months before now mingled with more casual listeners in Guns N' Roses T-shirts, all shoving and craning to see them across the cold, cavernous hall. Writing for *Uncut*, I noted Jack's "darkly manic, near hysterical mood . . . legs braced and black mane falling around his shoulders, he looks like a guitar hero from the darkest days of the Seventies . . . 'Hotel Yorba' is among the first songs transformed into White Metal . . . split in two by a blizzard of crackles and shrieks." At one point, Meg "is reaching up towards him as he leans down towards her, as if puckering lips for a kiss neither will allow, an embrace that is beyond them." The punk concision and sheer miracle of their sound at the Astoria in 2001 had noticeably loosened, *Elephant*'s indulgence in guitar solos "like this high-concept band . . . being stretched until it finally finds its limit, and snaps." Despite its external majesty, Jack was crestfallen to discover the so-called Palace was "an aircraft hangar". He had better luck at Blackpool's ornate, relatively intimate Empress Ball-room on January 27 and 28, where the band filmed their first live DVD, *Under Blackpool Lights*. Naturally, he insisted the shows were filmed with multiple Super-8 cameras, forcing pit-stop reel-changes every three minutes. The grainy film stock catches light and colours, and Meg's deliberately dramatic presence, feline as she curls her head back, or a matador benignly goading Jack with an averted face or jutting jaw, but always listening, and mouthing songs she's lost in. Sometimes she and Jack still slip slightly out of sync as they react to each other, abrasive grit rare in arenas. Following an ignored last *Elephant* single, 'There's No Place For You Here', 'Jolene' finally became an A-side on November 20 as the live single to promote the DVD, reaching number 16 in the UK.

Jack's gifts to Detroit friends continued. While Soledad Brothers Ben Swank and Johnny Walker house-sat in his Seminole mansion, he played their previous band Henry and June's lone single, 'Goin' Back To Memphis', on the DVD. Blanche were tour support, playing to tens of thousands, and staying at Renée Zellweger's expensive flat overlooking Hyde Park, where they toasted their luck with flutes of champagne (though an associate recalls a later falling out with Jack over "a redhead"). "Jack seemed to take it all in stride," says Dave Feeny, Blanche's steel guitarist. "But at Alexandra Palace, he introduced me to Jeff Beck. And almost every show in a big city was like that – Colin Firth, Adrien Brody, the Strokes, Winona Ryder, of course Renée."

While Jack had his demons back home, Meg also had her misgivings.

When *Elephant* was released, she still owned all her bar work outfits, not wanting to tempt fate by trashing them. "There's nothing I'm doing these days that I ever thought I'd do," she told *The Observer*'s Andrew Perry that November, sounding content, even proud. But there was a downside. "She was a night owl on tour," Dave Feeny remembers. "She'd typically be up and sometimes we'd chat a bit on the bus. Like most folks thrust into the limelight, she had trouble adjusting to all the attention and press they were getting." Troy Gregory saw her discomfort. "She came to a Dirtbombs show, and when some people tried to talk to her, you could see her squirm." He mimics clenching fists by her side. "When every time you've ever met someone they've been quiet and shy, I think she was completely uncomfortable with that fuss. I keep on hearing that she didn't dig that too much." The White Stripes' popularity "hit her like a ton of bricks," Steve Nawara confirms.

By contrast, when the Great High Mountain tour brought musicians including Ralph Stanley from *Cold Mountain* and *O Brother, Where Art Thou?* to Detroit's Fox Theatre on May 13, Tim Eriksen found guest-star Jack's callow nerves of two years before wholly gone. "He was there with," he laughs knowingly, "these girls. He was still sweet. He seemed to me more comfortable in his fancy clothes. I was happy for him."

The White Stripes proved their mainstream rock acceptance at Los Angeles' Staples Center on February 8 with Grammys for 'Seven Nation Army' (Best Rock Song) and *Elephant* (Best Alternative Music Album). Introduced by their friend Beck as "the sound of dead cell-phones and oil rigs, the sound of empty parking lots and school buses", they broke off 'Seven Nation Army' for another burn through 'Death Letter''s blues (to a watching Eric Clapton's bemusement, and just before BB King). The equanimity Eriksen saw in Jack was then tested when Bob Dylan played Detroit's State Theatre on March 17, and invited him backstage. "We've been playing one of your songs lately at soundchecks," the man Jack called his father, alongside God and Gorman Gillis, said. "I was afraid to ask which one," Jack later told the *Wall Street Journal*. Back at home, he nervously rang the theatre to speak to Dylan's bassist. "I was like, 'Bob said some things that I thought maybe – maybe I misconstrued. Was he meaning that he wanted me to play with him?'" That snowy St. Patrick's night, Dylan sang of 'Highway 61''s 'seventh son', then the phrase Jack had first heard in the song as a child was repeated in an encore of 'Ball And Biscuit'. Begun by Dylan at the piano with a full-throated sneer before Jack took over, it blended well with Dylan's own recent songs' blues reclamations. They hugged at the end, starting something like a friendship.

Jack supported *Van Lear Rose*'s release with TV appearances, including a May 3 *Letterman* performance of its single, the duet 'Portland, Oregon', where Lynn seems Jack's guest. Its video has her leading him and the Do Whaters at a honky-tonk, the pair sitting like lovers between sets. With the album barely played on country radio, Jack gave his audience to Lynn. A second project from 2003, Jim Jarmusch's film *Coffee And Cigarettes*, opened in the US on May 14. Jarmusch had met the White Stripes after their free New York gig in 2002. When Jack saw a book about electrical pioneer Nicola Tesla on the director's desk at a later meeting, an epic Jarmusch-directed Stripes video with Jack as Tesla and Philip Seymour Hoffman as his rival inventor Thomas Edison was planned, including Edison's electrocution of an elephant. When financial sense prevailed, Jack and Meg instead charmingly played their band selves in *Coffee And Cigarettes*' anthology of black-and-white two-handers. "C'mon, Jack, you dragged me all the way down here in your little red wagon," Meg says, demanding he tell her about the Tesla coil (a 19th century transformer he sought in real life). Grabbing goggles and gloves, Jack plays himself as an enthusiastic, impatiently snapping kid, a cranky know-it-all whose demonstration of the coil ends in carnage. His reverence for Tesla – a mis-understood, self-sufficient genius 'robbed' of credit for his inventions – gave a glimpse of the Jack who'd wished to build a Tesla coil as a child and still worked on eccentric inventions, only a few, like *De Stijl*'s Peppermint Triple Tremelo, ever reaching the public.

In September, Jack and Zellweger amicably split. And on October 24, 2004, the White Stripes' champion and friend John Peel died of a heart attack in Peru. The White Stripes turned out to be the last great link in a chain of stubbornly personal discoveries that improved music's course. Jack understood as he paid tribute to "the last important DJ in the world", who "bought our album because it was the same colours as his favourite football team . . . He was proud that he once met Kennedy and took his picture. After our session, we were proud that we once met John Peel."

Still, Jack looked back on a year when he "got to play or be on the same stage with Bob Dylan, Loretta Lynn, Beck, Jeff Beck, David Bowie and Iggy Pop" as his life's best. Even the relentless touring that made him shaky and homesick in 2003 was done; after January 2004's European gigs, only eight summer festivals remained ("We caught a cab this time," Jack joked when they finally reached Reading). Offers to lucratively tour *Elephant* into 2005 were firmly refused. But in a *Guardian* online interview with his *Coffee And Cigarettes* co-star Steve Coogan, Jack's response to a suggestion they meet, made in caps-locked typing that Coogan said felt like "shouting", confirmed a darkening frame of mind: "I'm sorry Stephen I can't do coffee with you . . . I would love to meet with you in principle but I'm not as trusting as, well, such as before I first came to England for example."

Detroit now dogged Jack's heels, as Jim Diamond sued him late in 2004 for a copyright share in the first two White Stripes albums. Diamond had already demanded payment for originally recording and playing sax on 'Danger! High Voltage', which Jack also played on for free, back when none of them had money or hope of it. "Jim did regret it," Troy Gregory says. "Because he felt it made him look like this horrible guy going after money. And he felt he did have things to do with those records, and Jack felt another way. I got called in to give a deposition on that shit. And I was very pissed off about it." He saw a more Detroit solution. "Those two guys should have met up at the bar, and if they couldn't work it out, they should have gone out the back and beat the shit out of each other, and then whoever lost buys the other guy a drink. And I like both guys. They asked me to name groups I'd worked with, to substantiate I was a musician. And it was a list of about 30 bands. Jack got a kick and started laughing, some of them he hadn't even heard of. But I hated it. And Ben [Blackwell, then a Dirtbomb with Diamond and Gregory] was of course very upset because it's his family, and Jim was a friend. It became a weird thing of taking sides, and hearsay. It was stupid, and it was really sad to see. And it did cause a wedge, because there was that problem that Jim had with the Electric Six, too. And that didn't go very well. They wanted to take the tapes and go to another expensive studio when a label picked them up. And Jim's like, 'Well you've still got to pay me for these tapes.' 'You're being a real dick! You're trying to steal from us.' It got really weird, because all of a sudden there was some money around, for some people."

Diamond's suit finally went to trial on June 12, 2006. Stollsteimer testified he'd found a magazine interview downplaying Jack's assistance to his band and an angry note from him pinned to his door with a knife, which Jack called "a laughable lie". Diamond claimed royalties and co-authorship of mechanical rights – the recordings, not songs – on *The White Stripes* (which credited him as co-producer) and *De Stijl* (which he merely mixed), one of his lawyers stating in court that he was "at that time, in that place, equally talented" in contributing to the band's sound. The jury threw the claim out in 20 minutes as Jack and Meg ate lunch. Asked by *Turn It Down*'s Rich Tupica in 2007 what he was proudest of, Diamond immediately answered: "Standing up to Jack White." To me he says: "I don't really want to talk about that any more. I'd say that was basically from the influence of a lawyer person that I knew who wanted to further his own career. I want to put that behind me. It's pretty much behind me." Asked how the boom-time affected Detroit, he sighs unhappily. "Oh, I don't know. Probably some people got big heads. I don't really remember . . . and then there were some doldrum years in 2004, 2005. I started working with more out-of-town bands." As Stollsteimer found, many Detroit bands wouldn't work with him once he fought Jack.

Jack despised Diamond's actions. They further poisoned Detroit's well for him, and hardened a heart he felt had been too open. In future years, former friends who crossed him financially would be cut little slack, as if his own now relatively huge wealth was irrelevant. On Third Man's website Jack claimed that Rocket 455's Jeff Meier wanted $10,000 for the first White Stripes session tapes (which Meier recorded), when Third Man decided to release an alternate take of 'Let's Shake Hands' in 2009. The element of survival in such actions suggested by Gregory was just greed to Jack's now untrusting eyes. The resultant single's run-out groove reads: "RESCUED FROM EBAY OUT OF THE HANDS OF AN EXTORTIONIST DETROIT ENGINEER" (any actual amount paid is unknown). Meier put some chairs Jack upholstered for him on eBay, too. Even Neil Yee, whose open-handed running of the Gold Dollar gave the White Stripes their first break, found Third Man bruising to tangle with in 2012, when they wanted his tapes of early gigs for their Vault vinyl subscription series. They at first offered $100 a show, he said, though amicable agreement was later reached.

On my way across the river to Third Man's Nashville headquarters on a summer night in 2015, I talk to Jeff Meier on the phone for about half an hour. Like Diamond, he seems a decent man. But he sounds delicate and shaken from his financial run-in with Jack. In the end, it's too enmeshed with even his happy memories of Detroit's early scene to bear to be interviewed. In the schism after Jack's unlikely success, people were left burned on both sides.

Jack found respite with a musician who remained devoted to him. Brendan Benson saw in Jack "something I think I once had . . . heart and soul", a quality the music business had "corrupted" in him, he told *Spin*.

Benson's attic home studio was on East Grand Boulevard, in another nice old house, but outside Indian Village amidst the East Side's despair. On one of Jack's visits in May 2004, Benson played a demo tape whose only lyrics were, 'find yourself a girl, and settle down'. Benson asked his friend to finish words he was "tapped out" on, handing him his songbook. With his usual fearless instinct, Jack scribbled verses and a new key phrase: 'Steady, as she goes'. He blended his writing into Benson's wish "to find the beauty in the clichéd phrases," he told *Uncut*'s Barney Hoskyns, dropping his often knotty, opaque Stripes style to ponder 'a simple life in a quiet town'. They recorded it that day. The next week, he played the tape while driving his default rhythm section, Greenhornes bassist Jack Lawrence and drummer Patrick Keeler, to Detroit to demo with Benson themselves. The four were soon recording in Benson's attic in 125-degree discomfort, Jack remembered approvingly. Finished on the first or second take by the ad hoc band, 'Steady, As She Goes' was "a little more rocking" than the demo, Keeler recalled. After his drums, the first sound you hear is the bass line removed from Jack's music for so long, followed by his guitar, sourly ominous then stinging. The title matches the piratical swagger of the happy, fuzzed-up choruses, complicated by the verses' hitching skips and doubts. This apparent ode to mature, married life asks you to 'settle for a world neither up or down', stability like 'glue', and the suspicion that finding a sympathetic partner means 'you tripped and fell'. "We're all getting older now and enough of goofing around," Jack told Hoskyns of their musicians' lives. "How much of this world do we stay a part of and how much do we reject?"

On its eventual release on January 30, 2006, as the debut by a band now called the Raconteurs, 'Steady, As She Goes' became the second biggest hit, albeit co-written, of Jack's life – number four in the UK, and beating even 'Seven Nation Army' in the US at 54 (a reminder that rock's minor part in 21st century pop remained true).

That first day in Benson's attic, he and Jack also demoed 'Broken Boy Soldier'. In its band form it's runaway, rattling Seventies rock, Jack's voice Robert Plant-high but also throatily cynical, as he sings disgustedly of putting away childish things (the very childishness the White Stripes had championed). He's no longer asking others for forgiveness 'and I want you to know this', rages a man who's 'through ripping myself off' with arrested development. Whatever Benson's part in these words, Jack meant them all. He was dumping the dead weight of "negative" opinions he'd always accommodated to "do what I need to do", he told *Spin*'s Dorian

Lynskey. "I was fighting a lot of losing battles . . . I just felt like giving up," he further explained his crisis to *Mojo*'s Stevie Chick. "I wanted to know why [ex-friends] hated me so much . . . I was hurting myself too much, being too open to all that."

The White Stripes record made between Raconteurs sessions, *Get Behind Me Satan*, became a "farewell to a lot of the parts of my personality that I didn't want to see any more." Named for his "favourite thing that Jesus ever said", he shortened the phrase "Get thee behind me, Satan" to bring out its ambiguity. Maybe he was spurning temptation. Or maybe he'd be better off if even Satan had his back. "The idea beneath all of this is get behind me, get with me on it," he told Pamela Des Barres.

"I got scared thinking if we recorded [*Elephant*'s follow-up] in Detroit it would have to feel like it was coming from my neighbourhood," Jack had told *NME*'s Julian Marshall. "The one I grew up in." The implied impossibility of that feeling showed his alienation now. Third Man Studios, a name that travelled with him, was applied to the main hall and stairway at Seminole, where the White Stripes anyway made their first hometown record since *De Stijl*. Songs were finished in the studio on acoustic guitar, piano and marimba, with electric guitars mostly moth-balled. They started in late February 2005 with their live engineer Matthew Kettle, meaning to be finished by March 18, but the album seemed "cursed", Jack told *Mojo*. Equipment mysteriously falling or breaking left him "close to scrapping the whole record." This spooked frustration suited a tortured, lonely album.

He said it was about "characters and the idea of truth". His poetic preface this time found transformative power in artifice, telling his fans that stories represented realisable dreams. *Get Behind Me Satan*, though, told tales of bitterness, denial and despair. After *Elephant*'s muscular rock, its music expressed ennui and doubt. "The riff for 'Blue Orchid' . . . turned the album completely around," Jack recalled. But its stiff, treated electric guitar sounds splintered and thin. What connects is his hectoring, resentful voice, demanding, 'How dare you? How old are you anyway?'

There are familiar pleasures. 'Little Ghost''s campfire folk recalls 'Hotel Yorba', played with Appalachian flair learned on *Cold Mountain*. 'My Doorbell' is the only real pop song, drums and piano pounding a staccato swing rhythm. But even here Jack sounds harassed, as he insists uncon-vincingly to a girl who never comes by that 'I've got plenty of my own friends, they're all about me.' 'Instinct Blues' is the distorted equivalent to 'Ball And Biscuit', Jack almost visibly egging Meg on. But it's a blustering blues. Though deep in blue moods, Jack needed new sounds for them. So this becomes an album of disparate experiments, tested then abandoned mid–song.

'Blue Orchid''s guitar cuts out in favour of the creepy, tiptoe melody of 'The Nurse', picked out on the xylophone's exotic relative, the marimba (which Jack was taught to play at Cass Tech). This murmured, quivering Gothic drama may be the strangest White Stripes song, partly inspired by the last, Alzheimer's-afflicted days of Rita Hayworth, whose life Jack seized on as a motif to make sense of a record threatening to defeat him. It's about a carer who could poison you as she's 'suspiciously dusting the sill', and weary promises ripe for betrayal.

'White Moon' then finds the singer 'needing' the redheaded Rita of her wartime pinup prime. This slow, elegiac piano song develops intensity over four minutes, as Jack moves through broken yearning, abandonment and flashes of bitter resentment, rising to a quickly dissipating climax as he thinks of Rita, finally an inaccessible, untouchable 'ghost'. Jack "felt a personal connection to her", he told *NME*'s Pat Long (before hurriedly backtracking), and Hayworth, who disguised her Latino background for fame, lets him consider its price: 'Easy come, easy go, be the star of the show/ I'm giving up all I own to get more'. 'Take Take Take', inspired by Hayworth's autograph of a napkin with a lipstick kiss and the words, 'My heart's in my mouth', completes the sequence. It's the best song about aggressive fandom since Eminem's 'Stan', as the sight of Hayworth in a club drives a stranger to ever more invasive lengths. Propelled by springy acoustic guitar, Jack plays this character with grating contempt.

The pain Jack's picking at predates his success. The introspective folk song 'As Ugly As I Seem' pines for 'a spot on the ceiling of my childhood bedroom' and the 'safe and warm' comfort of home. On an intimate album of vocal nuance, he reasons with tormentors who make him feel like a freak: 'Just let me alone to be in search of the truth myself'. The final song, 'I'm Lonely (But I Ain't That Lonely Yet)', seems more straightforwardly comic. But the last verse's barely audible murmur ends with near-suicide in a river. It completes an album Jack's frenetic energy barely keeps afloat. It's the White Stripes' most sonically inventive and weary record, its art found at his wit's end.

Over at Sire, the Von Bondies' *Pawn Shoppe Heart* follow-up took three years to be released on a different label, Stollsteimer being told it just wasn't 'emo' enough. Most majors would have ditched *Get Behind Me Satan*. But the White Stripes' contract let them ignore previous success, and pursue a quixotic path. Though 'Blue Orchid' debuted higher than 'Seven Nation Army' in the US at 43 (nine in the UK), the album's contrariness was compounded on its June 7 release by "anything but a textbook set-up for a blockbuster", *Billboard* dubiously noted. V2 bosses forced brave faces as US promotion was delayed for months, while Jack played an opera house in the Amazon.

13

The Gang

O N May 30, 2005, the White Stripes headed upriver, with excited talk onboard of Colonel Kurtz and *Heart Of Darkness*. It was the day before they played the 700-capacity Teatro Amazones in Manaus, Brazil, founded after an insane 19th century jungle journey repeated by Werner Herzog's equally ill-advised film *Fitzcarraldo*. A Peruvian fan's request for them to play put the idea in Jack's head. "I wanted to go to places where no one had ever seen us before," he told *Billboard*, "so we get that feeling back of those live shows where we used to have to prove ourselves." A 12-date Latin American tour had already visited Mexico, Guatemala, Panama and Chile, its unprofitability seeming to please Jack. He let his Detroit problems wash away on the current, as the White Stripes' boat cut its engine to drift up the Amazon's Ponta Negra tributary, rainforest on either side and giant dragonflies in the air. "He was stroking the belly of a baby crocodile," *Mojo*'s Stevie Chick remembers. "It's a surreal life, but the best ever," Jack said later. "I've never felt so comfortable." Chick observed this rare serenity. "His [road-]crew were his friends. He was boss, but it was his day off, and he wanted to hang out with his tour manager and merch girl. He was very jovial and funny, with a larger-than-life personality, which seemed like it came naturally."

Also on the boat with Meg and the tour crew was Karen Elson. The 26-year-old supermodel from Oldham was known as "Le Freak" since having her eyebrows shaved and red hair dyed a brighter shade for a shoot, emphasising her translucent white skin. A lonely outsider in a hometown she longed to escape who now lived in New York, she'd been a cover girl since 1997. She'd met Jack three weeks before, playing an Eve figure to his Satan in 'Blue Orchid''s video. On the morning of June 1 the pair went back on the water by canoe, to the confluence of the Ponta Negra, Salimones and Amazon – three rivers that become black and white as they merge for three reasons, Jack later explained. There, a shaman married them. Meg, who'd encouraged the wedding, was maid of honour. Back in

Manaus' Igreja Matriz cathedral, they were further blessed by a Catholic priest. There'd be a third, more formal ceremony at Nashville's country shrine, the Ryman Auditorium. "It was either gonna happen today, or a year from today," Jack told Chick of his most wildly instinctive act.

The night's gig would have been extraordinary anyway. "There were no ugly people in Brazil," Chick remembers fondly of the crowd for the opera house's first rock show. "All the kids looked like the Fonz, all the girls were astonishing, and they were all dressed up for a show that was massively sold out, with loads more kids watching on a big video screen in the car park." MTV's film *Under Amazonian Lights* shows Jack with white-studded red toreador trousers and black Gaucho hat, a pencil moustache and saturnine beard, the Forties Latin look that completed *Get Behind Me Satan*'s transformation (his interest in costume and persona, rare since fellow metro-Detroiter Madonna braved and received ridicule). "Well I tell you from my soul, this is a good day for Jackie White," he announces in the ornate yet intimate, pillared hall. He reaches out to still a cymbal during the quietly sung, personal blues 'Same Boy You've Always Known', as Meg looks up at him with sad-eyed concentration. Then they're laughing, eyes flashing happy looks between them as they sing the kids' folk song 'Little Ghost'. The eerie marimba intro on 'The Nurse' sounds like Pan pipes here. Jack rests his hat on an amp for a 'Screwdriver' as huge and hysterical as when the White Stripes began, watched by Meg with frozen hauteur.

The crowd start to sing 'I Just Don't Know What To Do With Myself' as Jack strums its intro. Then he decides, "Meg, can I do this one by myself for a second?" and steps to the piano for the 1920 ballad 'Apple Blossom Time'. His hokey crooning of a song once favoured by Barry Manilow doesn't detract from its sentiment now: 'One day in May we'll come and say happy's the bride the sun shines on today . . . Church bells will ring/ You will be mine/ In apple blossom time'. Meg smiles, and Elson cries and blows a kiss from the balcony. Then Jack completes Bacharach and David's song with redoubled passion.

In the hot night, some of the hundreds watching the screen pogoed against crash barriers. Jack, living as fearlessly in the moment as he ever had, went to them. "Jack took Meg's hand," Chick recalls, "and the two of them swept up through the aisle between two blocks of seats, and walked straight out of the venue, and we ran after them, and kids started getting up and following them too." Soon, Jack was playing 'We're Going To Be Friends' unamplified, perched with one leg dangling carelessly over a winding staircase. In the car park below, as someone screamed, 'Oh my God, Jack White!'', the barriers toppled. "He was just strumming away," Chick continues, "and Meg was playing on the bongos. And all these kids started swarming up the stairs." Elson, awed by Jack in action, cried out, "I've married such a wonderful man!" "We said, 'Karen, we need to get you out of the way,'" Chick recalls, "'because these kids are going to trample you to get to Jack.' It was this ecstatic, crazy, Beatles moment." As Chick feared for Elson's safety, her husband appeared to feel bulletproof, even as his trousers were ripped and medallions torn from his neck. Meg exhaled, exhilarated, once they'd raced back inside, where 'Seven Nation Army''s crowd-chanted riff inspired a delirious version, as excess fans pounded doors slammed by security. Riot police were hurriedly forming lines as the band slipped back to their hotel, where Meg downed cocktails with the crew. "The promoter had bought a massive wedding cake for Jack and Karen," says Chick. "And there ended up being a cake-fight. Meg was throwing cake at people. It was really giddy." Jack and Elson left them to it. "What a great day," he said, briefly satisfied. "It started with a marriage, and ended with a riot."

The White Stripes continued an early tour policy of investigating new places with Eastern European and Balkan gigs, beginning in Moscow on June 26. Forty-one dates in seated American and Canadian theatres followed, which Jack bitterly regretted for their sedateness. In Providence, Rhode Island on September 19, even wearing voodoo makeup to play the orchestra pit organ like Lon Chaney's Phantom of the Opera couldn't rouse the crowd. Such 21st century passivity at rock'n'roll increasingly exercised him. "Sometimes it's so bad that Meg and I have to ignore the audience and play to each other," he told *NME*'s Pat Long miserably.

The pair's own sense of community was strong when they headlined Glastonbury on June 24, as high as it was possible to rise in Britain from their 100 Club debut four years before. The Pyramid Stage exterior was lit red with a white tip. Red and white lights played over a black backdrop with stitched white foliage debuted in miniature in Latin America, and a marimba, piano and bongos relatively filled a huge stage they'd conquered with far less in 2002. Meg wore red and white, but the band's old crayon brightness didn't suit all-black Jack's mood. Full darkness after the festival's wretchedly muddy first day aided the crepuscular atmosphere. Then Jack ran at Meg, who smashed a starting-pistol beat.

There's no compromise in what follows. Watched by tens of thousands and TV millions, Jack starts 'The Nurse' with a spotlit marimba solo, as if

232

still practising it back at Cass Tech. He clambers onto Meg's drum kit, gabbling breathy gibberish, and signals to her for 'My Doorbell' as he abandons 'Ball And Biscuit', still running on intuition. Exploratory guitar sallies and *Satan*'s piano songs break up old moments of explosive intensity such as 'The Hardest Button To Button', here definitive, manic grunge. Meg's total comfort in front of the vast crowd is more remarkable. She sings her brief *Satan* vocal spot 'Passive Manipulation' three times with wholehearted strength, and finds childlike vocal union with Jack on 'Little Ghost'. An eight-minute 'Death Letter' is a majestic spectacle, Meg starting its acceleration as her long hair tumbles wildly over her face, then Jack shoving his back against hers on her stool, ex-lover intimate, as they climax the song together. Always encouraged by Jack, at this night's highest musical moments she matches him. The attic where they began has gradually grown over eight years to this biggest of rooms. But as Meg and Jack calmly discuss next moves onstage it's still as if only they matter, the din of success out in the dark kept at bay. The marriage didn't last. But as Steve Nawara speculated, what could be more personally powerful than these hours? No matter how huge the crowd, you can feel the human breath between them as they play.

Jack ensured he was in Poland for the first time as he turned 30 on July 7, and the crowd at Gdynia's Open'er festival sang 'Happy Birthday' in Polish as his family used to. The tour assumed more conventional shape as it progressed, finishing in the US with three more Masonic Temple gigs, their first Detroit shows in two years. The second night, October 1, saw Jack and Meg run on in conquistador helmets, a freshly absurd Latin look, and leave as the crowd roared the words of 'Boll Weevil' back at Jack: 'he's looking for a home.' They believed, as he'd promised here in 2003, that he was home.

But Jack's now rare interviews showed a stiffening resolve to pull away from the place of his betrayal. "Detroit is done," he told *NME*'s Pat Long, two weeks after the Masonic shows. "It's not healthy to be there any more." Was he lonely? Long asked. "I just stay at home," he answered mournfully. "There's nobody I care to see. I don't have any friends." He no longer "yearned" for the city immortally documented in *The White Stripes*, he told Andrew Perry, believing it "decrepit" and "corrupt". He'd later dismiss its "super-cool garage-rock scene", once like family, as inhibitions. "They were Satan," he told the *Daily Telegraph*'s Ben Thompson, in almost joyous renunciation. "It was them who were standing in our way all along."

The White Stripes' November UK tour returned them to Blackpool's

Empress Ballroom and Alexandra Palace, where Jack held court backstage on something like a throne, conversing with Detroit's Alice Cooper. Downloads of each night's 'The Denial Twist' could be bought, then burned onto custom-sleeved CDRs from a merchandise stand, which if you were lucky also sold some of 400 Triple Inchophone miniature turntables, and the otherwise useless 3-inch singles they played. These included 'Top Special', a primitive blast in early Stripes style originally recorded for Japan at Dave Feeny's studio. The title was a schoolyard Japanese term for best friend, but the sentiment of this sequel to 'We're Going To Be Friends' is betrayal, Jack's tape-sped, panicked vocal gasping: 'What? Why would you say something like that? But you're my best friend! It's not cool, it's not cool, it's not cool . . .'

'My Doorbell' was released conventionally on September 3, and 'The Denial Twist' on November 7. Michel Gondry returned to film the latter's video, the band's most imaginative since 'Fell In Love With A Girl', matching the song's theme of distorting truth with packed surrealism, in a funhouse-mirror-warped appearance on Conan O'Brien's chat show. Both singles briefly hit number 10 in the UK. But promotion couldn't change *Get Behind Me Satan*'s awkward introspection. After two years its US sales were 859,000, 1 million less than *Elephant*, whose global commercial triumph was halved.

Bruce Brand saw one of the London shows, four years after driving Jack and Meg from Gatwick Airport. "The last few times, when it was massive, and they had their own production team with palm trees everywhere, it was a bit of a distraction," he believes. "Before, it was completely focused on the two of them, almost playing in a vacuum. I missed the simplicity and the raw energy. But that's what happens."

Success didn't change the White Stripes' attitude to their first British friend. "Jack's always been right as ninepence to me," Brand says. "Oh," he remembers suddenly, "I've got one of his hats. Do you want to see it? This turned up on my doorstep from John Baker after a tour. There was a brown kipper tie with butterflies on it I assume he wore then, too. Many times I've thought about putting the hat on eBay. But then I thought, what if he wants it back?"

The forgotten memento is a homburg from Henry the Hatter of Detroit, inscribed: 'JW III. Size 7 3/8'. "Are you going to try it on?" Brand suggests. "Get some of Jack's DNA . . ."

The cap doesn't fit.

Tour's end was in Perth on February 2, 2006. On December 14, 2005,

John A. White III had bought a mansion in Nashville for a reputed $3,115,000. 1731 Seminole Street was put on the market in August 2006, a home he loved eventually selling in 2007 at a loss on his investment. But the Gillis stiff upper lip wouldn't keep him where he wasn't wanted any more. In 2006, he and his wife started a new life in the South.

Nashville, September 2015. Country music hits you between the eyes at the airport. Hank Williams, Hank Williams, Jr. and Johnny Cash are painted on a bar wall, and live gigs sometimes soundtrack your sprint to the gate. Arriving from Detroit's grey, glum terminal, Nashville International Airport is an *Oz*-like contrast of garish Technicolor, the brash gateway to a neon-bright, commercially confident, self-appointed Music City. Detroit beats it for brilliance and innovation. But thrusting Nashville doesn't care.

There's no statue of Iggy Pop or Aretha Franklin in the Motor City. The Motown Museum apart, its main glory is ignored. Cross the Cumberland River in the near-tropical Southern night, past the fecund, tree-lined riverbanks to downtown Nashville, and music's cheerful exploitation is endemic. The George Jones Museum honours country's most revered male singer with T-shirts, 'moonshine' liquor, a notable lack of records and the promise of a rooftop bar. Framed black-and-white photos and colourful murals memorialise conservative country's Fifties and Sixties stars almost everywhere. The imposing iron and concrete frontage of the Country Music Hall of Fame offers exhibitions on Flying Saucers Rock & Roll: The Cosmic Genius of Sam Phillips, and Dylan, Cash and the Nashville Cats - belated acknowledgements of rock's symbiotic connection to a city and music constituency that once despised it. A few days back, Jack and Loretta Lynn put their handprints in the Nashville Walk of Fame cement. And on Lower Broadway, rows of honkytonks jostle for drunken tourists like the curry houses of London's Brick Lane or the sex shows of Hamburg's Reeperbahn, blasting their wares into the street at high, competing volume. There's roughneck country rock in one, the band hemmed in by the bar and playing Led Zeppelin as the Stetsoned, good ol' boy singer accepts whiskey shots from the crowd, and a drunk woman grabs at him. At 2 a.m. in Robert's Western World, the North Hightop Allstars slap beautiful rockabilly from a battered double bass and sing a plaintive 'Lost Highway', for dollars in the tip-jar from the few remaining strays. Both bands are authentic in this town.

"They respect music, even the plastic country and western side," Jack told Pamela Des Barres. "I don't think anyone has a secret agenda here . . . They don't mind being on the side of a bus or a billboard here *at all*. That's the goal. So I'm not going to hurt their feelings." He put his relocation to a commercial musicians' Mecca more bluntly to Brian McCollum: "I can do what I need to do and not have to listen to any nonsense to do it."

Jack's sometimes seen at Acme Feed & Seed on Broadway. Portraits of Cowboy Jack Clement, the Highwaymen, the Louvin Brothers and Lynn line its stairway, with primitive paintings of Robert Johnson and Ryan Adams on the top floor bar, and a taxidermied stag's head on the ground floor where bands play at night. The young, after-work crowd in smart-casual clothes are a long way from the Lager House. It's hard to imagine Jack here, or see Acme's appeal to him. Until I look from across the street at its red-and-white-chequered walls and black-framed windows. Some things don't change.

He goes to bluegrass and country gigs "all the time", amidst audiences to whom he means nothing, but sadly knew from the start that seeking his old inspiration in another rock scene was "asking for trouble". "He's like a ghost," Nashville-based singer-songwriter Frankie Lee says. "No one hangs out with Jack. His band does, I'm sure. But he does the same thing in every situation. You don't see him, you hear about him. He's a private person."

Jack lives 11 miles and 18 minutes' drive from downtown, a short commute but a world away. Passing adverts for Sun Records in Memphis and a Civil War battlefield, warehouses and big ranch-houses, we're soon in an avenue of mansions on hills with tree-screened drives, stone gate-posts and lawns like small golf courses. Then we hit a quieter stretch of road. Jack's home is a two-storey, pillared, wide white house with a black roof, and a red outhouse to the right. It's not quite a *Gone With The Wind* fantasy, but a discrete upgrade from Seminole Street, with more privacy and country hush. A black fence shields its seven acres, which back onto woodland. Jack's near neighbours have included a Commissioner of Wrestling and a prosperous doctor. More suburban, older neighbours in his peaceful street first met him in October 2015, when he ventured out to the annual pot-luck lawn picnic. Most had no idea who he was as he mingled, relaxed and smiling. He apologised for not attending before, explaining he was often away.

"It was very hard for me to move," he remembered to Dan Rather. "I always imagined I was going to be [in Detroit] my whole life." He once confessed to his sisters that part of him expected all 10 siblings to return to 1203 Ferdinand one day, as if all the years apart had been a passing dream, and true home could be regained. "Home" was a word his lyrics obsessively repeated, he told Barney Hoskyns, till *Get Behind Me Satan* pushed the idea "to the absolute breaking point". "I've always felt like Detroit is my home," he considered to Brian McCollum. "But I've always felt like my soul came from some other place. And maybe it is from down South." Still it's hard to imagine him quitting on his own. Karen Elson had, like him, been a bullied, working-class misfit, but unsentimentally declared on leaving Oldham aged 16: "I'm never fucking coming back." And there was less drama in her account. They'd moved "on a whim", she said, and because Nashville seemed better than her New York home for raising a child. Scarlett Teresa White, perhaps decisive in Jack's wrenching change, was born on May 2, 2006.

He wasn't alone with his new family for long. As when Sixties counterculture king Ken Kesey was exiled from California, and his charisma's centrifugal force lured his Merry Pranksters to live out their days under his wing in Oregon, Jack gradually gathered everyone he needed from Detroit. His fellow Raconteurs followed first. One had reasons that made Jack's look paltry.

"So anyway, I was stabbed," Brendan Benson says, sitting smoking on the veranda of his east London hotel in 2009. Detroit's worst side had finally walked through his open door one winter day.

Benson's part of East Grand Boulevard, so near to Jack in Seminole, had been a ghost street. "I loved my house. I had no neighbours. It had bars on the windows. It was an impenetrable fortress. And inside, it was very cosy and beautiful. But I made the mistake of sometimes leaving the door open. Being naïve, I forgot about the crack addicts. I think once or twice people just came in my house, when I was there. It's really my fault for leaving the door open, I guess . . . I chased this one guy out of the house and down the street, in the middle of winter. I had a robe on, slippers, slipping and sliding on the ice. Finally I caught up with this guy who was three times my size, and screamed at him: 'What's in the bag, what's in the bag?' I knew he'd taken something. I saw something come up, and it was like he'd punched me in the arm. I didn't feel anything, but thought something was wrong. And sure enough he'd stabbed me with – like a shiv!" He laughs disbelievingly. "A screwdriver or something."

The rangy, sharp-featured 37-year-old stretches his legs in the sun as he talks, and orders another white wine. Detroit wasn't finished with him yet. "The final straw was when I was 50 yards from my house, pumping gas.

I'm watching the numbers on the pump, and the next thing I know I'm falling to the ground, without any concept of why – an eerie, gross feeling. I came to, and some guy's rifling through my pockets. I'd been hit on the head and robbed. I was semi-conscious when I drove to the hospital." He retreated to his mum's, head in bloody bandages, before moving to Nash-ville. "I was told about all these cool up-and-coming neighbourhoods. I didn't wanna bother. I said, 'Show me a neighbourhood that's up and come.'" There was no way back. "A friend said, 'You'll be sorry to hear that there's tumbleweeds blowing through your house, and the windows are busted out.' I was there for seven or eight years. That part of my life has been totally belittled."

He still thinks about the last attack – a spanner thrown at his head, it turned out, from which, if he'd stumbled home instead of to the hospital, he could have died. "When I pump gas, I have that eerie feeling. A flash-back, I guess. It's really traumatising. I couldn't believe that somebody would do that in the middle of the day and leave me for dead, and more-over no one would come to my aid. There were people walking by – 'I don't give a shit.' I'm angry about it. But I don't know who to be angry at. They're desperate people. And rightfully so. They don't have the same opportunities. They're doomed at birth, most of them. Born poor, living poor. What the fuck are they going to do?"

Benson's new album when we speak, *My Old, Familiar Friend*, is his first solo record since those attacks. Like the three before, it's full of lovingly crafted melodies redolent of the Seventies. Half the lyrics, though, have an undertow of betrayal and paranoia; only partly a response to almost dying. "For some reason I have this thing inside of me that's distrustful," he con-siders. "We learn soon, at an early age, that good things don't last. I've gone into relationships thinking that. The one I'm in now is slowly curing me. Being attacked is all part of it. I have the same naïveté going into a relationship as I do living in a war zone. And to this day, I still leave my car open. And my car was stolen from my backyard last month, in Nashville. And I probably won't change. I still wanna believe that people are trust-worthy, and that there's nothing to be afraid of."

Benson's faith was bolstered growing up in Louisiana's otherwise all-black housing projects, a life outside American ethnic norms much like Jack's more miserable one. At home, his young parents played Stooges, Roxy Music, Wings and Bowie records, before divorcing "when I was 12, 10 – maybe younger", he says vaguely. "My dad's impulsive, a childlike dreamer. We moved to Louisiana because he wanted to live in the South and be a redneck, he thought that was cool. I spent my first 12 years in a tenement, and I never had a white friend till I was 14. I think that's why I don't feel like a target, or an outsider [in black neighbourhoods]. Musically, though, I might as well have been in Detroit. I wasn't too appreciative, but now I'm way more interested in those records. It's hard to come by great music like that these days. Lennon and McCartney are the tiger and the lamb for me. All life's in them."

Benson's career began on a major label, Virgin, in 1996, "promised the world" but not sure he wanted it. He was dropped soon afterwards. Shattered, he vanished for five years. "But I'd bought a little attic home studio with the advance, and it never sat idle." That studio became a sanctuary, more comfort than family or friends. "I never left," he says. "To a fault, to my detriment. I didn't feel anxiety there. But I knew all the while it wasn't healthy. It was the best excuse not to have to go out and live life. In Nashville, I decided not to build a home studio, and I've discovered other things. That there are other people, that music is a group effort. The Raconteurs resocialised me, totally."

'Steady, As She Goes' has proved prophetic when we speak (as it was for Jack), Benson picking domestic life over the studio. "Music's all meaningless," he says. "I don't go around saying it much, because it's not very cool, or even pleasant to hear. But I think it's the sad truth. We make art to plug a void, to think that things make sense. That's why I do it. But in the last two years, I've discovered mundane things like doing the dishes, or mowing the lawn – a Zen-like, healing thing. And I really get off on that. Cutting my grass is just as fulfilling as writing a song. More, sometimes."

Jack's new home had a vegetable patch, but it's hard to imagine him having that thought. Still, his sole major writing partner, so languidly charming and phlegmatically wounded when I met him, brought these characteristics to their shared band. By February 2005, Benson was already talking excitedly to *NME* of a Raconteurs album he thought they'd finished. "It's a fucking brilliant record . . . A guy the other day said that he had heard Nirvana's *Nevermind* four months before it came out . . . he said, 'This feels just like that.' And that's how it feels for me. It's a cross between Deep Purple and Cat Stevens." In fact *Broken Boy Soldiers* was mastered in New York in February 2006 when the White Stripes finally finished touring, the end of three week-long sessions begun in 2004. The Raconteurs' March interview schedule dwarfed *Get Behind Me Satan*'s minimal campaign, as Jack sought to make them more than a side-project. Swiss journalist Hanspeter Kuenzler had one crucial opening question.

"First thing we need to know," he asked, deadpan. "You and Brendan, brothers or married?"

"This band will show people that there are a few misconceptions about me," Jack told *The Times'* Mark Edwards. "The restrictions, the minimalism that we purposely placed on ourselves in the White Stripes . . . that's not how I am the rest of the time." But though his bandmates were free, he set live limits and handicaps on himself. And all his Raconteurs equipment was copper. "Having everything in the White Stripes red, black and white . . . keeps me on that one path," he told *Guitar Player's* Jimmy Leslie. "Copper centred me on the Raconteurs."

"We avoided the obvious things," he told Kuenzler of co-writing. "Brendan would do a guitar part where I probably would have done." Jack or Benson might bring music or lyrics, and Benson wrote Jack's solo on 'Level'. But, 'Steady, As She Goes' and 'Broken Boy Soldier' aside, Benson's bruised, slightly sour voice dominated. Third single 'Together' was all fragile maturity, built on cushioned soft rock keyboards, and suggesting you work for happiness rather than wish for a life 'like the stories that you read, and never write'. 'Yellow Sun' was Lovin' Spoonful folk-pop, Jack's first-take vocal harmonising with Benson as they strummed acoustic guitars. 'Call It A Day' went in depressed circles, Benson doggedly ploughing on. Only 'Blue Veins' put Jack out front. This piano ballad's baroque, sultry melodrama recalled Lee Hazlewood (the band played a song arranged by him for Nancy Sinatra, 'Bang Bang', in concert). Jack's vocal took from Southern soul testifying and Screamin' Jay Hawkins with doo-wop harmonies, while a sudden burst of back-wards-tape phasing and Thirties Harlem piano passed without comment. But more than another outlet for Jack's writing, *Broken Boy Soldiers* saw him playing rough, percussive Hammond to egg on others' solos on 'Store Bought Bones', or participating in 'Intimate Secretary''s busy middle-eight. 'Hands' typified an album bursting with elegant detail, mixing psychedelia and glam on its guitars' optimistic climb.

What this most resembled in Jack's past was the Go. The Raconteurs were the gang he'd pined for then, in a triumphantly improved context – not near-divorced but newly married, and not fighting his paranoid corner in a band that could sack him. He was one of the boys on his own terms, studiously not using innate dominance. For all its resource-exploring Seventies styles, *Broken Boy Soldiers* was also, like *Whatcha Doin'*, ordinary next to the White Stripes. This was a good, old-fashioned rock record. No more.

On the LP's May 15, 2006 release, 'Steady, As She Goes''s success helped it reach number two in the UK and seven in the US (though sales tailed off). The Raconteurs' 70 gigs that year returned Jack to venues the White Stripes had long outgrown. Their live debut at Liverpool Academy on March 20 was followed by London's Astoria three days later, and a summer of festivals and theatres. They also supported Bob Dylan on eight arena dates, starting on November 9 in Portland, Maine. Benson preferred his taste of the relative big time to a warm-up act's "hard", "humbling" life. But like Jack, this was the gang he'd always wanted. "Ever since I can remember fantasising about playing music, it was always in a band," he told *Spin*'s Dorian Lynskey. "Solo guy . . . I mean who fucking cares? I'm tired of writing music by myself." The video for second single 'Hands' showed the spirit between them: a band on the run, stumbling on a school for deaf girls where they signed, played card tricks and happily rioted after dark.

The White Stripes' sixth album, *Icky Thump*, intervened. But the Raconteurs reconvened the week after it was mixed in April 2007 to record in the narrow, three-week window before the Stripes toured, then for three further weeks in February and March 2008. Their second album, *Consolers Of The Lonely*, was a response to tours where "we changed those first album songs so much, we pushed them really hard," Jack told Kuenzler. "And we also got into different areas that we could explore in this band that we couldn't in our others. For me, I can play guitar solos that I can't in the White Stripes, 'cause I'm the only person generating melody in that band." After *Broken Boy Soldiers'* 8-track attic taping, they stretched out in John McBride's lavish, vintage equipment-filled Blackbird Studio in Nashville, where *Icky Thump* had just been made. It was an "anything you could ask for kind of studio," Patrick Keeler dreamily explained. "John's got thousands of mics," Benson told Kuenzler. "There's instruments hanging on the walls you can't believe you're looking at. And you can play them! We spent a little more time on this one. And we were inspired to just experiment a little more. And really be artistic. We had the basic ideas of the songs, but wrote a lot in the studio. There were moments in songs where I didn't understand what was gonna happen, is this gonna work out? And in the end it did."

The album brims with confident, varied ideas, stretched arrangements and spliced styles. 'The Switch And The Spur' is typically outré: a spooky spaghetti western sung by Benson, in which a poisoned outlaw in a cursed land hallucinates while Attractions-style keyboards, stabbing mariachi brass and clanging drums give churning atmosphere. Benson's voice is more forthright and full this time, harder to separate from Jack's. 'Many Shades Of Black', especially, is a blowsy, ballsy ballad showcasing his inner Sinatra, punched home by the Memphis Horns and wailing, Brian May-style guitar. When it became the album's second single on August 25, 2008, the B-side saw XL labelmate Adele sing this natural showstopper.

Jack's presence, like Benson's, has become bigger. 'Top Yourself''s surly blues is a long way from his early songs' playground crushes, jeering: 'How you gonna get that deep / When your daddy ain't here to do it to you?' He sings 'Hold Up' and 'Five To The Five' as New Wave tear-ups surging with energy and pleasure, and 'Pull This Blanket Off' as sad-eyed country rock, mixing slide guitar, honky-tonk piano and Dean Fertita's clavinet to find a style equally suited to Ray Davies or Mick Jagger, circa 1970.

Nashville was a deepening influence. "American folk music, especially from the South, blues and folk and country and rock'n'roll, is incorporated in what we're interested in and how we're creating," Jack told Kuenzler. "And down here you hear a lot more bluegrass on the radio, in the car or restaurant or on TV. There is just a lot more roots music around. Where we're from, you couldn't go and see a bluegrass band play, or a western swing band. But you can here." Stephen Berkman's photos for the panoramic sleeve, shot in black and white with 19th century tintype technology, show the band as minstrels on a flatbed stage pulled by lions. It portrays the Raconteurs' range of Americana, and Jack's widened horizons with them. "This is really the colour of the songs," he told Kuenzler. "When we saw the tintype photography that Stephen uses, that is what the songs look like to us."

Third single 'Old Enough' was re-recorded in bluegrass style in January 2009 with singer Ashley Monroe (who Jack had heard on the Grand Ole Opry, then bumped into at Nashville Airport) and Eighties insurgent country star Ricky Skaggs on mandolin. And dominating everything on one of the strongest sets of songs Jack had played on is 'Carolina Incident'. This is the flowering of his roots in the coffee houses of Nineties Detroit, a violent country *noir* melodrama of extravagant, tightly coiled narrative invention. Dylan's *Blood On The Tracks* saga 'Lily, Rosemary And The Jack Of Hearts' is one precedent for the tall tale of a redhead's redneck boyfriend, a long-lost husband-turned-priest battling for his life, and a son's brave misuse of a milk bottle. *Cold Mountain*'s Dirk Powell returns on fiddle and the Flory Dory Girls add Morricone-style, spectral vocals, as the music swirls round cinematic scenes of underdog heroism and sly farce. Jack claims it's folk truth, with a wink.

Consolers Of The Lonely was released on March 25, 2008 with no prior promotion, an attempt to short-circuit tiresome industry norms from which it never recovered commercially. But the 71-date tour that began on April 14 proved how formidable the band had become. They used an auxiliary Raconteur, Mark Watrous, and a set-list on the piano, the White Stripes' hair shirt torn off by this more practical group. Benson sometimes scissor-kicked, getting off on his dream band. Jack, often in a black T-shirt's burly anonymity, turned his hunched back for long stretches like a giant trying to shrink, taking the contrasting chance to focus on playing. At Montreux's Miles Davis Hall on July 7 (released on DVD as *Live At Montreux 2008*), 'Blue Veins' has become a 10-minute epic in which Jack leans forward in the heart of the band's storm as he shreds and distorts, using a vintage mic to preach and pant from, ending breathless and wet with sweat. When Benson gives his crooned kiss-off on 'Many Shades Of Black', Jack is still pushing his guitar, finding his own space in this fuller band's relative privacy. Then 'Carolina Incident' is all him. He always says everything he does is a means of storytelling, and here it is stripped and raw, the crowd gripped as his voice conducts them, wide-eyed, through his words' high-wire twists. The Raconteurs made Jack more of a guitarist, and more of a folk singer.

Jack's resolve to spurn the strictures of the "super-cool garage-rock scene"' allowed other experiments outside the White Stripes. In 2005, he met Coca-Cola's request to use 'We're Going To Be Friends' in a TV ad by quickly writing a fresh song instead. He saw it as a rare opportunity to compose to order, and have a "globally positive" effect on an otherwise unreachable public. There was outrage he must have predicted, after the White Stripes' early refusal of a Gap ad. But as he bullishly told *NME*, he thought Coke "the greatest drink ever made by man." He'd enthused further, backstage at the Bowery Ballroom in 2002: "I always wanted to work for Coca-Cola. I have a Coca-Cola delivery man's jacket. They used to wear green uniforms and green hats. The guy let me offload Coke racks from his truck . . ." The kitsch artifice of Japanese pop artist Nagi Noda's ad, with its serial images of a red-and-white-dressed redhead bonding with nature, also appealed. Seeing it for the first time during the 'Blue Orchid' video shoot, he wrote 'What Goes Around Comes Around' in 10 minutes and played it to a redhead he'd just met, Karen Elson, in his room. Jack confessed Coca–Cola hadn't much liked his song. Its forgettable, flyaway optimism showed that, in the jingle field, his talent fell far short of the writers of 1971's 'I'd Like To Buy The World A Coke', as the ad's brief 2006 life proved.

Another commission, to write and produce the Bond theme he'd thought 'Seven Nation Army' could be, resulted in 'Another Way To Die'. *Thunderball* and *Goldfinger* played silently on TV as he recorded it in Nashville, aiming for the "powerful and slow" movement of the Sixties films, he told *Guitar Player*'s Jimmy Leslie. He played drums, bass and guitar, neo–soul singer Alicia Keys later adding duet vocals. The Memphis Horns returned from *Consolers Of The Lonely* for the quick brass stabs of its most John Barry moments, while Jack's interest in Bond's trade as 'a slick trigger-finger for Her Majesty' recalled Wings' 'Live And Let Die'. He fully mined the assignment's potential, designing instruments for a planned tour with Keys in which they'd both play white Gretsch Bo Diddley guitars, like Diddley and his stage foil the Duchess, till a slipped disc in his neck intervened. The song's uneven, improvised shape, normal in the White Stripes, anyway broke Bond convention. Though it hit European Top 10s on its October 20, 2008 release, it was viewed as dimly as the shambolic Bond it soundtracked, *Quantum Of Solace*. Jack was too distinct to be a writer for hire.

His quietly growing solo presence extended to three more films. He took a second acting cameo, as Elvis in Jake Kasdan's music biopic parody *Walk Hard: The Dewey Cox Story* (2007). Sporting a snakeskin jacket, curled lip and fiery Southern mumble, he warned: "Look out, man! It's called Ka–ra–teh, and only two kinds of people know it, the Chinese and the King!" Star John C. Reilly admired this improvised "country gibberish", a rare glimpse of Jack's goofy, often misunderstood humour. Martin Scorsese's 2008 documentary on the Stones' November 1, 2006 gig at New York's Beacon Theatre, *Shine A Light*, saw him guest on 'Loving Cup'. His twitching grin of nervous joy as he shares a mic with Jagger relaxes as he leans into a funk groove with Keith Richards. A word from Jack in Richards' ear was a conversation continued in a warm joint interview in *Rolling Stone*, and unreleased 2009 music, after which Richards said he was "wide open" to him producing the Stones. Jack valued talking cinema with Scorsese even more. His progress into his heroes' ranks continued with Davis Guggenheim's documentary *It Might Get Loud* (2009), centring on a January 23, 2008 guitar summit with U2's The Edge and Jimmy Page. Jack is shown nailing a primitive bottleneck guitar together on an isolated Tennessee porch, and writing and recording 'Fly Farm Blues' in 10 minutes with just his Kay guitar, a ribbon mic and reel-to-reel (it became his second, limited solo single on August 11, 2009). Though his real Nashville life was carefully obscured by such rustic set pieces, this became Jack's fullest film portrait, as he toured Mexicantown and expounded his fundamentalist music views. He and Page also taught each other 'Whole Lotta Love' and 'Seven Nation Army'. These old rock stars liked Jack visiting their club.

14

Xanadu

THE Raconteurs' success, especially, seemed to diminish the White Stripes in Jack's world, as other opportunities crowded in. He felt "equally compelled" to write for both bands, he told *Mojo*'s Andrew Male. Meg was also more detached from him than at any time since their wedding. No longer down the block, when he'd moved to Nashville she left for LA. "It's quieter than people think," she reported. She'd spent her months minus Jack "repeatedly cleaning the house till 3am" due to a filthy Chihuahua, *The Sun*'s Simon Cosyns heard. Then there was a novel she was pondering, if she could get her thoughts "to travel down onto the paper". But after the first Raconteurs tour neared its close in December 2006, Jack beckoned. "I talked with Meg as we were ending the tour and started writing songs with her," he told *Hot Press*' Peter Murphy. "We got distracted from the sessions a few times . . . the album was half-written in the studio."

One cloud as they began was the death of his father Gorman on November 30, aged 79. An obituary listed the surviving Gillis clan mostly gathered, like Jack, around his bedside in his last hours: "his wife of 53 years, the former Teresa Bandyk; daughters Barbara, Maureen and Anne; sons Raymond, Stephen, Joseph, Leo, Edward and Alan; 19 grand-children; one sister, and many nieces and nephews." Jack and his siblings cracked blackly comic jokes with their dad till he died. What he felt most, once more, was lonely. "I felt selfish for thinking it," he remembered to *Rolling Stone*'s Jonah Weiner, "but I said it out loud: 'When I die, none of you are gonna be here. I'm gonna be all by myself, and you'll already have gone.'" *Icky Thump* would include a long, valedictory thank you for the White Stripes' "ten wonderful, fortunate, and tumultuous years", an anni-versary he was keenly, proudly conscious of; thinking right back to one of the coffee houses that first let him perform, he thanked "Planet Ant for being open". The dedication was to "Good Guy Gorm".

Jack and Meg spent three weeks recording *Icky Thump* in January 2007, the most for a White Stripes record. Photos of Harpo Marx and Charley Patton flanked them at Blackbird Studio, a short drive from Jack's house, where Meg stayed. It was his first time there with engineer Joe Chiccarelli (both returned to for *Consolers Of The Lonely*). The set-up was like a millionaire's upgrade of Toe-Rag, stuffed with analogue gear but capable of anything, as they filled 15 tracks with over-dubs. "Jack really wanted to step things up," Chiccarelli told *Sound On Sound*'s Paul Tingen, "and do something that was more modern and punchier . . . to do Pro Tools-style editing, doing detailed, radical edits in the song, chop things up in ways that are unnatural, with dramatic changes. But he did not want to use a computer." The first problem confronting Chiccarelli in the large, red-curtained live room of Studio D was one Neil Yee had faced recording them at the Gold Dollar 10 years before: the emptiness of a two-piece sound that "wasn't powerful enough", requiring massed room-mics, compression and echo chambers to manufacture the White Stripes' thunder. Half-finished songs had new sections spliced in later, like 'Icky Thump''s instrumental bridge, blurring Jack's guitar with the analogue squeal of a 1959 Univox synth. He had his solo on the song punched in and out as he played, snipped to short, jagged phrases. After *Get Behind Me Satan*'s thin-aired introspection, this was the hot sound of a happy man, content at home and competing with his contemporaries.

Chiccarelli also witnessed something Jack often insisted was true: Meg's artistic assertiveness. The nervous amateur who'd dropped her sticks at Ghetto and dumbly followed Jack's orders was long gone. "Meg decided that she wanted a different drum feel, so we would punch in the drums," the engineer recalled, with '300 M.P.H. Torrential Outpour Blues' using two drum kits on her orders. "Meg did some of her own drum edits – she knows how to edit tape [Liam Watson had shown her, letting her splice some of *Elephant*]. They're both about making the music feel alive . . . while pushing themselves to try different grooves and drum feels." He admired the "big, wide pocket" of perfectly judged spaces she left, and the bass gaps she filled. "I have heard Jack play with other drummers, and he doesn't sound like the White Stripes. She is more than one half of the sound of that band."

Icky Thump matched *Elephant*'s Anglophilia, taking its title from Jack tweaking Lancastrian Elson's epithet "Ecky thump". He and Meg dressed as a Pearly King and Queen on the sleeve, and became a Steptoe-like double-act collecting junk on 'Rag And Bone'. Cockneys wearing pearls washed up from the Thames and rag-and-bone men resembled their music, Jack told *The Sun*. "You take things that other people aren't noticing and make something beautiful out of them, keeping them alive." He also went deeper into a Scottish heritage for which he'd suffered as a child, after going to his Mexicantown school's international day in a kilt. 'Prickly Thorn, But Sweetly Worn' is an airy, uplifting Highland fling that uses Jim Drury's bagpipes to find a new spot for Jack the folk singer to rest. The bagpipes flow into 'St. Andrew (This Battle Is In The Air)', a choppily overdubbed, psychedelic deathbed ascension like a Celtic 'She Said She Said', in which Meg's tape-sped, lost voice pleads: 'The children are crying . . . I'm not in my home . . . I travel backwards in ecstasy . . . St. Andrew, I've been true . . . never forget me.' "It's about my father dying," Jack told *Q*'s Michael Odell. "He died on St. Andrew's feast day. I'm imagining what it must be like to have that moment of reckoning."

Mexican traditions more genuinely around him growing up were referenced in Regulo Aldama's trumpet flourishes on 'Conquest', and the title track's story of a gringo coming unstuck with a señorita south of the border. Jack's fellow feeling in the latter even provoked a political outburst (something he usually found awkward and pointless, in pop and life, keeping his mouth shut when his new, conservative Southern neighbours held forth). "We're sorry we're from America," he'd begun at Glastonbury 2005, mortified beyond endurance by George W. Bush's presidency. Now, moves to wall off Mexican immigrants made him sneer like Eminem at 'white Americans': 'Why don't you kick yourself out/ You're an immigrant too.' 'Bone Broke', too, was a class-conscious boogie about poverty and privilege.

The classic rock impetus of the Raconteurs carried into *Icky Thump*. '300 M.P.H. Torrential Outpour Blues' hints at the circular fatalism of Dylan's 'Stuck Inside Of Mobile (With The Memphis Blues Again)', its weary singing and lounge organ roughened by snake-rattle percussion, and 12 seconds of viciously clawing guitar. Its phrase 'just play the victim' recalls 'Let's Play The Victim', a song Jack said he was writing while shaking from exhaustion and homesickness in Tokyo in 2003, but singing 'ugly cancer' in a last verse about mortality indicates (like *Icky Thump*'s several mentions of cemeteries) that his dad's death had worked its way in. 'Ice Cream Soda''s dense, scratchy twang suggests Sonic Youth. And when 'Catch Hell Blues' warms up, its rural slide guitar starts to sizzle, then bounds forward like a mountain lion with Meg's bass thud and Jack's tribal roar. *Satan*'s desultory 'Instinct Blues' is shown up by the high, taunting expressiveness of his guitar here. "Try and catch me," he goads, cocky as a rapper.

'You Don't Know What Love Is (You Just Do As You're Told)' could be Lynyrd Skynyrd, if it wasn't for the wrecking-ball drums punching it home and Jack's needling, overdriven solo. Written while touring with Dylan, it asks a woman concealing and demeaning herself with a man to shape up. This theme of shifting and false identities during romance links the album, set out in Jack's liner notes: "I once saw a man completely impersonate another man who was not unlike himself." 'Conquest', a cover of a Fifties Patti Page song often played in his Nineties upholstery shop, sees the male hunter become the hunted. Then 'I'm Slowly Turning Into You' rides into a slow whirlpool of heavy distortion and witchy female murmurs as Jack, at first wanting 'to keep my little shell intact', lists irritating traits he shares with his lover, till finally accepting: 'I'm proud to be you.' 'A Martyr For My Love For You' is one of his absurd, tender ballads about "the guy with no confidence, like me," he told *Q*. It's a teenage tragedy of a boy sacrificing love rather than disappoint its object, sung in an agonised whisper. 'I can tell a joke/ But one of these days I'm bound to choke' directly describes its writer's ongoing, tortured self-doubt.

Jack's notes also included lines supposedly inspired by a picture of an old acquaintance: "Feels like you never really were a friend of mine. Feels like ghosts do walk among us." The subject of 'Effect And Cause', perhaps, a "woman I was in love with a few years ago; nobody anybody knows," as he told *Q*. This could be the same woman he once mentioned loving for 10 years and partly inspiring 'The Nurse': an unknown love, requited or not, or camouflage, maybe, for Meg.

Icky Thump was released on June 18, 2007, licensed to the very corporate Warner Bros. in the US after V2 collapsed (the Raconteurs made the same switch). It was preceded by the 'Icky Thump' single, with its Spanish-subtitled video of Jack waylaid in a Mexican bordello by a red-headed Meg, and stumbling past America's 'Great Wall Of Mexico'. It peaked at 26 in their US Top 40 debut, and two in the UK, heavily helped by downloads. But Jack's long-term faith in vinyl startled pressing plants, as the then backwater industry's maximum 4,000 runs rocketed for 120,000 red 'Rag And Bone' 7-inches, given away with *NME* on June 6.

"Sadly Meg's idea of each copy of *NME* containing a reel-to-reel tape of the song wasn't practical," Jack advised. Hitting number one in the UK and two in the US and selling 400,000 in its first week, *Icky Thump* was similar to *Satan* in long-term impact. *Elephant* and 'Seven Nation Army' were the exception.

The White Stripes played their first gig in 15 months at Nashville's intimate Cannery Ballroom on May 18, then toured European festivals through June. But in the band's 10th year, Jack still bridled at the banal and rote, preserving what was left of his innocence by keeping even the drudgery of touring as freshly stimulating as he could. Their big London gig was at Hyde Park on June 14, with nearby Marble Arch draped in red and white. But Jack also asked to play a benefit gig at the Royal Chelsea Hospital on June 12 for the mostly octogenarian veterans the Chelsea Pensioners. "They know so much more about life than we do and I just want to meet a few of them," he told *The Sun*. He welled up as he sang, and thanked them for their service. That night, the White Stripes played in heat a little like their first London summer at the city's last, lushly velvet-lined Fifties ballroom, the Rivoli. Then on June 24, they began a North American tour that beat even 2005's Latin American one for imaginative adventure. Jack meant to play every province and territory in Canada, then every state in the US. "We wanted to play out-of-the-way towns," he explained in Emmett Malloy's documentary, *Under Great White Northern Lights*. "Something way more unique is going to happen, hopefully."

It took four buses and three semi-trucks to transport this two-piece band now. Some in the party had recurring nightmares of the Rockies, which had to be crossed on often treacherous roads, passing a Ford Mustang with its airbag popped, windows smashed and blood spattered along the way. They played hockey arenas just behind Toby Keith, the country star best known for his redneck-riling 9/11 response 'Courtesy Of The Red, White And Blue (The Angry American)' and its lines, 'we'll put a boot in your ass/ It's the American way'. Fake dollar bills with Keith's face in place of George Washington's – coupons for his sponsor Ford's trucks – were still on venue floors when the White Stripes arrived. In these Canadian equivalents of America's flyover states, there was little but doughnuts to eat after shows. Hotels were often filled for 100 miles around, to see a band whose arrival was front-page news.

In the more remote locations Jack desired, he and Meg flew in a red, white and black prop plane, with separate crew and equipment awaiting them. Meg looked like a Sixties jet-set starlet when they touched down in Whitehorse, Yukon, where Jack learned spear-throwing, and talked till 3am with the local softball team. At one of the free, afternoon "side-shows" they played to more fully experience such places, people stood under trees in the round as Jack sang the folk tale of romantic rivalry and pursuit 'Black Jack Davey'. In Yellowknife, Northern Territory, the mayor picked them up and talked buffalo hunting. Garden Bowl veteran Jack was more interested in the bowling alley. "Meg and I have been bowling all around the world," he said proudly. "Estonia, Panama, Argentina, Cleveland . . ." He strummed 'Little Apple Blossom' on his acoustic guitar at Yellowknife's log cabin Wildcat Cafe, led a singalong of 'The Wheels On The Bus' in a bus in Winnipeg and in Charlottetown sang 'Catfish Blues' from a boat, like young Louis Armstrong (first heard by many from a Mississippi paddle-steamer). At one night gig, Meg watched Jack with her mouth open, nodding as if out on her feet, trying to focus but spent, their stage sexual chemistry burned out. Jack was buzzing afterwards in the dressing room about the crowd's enthusiasm when they "don't even know the songs". Meg lay stretched out. They both closed their eyes.

By the time they got to Iqaluit's wet country airport tarmac, both were frayed by the self-imposed schedule, Meg's hair bedraggled and Jack tired and testy. As they drove past the trailers on the town's desolate, windblown outskirts, Jack half-jokingly wondered whose idea a meeting with Inuit elders was. "I don't wanna talk about it," Meg murmured. When someone in the car repeated something Meg said with her usual softness for Jack's benefit, he snapped, "I don't need your narration." But both were at their best at the coffee morning with Inuits who didn't know who they were, in return playing 'Lord, Send Me An Angel' and accordion music learned from Scottish whalers. Then Jack ate raw caribou, and Meg discussed polar bears. The cameras and imposing road crew in black gangster outfits muddied the scene's simplicity. Still, it was a folk moment Jack used his stardom to reach.

In the dressing room after that night's gig at the Arctic Winter Games Arena, though, Meg's quietness got to him. "Nobody can hear a goddamn word you say!" he yelled. "Now she won't repeat it," he further complained, clearly not for the first time. Meg said, a little louder: "Sorry I wasn't on my game tonight, Jack." Their tone of voice was a fundamental difference. And Meg still agonised over her drumming. "Randy Newman said short people got no reason to live," Jack concluded disgustedly. "Shit, he must've never met a quiet person." He was heard hollering after her at other times.

They had much better moments. He waited to take her hand when they left a Yukon stage, and again as they walked through a snowfield, Meg smiling fondly behind him (scenes later used in the video for 'I'm Slowly Turning Into You', in which they step out of neighbouring chalets, like the eternally linked couple in a Swiss weather clock). In Halifax, Nova Scotia, the province where Jack's Scottish forebears landed, they linked arms as a sergeant major taught Meg to give a "very loud", cannon-firing command. Jack looked serious in Scots uniform and kilt, eating up his Gillis heritage. Ten years after the White Stripes' debut, on July 14, 2007, he ensured they played the Savoy Theatre in Glace Bay, Nova Scotia. Distant cousins Buddy MacMaster and Ashley MacIsaac (looking like old lumberjack punks) and Allan MacInnis (a National Hockey League Hall of Famer) were flown in, among other family. Not everyone shared the celebrations. Support act Dan Sartain, who found the bonhomie of early Stripes tours miserably absent, danced with old ladies in the veterans' hall next door as they played. Then he ate doughnuts.

Backstage, Jack played *Get Behind Me Satan*'s 'White Moon' at the piano, singing one of his most old-fashioned tunes with moving simplicity. Meg sat beside him on the stool. Smiling, she looked at him, then looked away. At least one line, 'It's the truth and it doesn't make a noise', was about her. She nodded along supportively, as she always had. And thick tears rolled down her face. 'Good lord, good lord,' Jack sang on, not quite aware, 'the woman I adore, she's a ghost.' Meg wiped her eyes, and kept silently crying. He looked at a loss when he finished, a boy unsure how to react as the cameras turned. Then he ignored the world to put his protective arms around her, shielding her from whatever was hurting. She leant her head in and reached for his hand, and he stroked the back of her head. Enfolded, they clung to each other. This was their relationship's truth. Marriage had gone in a blink, but their love lasted as long as their band. They were some kind of family.

They played the world's shortest, one-note gig in St John's, Newfoundland, on July 16, the Canadian tour's last day. A week later, the band began a US tour that included Madison Square Garden, but again sought obscure corners. On July 31, instead of Memphis, they played over the state border at the Bank Grove Amphitheater in Southaven, Mississippi. "That's the last White Stripes show," Meg told Ben Blackwell afterwards. Neither told Jack. The tour had a natural break for the birth of his second child, Henry Lee, which came on August 7. Its scheduled resumption never happened. "Meg White is suffering from acute anxiety," it was stated, "and is unable to travel at this time." Jack theorised her going from "a dead–halt for a year . . . right back into that madness" was the fixable issue.

'Conquest' became *Icky Thump*'s final single on December 18 (bar a Spanish-language version, 'Conquista', in January 2008). The B-sides were from the White Stripes' final session, in Beck's living room. More lo-fi than when they began, 'Honey, We Can't Afford To Look This Cheap' is a hilarious country tune about penniless showbiz imposters, while 'It's My Fault For Being Famous' sees Jack fantasise revenge on intrusive fans ('She stuck a cell-phone camera right into my face/ With a flick of the wrist I peeled the nose from my Mace . . .'). 'Conquest''s video is equally amusing, as haughty toreador Jack fatally falls for a bull, watched by a yawning Meg.

The White Stripes appeared one last time as a favour to Conan O'Brien, on his final *Late Night With . . .* TV show on February 20, 2009. They both played guitar on 'We're Going To Be Friends', Jack teaching Meg the chords backstage. They looked and sounded like a rusty old vaudeville couple. On May 22, Meg remarried, to Jackson Smith (son of Patti Smith and the MC5's late Fred "Sonic" Smith), in a double-ceremony with Raconteur Jack Lawrence and photographer Jo McCaughey in the grounds of Jack's home.

The impression of a living band was maintained by the March 16, 2010 release of the *Under Great White Northern Lights* box set, including a DVD, live LP and hardback book. The DVD and live album – their first – were released separately, the latter beginning with a bagpipe skirl, the music often harshly abstract and unhinged, pushed and manhandled to its limit. In April 2010, asked about the White Stripes' return by *The Times*' Craig McLean, Jack was still saying: "I would like to. I don't think her anxiety exists any more." She was around as he pursued other projects, "still involved and everything". But long before they agreed their split's announcement on February 2, 2011, "to preserve what is beautiful and special about this band", Meg had made her decision. She had controlled her crippling shyness to accompany her ex-husband with often visible amusement, growing musicianship and a gnomic, glamorous persona that balanced him. But as she told Bruce Brand, she liked listening to music more than playing it. A marriage's miraculous afterlife was done.

Jack was frustrated by his silent partner, thinking back. "She's one of those people who won't high-five me when I get the touchdown," he complained to *Rolling Stone*'s Jonah Weiner. "I'm like, 'Damn, we just broke into a new world right there!' And Meg's sitting in silence." He was humbly grateful for her, too. "I would often look at her onstage and say, 'I can't believe she's up there.' I don't think she understood how important she was to me, and to the band, and to music." He knew his best work left with her. "That band is the most challenging, important, fulfilling thing ever to happen to me," he told the *New York Times*' Josh Eells. "I wish it was still here. To *Esquire*'s Miranda Collinge, he said, "I will always miss the White Stripes. My dad's dead; it's like saying, do you miss your dad? Of course, I always will." He put it more simply to Weiner. "Nothing I do will top that."

Nashville, 2015. Head away from the tourist honkytonks, past the Country Music Hall Of Fame, the Taylor Swift Education Center and the corporate Music City Center, cross Korean Veterans Boulevard and head downhill, and suddenly this is a different sort of working town. Amidst scrubland, a police precinct neighbours the Nashville Rescue Mission, a Christian homeless centre. It's a place of work and worklessness closer in spirit to the Cass Corridor than Broadway's glare. In an area of light industrial estates, next to an industrial paint store, 623 Seventh Avenue South is a one-storey, black brick building, topped by a lightning-flashing Tesla tower sign, as if something vital is beamed from here. A yellow-and-black Rolling Record Store van is parked outside, for taking vinyl on the road. This is Third Man Records, part of Jack White's Xanadu.

Its storefront, the Records and Novelties Lounge, was just a record shop when it opened on March 11, 2009. It sells Third Man Records' rapidly growing catalogue on vinyl (and, grudgingly, CD) in categories separated by heavy wood dividers, racked above a handmade black cabinet. There's a smart new wooden listening booth, and T-shirts on sale too. The ceiling is beaten tin, silvery and reflecting gold from yellow walls, and so resembling the opulent sleeve of the label's *The Great Gatsby* soundtrack, platinum and gold discs of which are framed nearby. There's a photo of Jack in front of the plane that took him into Canada, and a Lego Jack and Meg. The Novelty Lounge of vintage, token-operated machines, opened on November 23, 2012, in the back of this tiny store, includes a Scopitone (a video jukebox showing Third Man music videos on 16mm, with updated sound via laser), a fairground Mold-a-Rama producing miniature, wax-and-plastic Airline guitars, and a photo booth. Most impressive of all is a Forties Voice-o-Graph Automatic Recording Studio, inviting you to: "Step In! Record Your Voice. Hear It! Played Back. Play It! On Any Phonograph. Mail It! Anywhere." This wooden booth, the sort in which

Richard Attenborough's teenage gangster Pinkie left his vicious message for his lover in *Brighton Rock*, is of narrow phone-box dimensions. It's hard to imagine its most famous client, lanky Neil Young, folding himself in to record his LP *A Letter Home*.

On the way here, back on Broadway, I'd visited the Ernest Tubb Record Shop, which Jack saw in *Coal Miner's Daughter*. Still boasting of its midnight Opry shows, the late country star's store sells 8-track cartridges, yellowing Tubb 78s and a thin CD range, as paintings of ancient country stars look down. It struggles on, with its old-fashioned till and dusty charm. The closest thing to a Jack White Museum and Store, by contrast, is a hand-crafted cabinet of curiosities, which makes the analogue and the mechanical marvellous, colourful and covetable for a new century. It is part of Jack's stand for a world he desires.

Third Man Records had existed since 2001 as a label licensing Jack's music (and his friends Whirlwind Heat) to the majors. But he only explored its potential as the White Stripes wound down. As with most of his ambitious leaps forward, he preferred to remember a sequence of circumstances over which he'd had little control. He bought 623 Seventh Avenue South in 2008 with modest intentions, he told *The Tennessean*'s Brian McCollum. "I had 11 or 12 storage units all over town. Tour gear, things from Detroit, recording equipment. I just wanted to put it all in one place." Then he discussed reissuing the White Stripes 7-inches, whose US rights he'd regained post-V2, with Ben Blackwell, then back in Detroit, building useful experience by running Cass Records from his mum Maureen's house. "'That should be enough to keep a record label running,'" Blackwell remembered his uncle saying. Jack asked Blackwell and Soledad Brother Ben Swank, then in London, to move to Nashville to help start the label. "Maybe they'd move back home or something" later, he vaguely supposed. He also gave them a second job, recalled to McCollum as a further, meek speculation: "What if we put a buzzer out front and you could just sell a couple of records once a week if someone rings the buzzer, probably never happen." He was talking in 2014, when Third Man Records drew 300 daily visitors, and was the world's most important indie label. He tempered his pride with the defensiveness of a working-class man who hadn't known he could make records and whose peers disparaged ambition, but now acted almost unchecked. He added a darkroom and photo studio next, then a rehearsal stage for his bands also became a live venue. In six months, Third Man became "a giant conglomerate of so many ideas," Jack told *Rolling Stone*.

It's near closing time when I visit, and the shop feels calm and cool as a worker in a yellow, black and white dress (not one of the "statistically improbable" number of redheads *Mojo* found Jack employing) moves to change a jukebox 45. The bulk of Third Man's business and nervous energy lies behind a black connecting door of deliberate mystique from which, like a man from U.N.C.L.E. Ben Blackwell appears. "Evening, ladies!" he booms, even going home with a sense of theatre.

Through that door is a gold record-lined corridor, with a floor of bright yellow epoxy, a viscous resin workers had to be trained to lay, just because it felt good underfoot. Turn right at the end, and you reach four offices. Four graphic designers work on record sleeves in one, aided by Third Man's photo studio and darkroom, and Jack. "It's great for me," he told Pamela Des Barres, "because when I was younger I wanted to be a film-maker or an architect. I've been using that design desire to do album covers." "John A White III, DDS, Family Dentistry" is etched on the glazed glass of his tin-ceilinged office, Philip Marlowe-style ("The music business can be like pulling teeth," he reasoned to *NME*'s Emily Mackay). Visitors here have at various times noted Screamin' Lord Sutch's stage coffin, a giraffe head complete with neck, and a cowbell, *George Orwell Reader*, pocketknife and antique ice cream scoop scattered on a black leather-topped desk. A blown-up photo of Charley Patton is on one wall, with pictures by Jack's children proudly displayed, and a black skull flanked on a shelf by black-and-white photos of Son House and Slick Rick. Jack's thumb on a biometric scanner opens the nearby Vault, a fire-proof, climate-controlled room stacked to the ceiling with every master-tape he or Third Man have made; his most valuable possession. He let it be believed it was nuclear-proof, raw garage-rock reels and cock-roaches all that would endure.

Turn left at the corridor behind the shop, and a metal staircase runs down to a former car factory bought and combined with the first building in 2012. Its warehouse has a fake Forties motel wall, and workers in black and yellow packing 500 mail-order items a day. Also on the left is the Blue Room, where Jack has invited musicians from Mudhoney to Alabama Shakes to play to crowds of 300, at a loss-making $10,000 cost to Third Man. "Somehow in the great scheme of things it works out," he's said. Lab-coated engineers man the crow's-nest sound booth and vinyl master-ing suite glimpsed through a slit above the stage, which 2012's expansion made the only place in the world that can cut gigs direct to acetate vinyl, using a vintage lathe from James Brown's home, King Records. Like the

1947 Voice-o-Graph, this fulfilled a fantasy, Jack told McCollum. "It started to become: anything that I thought I was going to see when I was younger and got out on tour – what if that was here?"

Between Jack's house and tennis court, a row of outhouses in his idyllic grounds completed his kingdom. Missing the thinking time upholstery once gave him, he made his original workbench the centre of a new workshop, where he could be found replacing barstool seats with remembered craft. Its brick, like much of Third Man Records, replicated the yellow and black of his Hamtramck shop, colours that represented work to him. Next to this nostalgic sanctuary was Third Man Studio, a name that moved with him but found fruition here. The former artist's workshop had white bricks on its ceiling and a red alcove, the colours of the band that never got to record there continued throughout. A 16-track Neve mixing desk with Afrikaans instructions was from a Seventies South African TV station. The glitterball above an elk's head once belonged to Johnny Cash. The live and control rooms were deliberately minimal and cramped. Between Third Man Studio and Records, 18 minutes' drive apart, Jack had built everything he needed.

He christened his kingdom with a third band, the Dead Weather. As with the Raconteurs, and even the White Stripes when Meg asked to drum on 'Moonage Daydream', he liked to remember their formation as a happy creative accident, not professional business. In October 2008, he meant to record a solo 7-inch he'd produce and drum on in his newly finished studio. Jack Lawrence played bass, with Dean Fertita, the auxiliary Raconteur they shared with Queens Of The Stone Age who was staying at Jack's house, on keyboards and guitar. The Kills' singer Alison Mosshart was also in town, and came over. Her sleaze-rock duo with Jamie Hince had gotten close to the Raconteurs sharing their tour bus when, supporting them in 2008, their own bus was stolen by its driver ("He had stolen three or four tour buses before and gotten away with it," she absurdly explained). This new collaboration was "just going to be a project for one among a handful of 7-inches, but it blossomed into something bigger," Jack told *The Guardian*'s Will Hodgkinson. They started, as was his preference, with a cover version, Gary Numan's 'Are "Friends" Electric?'. By day's end, four or five new songs had begun an album, finished in February 2009. On March 11, they were the first live band in the Blue Room when Third Man Records opened. The 150 friends, family and fans present were given test pressings of the label's first single, the Dead Weather's 'Hang You From The Heavens', individually painted by different band members. In a statement of future intent, 'Texas-sized' 8-inch and glow-in-the-dark vinyl variants of TMR1 were also issued.

Having explored "structure and craftsmanship" in the "relaxed and poppy" Raconteurs, the Dead Weather let Jack be "guttural and dirty and forceful", he told Hodgkinson. They also allowed him into a "dark and murky area of the blues, a place where you find bands like the Gun Club", Barney Hoskyns heard. More importantly, he was the drummer again. Like a cricket all-rounder who insists on seeing himself as a batsman when it's plain to sane observers that bowling's his strength, Jack told *Uncut*'s Marc Spitz that "it was scary how good [drumming] felt. How much I preferred it to playing the guitar." It felt like "coming home", he told Hodgkinson. "Even during the White Stripes I thought: 'I'll do this for now, but I'm really a drummer.' That's what I'll put on my passport application." When the Dead Weather played, crowds pined for a song or two on guitar. "I know that," he told *Uncut*'s John Mulvey. "But I don't want to do that." The band used the white instruments custom-built for the aborted Alicia Keys tour, and he eagerly explained the kit Ludwig made to his design, with three drums on either side, of course, powerful 16-inch snares and cymbals standing elegantly "like statues", including one teenage Jack had saved for, and ridden his bike to Dearborn to buy. Like his upholstery workshop, this too was a nostalgic dream.

Jack clearly took his pleasure playing, because his writing was minimal. On the Dead Weather's debut, *Horehound* (released on July 13, 2009, and reaching number six in the US and 14 in the UK), Mosshart's voraciously sex-hungry, snarling persona dominates the funny, taunting perversity of second single 'Treat Me Like Your Mother', and the sultry cowpunk of 'So Far From Your Weapon', a sexual duel like the climactic gunfight between Jennifer Jones and Gregory Peck in King Vidor's 1946 Western *Duel In The Sun* (aka 'Lust In The Dust') – maybe also referenced in 'Treat Me Like Your Mother''s video, in which Jack and Mosshart bitterly machine-gun blood and bits from each other one desert morning. Their vocals shakily climax together in a co-written song about shame, 'Rocking Horse', too, though the relationship is distant and chaste next to the White Stripes' unspoken sparring. Third single 'I Cut Like A Buffalo' is Jack's sole solo writing credit, built on his androgynous lyric and Fertita's prancing reggae keyboard, weirdly punctuated by monkey-chokes and pig-wheezes. 'Will There Be Enough Water?', co-written with Fertita, is his other main contribution, a blues of worry and restrained menace, all slide, piano and single snare-cracks, seeming to shimmer in Texas heat.

After their debut public show at New York's Bowery Ballroom on April 14, the Dead Weather played 60 North American and European dates through November, initially passing back through clubs familiar from early White Stripes shows. On June 12, before playing the Magic Stick, Jack sat in the ruins of Cass Tech's old building and wept. He thought of his grandmother, believing it may once have been the factory where she worked on arrival from Poland, and of his past in his old city. "Those streets are so compelling to me," he later told Brian McCollum. "I couldn't take that that building had gone." He and Dave Zainea met as friends. In 2013, he'd give Zainea a framed disc dedicated to him and the Garden Bowl, commemorating Third Man's LP of a July 9, 1999 gig there by the short-lived Jack White & the Bricks. Zainea gave Jack the Garden Bowl alleys' old lights, so he could bowl in his Nashville home.

As with the Raconteurs, Jack pushed the Dead Weather's potential harder the second time. Touring flowed into recording in December 2009, and *Sea Of Cowards*, Jack's term for the trolls anonymously spitting ignorance on the internet he hated, was released on May 11, 2010, reaching number five in the US and 32 in the UK. Made, like *Horehound*, in three weeks, it was a denser sequel, further entwining Mosshart and Jack's clawing, cat and dog personas. They echo and egg each other on in first single 'Die By The Drop', which imagines marriage as war, Jack yelping their threatening vow: 'I'm going to take you for worse of better.' 'The Difference Between Us' shows the heavy influence of the early Eighties era of the Gun and Birthday Clubs, gliding and climbing on ominous, John Carpenter-style synths, and chopped at by processed and overloaded guitars, as Mosshart's competing vocal lines slap her to a standstill. Jack is more heavily committed to writing and playing, shrieking on occasional guitar, sneering a woman can't see or touch him on the Fertita collaboration 'Looking At The Invisible Man', and confrontational on the strutting, unruly 'Blue Blood Blues', with the sort of absurd hip-hop brag he was starting to relish: 'All the white girls trip/ When I sing at Sunday service . . .' *Sea Of Cowards* concludes with Jack's 'Old Mary'. Hammond organ carries this surreal, supernatural elegy's tune over hip-hop rhythms and a chittering cacophony. It comes from a stranger imagination than the rest of the album. But the personal vulnerabilities Jack let into his other bands, like the songwriting and storytelling he always claimed was central, were weakest in the Dead Weather.

They made his least memorable, most distanced music, but did explore an aesthetic: a western Gothic rock hybrid, taking from the Seventies and Eighties. This could be seen in the ritual masks on *Sea Of Cowards'* sleeve, and their best videos: the bloody, black leather jackets and dusty Californian town of 'Treat Me Like Your Mother' (directed by the visionary director of *Sexy Beast* and *Under The Skin*, Jonathan Glazer), Jack's own video for 'I Cut Like A Buffalo' (in which he's stalked through flashes of blue and darkness by carving-knife-wielding, veiled redheads), and Floria Sigismondi's 'Dead By The Drop', with Mosshart as a witchy Siouxsie Sioux at mystic war with magus Jack in the guise of their mutual hero, Captain Beefheart.

Forty-eight more gigs began on March 17, 2010. Back at Glastonbury's Pyramid Stage on June 26, Jack's low drum kit (modelled on Ringo's so "the screaming girls" can see, he'd half-joked) let him press and lead from the back, while Mosshart veered between lassitude and spidery, thin-limbed frenzy, in a jagged, dirty rock show with few rivals in the new decade. Jack's initial instinct for drum solos to replace his guitar centre-pieces had also settled down. He denied his dominating presence less than in the Raconteurs, but simply played his part in this band, a fantasy attempted in the Go, now fulfilled.

"This is it for me," a relaxed Jack told reporters when they reached Poland on July 4. "This is the last band I'll be a part of." Though the Raconteurs returned for six gigs between September 14 and November 13, 2011, by 2014 Brendan Benson deemed new records "off the table" and Jack, by then with a solo band, accepted it and the Dead Weather was "enough". But the Dead Weather, too, found little room in later schedules. When a third album, *Dodge And Burn*, finally arrived on September 25, 2015, Dean Fertita admitted a leftover "snippet or a riff" from earlier records was often seized for use, in just over three weeks at Third Man between 2013 and 2015. Mosshart wrote all the lyrics, though Jack's hand seems visible in 'Three Dollar Hat''s rhythmically hip-hop rewiring of the folk standard about a bad black man, 'Stagger Lee'. The best songs on earlier albums were Jack's. Here, it's her 'Impossible Winner', an untypical torch song given dark grace by a string quartet. In its video, the band are on a prison train with nightmarish guards. Jack, looking the sensitive type, finally gets the extra limbs his work rate needs, simultaneously sipping tea, typing and filing, while ruggedly handsome, bony Fertita and meek, bow-tied Lawrence fearfully watch Mosshart's defiance. Though the least of his 21st century bands, the Dead Weather look like one here, as distinctive as the fans who desire their strain of rock'n'roll.

A September 14, 2015 performance of 'I Feel Love (Every Million

Miles)' on *The Late Show With Stephen Colbert* was Jack's contribution to *Dodge And Burn*'s promotion. "Jack's just been going forever," Fertita told *Billboard* of his interview absence. "So he just needs a minute." But though time seemed to finally defeat Jack's efforts, he retained command. "I produced all of those albums – Dead Weather, Raconteurs, White Stripes," he told *The Tenneessean*'s Brian McCollum, comparing his role to Orson Welles' direction: sometimes also playing "a main character like *Citizen Kane*", sometimes "just a director. So in a way they're all my records. We just call them different things."

15

Empire

THE Dead Weather were also symptomatic of a time when Jack's own songwriting became relatively scarce. Five years passed between *Icky Thump* and his next full collection. His priorities had changed in Nashville. Just as Robert De Niro's monomaniacal acting focus slackened after founding the Tribeca Film Centre in 1989, Third Man and his family became Jack's main concerns. Another comparison was Dylan, whose true late masterpiece wasn't an album, but his ever-mutating, Never Ending Tour. Unable to musically beat the White Stripes, Jack's major work became Third Man, which might mean more. He built the label on the apparently redundant, unprofitable format of 45s, producing them all until 2012. Ringing musicians passing through town to suggest they come by his studio and play, further calls built impromptu bands from Nashville's surfeit of fine session players.

These ongoing Blue Series singles, with distinctive sleeve head-shots on blue backgrounds photographed and developed in-house, have ranged from Tom Jones' 'Jezebel' to Transit's 'C'mon And Ride', by a group of Nashville bus drivers. In my pile, I find Jack adding abrasive guitar pulses to Detroit rapper Black Milk's swirling 'Brain', and a drum solo to B-side 'Royal Mega''s surging, Curtis Mayfield-style soul; Detroit shock-rappers Insane Clown Posse tackling "freak" Mozart's 'Leck Mich Im Arsch' (which means what you think), and the Jack co-written, redneck meth rampage 'Mountain Girl'; Jack on guitar for Butthole Surfer Gibby Haynes' punk prank 'Paul's Not Home', with layers of squealing, high lead and distorted, throttled blues on its B-sides, amounting to an essential release; and Jack on acoustic guitar, drums and vocals on Beck's 'I Just Started Hating Some People Today', and drums on its cyberpunk noir B-side 'Blue Randy'. He just produced Laura Marling's straight covers of Jackson C. Frank's 'Blues Run The Game' and Neil Young's 'The Needle And The Damage Done', and Courtney Barnett's 'Boxing Day Blues (Revisited)' and its stunned-sounding, B-side version of Roland S. Howard's suicidal 'Shivers'.

Jack's drumming filled out the sound of Seasick Steve, whose blues make the White Stripes sound baroque, on a brace of Mississippi Fred McDowell songs. Seasick, aka Steve Wold, a former hobo and late-blooming, white-bearded UK festival star, also released a Third Man LP, *You Can't Teach An Old Dog New Tricks* (2011), aged 70. "Jack's a deep musician, and he's crazy," Wold told me in London. "He's like some genius kind of conductor – and his ideas are not stupid. It's like he's conducting something in his brain. He's full of himself, but he's also a genius, you know! He's very kind of, busy. And he probably wondered what I was about, because I was getting drunk and shit. He knows I have deep respect for him. But he's so in demand, I don't know if he had a lot of time to think about me, one way or the other. He's got 50 things going on at once, and all everybody in the world wants to do is talk to him or do something with him." Not everyone enjoyed the results. Dan Sartain spent a day making his single 'Bohemian Grove', only to discover an early take, ultra-slow on Jack's instructions, was being released against his wishes. Friends found him melting the loathed vinyl into bowls.

The mechanical-minded, ornery, quixotic rock star Neil Young, though, was a kindred spirit. After Willie Nelson recorded 'Red-Headed Stranger' with Jack in the Voice-o-Graph booth on April 18, 2013 (ahead of its move from Third Man's back corridors to public use on Record Store Day two days later), Young, too, tried it out, later recording *A Letter Home*'s LP of mostly Sixties covers with Jack. Released on April 19, 2014, there's a crackly warmth as Young uses the booth's original role of recording for loved ones to address his late mother. "My friend Jack has got this box that I can talk to you from," he explains, concluding: "And I miss you . . ." You can hear the mutual pleasure in Jack's barrelhouse piano on a raucous 'On The Road Again'; he then takes the higher part in the Everly Brothers' 'I Wonder If I Care As Much'. "*A Letter Home* in a Forties recording booth is an historic art project," Young told me, calling from his Californian ranch, Broken Arrow. "There was a direct feed out of the back of the booth, that went to an analogue master, that recorded the whole thing. When you listen to it, it sounds like it was made a long, long time ago. It sounds like it was made in 1940. Elvis made one like that. It was fun to work with Jack as co-producer. Jack is a very talented man."

Another series, *Live At Third Man Records*, saw bands from Mudhoney to Drive-By Truckers recorded in the Blue Room. The prize of 45 such releases by early 2016 was perhaps Jerry Lee Lewis, taped on a stage across the street. The inner sleeve, with the Killer looking thunderously unimpressed next to Jack, shows a priceless summit. Local high school bands also attend the Blue Room for vinyl education, recording songs pressed in the school colours, sometimes supervised by Jack. Then there's the Green Series of Spoken Word Instruction singles, begun in 2012 by Jack interviewing 84-year-old stripper Tempest Storm. This included a 'Bolt-a-Trope' card, which, helped by a glass and flashlight, saw Storm perform as the single turned (Jack played strip-club drums on the flip). There was every sort of coloured vinyl, too, including the Dead Weather's 'Blue Blood Blues' 12-inch, which you sawed open for the 7-inch inside, and Jack's liquid-filled solo 12-inch 'Sixteen Saltines' ("We had a lot of returns on that one," he confessed). Such novelties were initially sold at Third Man, or in the Vault series, which posts lovingly packaged rarities from Jack's career to quarterly subscribers. Since 2011, the Rolling Record Store has spread them wider. And on April 1, 2012, Jack's 'Freedom At 21' single was released outside Third Man as 1,000 flexidiscs tied to balloons. They were reaching people, Ben Blackwell explained, by letting vinyl "literally fall from the sky". Blackwell mostly oversaw these fantasias, a veteran record collector electrifying a community he understood (Ben Swank looked after the label's more practical side). "One of the big projects we've been working on for a while is the first record in space," Jack told Brian McCollum. "And we're coming close."

Adjusting Third Man Upholstery's old slogan, 'Your Furniture's Not Dead', Third Man Records declared that 'Your Turntable's Not Dead', evangelising for vinyl with passionate creativity. Its location was picked for its proximity to United Record Pressing, the largest vinyl factory left in the US (which had pressed the first White Stripes singles). Vinyl LPs were "the pinnacle of human expression", Jack told the *New York Times*' Josh Eells. They stood against "an age which is the antithesis of what I am trying to do artistically," he told *Uncut*'s Marc Spitz, admitting to Ben Swank that "in my head, I'm still living and working as if there is no internet." His disconnection with a "dead" generation was captured by this absurd, touching complaint to Eells: "Kids today never say, 'Man, I'm really into remote-controlled steamboats.' They never say that."

But Jack wouldn't give in. "I want to be a part of the resurgence of things that are tangible, beautiful and soulful," he told *The Guardian*'s Will Hodgkinson. He wanted, as with all his work, to "get my hands dirty". Third Man's vinyl, he told Hodgkinson in *Mojo*, was a device to lure people into "a mechanical, romantic relationship with music." And slowly, improbably, in alliance with Record Store Day (begun in 2007 to bolster independent record shops, and making White its "Ambassador" in 2013), the tide turned. Vinyl sales, flatlining throughout Jack's musical life, rose in the US from 1 million in 2007 to 17 million in 2015, becoming objects of desire again. "We actually did a lot, we pushed this really hard," Blackwell insisted to *Audioboom*'s Damian Abraham. "No one's going to say Universal really brought vinyl back, or Warner, killing it with vinyl." Jack's business managers warned him that Third Man would be a "money pit". But his tireless, eccentric creativity connected against the odds, as the White Stripes had. It was "incredibly profitable", he told *Rolling Stone*'s Weiner, "and the reason is because I don't care about that. If I'd done it to make money, it would have failed." Even without his records, he told Hodgkinson, Third Man "made sense financially". By 2015, its Nashville operation had released over 300 records, expanded into three buildings and employed 26 people. Jack saw its potential evolution as infinite.

On the evening of my visit, I pass through a silver door with evil-eye slits into the corridor that now connects the shop building and its neighbour. Tricks of paint and light on the black and red bulb-lit white walls give it a crooked, *Cabinet Of Dr. Caligari* perspective. There's a sort of greenhouse as I turn the corner, then I'm in the Blue Room. Beneath a red and white wall, black dungeon doors warn 'Employees Only', emphasised by Tesla lightning bolts. Jack and Meg Pearly King skeletons perch on a phone booth, and on another booth there's a stag's head. The elephant head used in *Elephant*'s promotion is on the back wall, behind a bar serving Tennessee beer from moonshiner jars, and popcorn. It's one of Third Man's monthly *Light + Sound Machine* nights, a collaboration with local arthouse cinema the Belcourt Theatre's James P. Cathcart. It expands Third Man's commitment to the tangible, communal and outré, declaring itself against digital distribution and on-demand viewing. Tonight, Memphis experimental filmmaker Lynne Sachs is here to introduce work going back to the Eighties. Some in the audience are here to peer inside Jack's world. Most stay for films they'd never otherwise see. But before we begin, there's a booming announcement. "Someone has parked their truck in *Jack*'s space. You *will* be towed . . ."

"I haven't seen this projected on 16mm for such a long time," Sachs says as the first film starts, on the creased screen in front of the small, chest-high stage, which Jack has played more than anywhere, post-Detroit. I hear the projector winding down and cranking up, and see the light overexpose the nude, hypnotically turning bodies in the divided frame of *Drawn And Quartered*. The centrepiece, *Investigation Of A Flame*, grippingly investigates the Catonsville Nine, priests who burned a draft office's files with napalm during the Vietnam War; one, Daniel Berrigan, later poured his blood on uranium in a nuclear protest at Oak Ridge, near where Jack lives. It's a warm, wonderful night of local art.

Third Man wasn't the Xanadu Jack had seen in *Citizen Kane*, a barren vista of baubles meaning nothing to their owner as he wasted away, but a continuation of the Gold Dollar and Zoot's promotion of the underground and the honest, writ large by his success. "We're here to make things exist that we think are beautiful," he told *The Guardian*'s Dave Simpson. "Some people might go out and buy a Ferrari or something, but I would rather spend my time and energy in releasing these records . . . If anyone can learn about art and creativity through something we made exist, that's very fulfilling and worth every penny."

New acts had records released, usually local, such as Pujol, whose 'Black Rabbit' 7-inch is speeding post-Clash punk, energised by Jack's production. In 2012, he eased off the reins to allow recordings he didn't produce (Radiohead, whose pre-show playing of Son House transformed his life, got the keys to Third Man Studio that June 7). Mediocre garage bands were given a shot (mostly by Blackwell or Swank) along the way. Nashville-based Margo Price's 2016 debut *Midwest Farmer's Daughter*, though, is fiercely honest country by a superb singer expressing the injustice of working-class American lives, her own especially. She sold her car and wedding ring to record it straight to acetate at Sun Records, Memphis. In country's capital city, every label but Third Man turned down a potential star they can be proud of.

Before Price, Third Man's most legitimate new album outside Jack's bands, and one of his most delicate production jobs, was the debut LP by his wife. Elson learned guitar in New York's East Village, where she co-founded the political cabaret group Citizen's Band, and had privately written music with ex-Smashing Pumpkin James Iha. "Why have you been hiding this from me?" Jack asked when he overheard her in her walk-in wardrobe, singing songs she lacked the nerve to make public. The next day, he took a second wife into a marital home studio, producing and drumming on *The Ghost That Walks* (a sneering school nickname for the lanky, pale Elson). Influenced by her love of Nick Cave, PJ Harvey and Mazzy Star, John Steinbeck and frontier writer Willa Cather, Elson's folk ballads and country waltzes are sung in a strong, natural voice, over airy, autumnal arrangements (Jack's, around her guitar parts). 'Mouths To

Feed' is typically poetic: 'the dust has come and sugared my lungs.' She perhaps had more traditional musical talent, and certainly need, than Meg, and was immensely grateful for Jack's push. "I knew I had more in me than just standing up and having my picture taken," she told *The Guardian*. "I've finally got all this shit off my chest."

Elson gigged in March 2010 ahead of *The Ghost That Walks*' May 24 release, while Jack produced an album with Fifties rockabilly queen Wanda Jackson, then toured *Sea Of Cowards* in Australasia. Elson left to model twice a month, and Jack restricted touring to two-week stints where possible, or else followed Paul McCartney's Seventies example by bringing their children along. One parent was always at home. With Third Man's creative sustenance on his doorstep, life appeared idyllic in Jack's peaceful Southern home.

"Anyone who knows us knows we're very well-suited," Elson had reassured *The Guardian* of their relationship in 2008. But in June 2011, these invites were sent: "Karen Elson and Jack White kindly request the presence of [GUEST] at a party to celebrate their sixth anniversary and upcoming divorce, with a true, swing bang humdinger . . . no plus-ones or deadbeats." It seemed the sort of bloodless 21st century 'uncoupling' later patented by Chris Martin and Gwyneth Paltrow. "We should be pals, and not pretend we're something bigger," Jack told the *New York Times* a year later, when Elson was back at his house, helping to tend the children's whooping cough. She termed him "a dear, dear friend".

The album he began a month after this announcement told a different story. When the Wu-Tang Clan's leader, the RZA, failed to show for a Third Man Studio session in July 2011, Jack didn't waste the band he had ready – Michigan drummer Daru Jones (taken from rapper Black Milk), Jack Lawrence on bass and guitarist Jake Orrall. They recorded three songs, including 'Trash Tongue Talker', with Jack's roadhouse boogie piano and vocal leading a high-energy kiss-off of lowdown, gossiping enemies. For the rest of 2011, having reluctantly removed the White Stripes' shadow by announcing their split that February, he began his solo life. Studio personnel varied, but were built around female musicians – Carla Azar (drummer with a Stripes support act, Autolux), veteran bluegrass and country double-bassist Bryn Davies, and especially Brooke Waggoner, a Nashville-based keyboardist with two albums of her own. He credited producing Wanda Jackson's *The Party Ain't Over*, in which he marshalled a large band for an elaborate, soul-based sound, as crucial preparation. "That production attack really paved the way for me to do my own thing," he told Brian McCollum. Lacking his duo's natural restraints, he now invented new straitjackets, forcing himself to improvise songs in the studio, telling the band he had them when he didn't. "These songs feel like they could only be presented under my own name," he wrote when *Blunderbuss* was released as his debut solo LP on April 14, 2012, the year he turned 37. "[They] had nothing to do with anything or anyone else but my own expression, my own colours on my own canvas."

That canvas was blue, his chosen solo colour. On the blue, black and white sleeve, his eyes look bleakly down, and a vulture perches on his shoulder. In another photo he's out of focus, parts of his face whited out. Death, he realised as he finished *Blunderbuss*, "was overwhelming through-out the lyric writing". His brother Ray, the sometime priest and private eye who had thought to take Jackie Gillis to the movies, had died suddenly in April 2011, aged 54. Jack's blurted fear at his father's deathbed that he would be the last sibling to go, alone and abandoned, was coming true. "Dropping like feathers like flies," began the liner notes by a man "blue from the held back breath"; "Friends die while you're talking to them. Lovers lie while you're lying with them. How long is life supposed to be?"

He refused to admit his other recent loss as his album's subject. "Come on, man, I'm not so simple that I'd write open letters and give them away to the public," he told *Uncut*'s John Mulvey, before perhaps inadvertently opening up a new confessional line. "Any song that people think is about divorce could just as easily be about me and Meg." At any rate, Jack sounds more depressed on *Blunderbuss* than ever before, and repeatedly states a possible cause. 'Missing Pieces' recalls his recent experience of a nose-bleed only noticed on seeing his bloody face in a mirror. He analogises this to being butchered by someone who, having said they can't live without you, takes 'a part of you with them' when they leave. 'Sixteen Saltines' finds him missing the whistle that once let him know his wife (let's say) had returned to their now broken home. It's only when he stops working, and is in that home alone, that he thinks of 'nothing else' but another touching her. The title song is a hazy tale of an affair. Even 'Free-dom At 21', a brooding rant about a careless new digital generation, per-sonalises it as a woman slicing off the soles of his feet. On 'Love Interruption' he wants his fingers slammed in a door, face ground in the dirt and own mother murdered by love, which he wants to put behind him, like Satan.

Just as these lyrics tell a consistent story, their music has a sullen, static gloom. Jack only plays lead electric guitar on three songs (plus three solos), and the fight he brings to the instrument is lost. Keyboards and piano dominate, and it's Brooke Waggoner's romantic cascades that keep the emotional lights on. A funked-up cover of Detroit R&B star Little Willie John's 1960 'I'm Shakin'' then 'Trash Tongue Talker' do considerably perk up *Blunderbuss'* second side. 'Hip (Eponymous) Poor Boy' is best of all. Like the often melancholy, eventual suicide Nick Drake's wry 1971 'Poor Boy', it tips the wink to the mood elsewhere, helped by Waggoner's joyful honky-tonk piano, and Jack's lightly sung relish of his words. He told *Uncut*'s John Mulvey it "explores the way people can sell themselves as authentic and make money off it at the same time". But the man thought mad for 'doing all the things that I don't need to', and who's 'turned on' with a 'cold shiver' when a song overwhelms him, is Jack. A home straight of 'I Guess I Should Go To Sleep', 'On And On And On' and 'Take Me With You When You Go' (in which the singer 'can't catch a breath or a break'), for all their warmer musical variety, then confirms *Blunderbuss'* true, depressive confession. As the first album with his name on it, it still became his first US number one.

Jack prepared for his first solo tour by rehearsing with two bands, on opposite sides of town. The all-female Peacocks were Brooke Waggoner, Bryn Davies, Carla Azar, Grammy-nominated Nashville soul singer Ruby Amanfu, Lilli Mae Rische (fiddle) and Denmark's Maggie Bjorklund (pedal steel). The all-male Buzzards were Daru Jones, multi-instrumentalist Fats Kaplin, Mars Volta organist Ikey Owens, Old Crow Medicine Show mandolinist Cory Younts and bassist Dominic Davis, formerly Suchyta, Jack's childhood best friend, who'd been handed a bass and informed it was his instrument by Jack in the attic at 1203 Ferdinand, when both were 11. Davis moved to Nashville in 2013. "All of these people have moved here or want to move here now," Jack told *The Tennessean*'s Brian McCollum happily. "It's become a real music-based family." Jack, of course, was its progenitor and paternal chief.

He had added to the White Stripes' inherent struggle by placing his guitar picks at the stage's rear, he'd explained in *Under Great White Northern Lights*, and the organ "just far enough away that I have to leap to get to it . . . all of those things build tension". As he asked Conan O'Brien, "What good can come from comfort? It's not going to be art." Now, after debuting both bands on *Saturday Night Live* on March 3 and at Third Man on March 8, he toured with both at great expense, announcing who'd play each gig over breakfast. Musicians less loyally attuned to him than Meg sometimes bridled. "They would get pissed off," he admitted.

Carla Azar recalled the set-up to *Tom Tom*. "The men play differently to Jack than the women do. And Jack plays differently . . . There's definitely more sexual chemistry between the females and Jack." She loved his bandleading. "He doesn't seem to have the second-guess-yourself chip . . . He lets musicians be who they are, doesn't try to control them or the situation – while completely maintaining control the whole time . . . He chooses people he likes to play with and brings out the best in them."

The tour included music from all Jack's bands, finally adding electric bass to White Stripes songs, a trick Dominic Davis found as tough as Steve Nawara had a decade earlier. Other aspects, though, were unrecognisable from the band that had baffled the 100 Club by arriving with little more than an amp, as singer-songwriter Frankie Lee observed backstage at the Lollapalooza festival in Chicago's Grant Park, on August 5, 2012. "They stripped the stage, which is rare at a festival because it takes so long," he remembers. "Everyone else playing there had typical road-cases. And Jack's were huge, probably 10-feet tall, and we all wondered what they could be for. And the guys who were wheeling them around looked like little Oompa-Loompas in blue-and-black suits, bowler hats and dyed-black hair, and they didn't talk to anybody, and that created suspense. He had two buses backstage, and I don't think he was on either bus. And I saw a couple of girls from his band walking around, all in baby-blue and long black hair, they looked like witches and they weren't talking. And by the time the show came round, you almost didn't need it to happen, he'd created so much expectation, like a freak show. There was a spotlight, and he came running from the side of the stage, and hit his first chord, and the whole place went crazy. A drape drops to show the Third Man sign huge behind him, the amps are blue and the band are blue, and he's super-charged, like a boxer. Throwing away guitar picks and going to the back of the stage to get another, and sitting back-to-back with someone at the keyboard – no one plays music like that. He's an entertainer. You don't even think of the music, it's just fun to be at a show where someone takes it that seriously, from the details of the road-cases to the shoelaces of your roadie. And that's just one show, you know?" "I think about the person who's looking at all the equipment on stage before the band get there," Jack typically admitted.

He disliked, though, having to provide such spectacle, and playing to such huge audiences. He was also dismayed by fans who now passively watched him with, as he'd sneered in 'Freedom At 21', 'two black gadgets in her hand'. With phones never pocketed, and gigs experienced through their screens, that left the sound of one hand clapping. At Radio City Music Hall on September 30, 2012, Jack quit the stage after an hour, finally goading the crowd into animated cries of, "Fuck Jack White!" A ticket wasn't "an emblem of entitlement," he told *Esquire*'s Miranda Collinge afterwards. "I've always felt like I'm a stand-up comedian," he told Conan O'Brien, free-forming his set based on crowd responses. Now, though, they were "lying to me . . . I have no idea what to do". This tide defeated him. Three years later, at Lollapalooza on April 12, 2015, he was trying to "get this show to transcend the people," asking those people almost despairingly to "put your cell-phones down for five seconds" because, he pleaded three times, "music is sacred". He quit touring for a while, soon afterwards.

He also took a break in 2013, focusing on what he called a "pivotal year" for Third Man. In March, a deal with the source of the first blues records he'd bought, Document Records, began the vinyl reissue of Charley Patton, Blind Willie McTell and the Mississippi Sheiks' complete works, with Rob Jones' striking red, white and black sleeves – the music was "Library of Congress-type material", Jack told *Rolling Stone*'s Patrick Doyle. Later that year, a partnership with Revenant Records produced *The Rise And Fall Of Paramount Records 1917–1932, Volume 1*, a cornucopia of LPs, books and an innovative USB stick in a hand-crafted, velvet-upholstered wooden cabinet. Along with a second volume in November 2014, it compiled Paramount's almost inadvertent recordings of American pop's vernacular, visceral foundations, from Louis Armstrong to Son House, novelty folk to funereal country. Priced at $400, this was back-country music produced with a Persian rug's care. *Why The Mountains Are Black: Primeval Greek Village Music 1907–1960* would be an equally landmark release in 2016, collecting ritualistic, haunted 78s from a vanished world. Jack also took frequent meetings with artists and producers in 2013, signing Illinois roots musician Pokey LaFarge on a broken Jimmie Rodgers 78. "I'd rather, at some point, my name not have to be attached to it," he told Doyle of his dreams for Third Man.

Life at home was less happy, as his "swing bang humdinger" celebration of divorce soured. On July 22, 2013, Jack was served a restraining order barring him from "any contact with wife whatsoever except as it relates to parenting time with the parties' minor children". Quickly reported by the press, the restraining order affidavit claimed Jack had a violent temper and tendency to harass by barrages of phone calls, emails and texts, "pressuring [Elson] about the settlement terms for divorce"; "This pattern of husband's bullying wife into submission was a contributing factor in the demise of their marriage . . . Wife fears for her and the children's safety as a result of this harassment". Several of Jack's unguarded emails were quoted. "I'm not extending this anymore," he wrote of settling. "And we're not getting lawyers involved to rip me off." He refused Elson's requests to attend family counselling, and resented her lawyer, who filed a motion for custodial psychological evaluation.

There was nothing exceptional in such vicious exchanges in the midst of divorce. In an email to *Rolling Stone* the next year, with the settlement and especially shared custody rights agreed, Elson called Jack "a wonderful father", with "fierce" love for their children. "Those who gain off of a marriage ending helped to create a downward spiral at my most vulnerable," she stated. "The vultures came out and pecked on our bones at our weakest." "When shitty lawyers are in a situation like divorce," Jack told *Rolling Stone*'s Jonah Weiner, more acidly, "their goal is to villainise. Go ahead and villainise me, crucify me. You're not gonna get me." Not every charge rang false, though. "I'm a very provocative person and very intimidating," he told *The Guardian*'s Tim Lewis. "I don't blame anyone who doesn't want to be around me – it's expected." He could simply be tiresome, he told Pamela Des Barres. "People see me onstage . . . and I'm going for it, and it's 100% . . . But they don't want to live with that guy. Because that intensity goes to when we're driving down the street and I can't stand the fact that all the people are wearing flip-flops now . . . it goes on and on and on." Considering Elson's wish for him to have counselling, he told Lewis he'd tried therapy in the past. "Loss hurts, insults hurt, death hurts," he said, suggesting his fundamental wounds. "You can't change that, you can only change your perspective on it . . . I haven't been to [a therapist] in many years, because it just doesn't do anything for me anymore." Instead, he tried to think his way through the pain by himself. "My problem is that most of it is private," he said, "so I don't really want people to know about it."

The most absurd insecurity Jack's divorce emails revealed was his antipathy towards the Black Keys, a Midwestern, blues-heavy, guitar-drums garage rock duo formed in 2001, who'd honestly toiled till their seventh and most popular album, *El Camino*, hit US number two in 2011, the year of Jack and Elson's divorce. In 2010, Black Keys guitarist Dan Auerbach and drummer Patrick Carney had also moved to Nashville, where Auerbach and Jack's children shared a private school. In 2013, Jack emailed Elson to demand their children switch schools, reasoning: "That's a possible 12 fucking years I'm going to have to be sitting in kids' chairs next to that asshole with other people trying to lump us in together. He gets yet another free reign [sic] to follow me around and copy me and push himself into my world." The restraining order also mentioned Jack's annoyance at Elson attending the wedding of another performer who had "ripped him off". Rounds of Jack publicly slighting the Black Keys and making clenched-teeth retractions would climax in the early hours of September 14, 2015, in New York, with the Dead Weather in town for their appearance on *Stephen Colbert*, and Carney relaxing at the Cabin Down Below bar, when Jack walked in. Carney's early morning tweets told the story. "I've never met Jack White. Until last night. He came into a bar in NYC . . . and tried to fight me. I don't fight and don't get fighting but he was mad!!! He is why I play music. The bully assholes who made me feel like nothing . . . A 40-year-old bully tried to fight the 35-year-old nerd. It might get loud but it might also get really really sad and pathetic." "Nobody tried to fight you, Patrick," Jack soon responded. "So quit whining to the Internet and speak face to face like a human being." This idiocy ended when Jack rang Carney that day, and had his first conversation, for an hour, with a man he thought he despised. "He's cool. All good," Carney tweeted afterwards. "From one musician to another," Jack concluded, tweeting with antique gravitas, "you have my respect Patrick Carney." He had similar petty rows over the years with Ryan Adams, Justin Townes Earle, his own online fans and Billy Childish (who Jack fell out with after Childish said he disliked his music in *GQ*, but also later made peace with in a phone call). The Jack who itched to take direct action, justified or not, and who assaulted Jason Stollsteimer, still lived inside him.

In the 18 months between releasing *Blunderbuss* in 2012 and early 2014, Jack also worked on its follow-up. "Things are different when you're in a band . . . and you're in motion," he told *Uncut*'s Jason Anderson. "I'm not under so much pressure to make a next move if I don't feel like it." In the collapsing music industry of the 2010s, he planned to just "put things out whenever they make sense". The pull of his family, and his secure success, also left him less inclined to tour heavily. When he got up at 6am, Third Man anyway left him plenty to do. But what he claimed in *Rolling Stone* was "the challenge of working on something for a long time" proved unnatural for the man who made *White Blood Cells* in three days. He increased the pressure of *Blunderbuss*'s studio-improvised songs by writing on an LA painter friend's piano while they listened and, faced with a growing backlog, memorised melodies instead of recording them, to "filter out the garbage". But when he tried to write lyrics months later, the meaning of the music was fading. His solution was to use "this pile of mediocre writing that I'd done as a teenager", he told Anderson, splicing its characters and sentences into his present. "Collaborating with my younger self", he'd build new lyrics on 19-year-old John Gillis' foundation. This was the age at which a violent psychic crisis had defined him, and pushed him onto his creative path. Comparing himself now to that tortured, trapped, yearning young man, he seemed to envy him. "The harsh reality is," he told *NPR*'s Bob Boilen of his youthful characters, "when that person gets to the end of that tunnel, there's nothing there. Whereas when I was writing when I was 19, I thought, 'Oh, no, when you get to the end of that tunnel, something beautiful and romantic might happen . . .'"

Perhaps as important to what became *Lazaretto* were Jack's widening musical horizons. Just as absence from Mexicantown had made him fonder of a culture he paid tribute to in *Get Behind Me Satan*'s toreador look and Latin American tour, 'Icky Thump' and 'Conquista', so he'd opened his heart to hip-hop. Jay Z had rapped over one of his unfinished tracks, Kanye West (who gave maybe "the greatest show" Jack had ever seen in Nashville) asked him to contribute to his 2013 album *Yeezus*, though forgot to follow up. Jack now saw these two men, Dylan and Neil Young as his peers. He envied the rappers their unchecked egos, the hubristic strut that made Kanye "100% honest", he said, and which he distrusted in himself. But when he pulled into his parking spot at Third Man blasting out Ol' Dirty Bastard, or listened to mournful Texan shock-rappers the Geto Boys, his inhibitions were half-released.

The astonishing video for 'Freedom At 21', by Kanye's regular director Hype Williams, had made this change public. It shows Jack as a gangster rock star in shades at the wheel of a green sports car, pulled over by a black female cop in hot pants and high-heeled boots. In his cell, he's an anaemic-blue iceman, impassive as he's stripped and snaked over by a busty jailmate. All this CGI-heavy, highly sexualised action, standard for hip-hop, was spliced with Jack's cybernetically gloved left hand peeling off jittery guitar riffs. The video for *Lazaretto*'s title track and first single fetishised his instrument still more, as a plectrum smashes glass into slow-motion shards, matching the music's sharply crystalline sound, and a sports car spins and a bull paws the ground at Jack's barbed, snorting solo, till the guitar shatters itself. It could have been designed to show the Mexicantown neighbours who'd derided his porch guitar-strumming, and all those who'd turned rock into hip-hop and R&B's poor relation, that it could live in their world.

As a single, 'Lazaretto' was a Frankenstein's monster, stitched together with wild-eyed cunning from mismatched parts. Heavier sounding on 45, it's densely layered and morphs through styles, topped by Daru Jones' shuffling funk beat, and tailed by Fats Kaplin's dancing bluegrass fiddle. Jack the blues evangelist credited his hybrid touring bands with influencing him in "16 different ways", beyond genre. He focused on Jones, a charismatically energetic Michiganite steeped in jazz and hip-hop (as was bassist Dominic Davis). With American music history absorbed he was, he told Brian McCollum, "trying to move forward to the next stop".

Lazaretto defined Jack's solo stance, where *Blunderbuss* failed to. 'Three Women' toys with and rewrites Blind Willie McTell's 'Three Women Blues' more confidently than the White Stripes used his songs, Jack singing 'Lordy, lordy, lord' over hip-hop beats and chopped-up harmonica with a glee beyond minstrelsy. The lyrics' enviably packed love life was, he noted, unlikely to have been factual for the original's blind writer in the Twenties. The song's subject became "who the singer is . . . and reality was for the blues", he told McCollum. "How much of it is something that never really happened to any of these people?" This was closer to *In Search Of The Blues*' debunking than his misty Delta dreams of 15 years before. 'Would You Fight For My Love?' could be more scenes from a disintegrating marriage ('It's such a pleasure, to sing with you together/ Making love when there is nobody home'), but Ruby Amanfu's spaghetti western operatic backing vocals, and Ikey Owens' and Brooke Waggoner's duelling keyboards in a big 12-piece band, balance its conflict with energetic imagination. 'Temporary Ground' is a nightmare of static, rootless, Godless existence made gorgeous by Lillie Mae Rische's fiddle and twanging Tennessee vocal. The basically instrumental 'High Ball Stepper' combines a wordless Amanfu vocal based on Rische's screeching fiddle tune-up, backwards pedal steel and speaker-splitting guitar. 'That Black Bat Licorice' is a dizzying, word-drunk rap, spiked by clavinet, fiddle and harp.

Inspired by the musicians he'd drawn to him in Nashville, Jack's solo style here was a fresh mutation. Having insisted on rock's blues roots for so long, he now nurtured them with a sound filtered through hip-hop and country. The studio result was like a pressurised, compacted version of

Elvis Presley's Seventies live shows, which self-consciously encompassed most American styles. For those who missed the White Stripes' early, bludgeoning attack, a cover of Elvis' 'Power Of My Love' on 'Lazaretto''s B-side was among Jack's most visceral performances. The yelping screech some laughed at when he started now neared Elvis' throaty, adult roar, his guitar whipped and scalded, and the song had steamroller might.

Familiar themes resurfaced. 'Entitlement' was provoked by "the sound of voices of teenage kids at the mall now . . . when they say 'like' every three words", and their inflated sense of human rights, he told NPR's Bob Boilen. The song retorts: 'We don't deserve a single damn thing.' 'Want And Able' similarly accepts an unfulfilled, circumscribed life. It ends this album made as a divorce became brutal with the singer longing to lie by a certain woman, and touch her in his dreams: 'But that's not possible/ Something simply will not let me.' The sound of Fifties hunting records, made to flush birds to the slaughter with recordings of crows dying or fighting, begins the song, and concludes the vinyl album in an unending, ugly, cawing locked groove.

Lazaretto followed *Blunderbuss* to number one in the US. More remarkable were its vinyl sales there – 40,000 in its first week, with a similar story in the UK on its June 10, 2014 release. This was helped by its Ultra edition, a carnival of vinyl trickery, including secret songs that played at different speeds pressed under the centre labels, a hologram, one side which span in reverse from the centre, alternate and locked grooves. With jokey but involving drama, 'Lazaretto' was also recorded and cut live at Third Man on the morning of April 19, pressed then personally sold by Jack outside his shop in 3 hours and 51 minutes – the world's fastest record.

Lazaretto's sleeve, with Jack a grim, blue-suited, perhaps undead rock monarch, resting on cemetery angel statues whose bowed heads avoid his gaze, confirmed his solo work's darkened, if playful, tone. One of its songs, 'Alone In My Home', matched this image of him ruling an empty kingdom of stone. It was a New Wave country ballad, so appealing you might miss Jack's eternal fear, aged 19 or 39, of somehow self-inflicted loneliness (even as *Lazaretto*'s title referred to a quarantine island, which Jack, who ached to restrict his consuming creativity, said would be "nice"). Having grown up in the safe chaos of nine siblings, adult life apart from them could be insufferable. "The notion of being alone in my home is very, very hard," he told Brian McCollum. "Whenever I'm by myself in a hotel room in Japan, it's very hard . . . I create family when I can, and I try to encourage family all around, and there's times where I have to be by myself." A solo career delayed till he was 36, and its desolate themes, make sense in this light. Referring to all the musicians he drew to Third Man as "family" showed his longing. This wasn't just personal. It went to the heart of his desires for music, and America. 'Oh say does that star-spangled banner yet wave, o'er the land of the free and the home of the brave?' he sang to *Esquire*'s Miranda Collinge, explaining that those lines in the US national anthem could make him cry. Then they did. "To make the people *ask* the same question *out loud*," he tried to explain. "The idea that you're involved together. Not alone. Not by yourself. As a culture." Swallowing tears, he suggested this was "very beautiful".

"Sometimes your physical body and your mental body, your spirit, is drifting too," Jack also told McCollum. "And maybe no place is comfortable. And . . . you can really become very depressed." His response was to "constantly create my own environment" to help the next stage of his endless work. "I had to just invest in something solid," he told Pamela Des Barres of the life he built in Nashville. After exile from Detroit, Third Man helped moor him against psychic drift. Its presence in an initially rundown neighbourhood in country's capital also magically transformed both, drawing hip rock musicians and gentrifying money in his wake. "Nashville's resurgence probably starts very close to when he set up shop," says one recent arrival, Frankie Lee. It was his second time in "supposedly the 'coolest city in America,' " Jack worried to *Nashville Scene*.

He now expected the things he most desired, from the White Stripes to marriage, to fail. The boyish, giddy idealist of his twenties was battered by defeats as he turned 40 in 2015. He told *The Guardian*'s Tim Lewis in a flash of bitter self-knowledge that "the overwhelming goals of my life are to create community, create family", despite having a "tragic Greek" personality "that will possibly destroy it, and perhaps that was my plan all along".

A late-starting romantic life that left him wonderfully entwined with Meg for a decade had, like so many things, become less inhibited for him as he reached middle-age. "I can sleep in a bed with them or go to lunch with them," he told *Uncut*'s John Mulvey of the women in his life, when newly divorced in 2012. Saying to them "you're my friend, you're my wife, you're my girlfriend, you're my co-worker" felt ridiculous, he expanded to the *New York Times*' Josh Eells in 2014. Having abandoned monogamy "a long time ago", "those rules don't apply any more". This potentially polyamorous life was another refusal of convention, which some others shared, and could be more meaningfully liberating than simply sleeping around. The alternative, anyway, had failed.

Jack's life and music were now both remarkable self-creations. Both were also as difficult as they had been for John Gillis. But they were no tragedy. His charmingly boyish, near-daft enthusiasm and drive was still on display in Bernard MacMahon's 2016 documentary *The American Epic Sessions*. Jack was an executive producer and key participant in intensive sessions in a resurrected 1931 Hollywood recording studio, using an electric amp, mic and pulley-driven recording lathe of the sort used on Charley Patton's records. T Bone Burnett was also a producer, but as Jack played piano with rapper Nas or guitar with Elton John, and welcomed Willie Nelson and Merle Haggard to the studio, the callow figure he had cut among his seniors during the *Cold Mountain* sessions was a lifetime away. Yet when he eagerly explained the beauty of this electric technology, and stepped even further back through the last century to make an acoustic recording into a recording horn, he was still the boy of two decades before. And when the leather strap holding the pulley's huge weight snapped, he rushed to a nearby seatbelt-repair shop, for some nostalgic, restorative upholstery. "Some great guitar players started off in upholstery and lost fingers – Django Reinhardt, Jerry Garcia," he told MacMahon, still fabricating yarns as he snipped away.

His peaceful, sunlit mansion was also wholly different to the graveyard where *Lazaretto*'s blue Jack glowered. There, he spent as much time as he could playing with his children. Teresa was five and Henry – now called Hank – almost four when the *New York Times* visited in 2012. "They're little vaudeville kids," he said proudly. They'd formed a band called Coke though, unlike Jack, they'd never drunk it, just as he denied them the addiction to digital screens of their peers, only permitting mechanical games. The children were six and eight when *Rolling Stone* visited in 2014. Teresa enjoyed Monty Python and W.C. Fields with him now, in between a wide range of pop. They were by then too old for the magical comfort he'd shared with them two years before when, wanting to hear the sound of rain that never reached his bedroom to help his lonely sleep, he'd had microphones installed, to relay its patter. When he first turned the sound up, with his children dozing in his bed, his daughter asked if he could turn the sun up, too. He wasn't always alone in his home.

Epilogue

Return of the King

THE Lager House, September 2015. You can read Detroit's rock history on the walls, from a poster for a John Sinclair Freedom Rally attended by John and Yoko, to one for 'I Just Don't Know What To Do With Myself'. The black stand-up rasping social critique from the side of his mouth on the back-room stage where Jack and Meg once saw bands is looking for a lift home as, even in Corktown, it's chucking-out time. Almost everyone at the bar is in one band, or three. This enduring neighbourhood joint is as close as you'll get to how things were. It shows how things have changed, too. An old friend of Ben Blackwell, hipster-bearded and still in his suit from attending a congressman's funeral, is rowing with a drunk woman on the next barstool about which of them is the realest Detroiter. She fires an immortal parting shot: "Oh, so I'm too troublesome to be fuckable!" The regulars stare in amazement at the business card left behind by this sociology professor.

Remnants of the garage-rock gold rush expired suddenly in 2015. The Magic Stick I visit in December 2014 has become the smarter, slicker dance club Populux when I return the next summer. "It got really hot '98 up to 2005," Dave Zainea recalls, "but by 2008 I could see it diminish. Those bands got older, and the scene changed. The average attendance decreased from 350 to 40–70, so we moved that scene into the Majestic Cafe and Theatre. You gotta survive. But we're not giving up on rock'n'-roll." Faced with rocketing rent, Ghetto Recorders' final session was on May 1, 2015. Jim Diamond has traded Detroit for the south of France. "I'm 50 and I want to move on," he says. "There are people from California and Brooklyn coming here with money. Back in the old days no one had any money. It was fun, I was younger, but I don't dwell on that time."

"There are still a lot of good bands," Troy Gregory councils me, as we sit in his darkening Ferndale front room. "It's just whether anyone's making a stink about it. A lot of record companies came sniffing around, and they thought all the bands would be the same as the White Stripes.

279

They found out they were all different, made by people with the audacity to feel that what they're doing is just as important as Roxy Music or the Kinks. That's how I feel. But because there was an interest, there's this idea that, 'The thrill has gone.' I'm sure if you and I went around the clubs now, even on a weekday, we'd find a good band."

"Music is getting really good, and it's hard for me to not go out every night," Steve Nawara informs me of Detroit's changing times. "It's very exciting, and not only because of all the development and new people moving in. But I don't recognise my own town. There are so many great things about Detroit that are now gone, like the old blues places. They were so organic, created over decades. There's a pop-up something or other, but it lacks the balls, the soul. There's definitely resentment from people who lived here their whole lives. All the traditions in America are being wiped clean. I'm a Corktown resident still, and it's been gentrified very quickly, with lots of dudes with long beards. God bless the Lager House. It's the wild side, though, and the freedom of it all that's going. Right now Hamtramck is the place to be."

Walking through downtown Detroit now feels odd in a way I've never experienced elsewhere. The people stepping out of the revived hotels and the Sunday morning joggers exist in a parallel reality to the black Detroiters who remain, each not recognising and almost passing through the other, like ghosts. "I had that impression too," Matt Smith agrees, "when I first saw people from the suburbs down Michigan Avenue. Wow, these people are walking around, and no one's shooting them! This is fascinating! It's nice to see things being redeveloped, in a way. But as part of that, neighbourhoods are being devastated with mass foreclosures, and houses left deliberately unoccupied. Are they just creating the same climate of 1967, before the riots?"

Nawara's focus is on Detroit's new music. His Beehive Recording Company intends to tape every band he can, from a sense of mission in this special place. "The Gold Dollar was like looking into a fishbowl of great bands," he explains, "but there's some I can barely remember the names of. So at least this will be a permanent time-capsule of Detroit music from here on out."

A month later, Detroit's fiercest rock hope since the 2000s, Proto-martyr, are playing Brighton's packed Green Door Store. Singer Joe Casey's cheek bulges with bile and indignation. When not red-faced and raging, he sings quietly, slipping his words out beneath the band's music. Though drawing on post-punk strands rarely heard in Jack's day,

Protomartyr continue the individual, dissatisfied expression of work-ing-class, rock'n'roll Detroiters. One song, 'Pontiac 87', recalls the Papal visit when Jack met the Pontiff. Before the gig, Casey recalls his excite-ment at the specific Detroit references in *The White Stripes*. A decade older than his bandmates at 38, this new hope is, it turns out, the Gold Dollar's last refugee, having seen the White Stripes there before they conquered the world. He and guitarist Greg Ahee consider Jack's lasting impact back home.

"I remember seeing [legendary label boss] Seymour Stein at the Lager House," Casey says. "And now, there's not that much of a garage-rock scene, but people come expecting to see it. [Outkast's] Andre 3000 just came in to mix Aretha Franklin's record, but he went, 'Where's the garage-rock?' It's like when people go to Paris, and want to see berets."

"One thing they had in that scene was a unified aesthetic," Ahee con-siders. Protomartyr's LP sleeves and collaged posters also offer a complete world. "And musically, what I take from the White Stripes is a maximum minimalism. We push what we can do with bare essentials as far as we can. I don't think I consciously said, 'Jack did this so I'm going to.' But we went to see *Under Great White Northern Lights* in Detroit, and he talked about how he'll have one guitar pick, and move the back-up far away. And when I play, I only have one pick. Having boundaries makes you more focused and determined. There's this Detroit rapper, Danny Brown, who talks about doing the most with the least. That's a common thread through a lot of Detroit artists. And I would say a lot of that comes from the White Stripes."

"There are a lot of really talented guitar players that have come up since then," Matt Smith says, considering the man he knew best as the Go's guitarist, "in bands like the Crooks and the Pizazz. These kids all told me that the only reason they picked up a guitar is because they heard the White Stripes. There's a whole generation who told me if it wasn't for Jack White they'd have been DJs. I don't know if Jack's aware of that. But I've heard that again and again from younger musicians."

"I feel like that's a question you'll have to wait another 10 years for," the Hentchmen's Tim Purrier says, asked if the scene his band helped found left a mark. "In high school we were into stuff at least 10, 20 years old. Hopefully the seeds are starting to grow."

"There's a lot of people from Detroit here," Third Man's Noah Uman tells me in Nashville, as the *Light + Sound Machine* ends, and the Blue

Room empties. "And I know they miss it like hell every day." Alongside Jack's nephew Ben Blackwell, his school friend Dominic Davis, Michiganites Daru Jones and Dave Swanson (now a photographer and unlikely Third Man fashion designer), Kevin Carrico, who Jack filmed car ads with aged 17, came to Nashville to work on *A Letter Home*. Another nephew, Josh Gillis, also now lives in Jack's county, Davidson (so maybe his lonely home). He played guitar on *Lazaretto* B-side 'Blue Light, Red Light (There's Someone There)', and edited *Acknowledge*, a poetry anthology by homeless contributors to Nashville's version of *The Big Issue*, *The Contributor*, for a new branch of Jack's empire, Third Man Books. This imprint, heavy on carefully crafted, Nashville-printed underground poetry and expression, is edited with Ben Swank by Chet Weise, ex of Stripes blues-punk compadres the Immortal Lee County Killers. "Anyone can design a record cover," Blackwell told the *Metro-Times* of this tight circle, "but who do you really want to also hang out with?"

Jack still pined for his hometown, though he felt spurned by it. "I've cried there, on tour, pulling in," he told *Rolling Stone*'s Jonah Weiner. "I've missed it incredibly. And, at the same, time, I've thanked God I don't live there." This was typical of someone as proud of their roots in a tough place as they were relieved to get out and flourish. But Jack never forgot. In September 2007, Ben's father Morris "Coach Mo" Blackwell revealed his certainty that the anonymous donor of $170,000 to renovate Clark Park's baseball ground was the man who as Jack Gillis had walked three blocks from his childhood home to hone a "smooth left-handed swing" there. In 2013, he again attempted anonymity in saving the Masonic Temple from auction by paying its $142,000 back-taxes. The complex where his mother had ushered gratefully renamed one of its grand venues the Jack White Theater. On July 29, 2014, while in Detroit playing the Fox and the Masonic, Jack threw the opening pitch before a Tigers baseball game, and took Scarlett and Hank to learn in Clark Park with "Coach Mo". Then in June 2015, Third Man's most significant expansion was announced. It would return to the Cass Corridor.

"Six years ago, there was clearly bad blood," *Metro-Times* music editor Mike McGonigal told NPR of the hometown scene's relations with Jack. His donations softened hearts. Third Man Cass Corridor's speedy hiring of Dave Buick, whose Italy Records had given the White Stripes their start also had "huge" significance, McGonigal believed. "They had a falling out that was tough. I'm friends with Dave and . . . to me that meant, 'Oh, this guy is really mending fences and coming home.'" The Cass Corridor name also resisted the area's insidious, a historic rebranding by big business as 'Midtown'.

As summer 2015 turned to autumn and his plans took shape, Jack was regularly seen at downtown Detroit's "fancy joints", the Majestic's barman Josh tells me. In August, he, Blackwell and Buick ate at the Republic Tavern, a stone's throw from Cass Avenue. Jack spent Friday October 11 dining not far from the Lager House, and the following night was back in Mexicantown. The week before my September Detroit arrival, he caught a Tigers game with a recent songwriting confidante, Paul Simon.

When I take the short walk from the Majestic to Third Man's site at 441 West Canfield Street, I'm astonished by an environment very different from the nearby ruins of the Gold Dollar, or anything I've yet seen in Detroit. Third Man Cass Corridor is boarded up and shrouded in black, marked only by a giant label sign inscribed by the local Golden Sign Co., a padlocked mystery like Kubrick's obelisk. Opposite is the Motor City Brewing Works and Winery. Next door is Shinola, whose founder Tom Kartsosis co-owns the building with Jack. Inside Shinola, past the frosty security guard, luxury wristwatches and pricey bicycles assembled in Detroit, is a ping-pong table. Third Man's other neighbour is the newly opened Jolly Pumpkin Artisan Ales bar where, in the shadow of Wayne State, whose students were once routinely mugged, young white families sit outside in the sun served by long-bearded waiters. This corner of the old ghetto is now Yuppie Central.

"Gentrification's starting here in the Cass Corridor and its spreading out," barman Josh tells me back at the Majestic. "It's keeping the crime rate down, but removing the culture that made it special in the first place." Third Man's alliance with Shinola, who Blackwell admitted to WDET "are no stranger to people giving them shit", also wrankles. "People are getting suspicious of some of the corporate types Jack's doing business with." Protomartyr's Ahee agrees. "Hopefully some good will come out of Third Man being there, but Shinola represents everything I hate about New Detroit. It's a very manufactured idea of Detroit credibility. That's the opposite of what I liked about the White Stripes, and what Jack stood for to me."

Jack sharing a stage on March 30, 2015 with Jay Z, Kanye West, Madonna, Beyoncé and Rihanna at the launch of the artist-owned streaming service Tidal also bothered some. Anyway, he chose his own company now. And if his business moved in glitzy, upmarket circles to further its success, the benefit for once truly trickled down. On October 30, Timmy's Organism (the latest outfit of musician-artist and oft-banned Gold Dollar wild man Timmy Lampimen) and Wolf Eyes both released Third Man albums. The former's *Heartless Heathens* was a classic slab of Cass Corridor, Cro-Magnon glam-punk with an artist's heart. Like the exotic drone-collages of Michigan noise veterans Wolf Eyes' *I Am A Problem: Mind In Pieces*, Blackwell brought them to Third Man. A label-sponsored joint tour, Audio Social Dissent, introduced these extreme outriders of the White Stripes' scene to America. Danny Kroha's mostly home-recorded solo album *Angels Watching Over Me* (2015) further developed the late Nineties scene's blues obsessions. A new Gories single, 'Be Nice', even found Jim Diamond mixing a Third Man record. The label also began reissuing Tamla 7-inches from 1959–62, prior to Motown's slicker production, which Detroit's most successful music mogul since Berry Gordy never liked.

Family and most of the musicians Jack was still friends with joined his party at Third Man Cass Corridor on November 26, the night before it opened. "Everything in this neighborhood seems to me like the perfect place for the renaissance and the rebirth and the regrowth from the ashes that Detroit is going to rise from," he promised, raising a glass on an auspicious night. Having left suddenly and bitterly, the exiled son now returned a king.

The Gories brought Detroit music full circle when they took to the store's stage the next night, alongside Lillie Mae Rische and Margo Price. Hundreds queued to enter the yellow-and-black-liveried shop, at 4,300 square feet more than quadruple the Nashville prototype's size. That left plenty of room to sell label-branded hockey shirts, pet leashes, frisbees and keyrings amidst the Mold-a-Rama machine and records, in a more commercial, tourist-friendly branch. The globe in Third Man's insignia started to seem prophetic. A January 17 night of Detroit poets, though, like the store's drive to supply water to the state-poisoned citizens of nearby Flint, were not corporate acts.

Cass Corridor's most astonishing innovation was visionary, and local. The Third Man Vinyl Pressing Plant would open behind the store in 2016, with the first eight new record presses for at least 30 years sitting amidst its yellow floors and blood-red beams. Jack had helped create a worldwide backlog in vinyl. Now he, not the opportunistic majors clogging up production, stepped in to solve it. United had reserved a press for their most valued customer. Now he owned his means of production.

Dave Buick, looking after Detroit reissues, found his late Nineties Italy catalogue among the first releases. Other employees focused on new Detroit artists and publishing. Ben Blackwell hoped Third Man would be a local facility for "a little punk band to make 300 copies of a 7-inch", like the White Stripes when they began.

Jack was just visiting his old home. Meg, continuing the strange symmetry of their lives, had divorced her second spouse, Jackson Smith, in July 2013. She now lived back in Detroit. "I don't think anyone talks to Meg," Jack told *Rolling Stone* in 2014. "She's always been a hermit." But this was no longer true. "I see Meg quite often," John Krautner informs me. "She's always been very friendly. She doesn't do much playing. But she's always up for getting together and listening to records. That's mostly what she does, I think, listens to records, and hangs out – that's her life-style! She was doing well last time I saw her." Steve Nawara agrees. "She's happy and she's quiet and she has a beautiful life and a beautiful home. I'm very proud of her."

During his October 2015 week revisiting Corktown and Mexicantown, Jack had also watched Protomartyr play the Marble Bar, a rare return to the sort of gig that filled his nights when Detroit was his town. It drew the hassle he'd feared. "It's funny," Greg Ahee reflects, "because Meg can still be anonymous. We run into her frequently. She goes out a lot, and we all have a lot of mutual friends with her. And she finally seems comfortable. It's almost the opposite of how it seemed when the White Stripes were onstage and Jack was loving it, and she was terrified, it seemed. But now, in the times I've seen him out in public, he does not look comfortable. And we all know who she is, but nobody bothers her that much. She always seems to be having a good time at parties. She left the band because it wasn't for her. Hopefully she can live off their success, and just do what she wants to now. Jack will always be in that celebrity prison, for want of a better word."

"There's that bar right around the corner with all the dead celebrities up on the wall," one of Ahee's bandmates observes of Brighton's Prince Albert, with its evolving mural of Hendrix, Cobain, Peel and the rest. "And someday, Jack White's going to be spraypainted up there. That's the way it goes."

In the meantime, Jack White worked. He appeared suddenly in flickering conference calls that snapped his Cass Corridor staff to attention, when not commuting between his kingdoms. And he toured ampless and acoustic in the five US states he'd so far missed, singing into a ribbon microphone in Alaska, continuing his fascination with pure sound. And he marched through his mansion, playing with his children, or helplessly picking out a new tune at the piano. And he sat outside, listening to his latest music beamed to a radio so he'd never overestimate how it sounded, in his electric car from a company named for his thwarted hero, Tesla (in 2016, there was a surge of 250,000 orders for these vehicles. Maybe, like vinyl, he'd be right again). He was a sometimes lonely, benign emperor of the blues, and he was doing more with each day of his life than anyone else had thought possible.

Acknowledgements

This book began and ends in the great city of Detroit. Brett Callwood pointed the way, and Noel Ireland let me see the Magic Stick after hours then drove me home. Stacey Shelley, my best friend through three books now and for life, gave me the crucial nudge to return to the city a second time. Troy Gregory then waited for me on his Ferndale porch, and spent three hours telling me hip history that opened everything up. Steve Nawara, John Krautner and Matt Smith were thoughtful raconteurs about the Go, the White Stripes' early days and Detroit at the turn of the century. Jim Diamond gave me an unexpected, amusing trip to the south of France, and the lowdown on Ghetto and *The White Stripes*. Among the typical wealth of Motor City hospitality, thanks to all at the Lager House for a memorable night and maintaining Corktown's true spirit, to Dave Zainea and everyone sitting at the Majestic bar, and brother Joe's hummus.

London was where I met the charming Dan Kroha after a Gories gig. For discovering exactly how Jack and Meg conquered Britain, I'm indebted to Bruce Brand, Simon Keeler (also a kind conduit to Third Man gear), Russell Warby, Stevie Chick, Holly Golightly, PJ Crittenden, Matt Hunter and John Mulvey. Tim Eriksen thought hard about Jack in Nashville and Transylvania, while I nursed a Scotch. Thanks also for their time and insights to Dave Feeny, Tim Purrier, Stuart Sikes, Wade Ogle, Protomartyr, Doug Coombe, Seasick Steve, Neil Young, Bernard MacMahon, Marybeth Hamilton and Frankie Lee, and to Jakub Blackman, Chris Carr and Tones Sansom for turning keys. Parts of my interview with Brendan Benson first ran in *The Independent*.

Swiss king of the opening question Hanspeter Kuenzler kindly lent me cuttings, and allowed use of the transcripts of his two Raconteurs interviews. The websites Expecting and golddollar.com helped me piece together Jack's early live career. At Third Man in Nashville, Noah Uman was a kind host. In a story played out on vinyl, fine record stores helped me on my way: Resident Records, Brighton; Block Street Records, Fayetteville, Arkansas; UHF Records, Royal Oak, Michigan; and Hello

Records, Detroit. The British Library and Jubilee Library, Brighton were vital, as all libraries are.

The music editors and writers of the *Detroit Metro-Times* have written the weekly history of their city's musicians during the period this book covers. As with the *Detroit Free Press*' Brian McCollum, and the late Jim Ridley's *Nashville Scene*, these journalists got there first. Radio New Zealand's documentary *The White Stripes In New Zealand* filled a vital gap. Interviews by Brian McCollum, Barney Hoskyns, Pamela Des Barres, Andrew Male and Andrew Perry drew valuable details from Jack about his childhood. Like the many other magazine and newspaper sources quoted, they are credited in the text.

Thanks to my editor Lucy Beevor for generous support, and David Barraclough for saintly patience.

Deborah Nash gave me something to look forward to when it was done.

Bibliography

Parts of the following books were consulted:

Hamilton, Marybeth. *In Search Of The Blues: Black Voices, White Visions* (Cape, 2007). A revelatory, essential book on how the music came to mean what we think it does.

Handyside, Chris. *Fell In Love With A Band: The Story Of The White Stripes* (St. Martin's Griffin, 2004).

Miller, Steve. *Detroit Rock City* (Da Capo Press, 2013).

Peel, John. *Margrave Of The Marshes* (Transworld Press, 2005).

Sugrue, Thomas J. *The Origins Of The Urban Crisis: Race And Inequality In Postwar Detroit* (Princeton, 1996).

True, Everett. *The White Stripes And The Sound Of Mutant Blues* (Omnibus Press, 2004).

And on the De Stijl movement, these:

Alber, Volkus, Kras, Reyer and Woodham, Jonathan M. *Icons Of Design: The 20th Century* (Prestel, 2004).

Sparke, Penny. *The Genius Of Design* (Quadrille Publishing, 2009).

Sparke, Penny. *A Century Of Design* (Mitchell Beazley, 1998).

Wilk, Christopher (ed.). *Modernism: Designing A New World* (V&A Publishing, 2006).

Woodham, Jonathan M. *20th Century Design* (OUP, 1997).

Discography

(UK chart positions follow where applicable; singles are 7-inch vinyl unless otherwise stated. "Vault only" denotes subscription-only vinyl from Third Man; of these, only releases with otherwise unavailable material are included)

GOOBER & THE PEAS
ALBUM

The Jet-Age Genius* Of Goober & The Peas (Detroit Municipal Recordings, 1994)

THE GO
ALBUM

Whatcha Doin' (Sub Pop, 1999)

THE WHITE STRIPES
ALBUMS

The White Stripes (Sympathy For The Record Industry, 1999)
De Stijl (Sympathy For The Record Industry, 2000)
White Blood Cells (Sympathy For The Record Industry, 2001)   55
Elephant (XL, 2003)   1
Get Behind Me Satan (XL, 2005)   3
Icky Thump (Third Man/XL, 2007)   1
Under Great White Northern Lights (Third Man/XL, 2010)   25
The Complete John Peel Sessions (Third Man, 2016)

Subsequent White Stripes albums are Vault only:
Under Great White Northern Lights B-Shows (Third Man, 2010)
The White Stripes Live In Mississippi (Third Man, 2011)
Live At The Gold Dollar (Third Man, 2012)

Discography

Nine Miles From The White City (Third Man, 2013)

Live Under The Lights Of The Rising Sun (Third Man, 2014)

Live At The Gold Dollar III (Third Man, 2015)

Under Amazonian Lights (Third Man, 2015)

SINGLES

Let's Shake Hands/Look Me Over Closely (Italy Records, 1998)

Lafayette Blues/Sugar Never Tasted So Sweet (Italy Records, 1998)

The Big Three Killed My Baby/Red Bowling Ball Ruth (Sympathy For The Record Industry, 1999)

Hand Springs/The Dirtbombs – [split-single with the Dirtbombs – Cedar Point '76] (Extra Ball Records, free with *Multiball* fanzine, 1999)

Hello Operator/Jolene (Sympathy For The Record Industry, 2000)

Lord, Send Me An Angel/You're Pretty Good Looking (Trendy American Remix) (Sympathy For The Record Industry, 2000)

The Party Of Special Things To Do/China Pig/Ashtray Heart (Sub Pop, 2000)

Hotel Yorba/Rated X (XL, 2001)   26

Fell In Love With A Girl/I Just Don't Know What To Do With Myself (Live) (CD2 + Love Sick (Live) (XL, 2002)   21

Dead Leaves And The Dirty Ground/Stop Breaking Down (Live) (CD + Suzy Lee (Live) (XL, 2002)   25

Red Death At 6.14 (XL Recordings, 2002 – free with *Mojo* magazine)

Candy Cane Children/The Reading Of The Story Of The Magi/Silent Night (XL, 2002)

Seven Nation Army/Good To Me (CD + Black Jack Davey) (XL, 2003) 7

I Just Don't Know What To Do With Myself/Who's To Say . . . (CD + I'm Finding It Harder To Be A Gentleman (Live) (XL, 2003)   13

The Hardest Button To Button/St. Ides Of March (XL, 2004)   23

There's No Home For You Here/I Fought Piranhas (Live)/Let's Build A Home (Live) (XL, 2004)

Jolene (Live Under Blackpool Lights)/Do (Live) (CD + Black Math (Live) (XL, 2004)   16

291

Blue Orchid/The Nurse (CD + Though I Hear You Calling, I Will Not Answer, CD2 + Who's A Big Baby/You've Got Her In Your Pocket (Live)) (XL, 2005)   9

My Doorbell/Same Boy You've Always Known (Live) (CD + Screwdriver (Live)/12″ + Blue Orchid (High Contrast Remix)) (XL, 2005)   10

The Denial Twist/Shelter Of Your Arms (7″ 2 The Denial Twist (Live)/As Ugly As I Seem (Live)) (XL, 2005)   10

Walking With A Ghost (V2, 2005)

Top Special (3″, tour only) (Third Man, 2005)

Icky Thump/Baby Brother (CD + Catch Hell Blues) (XL, 2007)   2

Rag And Bone (free with *NME*) (XL, 2007)

You Don't Know What Love Is (You Just Do What You're Told)/A Martyr For My Love For You (Acoustic version) (7″ 2 + 300 M.P.H. Torrential Outpour Blues) (XL, 2007)   18

Conquest/It's My Fault For Being Famous (7″ 2 B-side Honey We Can't Afford To Look This Cheap, 7″ 3 Conquest (Acoustic Mariachi version)/Cash Grab Complications On The Matter) (XL, 2007)   30

Conquista (Third Man/XL, 2008)

Subsequent White Stripes singles are Vault only:

Let's Shake Hands (Alt. take)/Look Me Over Closely (Alt. Take) (Third Man, 2009)

Signed D.C./I've Been Loving You Too Long (Third Man, 2011)

The Hardest Button To Button (Beck remix)/The Dead Weather – Hang You From The Heavens (Josh Homme and Mark Lanegan remix) (Third Man, 2012)

Dead Leaves (Alt. Take)/Let's Build A Home (Alt. Take) (Third Man, 2012)

Live On Bastille Day [First White Stripes performance] (Third Man, 2012)

Rated X [studio version]/Whispering Sea (Live) (Third Man, 2015)

THE UPHOLSTERERS
SINGLE
Makers Of High Grade Suites (Sympathy For The Record Industry, 2000)

Discography

THE RACONTEURS
ALBUMS
Broken Boy Soldiers (XL/Third Man, 2006)   2

Consolers Of The Lonely (XL/Third Man, 2008)   8

Subsequent Raconteurs albums are Vault only:

Live In London (Third Man, 2009)

Third Man Live 04-17-2010 (Third Man, 2010)

Live At Third Man Records (Third Man, 2012)

Live At The Ryman Auditorium (Third Man, 2013)

SINGLES
Steady, As She Goes/Store Bought Bones (XL, 2006)   4

Hands/Store Bought Bones (The Zane Rendition) (7" 2 + It Ain't Easy
(Live), CD + Intimate Secretary (Live) (XL, 2006)   29

Broken Boy Soldier/Headin' For The Texas Border (Live) (7" 2 + Blue
Veins (Live) (XL, 2006)   22

Salute Your Solution/Top Yourself (Bluegrass Version) (XL, 2008)

Many Shades Of Black/Many Shades Of Black (with Adele) (XL, 2008)

Open Your Eyes/You Made A Fool Out Of Me (Third Man, Vault only,
2012)

THE DEAD WEATHER
ALBUMS
Horehound (Columbia/Third Man, 2009)   14

Sea Of Cowards (Warner Bros/Third Man, 2010)   32

Sea Of Cowards Live At Third Man Records (Third Man, Vault only, 2010)

Dodge And Burn (Third Man, 2015)   21

SINGLES
Hang You From The Heavens/Are 'Friends' Electric? (Third Man, 2009)

Treat Me Like Your Mother/You Just Can't Win (Third Man, 2009)

I Cut Like A Buffalo/A Child Of A Few Hours Is Burning To Death (Third Man, 2009)

Forever My Queen/Outside (Third Man, Vault only, 2009)

Die By The Drop/Old Mary (Third Man, US only, 2010)

No Horse (First Take)/Jawbreaker (First Take) (Third Man, Vault only, 2010)

Live At Third Man Records (Encore) (Third Man, Vault only, 2010)

Blue Blood Blues/Jawbreaker (Live) [12″ B-side is No Hassle Night/Just Want To Make Love To You (Live)] (Third Man, US only, 2010)

Open Up (That's Enough)/Rough Detective (Third Man, Vault only, 2013)

Buzzkill(er)/It's Just Too Bad (Third Man, Vault only, 2014)

I Feel Love (Every Million Miles)/Cop And Go (Third Man, Vault only, 2015)

Impossible Winner/Cop And Go (Third Man, Vault only, 2015)

JACK WHITE
ALBUMS
Blunderbuss (XL, 2012)   1

Live At Third Man Records (Third Man, Vault only, 2012)

Lazaretto (XL, 2014)   4

Live From Bonaroo 2014 (Third Man, Vault only, 2014)

Acoustic In Idaho (Third Man, Vault only, 2016)

SINGLES
Fly Farm Blues (Third Man, 2009)

Love Interruption/Machine Gun Silhouette (XL/Third Man, 2012)

I'm Shakin'/Blues On Two Trees (Third Man, tour only in UK, 2012)

Sixteen Saltines/Love Is Blindness (XL/Third Man, 2012)

Love Interruption/Machine Gun Silhouette (Third Man, 2012)

Blunderbuss Demos (Third Man, Vault only, 2012)

Lazaretto/Power Of My Love (Third Man, 2014)

Alone In My Home [demo]/Entitlement (Third Man, Vault only, 2014)

Lazaretto Demos (Third Man, Vault only, 2014)

Would You Fight For My Love?/Parallel (Third Man, 2014)

That Black Bat Licorice/Blue Light, Red Light (Someone's There) (Third Man, 2014)

You Are The Sunshine Of My Life/You Are The Sunshine Of My Life [with *Muppet Show* house band the Electric Mayhem, from Jack's appearance on the show] (Third Man, 2016)

JACK WHITE AND THE BRICKS
ALBUM

Live On The Garden Bowl Lanes: July 9, 1999 (Third Man, Vault only, 2013)

Live At The Gold Dollar (Third Man, Vault only, 2016)

TWO-STAR TABERNACLE
ALBUM

Live At The Gold Dollar (Third Man, Vault only, 2016)

SIGNIFICANT JACK WHITE GUEST APPEARANCES
ALBUMS

The Hentchmen – *Hentch-Forth* (Italy, 1998). Jack guests on bass.

Loretta Lynn – *Van Lear Rose* (Interscope, 2004). Jack produces, plays guitar, and duets on 'Portland Oregon'.

Danger Mouse and Danielle Luppi – *Rome* (Parlophone/Lex/EMI/Third Man, 2011). Jack sings 'Two Against One', 'The Rose With The Broken Neck' and 'The World'.

Various Artists – *The Lost Notebooks Of Hank Williams* (Columbia/Egyptian/Third Man, 2011). 'You Know That I Know' is Jack's contribution to a Dylan-organised album completing unfinished Hank Williams songs.

Various Artists – *Song Reader* (Capitol, 2014). Beck songs originally released as sheet-music. Jack sings 'I'm Down.'

SINGLES

The Hentchmen featuring Jack White – Some Other Guy/Psycho Daisies (Italy, 1998). Jack guests on guitar.

Andre Williams & Two-Star Tabernacle – Ramblin' Man/Lily White Mama And Jet Black Daddy (Bloodshot, 1998). Jack is on piano and backing vocals.

Alicia Keys & Jack White – Another Way To Die/Another Way To Die (Instrumental version) (XL, 2008)   9

Tempest Storm – The Intimate Interview/Advice For Young Woman (Third Man, 2012). Jack interviews Storm, the world's oldest stripper.

Brendan Benson & Jack White – Steady, As She Goes [original demo]/The Same Boy You've Always Known [demo] (Third Man, Vault only, 2013)